Enhancing Learning and Teaching in Higher Education

Enhancing Learning and Teaching in Higher Education

Engaging with the Dimensions of Practice

Edited by John Lea

 Open University Press

Open University Press
McGraw-Hill Education
McGraw-Hill House
Shoppenhangers Road
Maidenhead
Berkshire
England
SL6 2QL

email: enquiries@openup.co.uk
world wide web: www.openup.co.uk

and Two Penn Plaza, New York, NY 10121-2289, USA

First published 2015

A catalogue record of this book is available from the British Library

ISBN-13: 978-0-33-526416-2
ISBN-10: 0-33-526416-6
eISBN: 978-0-33-526417-9

Library of Congress Cataloging-in-Publication Data
CIP data applied for

Typeset by Transforma Pvt. Ltd., Chennai, India

Fictitious names of companies, products, people, characters and/or data that may be used herein (in case studies or in examples) are not intended to represent any real individual, company, product or event.

Printed and bound by CPI Group (UK) Ltd, Croydon, CR0 4YY

Praise for this book

"This volume not only brings together a huge volume and range of research and scholarship on teaching and learning but does so in an extremely accessible and engaging way. This is a book that seeks to encourage thinking, and thinking oriented to helping to enhance higher education and everyone's experience of it at that. It is a splendid book from which everyone can gain."
Ronald Barnett, Emeritus Professor of Higher Education,
UCL Institute of Education

"John Lea's book explores a rich spectrum of themes relating to teaching and learning in higher education in general, and to the notion of professionalism in HE teaching in particular. Not shying away from the profoundly contested nature of higher education, it offers a comprehensive picture of current issues, with contributions from an impressive range of scholars and practitioners. The text stimulates critical, intellectual analysis, but also provides research-informed, practical examples of creative ways forward for the sector."
Dr Dilly Fung, Director of the Centre for the Advancement
of Learning and Teaching, UCL

"This book is a long overdue and hugely welcome addition to the literature on HE professional practice: a text that provides a clear and highly engaging introduction to debates about how academic practices shape university teaching. For far too long introductory HE teaching programmes and their associated texts have tended to provide hints and tips, tools and answers; they have closed down debate and ignored critical voices. Such an anti-intellectual approach rightly generates frustration and cynicism. John Lea's book explicitly sets out to showcase key debates, disagreements and differing voices, opening up the discussion and reflective critique that should be at the heart of enhancing professional practices in learning and teaching in HE. The novel construction provides expert introductions to key themes in academic practice each followed by equally magisterial critical

responses. Further contributions from students and explicit links to the UK Professional Standards Framework for Teaching and Supporting Learning in HE remind us that these are not just theoretical debates but central to the purposes of HE, our intentions and actions as educators and the learning experiences of our students. This book should become a core text for new lecturer programmes and is essential reading for anyone with an interest in the nature and purposes of Higher Education."

Dr John Peters, Head of Academic Practice,
Newman University, UK

Contents

Illustrations

Figures

Tables

Preface

This book has two broad aims. First, it speaks directly to the contested nature of all aspects of higher education, and invites readers to interrogate the evidence which supports the various claims being made, particularly about how aspects of academic practice relate to learning and teaching. Second, and as a consequence of that interrogation, it is designed to help academics – and others who support learning and teaching in UK higher education (HE) – put together applications to become fellows of the Higher Education Academy (HEA). This might be through an application directly to the HEA; within a university or college accredited framework; or as part of a taught programme, such as a PG Cert HE programme. If the book is instructive, its general aim is to give readers some things to think about rather than tell them what to think, and is designed not to appear too much like a textbook. The subtitle of the book also alludes to these two broad aims in being a reference to the three dimensions of the UK professional standards framework (UKPSF) (see Chapter 1) and also to academic practice in general.

Chapter 1 on The Scholarship of Teaching and Learning in Higher Education, and Chapter 8 on Becoming a Fellow of the Higher Education Academy, introduce and conclude the book. Both are practical in focus, aimed at explaining the role of the HEA and the UKPSF as means to enhance the scholarship and effectiveness of teaching and learning in UK HE. Chapter 1 focuses more on the ways in which the UKPSF can be used to benchmark both individual and institutional continuing professional development (CPD). It also offers advice to help practitioners decide which category of fellowship is the most appropriate for them given their role – associate fellowship, fellowship, senior fellowship or principal fellowship (see Chapter 1 for detailed information). Chapter 8 focuses more on the mechanics of actually putting an application together.

The middle chapters of the book look in detail at different aspects of academic practice and how they relate to learning and teaching, beginning with ideas centred on enhancing student learning and finishing with a look at the broader landscape of UK HE and the implications for learning and teaching. Other chapters focus on the nature of academic identity; learning landscapes; academic knowledge; and students as partners respectively. Each chapter begins with an overview and includes case studies, practical examples and activities. Each chapter finishes with a range of stimulus pieces including:

- an opinion piece;
- a debate presenting two opposing arguments;
- student-authored 'Dear Lecturer' pieces;
- extracts from successful fellowship applications relating to the themes of the chapter.

The book was not written to compete with, or replace, existing books aimed at enhancing learning and teaching in higher education, for example, Ramsden (2003); Biggs and Tang (2007); Fry, Ketteridge and Marshall (2014). Indeed, this book assumes that readers will be either familiar with those books, or will access them if they require more information on some of the underpinning conceptual and practical applications of relevant pedagogical tools and ideas. Also, in a book such as this, it is naturally impossible to offer tailored support for individual applications for fellowship status with the HEA, in which case it is important to seek out those colleagues within each university or college who can offer that kind of support, particularly where an application is being made within a specific university or college accredited scheme. In the case of those who work independently from an employing institution, the HEA also has its own support services.

The book is avowedly centred on UK HE, but this comes with two important caveats. First, although one of the key aims of the book is to offer advice on the fellowship application process with the UK-based HEA, the book may also be of interest to readers around the world, particularly where similar learning and teaching accreditation schemes are in operation, and/or where concerted efforts are being made to raise the profile and scholarship of teaching and learning. And, second, many of the reforms that the book discusses might be best characterised as an 'English experiment' rather than being UK-wide. Here, I simply ask for a sympathetic ear from those practitioners living and working in the UK but outside of England, and hope that some of the general direction of travel for UK HE might be at least gleaned from what has been happening in England.

It is also important to remember that a lot of higher education takes place outside of designated universities, in which case I have tried to use the word 'university' only when it was merited by the context of the accompanying sentences. In all other cases I have used the term 'higher education' as a better, more inclusive, term.

Contributors

Patrick Ainley is Professor of Training and Education at the University of Greenwich School of Education and Training (as was). He blogs and publishes free downloads with Martin Allen at: http://www.radicaledbks.com/. Their latest book, *Work, Class, State, Education: New Inequalities in Uncertain Times,* will be published by Radical-read in June 2015.

Jane Allcroft is in her final year of a BA Hons English degree at Newman University, Birmingham. She works part-time in the university as a note-taker and Writing Mentor. A working single mum; she came to university following redundancy and hopes to have a future working in HE.

Wayne Barry is a learning technologist at Canterbury Christ Church University where he is actively involved in enabling learning mediated through the use of educational and social technologies. Wayne's research interests include social media, e-portfolios, learning spaces and professional learning. He is an Associate Fellow of the HEA.

Helen Beetham has been writing, researching and consulting in the field of e-learning since 1999, including on Design for Learning, Open Educational Resources and Digital Literacies. Her edited volumes, *Rethinking Pedagogy for a Digital Age* and *Rethinking Learning for a Digital Age* (Routledge, 2007; 2010) are widely used set texts.

Catherine Bovill is a Senior Lecturer in the Academic Development Unit, University of Glasgow. She has extensive experience of co-ordinating and teaching programmes of study for new academics. Her research focuses on students and staff co-creating curricula; conceptualising curricula; peer observation of teaching; and the internationalisation of higher education.

Cordelia Bryan SFHEA, is a freelance HE consultant with broad experience gained in the secondary, further and higher education sectors. She has led four successful Higher Education projects enhancing different aspects of learning, teaching and assessment and co-edited *Innovative Assessment in Higher Education* (Routledge, 2006).

Colin Bryson is Director of the Combined Honours Centre at Newcastle University. He is a researcher, advocate and practitioner of student engagement and partnership, and privileged to work with outstanding students and colleagues. He co-founded and chairs RAISE and was awarded an NTF for this work in 2009.

Martha Canfield is a PhD student in Psychology at the University of Roehampton where she is also teaching a few research topics for Psychology undergraduate students and carrying out tutorial activities.

Jenni Cannon is a recent graduate from Newcastle University where she studied Combined Honours in English Literature with Psychology, and was keenly involved in student engagement and representation. Jenni is now on the Civil Service Fast Stream graduate programme.

Jonathan Eaton is Research and Engagement Manager at Newcastle College. He completed his PhD at Queen's University Belfast and has taught in FE, HE and adult education. Jonathan is a Senior Fellow of the Higher Education Academy and a Fellow of the Royal Society of Arts.

Yaz El-Hakim is the Director of Student Engagement at the University of Winchester, Co-Leader of the Transforming the Experience of Students through Assessment (TESTA) national project, and the Vice-Chair of SEDA. His teaching and research interests are: Assessment and Feedback, Technology Enhanced Learning, Learning Environments and Student Engagement.

Frank Furedi, is an Emeritus Professor of Sociology at the University of Kent. He is the author of *Wasted: Why Education Is Not Educating*. His study of the history of teaching reading will be published by Bloomsbury in October 2015.

David Gosling is Visiting Professor of Higher Education at the University of Plymouth. He has written widely on topics relating to educational development, learning and teaching in higher education and in applied philosophy. He is currently engaged in supporting the Southern African Universities Learning and Teaching (SAULT) Forum.

Katja Hallenberg is a Senior Lecturer in Criminal Psychology, Criminology and Police Studies at Canterbury Christ Church University which she joined in 2012 after completing her PhD at the University of Manchester. Her key research interests include police education and professionalisation, and the links between justice and sustainability.

Dennis Hayes is the Professor of Education at the University of Derby. He is the founder of the campaign group Academics For Academic Freedom (AFAF). His publications include *The McDonaldization of Higher Education* (2006), *The Dangerous Rise of Therapeutic Education* (2009), and *The 'Limits' of Academic Freedom* (2015).

Mick Healey is an HE consultant and researcher, an emeritus professor at the University of Gloucestershire, visiting professor at UCL, and adjunct professor at Macquarie University, Australia. He was one of the first to be awarded a National Teaching Fellowship and to be made a Principal Fellow of the HEA.

Trevor Hussey is an Emeritus Professor who has taught philosophy and some psychology in Buckinghamshire New University and philosophy in the University of Oxford. He has published work in philosophy of science, the philosophy of nursing and of education, including *The Trouble with Higher Education* with Professor Patrick Smith.

Alan Jenkins long taught and researched geography and was a founding editor of the *Journal of Geography in Higher Education*. He is now an educational developer and Emeritus Professor at Oxford Brookes University. His expertise is on the relations between teaching and discipline-based research and embedding undergraduate research (http://alanjenkins.info/).

Ruth Lawton is University Learning & Teaching Fellow for Employability at Birmingham City University. Ruth joined the university as a careers adviser in 1991 but is now Programme Director for the PG Cert Learning & Teaching in HE, and is also MEd module lead for 'Embedding Employability in Your Practice'.

John Lea is Head of Academic Professional Development at Canterbury Christ Church University. His previous books include: *Political Correctness and Higher Education: British and American Perspectives* (Routledge, 2009) and *Supporting Higher Education in College Settings* (SEDA, 2014). He is a Principal Fellow of the HEA, and a Fellow of SEDA.

Diane Locke is a third year undergraduate studying youth and community work at Newman University, Birmingham. She is interested in the emergence of dyslexia as a positive attribute rather than a difficulty that needs support, and in using creativity in the curriculum as a means to engage students.

Sam Louis is a recent graduate of Newcastle University in English Literature, Business and Psychology. He is currently planning an extensive trip across Canada, after which he hopes to start his own business venture.

Bruce Macfarlane is Professor of Higher Education at the University of Southampton. He has previously held chairs at universities in the UK and Hong Kong. His publications have developed concepts related to academic practice, ethics and leadership. He is a Fellow of the Society for Research into Higher Education.

Anna McCormick graduated from Trinity College, Cambridge in 2010 with a degree in English Literature. She now works in strategy and project management in London.

Emily McCormick is a third year undergraduate at Loughborough University. She is currently in her placement year working at King's College Hospital in London as an information and performance analyst for paediatric neurosciences, creating and developing data management processes within the NHS.

Mike Neary is Professor of Sociology at the University of Lincoln in the School of Social and Political Sciences. While Dean of Teaching and Learning at Lincoln (2007–2014), Mike promoted the development of Student as Producer in higher education.

Ralph Norman is Principal Lecturer in Theology at Canterbury Christ Church University. His teaching concentrates on aspects of Philosophy of Religion and Historical Theology, and has included a series of seminars on Newman's *The Idea of a University*. His most recent publications have been on the history of British philosophy.

David Palfreyman is the Bursar and a Fellow of New College, Oxford, and the Director of the Oxford Centre for Higher Education Policy Studies. He is co-author of *The Law of Higher Education* (OUP, 2012) and *Reshaping the University: The Rise of the Regulated Market in Higher Education* (OUP, 2015).

Celia Popovic is Director of the Teaching Commons at York University, Toronto. Celia enjoyed a 20-year career in HE in the UK before moving to Canada in 2011. She has taught across numerous subjects in schools, colleges and universities giving her an eclectic view of education.

Nigel Purcell joined the HEA in 2011 as Academic Lead for the UKPSF/Recognition, after a career teaching in Further Education and then Medical Education development. His first task was to help oversee the launch of the revised UKPSF and he continues to be closely involved in its subsequent development.

Kate Riseley recently graduated with a 2:1 in English Literature from Canterbury Christ Church University. While studying she engaged in various Student Engagement initiatives which fuelled her desire to pursue employment in HE. Her interests for further study include exploring the notion of 'Being, Belonging and Becoming' through narrative accounts.

Patrick Smith is an Emeritus Professor at Buckinghamshire New University. Author of several books, more recently on work-based learning, he was also responsible for the development of the University's highly successful MA in Leadership and Management. Patrick has worked in the UK and abroad as a programme designer and facilitator.

Chris Stevens is an historian who taught history and politics at successively QMUL and Teesside University, between 1981 and 2001. He is currently Director of Quality and Standards at Canterbury Christ Church University. His publications include work on grass-roots conservatism in the late nineteenth century and electoral change in the twentieth.

Brigitte Stockton is Director of Programmes at the Winchester School of Art, University of Southampton, Dalian Campus, China. Her current research and publication interests

are in: transnational education; pedagogy and assessment in the arts; and sustainable consumer cultures.

Ted Tapper is an Emeritus Professor of Politics, University of Sussex, and currently a research fellow at the Oxford Centre for Policy Studies, New College, Oxford. His research embraces the politics of higher education and the political struggles generated by the relationship of the private and public sectors of schooling.

Dave Thomas is an Occupational Therapist employed at Canterbury Christ Church University and currently studying an MSc in Public Health. Last year, as an undergraduate, he was a pioneering Student Ambassador for Learning and Teaching (SALT), where he undertook a project exploring the inclusivity of the HE curriculum.

Figure credits

Acknowledgements

This book is very much a collaborative effort. Although I am the main author and the editor, it never made any sense to me, from conception to execution, to see this book as anything other than being wholly dependent on the contributions made by all the authors who agreed to take part in the project. I am extremely grateful for every contribution, both large and small.

On the large contribution side, those from Cordelia Bryan, Mike Neary, Helen Beetham, Mick Healey, Alan Jenkins and Cathy Bovill were integral to giving the book its overall coherence. I also wish to formally thank them for the speed and diligence they all exercised in turning my sketchy outlines into the fully formed chapters they became. I am also extremely grateful to Nigel Purcell, from the HEA, who worked diligently and patiently with me on Chapter 1 and Chapter 8, and particularly when my ideas were in danger of becoming unwieldy (which happened regularly).

On the opinion pieces and the debates I am hugely indebted to every author, none of whom needed much persuasion, and none of whom wrote beyond the word limit of 1,000 words, making the job of editing extremely straightforward. It should also be noted that for the debate pieces no authors read the opposing author's piece in advance of writing their own, which, again, made the editing task much easier, and prevented any catfights about who should go first and second in the debate; that decision was left to me, and I am grateful to everyone for that.

Two of the most distinctive features of the book are the contributions from the student authors and the extracts from successful fellowship applications. On the former I am extremely grateful to the students who enthusiastically took part in this project, both by reading drafts chapters of the book, and then contributing as authors. And on the latter, I am naturally indebted to colleagues up and down the country who agreed to allow me to use extracts from their successful fellowship applications (which I anonymised).

I am also grateful to the many colleagues who agreed to look at drafts of various parts of the book, particularly Anita Cooper, Jonathan Simmons and Phil Poole, and to Nicky Galer who helped with the various figures and checked the referencing before submission of the manuscript. I am also extremely grateful to the Higher Education Academy for their help and endorsement of the project, particularly

Stephanie Marshall and Raj Dhimar. I am also indebted to Fiona Richman, at the Open University Press, for trusting me to pull all this together, and particularly at those points when it must have looked like a publisher's nightmare. And, finally, I wish to thank Tris Ariss enormously for doing an amazing job on re-presenting my rather amateur drawing of the transport map, which appears at the end of the book.

John Lea, March 2015

1

Introduction
The scholarship of teaching and learning, the Higher Education Academy, and the UK Professional Standards Framework

John Lea and Nigel Purcell[1]

The scholarship of teaching and learning (SoTL)

> *What we urgently need today is a more inclusive view of what it means to be a scholar – a recognition that knowledge is acquired through research, through synthesis, through practice, and through teaching. We acknowledge that these four categories – the scholarship of discovery, of integration, of application, and of teaching – divide intellectual functions that are tied inseparably to each other.*
>
> (Boyer 1990: 25)

Twenty-five years on from this statement it is tempting to say that things have moved on enormously in the direction of Ernest Boyer's revisioning, not just in the United States (the country that Boyer was primarily referring to), but throughout higher education around the world. However, one might equally argue that things have changed very little. Ask a random group of academics today to whom or to what they owe their primary allegiance and you are probably still more likely to hear them refer to their subject-based research than any scholarship related to teaching and learning. Pursue this further with the same group and you might also discover that though some of them will not be happy with that situation, it is a case of needs must. That is, reward and recognition, and career progression in general are more likely to occur the sooner one turns Boyer's proposed *cycle* of academic activities back into the linear ladder he was arguing against; with the scholarship of discovery (or original research) on the top rung, and the scholarship of teaching and learning (SoTL) on the bottom (and the other forms of scholarship somewhere in the middle) (Figure 1.1).

We will be exploring this issue in some detail in Chapter 2, but for now it will serve as an introduction to the whole book, and for two reasons. First, it highlights the contested nature of some of the primary aims of higher education, and this notion of contestability will be a consistent theme running throughout the book. And, second, it raises the question of the relationship between learning and teaching and all other aspects of academic practice. In this regard, each chapter of the book looks at how the status of learning and teaching might be enhanced within academic practice overall,

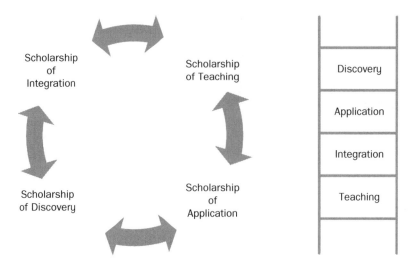

Figure 1.1 Depictions of Boyer's (1990) four scholarships.

but also how the various dimensions of academic practice might be better integrated. To begin this process, and after explaining the structure of the book, the rest of this introductory chapter will focus on the role of the Higher Education Academy (HEA) and the UK Professional Standards Framework (UKPSF) in seeking to raise the profile of learning and teaching in UK HE along the lines that Boyer advocated.

Academic practice and the main themes of the book

Apart from Chapter 1 and Chapter 8, the book is divided into six chapters, reflecting different aspects of academic practice and how they relate to teaching and learning: Chapter 2, 'Enhancing Student Learning'; Chapter 3, 'the Nature of Academic Time'; Chapter 4, 'the Nature of Academic Space'; Chapter 5, 'the Nature of Academic Knowledge'; Chapter 6, 'Students as Partners in Learning'; and Chapter 7, 'the Landscape of Higher Education'.

The first of these (Chapter 2) looks at the theme of learning, teaching and assessment: how the three are related; how they affect each other; and how ideas relating to each dimension have changed over the years, particularly in them all becoming more student-centred. In Chapter 3, we look at the question of academic identity and academic allegiances, and the contested nature of academic work; that is, what academics do with their time. The fourth chapter will look at the changing nature of academic space; how the architecture of higher education is shaped and is being reshaped in both face-to-face situations and in terms of digital space. Chapter 5 explores issues associated with academic knowledge and asks whether an expanded understanding of what constitutes knowledge is enhancing or diminishing the nature and aims of higher education. In Chapter 6, we look at the various ways in which we might enhance the role of students in all aspects of academic life, including the role of students as scholars – involved in the production of knowledge – rather than simply as consumers of knowledge. Chapter 7 looks at the changing landscape of higher education in

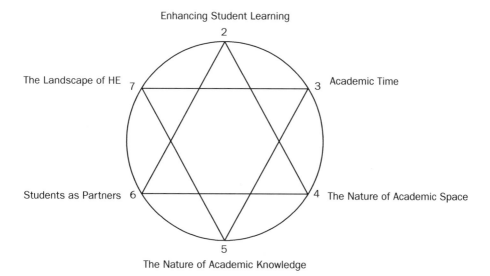

Figure 1.2 Depiction of the rationale for the book's chapters.

general, including the expansion of higher education outside universities, and the movement towards increased marketisation in the sector. Chapter 8 will return to the main themes, but couched squarely this time in the context of providing practical advice to readers on preparing an application to become a fellow of the HEA.

Figure 1.2 depicts the rationale for the order of the chapters. At the top, Chapter 2 links directly to Chapters 4 and 6, with a focus on the immediate learning context. At the bottom, Chapter 5 links directly with Chapters 3 and 7, with a focus on the wider aspects of academic practice and how they relate (or could be better related) to learning and teaching. But each chapter contains threads and themes from previous chapters to explore the means to integrate all the aspects of academic practice, and this is depicted by the outer circle.

Each chapter begins with an overview of the main themes, mapping out some key ideas and concepts and referring to relevant academic and policy literature on those themes. This is followed by more punchy, polemical, opinion pieces where the authors offer their own perspectives on a key theme of the chapter. Then follow debate pieces where the contributors were chosen precisely because of their opposing stances on an issue that relates to each chapter. Next there is a 'Dear Lecturer' piece written by students in response to the main themes of the chapter. The text is peppered with activities demonstrating how the themes of the chapters might be incorporated into applications for fellowship status with the HEA. And each chapter ends with quotes from anonymised successful fellowship applications.

The Enhancing Learning and Teaching Transport Map

In Appendix 3, you will also find a 'transport map' which depicts each of the chapters as an underground line and the main concepts used in each chapter as the underground train stations on that line. Transfer stations on the map indicate where different chapters have some key overlapping conceptual discussion and, again, the aim here is to show how the wider aspects of academic practice are interrelated and can be drawn together to enhance learning and teaching in Higher Education (HE). At the end of the book you will also find a glossary of these key concepts (stations) where the relevant concept is discussed.

The role of the Higher Education Academy (HEA) in the changing HE context

The HEA is the national body for enhancing learning and teaching in higher education (HE). We are committed to excellent learning and teaching, supporting UK HE organisations with an emphasis on improving the student experience.

With a robust evidence base to underpin all our work, we: help individuals realise professional learning and teaching ambitions; support organisations to achieve their strategic ambitions to enhance teaching and learning; work across the sector to shape the future of HE.

(HEA website)

The HEA was formed in May 2004 from a merger of the Institute for Learning and Teaching in Higher Education (ILTHE) and the 24 subject centres of the Learning and Teaching Support Network (LTSN) and the National Coordination Team for the Teaching Quality Enhancement Fund. The ILTHE was founded in 2000 as a result of the report of the National Committee of Inquiry into Higher Education (Dearing 1997), and in this regard the HEA can be considered a natural extension of a much broader movement in the UK aimed at raising the profile of the scholarship of teaching and learning, and in keeping with the initial critique and subsequent revisioning of academic practice, as undertaken by Ernest Boyer and his colleagues in the USA in the 1980s (Boyer 1990).

The HEA is a registered company, limited by guarantee and is a registered charity in England and Wales, and is owned by Universities UK (UUK) and GuildHE. It is publicly funded by the four HE Funding Councils in England, Northern Ireland, Scotland and Wales and by subscription from universities, colleges and other organisations with a vested interest in HE teaching. It also offers a range of bespoke services commercially to HE providers in the UK and overseas. As a professional body, it is therefore not owned by its individual members, and the members do not pay an annual registration fee (as in the case of many professional bodies). However, and like most other professional bodies, it is moving in the direction of requiring its fellows to produce annual evidence of 'staying in good standing', with reference to an accompanying professional code. It is also not the only professional body representing higher education learning and teaching. For example, the Staff and Educational Development Association (SEDA) has been running since 1992, and has its own fellowship scheme aimed at educational developers, but also has a much wider professional development framework aimed at anyone teaching and supporting learning in higher education.

The UK Professional Standards Framework (UKPSF)

Either as an academic, or as someone working in the professional services which support learning and teaching in higher education, you will probably be involved in a wide range of professional roles at any one time and throughout your career. Taking Boyer's work as a starting point, you may at times be a: teacher, tutor, supporter of learning; leader and manager at the curriculum, faculty/school, or institution-wide level; subject-based and/or pedagogic researcher and scholar; and/or consultant for a community or company and/or public intellectual. The UK Professional Standards Framework (UKPSF) provides a conceptual framework – written from the perspective of the practitioner – to aid understanding of this full range of teaching and learning roles, aimed at helping support the enhancement of scholarly approaches to teaching and learning, and encouraging practitioners to reflect on how these roles can be integrated into the wider aspects of academic practice, including aspects of leadership and management, consultancy, and work as a public intellectual.

It was also developed to support both institutional and individual responses to the rapid and substantial changes to the role and nature of higher education, and specifically in relation to how those that impact directly on teaching and supporting learning. These changes include:

* increasing student numbers;
* the implications of widening participation, particularly in respect of non-traditional learners, and first generation entrants to higher education;
* the increased involvement of students in all aspects of higher education provision;
* the major changes to fee and loan structures, particularly in England, and the increasing policy divergence among the UK nations;
* reductions in per capita teaching budgets, which, for example, will be close to 6 per cent for 2014–2015 (Grove 2014);
* substantial innovation in learning technologies and the rise of massive online open courses (MOOCs) and online learning in general;
* increasing diversification of HE institutions (HEIs), including a growing college-based HE (CBHE) offer and the development of the private sector university;
* issues regarding employability and what employers are looking for in graduates;
* changes in societal attitudes to professionals, including a perceived loss of trust and an increasing expectation of external accountability in the performance of professional roles;
* increased concern over issues relating to sustainability, both within and outside the formal curriculum;
* the positioning of UK higher education within an increasingly globalised HE sector.

Some of the dimensions and implications of this last point are featured in the first opinion piece in the book, which appears at the end of Chapter 1, and the issue of sustainability will be the subject of the final opinion piece at the end of Chapter 8.

The UKPSF began its life in 2005 when the HEA ran a consultation exercise on the establishment of a professional standards framework for UK HE focused on learning and teaching. The subsequent framework (known as the UKPSF from that point) is housed by the HEA but was designed to be used flexibly by universities, colleges and individuals as a means to benchmark their own continuing professional development (CPD) activities, aimed primarily at enhancing the effectiveness and scholarship of learning and teaching in UK HE. The first version of the UKPSF was published in 2005 and was strongly influenced by the earlier ILTHE set of standards. Following an extensive consultation process with the sector in 2010–2011, the 2005 edition was revised and the current version was published in November 2011 (HEA 2011). The UKPSF is endorsed by all major HE sector bodies including, Guild HE, the Scottish Funding Council, the Department for Employment and Learning, the Higher Education Funding Council for England, the National Union of Students, the Higher Education Funding Council for Wales and Universities UK. As such, it enjoys a legitimacy in the sector which greatly enhances its value at a national level.

Its five stated aims (HEA 2011) are:

1   To support the initial and continuing professional development of staff engaged in teaching and supporting learning.

2   To foster dynamic approaches to teaching and learning through creativity, innovation and continuous development in diverse academic or professional settings.

3   To demonstrate to students and other stakeholders the professionalism that staff and institutions bring to teaching and support for student learning.

4   To acknowledge the variety and quality of teaching, learning and assessment practices that support and underpin student learning.

5   To facilitate individuals and institutions in gaining formal recognition for quality-enhanced approaches to teaching and supporting learning, often as part of wider responsibilities which may include research or management activities.

The language and structure of the UK Professional Standards Framework

The Framework has been developed by the HEA on behalf of the sector as a whole and so it is the property of all of those with a direct interest in the HE sector.

(HEA website)

In describing the professional role of teaching and supporting learning in higher education, the language employed in the UKPSF is intentionally descriptive rather than evaluative. It is not highly technical or jargon-laden and for a document of its kind, it is very concise. This allows it to be used flexibly by, and within, institutions wishing to develop their own emphases and interpretative principles, albeit within the wider constraints of the national standards coordinated by the HEA through their fellowship scheme (see below). It is important to note here that though the UKPSF itself can be interpreted in a number of ways, the fellowship scheme belongs to the HEA, and therefore those seeking HEA fellowships must engage with that scheme in the manner prescribed by the HEA or as prescribed by the various HEA-accredited fellowship scheme frameworks running in universities and colleges throughout the UK.

The UKPSF is not directly based on any particular theoretical framework, though it does tie in with Boyer's (1990) suggested four levels of scholarship (see above), the implications of which will be discussed throughout this book. It is targeted specifically at teaching and learning support and, indeed, has been criticised because of this narrow focus, but its avowed intention is not to undermine other aspects of academic practice but to seek ways in which the scholarship of teaching and learning (SoTL) may be enhanced within a holistic and integrated approach to academic practice. And it recognises 'that the scholarly nature of subject inquiry and knowledge creation, and a scholarly approach to pedagogy, together represent a uniquely embedded feature of support for student learning in universities and colleges' (HEA 2005).

The UKPSF thus encourages and facilitates an *integrated* approach to academic practice through its emphasis on both discipline and pedagogic scholarship, and particularly since the revision in 2011, with an enhanced emphasis on management and leadership responsibilities, particularly in the new Descriptor 3 and Descriptor 4 categories (see below). Finally, and while recognising that pedagogy, as both a generic discipline, and through subject pedagogies (i.e. teaching and learning as related to particular discipline contexts), will have conceptual and theoretical underpinnings, the framework's key orientation is towards *applying* scholarship directly to the enhancement of practice in teaching and supporting learning in HE; put simply, the framework seeks to enact theory *in* practice.

It is also important to emphasise that it is a framework *for*, and not a set *of*, standards. It does not attempt to specify detailed performance criteria (as in a competency approach) and this has made it a much more flexible and adaptable tool for a wide range of CPD. In this context, the framework may also be contrasted with other professional standards frameworks which have been developed for the wider post-compulsory education sector, including by Lifelong Learning UK (LLUK), and by the National Council for Vocational Qualifications (NCVQ). The National Vocational Qualification (NVQ) system with its elements, performance criteria, evidence requirements and knowledge and understanding statements are all designed to comprehensively outline in specific detail exactly what is required in order to meet the relevant standard. This inevitably leads to very extensive documentation, for example, the logbook for an Edexcel NVQ in Learning and Development Level 4 is 263 pages long (in contrast to the 183 words for the entire UKPSF description). And while this approach to professional development, and education and training in general has been robustly defended (Jessup 1991), it has also been the subject of vociferous critique (e.g. Hyland 1994; Grugulis 2000).

The old LLUK standards (2005–2012), aimed mainly at further education college (FEC) lecturers, have also been contrasted with the UKPSF in two related projects undertaken for LLUK and the HEA respectively:

> the LLUK framework contains several references to the need to be 'compliant with', as opposed to 'engage with', which seems to be the general inference in the UKPSF. Following on from this, it could also be inferred that the LLUK framework

tends to define professionalism in terms of effective engagement with the roles and activities it specifies, whereas the UKPSF tends to define the professionalism in terms of one's commitment to the reflection and evaluation of one's own practice.

(Lea 2011: 9)

The LLUK standards are considered to be outcome- or competence-based standards whereas the UKPSF is regarded as a descriptor-based set of standards. The latter set out to assess the capability of individuals to engage with and make sense of aspects of the student learning experience for themselves within the parameters of their subject discipline and broader pedagogy. The former appear to require professionals to demonstrate that they respond to dozens of behaviourally-oriented expectations. The forerunner to the LLUK standards, the FEnto standards, were often criticised as leading to the atomisation of learning programmes mitigating against a holistic and coherent learning experience that may inhibit personal and professional development.

(Price 2011: 9)

While it may be possible to use the UKPSF as a structure for defining and applying standards, in itself it is probably insufficiently detailed and lacks the qualitative statements which would be needed to specify a standard. Rather, it is much better viewed as a framework through which a wide range of professional practice in teaching and supporting learning in HE can be reviewed, evaluated and developed. In this regard, it is designed to facilitate the kinds of critical reflective practice inspired by the work of Donald Schön (Schön 1983). And what seems clear from the two aforementioned projects is that the UKPSF appears much more developmental, and even *ipsative* in its approach, in that it provides opportunities for individuals to benchmark their own CPD, rather than provide evidence that someone is fit, or competent, to practise (albeit within the constraints imposed by the various fellowship schemes and frameworks in terms of how that CPD needs to be documented).

In summary, we offer Figure 1.3 as contrasting statements concerning the two approaches to standards.

The UKPSF has two key components:

1   the three dimensions of practice;
2   the four descriptors (D1–D4).

The three dimensions of practice

The dimensions provide three complementary perspectives reflecting the complexity and multi-faceted nature of the professional role of staff engaged in teaching and supporting learning. They are intended to cover what are considered to be the three fundamental aspects in the professional role of teaching and/or supporting learning.

A competency approach:

1. Tends to fix the definition of a specified role, which unavoidably reflects the views and opinions of the authors of the framework (subject to consultation). Even if this is well done, it will tend to embed a consensus view of a profession and be resistant to more radical minority approaches and is thus likely to be conservative in its approach.

2. Is necessarily generic and may therefore not be fully appropriate for the particular circumstances, policies, systems, culture, etc. of an individual or institution.

3. No matter how detailed and carefully written, is unlikely to cover all eventualities of any complex professional role and specific phrases, and terms will still remain open to variations in interpretation, possibly leading to ambivalence and potential confusion.

4. In a rapidly changing professional environment it can crystallise standards which become out of date leading to awkward misalignment with real practice (and which it is not practical to correct more frequently than every few years).

5. Particularly where the evidence-gathering process is very detailed, is very likely to succumb to a tick box approach to compliance.

The UKPSF 'Framework' approach:

1. Does not privilege one particular approach or methodology and therefore allows alternative, and perhaps minority approaches to be used and recognised.

2. Allows individuals, teams and organisations to fully contextualise their interpretation of the framework to their particular circumstances, roles and institutional contexts and strategic objectives.

3. While recognising there may be some difficulty in interpretation of specific elements in the framework, it produces a set of statements from which to begin the interrogation, and subsequent enhancement, of one's own teaching and learning regime in relation to other aspects of academic practice.

4. Recognises the need to update (on a five-year cycle) but mid-cycle it is fully adaptable to current practice, in only ever outlining the broadest range of dimensions of practice.

5. Recognises that alignment with a Fellowship category is a demanding but thoughtful process of critical reflection on one's own practice. The Framework encourages practitioners to adopt a scholarly and developmental narrative account, which is authentic and meaningful.

Figure 1.3 Contrasting a competency approach to standards with the UKPSF.

The three dimensions are:

1   *A: the areas of activity* undertaken by teachers and supporters of learning within higher education (with the emphasis on 'what you do');
2   *K: the core knowledge* that you need to gain and apply to carry out those activities at the appropriate level. This includes both relevant factual and propositional knowledge as well as the practical skills to put that knowledge into practice (with the emphasis on 'how you do it').
3   *V: the professional values* that you embrace and exemplify in performing these activities (with the emphasis on 'why you do it').

The three dimensions are often depicted in a cyclical way in order to encourage practitioners to consider them holistically, that is, how aspects in one dimension can be related to the others. For example, in developing a new mode of assessment on a course, this might have been informed by a recognition that some (if not all) students were previously being inhibited by the ways in which they were asked to engage and demonstrate their learning. Here the elements A3, K3 and V2 are being combined (see Appendix 1). And in a particular narrative context, this might also include engagement with A2, K2 and all the other values. Appendix 1 illustrates the different dimensions of practice and elements found in the UKPSF. The extracts from the HEA fellowship applications show these dimensions, added.

Apart from the values (which, obviously are value-laden), the areas of activity and the core knowledge statements are almost wholly descriptive, apart from the very mild adjectives like 'effective' and 'appropriate' (which are themselves open to interpretation by individual practitioners), and the values are intended to invite interrogation and interpretation of their meaning in practice.

The dimensions, particularly the core knowledge, are intended to describe knowledge in action rather than just propositional knowledge – 'knowing how' rather than just 'knowing that' (see Eraut 2000), in which case, the framework encourages practitioners to look for examples of where conceptual and theoretical understanding have been applied in practice.

Some illustrations of how the areas of activity might be interpreted in practice

When you prepare to teach or support students, you would typically design and plan at least an outline of the intended learning experience(s) in advance (A1). Then put your plans into practice (A2), either in the classroom or other physical or virtual environments as appropriate. As part of this support, you would generally undertake some kind of assessment of the learning; sometimes before the activity, to gauge prior knowledge; sometimes during the learning process, to evaluate progress and adapt the experience appropriately; and sometimes afterwards to ensure the intended learning has taken place, to identify gaps and in some cases to provide a summative – perhaps certificated – assessment of outcomes (A3).

The environment both real and virtual, of course, strongly influences the learning experience and you would plan for and effectively use it during delivery (A4a). And, generally, as your students engage with learning, whether in formal sessions or in other locations, you would seek to provide careful and sensitive support to help them with their questions and issues (A4b).

And as part of your commitment to do the best for your students, you would be careful to keep up to date with the relevant subject matter, to evaluate by various means the methods you have employed and to modify and develop your approaches and methods as appropriate (A5).

It would be an oversimplification to represent the five areas as a straightforward linear sequence in which you always begin with design, followed by delivery, etc., and not forgetting, of course, each individual has a unique teaching profile. In practice, you may well be responsible for teaching/supporting a number of different groups of learners (or individual learners) simultaneously. So at any one time you may be at different stages in the activity cycle in respect of different groups.

Some illustrations of how the core knowledge might be interpreted in practice

Clearly, you would generally have a full grasp of the relevant content of any subject you are teaching and/or supporting and would use all of the usual means to keep up to date with your subject (K1). You would also have a good knowledge of a range of appropriate methods for teaching, learning and assessing in your discipline area (K2) and your choice and application of methods and approaches will be determined by your understanding of how students most effectively learn in your discipline (K3) and of the potential of current technologies to enhance learning (K4).

In order to continue to develop and enhance your teaching or learning support role, you would generally evaluate your progress and performance and make changes in response to the information from those evaluations (K5). And all of your work is, of course, set in a wider higher education context of policy reform, which you need both to be aware of and to respond to appropriately (K6).

Some illustrations of how the values might be interpreted in practice

'Respect for individual learners and diverse learning communities' (V1) influences your attitude towards your students and to the various learning communities with which you engage. The key term in that element is 'respect' and while this term is not unproblematic and is open to a range of nuances in interpretation, the fundamental principle of seeking to do your very best for your students and of acting in their interest is surely not in dispute.

'Promote participation in higher education and equality of opportunity for learners' (V2) focuses on your commitment to establishing and enhancing inclusive educational practice. Again, these terms are open to a wide range of interpretations and it is important to realise that they are to be understood and applied in context. But the broad principle that all students (including prospective ones) are entitled to appropriate support and help to engage with their learning, regardless of potentially discriminatory/limiting characteristics, is surely uncontroversial.

'Using evidence-informed approaches and the outcomes from research, scholarship and continuing professional development' (V3) emphasises your commitment to your own development and in particular to you taking a thoughtful, reasoned, and scholarly approach to your teaching and supporting learning activities. To do this, you will draw on a range of sources in evaluating and enhancing your practice and seek to keep up to date with methods, approaches and issues in teaching and learning in your field, and possibly contribute in a variety of scholarly ways to that evidence base.

'Acknowledge the wider context in which higher education operates, recognising the implications for professional practice' (V4) stresses the need for you to be aware of the wider context in which HE operates, globally as well as nationally, and to be able to respond appropriately – within your discipline and professional context – to policy reform and general social trends which impinge on higher education provision.

The UKPSF Descriptors

The Descriptors are four set of statements which draw on the dimensions of practice to outline the key characteristics of staff performing at four broad categories of typical teaching and learning support roles within Higher Education (see Appendix 2).

Appendix 2 presents the UKPSF Descriptors (D1–D4). Each category corresponds with a fellowship category: D1 Associate Fellowship; D2 Fellowship; D3 Senior Fellowship; D4 Principal Fellowship, and the descriptors thereby outline what somebody, typically, would need to demonstrate evidence of doing, in their everyday practice, in order to make a claim (in a fellowship application) to be awarded the relevant fellowship.

It is important to stress that the four fellowships are not intended to be viewed as a hierarchy. Rather, they correspond to the activities that practitioners typically engage with in their everyday practice. In this regard they are role-related, but not necessarily *job*-role related. That is, it is your role in enhancing learning and teaching which the descriptors seek to capture. For example, a Professor of (say) Chemistry might be an internationally renowned scholar in their discipline context, but may have little or no responsibility for assessing students' work; little or no responsibility for institution-based learning and teaching strategies; or have a research profile that relates only to Chemistry as a subject, not its pedagogical implications. In this example, Associate Fellowship would probably be the most appropriate fellowship category for this professor.

Related to 1 and 2 above, the descriptors are also designed to help prospective fellows engage with the three dimensions of practice in appropriate ways and in accord with their roles. Each fellowship category is there to enable a practitioner to seek recognition for what they either actually already do in this respect, or might do (as forms of CPD) in seeking to become a fellow of the HEA. Once again, all fellowship categories are equal in status in that respect. And here, the descriptors would perhaps be better always depicted horizontally rather than vertically. That said, a change in role might well prompt someone to consider making a further claim for a different category of fellowship than one already held.

If you are unsure which fellowship category you might consider applying for, here is a quick reference guide followed by some key questions to ask yourself:

- *Descriptor 1* is appropriate for all 'Individuals able to provide evidence of effectiveness in relation to their professional role(s) which, typically, will include at least some teaching and/or learning support responsibilities. This teaching and learning role may sometimes be undertaken with the assistance of more experienced teachers or mentors.'

- *Descriptor 2* is appropriate for all 'Individuals able to provide evidence of broadly based effectiveness in more substantive teaching and supporting learning role(s). Such individuals are likely to be established members of one or more academic and/or academic-related teams.'

- *Descriptor 3* is appropriate for 'Individuals able to provide evidence of a sustained record of effectiveness in relation to teaching and learning, incorporating for example, the organisation, leadership and/or management of specific aspects of teaching and learning provision. Such individuals are likely to lead or be members of established academic teams.'

- *Descriptor 4* is appropriate for 'Individuals, as highly experienced academics, able to provide evidence of a sustained and effective record of impact at a strategic level in relation to teaching and learning, as part of a wider commitment to academic practice. This may be within their institution or wider (inter) national settings' (UKPSF 2011).

You might also ask yourself the following questions:

- *D1 or D2?* – When looking at the five elements in the areas of activity are there any that you know you have no responsibility for in your current role/range of activities? To make a claim for Associate Fellowship you only need to demonstrate engagement with two areas of activity.

- *D2 or D3?* – Do you have a leadership role in your current practice related to teaching and learning? For example, do you have responsibility as a programme, course, or framework director, or do you mentor colleagues in some capacity? If you answered yes here, then D3 may be the appropriate descriptor to look at more closely.

- *D3 or D4?* – Have you had some responsibility for, and could demonstrate clear impact on, teaching and learning-related strategies which are institution-wide, or do you have a national/international profile/standing with respect to learning and teaching within your discipline context or HE in general? If you answered yes here, then D4 may be the appropriate descriptor to look at more closely.

Engaging with the UKPSF

It is important to remember that the UKPSF is a framework which can be used in a number of ways. For example, an individual might use it informally to help him or her put together an application for an academic post, using it to demonstrate the nature of engagement they have had with a range of teaching and learning activities. Or an institution might use it as part of a CPD framework, which individuals are either encouraged, or mandated, to engage with in some capacity (and which may be related to promotion opportunities). In both of these cases there may be no formal qualification or claim for fellowship attached to these activities.

Alternatively, an institution may have had their CPD framework accredited by the HEA and thereby be enabled to award HEA fellowships to their staff, and in accord with how that institution expects the engagement with the UKPSF to be demonstrated. For example, you may be required to present your case for fellowship orally in front of a group of peers, or by written application, or by registering for a taught award (and achieve a fellowship upon successful completion of that award), or by choosing from any number of options which the institution in question permits.

For those who work independently of an employing HE institution, or who work for an institution which does not subscribe to the HEA, you may still be able to access an accredited-institution scheme which uses the UKPSF (or awards fellowships) by approaching the person responsible for the scheme. Indeed, this might be encouraged where there is a partnership agreement between a number of universities or where, for example, there is a university and further education college consortia, particularly where the latter offers degree programmes validated by the university. In these cases always ask about what fees might apply in your individual case. And of course, all individuals working to support learning in any capacity in a higher education context can apply for a fellowship directly through the HEA's own fellowship scheme.

Conclusion

The UKPSF provides a comprehensive and coherent framework for considering all types of teaching and learning support roles in HE. It is practical, it is widely accepted within the sector, and it can be used developmentally both by individuals and strategically by HE institutions. However, it is not without its detractors, particularly those who view the HEA as a kind of watchdog or quango, who have been charged with overseeing and implementing a robotic approach to teaching and learning in HE, by making HE teachers subscribe to a prescriptive and limiting set of competency-based standards for teaching and learning, and in the process leading them away from a research-led approach to teaching and learning in UK HE. Yes, it may be possible to use the UKPSF in this way, but because individuals and institutions are free to use it in a range of ways, our hope is that it will continue to be used in a much more personally reflective (and possibly *ipsative*) manner, and in keeping with the aspirational and non-prescriptive way in which it was originally conceived. On this point it is worth noting, as recommended in the two Lingfield Reports (Lingfield 2012a, 2012b), that the wider post-compulsory sector in England has now adopted an approach to standards which is very similar to the UKPSF (Education and Training Foundation 2014).

That said, the HEA does own the fellowships – after all, practitioners are becoming fellows of that body – and we should not forget the HEA's wider remit to help raise the profile of learning and teaching in HE and the scholarship of teaching and learning (SoTL). On the fellowships, the HEA encourages universities and colleges to have accredited a range of activities and approaches to CPD, and thereby enable fellowships to be awarded in a number of different ways and to suit the requirements of particular institutional contexts. However, on its wider remit, we quickly find ourselves back on much more contested terrain. For some, the HEA's expansion of the work of the original 24 subject centres, and its sponsorship more generally of a wide range of pedagogically related research and other collaborative projects, have all been of enormous service to the sector. But, for others, it has been easy to find evidence that none of these activities has produced what one might call a 'step change' in the nature of the profile of learning and teaching in UK HE.

Clearly the jury is still out on how best to raise the profile of learning and teaching, and it may well be out for some time to come. There may be several reasons for this. It may take many years to adjust reward and recognition within higher education to better reflect the efforts of those who excel in teaching and learning-related activities as opposed to subject-based research activities. Some universities now have routes to readerships and professorships which fully recognise contributions to the learning and teaching landscape, but others don't, relying on the traditional measures related much more closely to what Boyer referred to as the scholarship of discovery. But this whole area is further complicated by contested notions of desired relationships between teaching and research generally in higher education. Some of these issues will be discussed in more detail in Chapter 3.

Furthermore, the whole question of HE pedagogy is itself a contested notion. Is there actually a pedagogy associated with higher education, which is different, say, from further education? Are there any generic pedagogic principles and theories upon which we can all agree, or are there only subject pedagogies, and are these based on sound epistemological foundations, or merely conventions of narrowly focused discipline practice? And what is the best way to prepare academics for teaching roles – through generic teaching awards; through PhD programmes; through informal forms of mentoring? Can teaching be viewed as a science, based on hard experimental and accumulated knowledge of how people learn, or is it better viewed as a craft, or something entirely different altogether, and better conceived in terms of critical reflective (or reflexive) practice – in the spirit of authors like Schön (1983) and Mesirow (2000)? Evidence can be found to support claims in all these directions, and much of it is contained in the following report.

Relevant HEA project

Parsons, D., Hill, I., Holland, J. and Willis, D. (2012) The impact of teaching development programmes in higher education. Available at: www.heacademy.ac.uk/sites/default/files/resources/HEA_Impact_Teaching_Development_Prog.pdf

Using the following chapters in support of making a fellowship claim

We hope that each chapter will provide some food for critical thought on how aspects of your academic practice already relate to, or could be better related to, aspects of learning and teaching. To aid this process we begin each chapter with some comments from colleagues who speak negatively to the themes of that chapter. This device is used to offer a challenge to the contributing author(s) to respond to those comments. Chapter 1 starts somewhat uncontroversially with the theme of enhancing student learning, but even here it is clear that we need to consider carefully what it means to be 'effective' as 'higher' education teachers, because both terms are themselves contestable. More broadly, the chapter also raises the question of whether we might be in a position to say that 'we are all now student-centred in our approach to teaching and learning' (and what that might actually mean in practice).

We also hope that the open way in which we have presented the UKPSF in this Introduction will be viewed as a tandem invitation to openly engage critically with the contested nature of *all* aspects of academic practice (particularly as they relate to teaching and learning), and to use this in the construction of a coherent, critically reflective, and scholarly narrative account of your own professional practice, and for this to form the basis of a claim for a HEA fellowship. Chapter 8 will then return to the fellowship application process itself, offering some practical advice on preparing an application – be it within an accredited scheme or directly through the HEA. Each chapter also contains some self-assessment questions (activities). Each of the activity exercises (four in each chapter) is split between a question aimed more at people considering an application for Associate Fellowship/Fellowship, with a follow-up question aimed more at people who might be considering Senior Fellowship/Principal Fellowship.

Each chapter finishes with some quotes from successful fellowship applications, which we hope will also be useful in encouraging engagement with the various elements of the UKPSF. These extracts were randomly chosen from those that were kindly made available to us, subject to two simple selection criteria: (1) they should come from a range of discipline contexts; and (2) they should represent the full range of fellowship categories. The applicants supplied their complete applications, some of which were direct applications to the HEA and some were from university-based accredited frameworks. We then chose the actual extracts to reflect a range of engagements with various aspects of academic practice and the dimensions of the UKPSF. Four of the applications were from Senior and Principal Fellows, but the extracts we chose from these applications reflect in equal measure their engagement with aspects of learning and teaching as well as their academic leadership. The extracts were taken directly from the applications and only slightly edited where particular sentences didn't make sense out of the institutional context in which they were written.

We anonymised the applicants, using the following identifiers: Dr Brown (Senior Fellow) – Senior Lecturer in Psychology; Mr Blonde (Associate Fellow), Learning Technologist; Dr Blue (Principal Fellow) – Associate Dean Business and Law; Dr Orange (Fellow) – Lecturer in Forensic Chemistry; Mr Pink (Senior Fellow) – Senior Lecturer Art and Design; Ms White (Principal Fellow) – Head of Professional Development. Chapter 8 also includes three more sets of extracts from different applicants, which we used to exemplify forms of reflective writing in general, and across the range of fellowship categories. In all the quoted application extracts used throughout the book, the applicant has added the lettered references to the various component parts of the UKPSF.

To introduce these extracts, here is Mr Blonde, in his role as a learning technologist, reflecting on how he worked with academic staff to support their engagement with various learning technologies through the university's Digital Experience Building in University Teaching (DEBUT) project.

Mr Blonde (AFHEA)

From my own evidence-informed practice (see Ferman 2002; Sharpe 2004; Knight et al. 2006; Mainka 2007) and from staff feedback and evaluations on the learning activities that have been devised (especially from the evaluative work undertaken as part of the DEBUT programme), I know that academic staff are most engaged when they find the subject material intellectually stimulating and pertinent to their teaching practice; they have an opportunity for discourse and debate; and are able to share practice with colleagues who work within different faculties or subject disciplines [K1, K5, K6, V3, V4]. In the seven years that the DEBUT programme has been running, over 150 staff from academic and professional services departments have been introduced to a range of technologies of their choosing, which have been situated within their own personal and professional context [K1, K2, K4, V1, V2, V4]. The programme specifically builds in the chance for staff to 'play' with the technologies within a 'safe immersive environment'; opening up a discourse among the participants; enabling the sharing of 'good practice' within a rich multidisciplinary forum; and providing networking opportunities for staff from multi-campus sites [K2, K3, K4, K5, V1, V2, V3].

Alongside the contributions from student authors and the debates on various aspects of academic practice, each chapter also contains a short (1,000-word) opinion piece. To introduce these, here Brigitte Stockton looks at the notion of 'Brand UK HE'; how UK higher education has managed to position itself as a 'quality' provider in an increasingly globalised HE market place and knowledge economy (issues relating to which, will be discussed in Chapter 7). The piece refers to the role of the Quality Assurance Agency (QAA) in these developments, which will be discussed in Chapter 3. It also refers to some of the ways that UK HE providers have been able to articulate a distinct (albeit to some, western) learning experience for students, the essence of which will be discussed in detail in Chapter 2.

Opinion: On internationalisation

Brand UK HE: a global experience

Brigitte Stockton

Internationally valued, globally renowned and historically respected, UK higher education may be viewed as a profitable and reliable brand, offering a variety of products (mainly qualifications). Through association and collaboration, transnational host countries have invested in this brand to provide a gateway for postgraduate success and ultimately, to develop the skills and knowledge of future generations. For host countries, this investment is a demonstration of progressive behaviour and a statement of confidence in their continuing growth.

Recently, the Department for Business, Innovation & Skills (BIS) concluded that 'the dominant motivation ... for study in the UK [was] to lead to impact once they [students] returned home' (CRAC 2013). And outside of the Bologna Agreement boundaries, UK higher education (HE) providers have expanded to meet this demand. But, in some countries the initial enthusiasm for collaboration along with the sometimes rushed, ill-conceived, programmes have threatened relationships, the quality of provision, and ultimately the brand name of UK HE. However, a clearer informed vision with informed expectations is emerging. So is now the time to establish alternative motivational drivers and debate the expectations of both parties?

Counting the cost of off-shore management and resources, many UK higher education providers have discovered the significant economic benefits envisioned are less lucrative than initially forecasted. This realisation creates an opportunity to shift the focus away from consumerism and economic gain to establish alternate institute, social and academic rewards, exemplified through unique student experiences that evolve within a diverse cohort, alternate platforms for staff development, opportunities for collaborative global research and promotion of equality and cross-cultural understanding.

To reproduce this desirable authentic UK experience it is now recognised that a shared understanding of quality standards and the removal of misconceptions and misapprehensions are required. Superficial processes built through egotistical or unsound ideologies quickly unravel when placed under the Quality Assurance Agency UK Higher Education (QAA) spotlight in a higher education review. And effective risk management from the onset will ensure the UK Quality Code (QAA 2013a) acts as a reference tool from which collaboration can evolve, thereby avoiding potential confrontation and an air of postcolonial superiority, which can occur once programmes are running and processes are imposed as an afterthought.

QAA international reviews (QAA 2013b, 2014) strongly recommend onsite leadership and management of an overseas campus, ensuring 'rigorous, comprehensive and systematic' quality processes led from within the off-shore campus; with external UK support being essential for overall success (Fielden 2011). Thus, this highlights how proactive, rather than reactive, onsite management tackles or identifies potential problems while acknowledging the holistic impact. By contrast, a reactive satellite management system is often unaware of, or can misunderstand, localised trends, causal effects and the true context or extent of a problem.

A celebrated component of the brand may be the advertising catchphrase of the 'UK-style learning experience'. Unfortunately, this phrase can be misunderstood. In some cultures there is an ingrained expectation that this implies application of didactic pedagogies or conservative prescribed learning outcomes, unaware of the variable norms of UK HE, the reality of experimentation, seminars and the use of timetabled self-directed study aimed at promoting the independent learning of academic or technical skills, all of which are integral to education in the UK, and this misunderstanding can be disconcerting for all parties. In countries where the collective voice is predominant, or there is a culture of non-verbalised debate and unspoken thought, these attributes may not be valued or fully understood by students, parents and possibly the collaborative partner. However, this cultural shift in learning is essential if the environment is to mirror the UK higher education experience, where self-expression, debate between peers and professors and individual academic direction underpin the success of graduates. This cultural shift enables attributes such as time management, active learning and confidence to develop and be evidenced; creating opportunities for students to demonstrate emotional maturity and intelligence through engagement, retention and successful attainment. Whether this divergent methodology evidenced through pre-defined UK parameters is suitable across all cultures continues to be debated across subjects, yet currently this methodology remains a prerequisite for most qualifications and essentially a key component of the brand.

Whereas a brand may have national differences, it is in the curriculum content where this can be observed to effectively embrace cultural differences and the application of international perspectives on localised events, shifting cultural learning styles through familiar subjects to achieve the desired brand outcome. Yet this can only be achieved through empathetic staff mentoring and training that support the initiation of an inventive curriculum that positively explores ideologies and collective or individual responses.

We recognise that the transnational brand experience will continue in variable articulation, collaboration and progression agreements and the holistic student journey will take many forms. One argument that supports the idea that the western learning culture should remain unchanged is the familiarity it offers students during their transition in the UK, for example, expectations of engagement are already established, communication methods pre-activated with consistent email addresses, known student voice platforms and awareness of support mechanisms. This reduces the difficulties observed when creating diverse teams and which are at times replicated in the studio/classroom: 'reduced interaction, conflict regarding task allocation, high turnover, absenteeism, reduced cooperation and commitment ... [and taking] time for the benefits of diversity to show through' (Leadbeater 2008).

Whether the brand can be led by these drivers and focus on individual elements will continue to be debated. What is acknowledged is how the UK Quality Code for Higher Education can become the reference guide that promotes consistency, if consistency is required, regardless of the location. However, the recognition that the collaborative partner may offer opportunities to improve the brand through autonomy in pedagogy, delivery and research should not be overlooked. Thus, this ultimately ensures a global student receives a UK higher education experience to support their progression and to become a global graduate.

Note

1 Throughout this chapter Nigel Purcell writes in a personal capacity and not as a representative of the Higher Education Academy.

2

Enhancing student learning

Cordelia Bryan

There's just no evidence that one method of teaching is any better than another, is there?

Surely, teaching sociology isn't the same as teaching engineering, so is there any point in talking about generic principles?

What's the point of students marking their own work? Won't they just award themselves high marks?

Introduction

The assumptions inherent in the statements above may well need to be challenged, but they also highlight how our professional practice can get rooted in our everyday customs, routines and experiences, sometimes producing tacit forms of knowledge, and often leaving those customs unquestioned (Polanyi 1967; Eraut 2000). This chapter looks to open up some of these unexamined aspects of teaching and learning practice in higher education.

The word 'unexamined' is, however, a tricky one. For example, I heard a young lecturer say this recently in a PG Cert HE taught session: 'Facilitating student learning is a bit of a cop-out as the lecturer doesn't need to prepare as much material compared with a traditional lecture or seminar.' The comment is clearly reflective, but it is debatable whether it was designed to interrogate existing practice or simply to defend it. The response from another lecturer at the time was that, far from being a cop-out, facilitating learning requires not only a thorough knowledge of the subject material, but also some knowledge of *how* students learn.

This chapter will focus on this question of how students learn by looking at current pedagogic literature and examples of practice which are informed by that literature. This will be preceded by looking, first, at various dimensions of the notion of student-centred learning, followed by learning activities aimed at enhancing student engagement, and finally by looking at how forms of assessment and feedback might best complement these ideas and principles of learning. But before we embark on this, there is another comment I have not heard voiced as often as I would like: 'What can we learn by looking at some of the great pedagogic thinkers and reformers of the past?' Like all disciplines, pedagogy has a history and this chapter begins by looking at the influence of key thinkers and reformers of the university upon whose shoulders we stand. The ideas of these thinkers will also feature throughout the book as underpinning threads.

Some key thinkers on teaching and learning in higher education

In the eighteenth century, Wilhelm von Humboldt, a liberal thinker and German man of letters, posed questions relating to the purpose of university education. His questions are as relevant today and still occupy governments, policy-makers, teachers and students (Mueller-Vollmer 2011). Von Humboldt asked, What is education good for? What are you supposed to get from your university studies? Is it a liberal arts education which forms you into a good, knowledgeable and democratic citizen? Is it science/ technology/economics forming you into a part of a production wheel in society's economic growth? Is it a road to free your creative spirits and intellectual capacity?

Von Humboldt lay the foundations of a new educational system in Prussia, leading to the liberal arts education of the twenty-first century. His ideas on a modern education theory have been attracting increasing attention in recent years and may have a renaissance in our new information age. In the short period from 1809 to 1810, as head of the section for ecclesiastic affairs and education in the Ministry of the Interior, von Humboldt was able to institute radical reform of the Prussian educational system from elementary and secondary right through to the university level. His reforms were based on the principle of free and universal education for all citizens. His radical idea of combining both teaching and research in one institution guided him in establishing the University of Berlin in 1810 (today's Humboldt University) and the structure he created for this institution became the model not only throughout Germany but also for modern universities in most Western countries (Mueller-Vollmer 2011).

In the nineteenth century, John Henry Newman wrote in his discourses, published as the *Idea of a University* (Newman [1852] 1996) that university is a place of *teaching* universal *knowledge*. In order to achieve this, he believed that the university required a close relationship with the church. He was not advocating that the main characteristics of a university should be changed by its incorporation of church, but rather that its performance in its office of intellectual education would thereby be steadied. The steadying influence of the church for Newman is about integrity and pursuing truth: University, he asserts, 'educates the intellect to reason well in all matters, to reach out towards truth, and to grasp it' (Newman [1852] 1996: 92).

The ever increasing marketisation and managerialism pervading all aspects of university life (see Chapters 3 and 7 in particular) cause deep concern to those who still hold dear the liberal ideals of Newman and von Humboldt's university. Some fear an erosion of the fundamental ideals of universality, academic freedom and 'pure research' which do not easily sit within current Quality Assurance mechanisms. Mittelstrass (2010), addressing a European HE Conference, talks of the dangers of seeing teaching and research as just another job rather than Newman's ideal of pursuing *truth as a way of life*. The current discourse of the university with its strange administrative and economic language, he argues, no longer corresponds to *any* theory or idea: 'We need to beware of letting the university system erode in this manner. Such a system would lose research to extra-university institutions once and for all, and universities would evolve into mere teaching institutions' (Mittelstrass 2010: 188).

The teaching–research nexus has long been debated (e.g. Boyer 1990; Neumann 1992; Ramsden and Moses 1992; Jenkins et al. 1998; Light 2003; Nicholls 2005; Brown and Smith 2013) and more recently also includes students' perceptions in its discourse (Healey et al. 2014a) (see Chapters 3 and 6 for further discussion of these dimensions of academic practice). This is also being further complemented by forms of cooperative scholarship where our teaching practice is both informed by research findings of others and is the *subject* of our own research, and often undertaken in active collaboration with students, where they are true participants rather than just respondents, as in most forms of action research (AR) (McNiff 2001).

Unlike a lot of other empirical research, AR places the researcher at the centre of the enquiry in a self-reflexive capacity where s/he is continually self-evaluating practice in relation to pedagogic theories. AR often begins with an idea or hunch that is then developed (e.g. the feedback I provide doesn't seem to be making much difference to student performance). The teacher/researcher interrogates her/his own work, questioning why things are done a particular way and whether that way best serves the intended student learning. Data may also be generated by asking the students for their views and experiences and, in some cases, even including them in the tutor's self-reflexive process in focus groups or individually. In this model of AR, the teacher is not only sharing and modelling the research journey but also exposing his/her vulnerability as the person at the centre of the whole process. Engaging students in self- and peer assessment and other collaborative approaches to their learning is steadily gaining ground with compelling arguments for a system that supports symbiosis rather than competition and conflict (Brown and Smith 2013). And these approaches might also become an integral component in your own claim for HEA fellowship status (see Chapter 8).

Boyer (1990) made a compelling pedagogic case for teaching and research to be better integrated as complementary activities which, together, should be able to enhance the professional and scholarly practice of the career academic. As we saw in the quote which began the first chapter to this book, he identified four distinct types of scholarship pursued in universities: the scholarship of *discovery*, of *integration*, of *application* and of *teaching*. He makes a case for each to be considered as equal in status and advocates that academics be afforded the career opportunities to engage with all four, rather than becoming experts in only one. Advancing arguments for a more holistic and integrated view of academic practice, such as Boyer's, will be a recurrent theme throughout this book (and will be a particular focus in Chapter 3).

In von Humboldt and Newman's idea of the university, epistemological concerns were paramount. There had until this point been little or no mention of the part the *learner* plays in the acquisition of knowledge and search for truth. Their work acts as a significant corrective to that, but more on the level of the acquisition and pursuit of knowledge. Considering how, for example, life experience, state of mind, motivation and aspirations of the learner might affect his/her capacity to learn is a more recent interest of higher education research. What has become known as the student-centred approach to learning builds on the work of the psychologist, Carl Rogers (1989) and his client-centred approach to therapy which he developed and applied in an educational context. Rogers claims that a person cannot teach another person directly; a person can only facilitate another's learning (Rogers 1957: 301). The belief is that what the *student* does is more important than what the *teacher* does, and this might be argued to enrich the von Humboldt and Boyer notions of scholarship. But it also recognises that each student will process what s/he learns differently depending on what s/he brings to the classroom.

Rogers' person-centred approach brought about a conceptual shift in the focus of subsequent pedagogic research. Interest began to be focused on the learner, identifying, for example, multiple learning styles, cultural, gender and economic influences and prior educational experience as some of the key factors that might determine how a student approaches his/her learning when entering university. This paradigm shift in our understanding of how students learn has had huge implications for academic practice, which the rest of this chapter aims to highlight.

Student-centred learning

> The illiterate of the 21st century will not be those who cannot read and write, but those who cannot learn, unlearn and relearn.
>
> (Alvin Toffler, available at: http://www.alvintoffler.net/?fa=galleryquotes)

Student-centred learning is not new, as the connection between the work of von Humboldt and Rogers demonstrates. If we place that history lesson alongside the current practices of student-centredness we can see that the combined effect has been to slowly discredit the 'knowledge transmission' model in which the teacher simply lectures *to* students in the erroneous belief that they are learning what s/he wants them to learn. Students *may* share some common understanding of the lecturer's input but we have only limited ways of knowing to what extent, if any, individual student learning has occurred as a result of such lectures. Traditional forms of assessment have not helped in this regard – regurgitation of lectures in exams cannot be said to equate with or promote an appetite for 'life-long learning'.

Dear Lecturer

On student-centred learning

Jane Allcroft

I have learned more when I have had the opportunity to discuss ideas with lecturers in seminars and tutorials; where their greater knowledge and experience were used to prompt me into new ways of thinking, to challenge my initial reactions to concepts and, through discussion, to allow me to find new ways of understanding. The least useful approach has been the traditional didactic lecturer as fountain of all knowledge regurgitating it to a room full of people. For instance, we had one lecturer who simply put up PowerPoint pages and read them out to us. If the way to understand new concepts is to have them read aloud, then there would be no need for lecturers at all – we could simply read the information aloud to ourselves or each other. The chance to ask questions, to have space to flounder and experiment with approaches and ideas, to hear other students' questions and the lecturer's answers – these are the ways in which new concepts become meaningful to me.

To develop this one step further, I have found that to fully embed new knowledge and understanding I have needed to apply it, or discover it, through active engagement. For instance, I can recall and discuss knowledge gained through conducting my own research, in partnership with university staff, whereas information found only to use in an essay or worse, an exam, enters my short-term memory for the period during which I need to use it and is then gone and forgotten.

It is worth just flagging up that the term 'student-centred' is carefully crafted for linguistic effect, not unlike 'pro-choice' for abortion or 'non-violent' to describe a radical form of communication. Each is crafted to portray an opposite which is intended to be seen as undesirable or even ridiculous – *against* choice or *pro-violent-communication*. Like its political counterpart, the educational debate around student-centred approaches is more complex and nuanced. While strong pedagogic arguments are made here, and throughout the academic community, for adopting a student-centred approach, it is not the intention of the authors of this book to present *any* pedagogy as uncontested. We would encourage the continuation of discussions in favour of teacher-centred or non-student-centred teaching philosophy and practice if or when there may be legitimate claims to be made for its effectiveness.

I have, for example, run staff development workshops where the focus has overtly been teacher-centred with titles such as: 'How to survive the increasing pressures of large-group facilitation: a teacher-centred perspective'. If tutors are becoming ill because of the daily pressures placed upon them, their well-being, or indeed professional survival, is obviously worth considering as a priority. A workforce consisting of exhausted, demoralised or long-term absent academics serves nobody, least of all those at the heart of our student-centred world. Addressing teacher concerns head-on with workshops reviewing pedagogic practices which might help to alleviate the pressure they experience by reducing their workload, I claim, is a legitimate teacher-centred approach to the situation.

Reducing teacher input and enhancing student engagement in tutorials

In both 1:1 and group tutorials, require your students to come 'primed' and ready to discuss key issues about their work on which they would like help and support. This approach is moving in the direction of the 'flipped classroom' which will be discussed later in this chapter.

To begin, for first year students, you might devise a set of questions/tasks to help them identify exactly what it is that they need and post this on the VLE, e.g.:

- In your own words, write a couple of sentences explaining what you understood from the feedback you received and what, if any, action you have subsequently taken.
- What aspect of the feedback did you find hardest to deal with?
- Can you explain why you found this most challenging?
- What would help you most in improving this piece now and after the session?

Pair up students so that one acts as scribe, noting suggested actions or records the conversation while the other's work is being discussed. Having a good record of tutorial discussions is particularly helpful when students are working independently and struggling to know where to begin or how to improve their work.

Activity 2.1

- With reference to your own discipline context, in what ways have you sought to actively manage the continuum from teacher-centredness to student-centredness?
- In what ways have you been involved in seeking to articulate a distinct learning and teaching strategy for your school/faculty or institution overall?

Teaching as facilitation of learning is a much richer and more complex business than the old knowledge transmission model. Factors which pointed to the need for a different approach to teaching included the mass expansion of UK HE from around 8–10 per cent in the 1980s to a target 50 per cent (set by the then Prime Minister Tony Blair in 1999, as a target for 2010, and discussed in Chapter 7). Widening participation (WP) attracted students from more diverse economic, ethnic and social backgrounds. Despite the fact that many more students from higher-income backgrounds participated in HE before the recent expansion of the system, the expansion acted to widen participation gaps between rich and poor (Blanden and Machin 2004).

The increasingly diverse student population required of its lecturers a radically different approach to their teaching and it quickly became evident that a large proportion of students were no longer served by the teacher-centred approach to teaching. Perhaps for the first time in higher education, lecturers were faced with the same challenges commonly experienced by teachers in schools and in further education, for many of whom diversity was, and is, the norm.

As universities embraced diversity and academics began serious pedagogic research in the 1980s and 1990s, there was a gradual acknowledgement that studies were needed to broaden concepts of HE learning and seek innovative ways of engaging *all* students within the changing HE demographic. (e.g. Boud et al. 1985; Warner-Weil and McGill. 1989; Duke 1992; Bryan and Assiter 1995; Bourner et al. 2000; Thomas 2001; Savin-Baden 2003; Knight and Yorke 2003; Haggis 2009; O'Mahony 2014).

Sandwich courses and other work-based learning (WBL) schemes began to be seen not only as important to provide students with 'real-life' experience, but also as potential organisations of HE learning (Watson 2000). While it had long been recognised that such schemes enhanced students' inter- and intra-personal skills, such as self-confidence, leadership and team working, researchers now set out to ascertain whether work-based learning might also enhance students' cognitive, higher-order thinking skills, previously perceived as exclusively the domain of higher education. Once it had been ascertained that cognitive learning could and did occur outside the university, questions of how this learning might be better facilitated, formally recognised and accredited by institutions were addressed (Bryan and Assiter 1995). Today WBL is common practice and even becoming successfully embedded within humanities courses with no obvious employer connection or direct relationship (Stibbe 2013).

APEL (Accreditation of Prior Experiential Learning) was another development in response to diversity. APEL was to provide a route to higher education for young and mature people who might not have the required formal qualifications but who could prove that they had equivalent knowledge, skills and potential to benefit from HE study. Although sound in principle, APEL was never taken up in a big way, mainly because of the time-consuming nature of collating, assessing and processing individual claims (Warner-Weil and McGill 1989). Another problem was, in order for academic credit to be granted, the experiential learning had to be 'appropriately' framed. Presenting appropriate evidence for APEL required an ability to critically reflect on one's experiences as well as a sophisticated knowledge of academic language, thereby often excluding the very people it was designed to serve.

However, initiatives such as APEL and WBL marked a significant regulatory shift towards a more accessible university system. Pedagogic pioneers, initially in the polytechnics (before 1992) where the student demographic was changing most rapidly, became focused directly on student learning – wherever this may have taken place. Educational developers committed to widening participation in HE and keen to accept non-traditional students were often at the forefront of the WP initiative.

The scholarship of teaching and learning (SoTL)

The notion of a higher education pedagogy, and the development of a scholarship of teaching and learning (SoTL) seemed to take off in the 1980s and 1990s – pioneered in the UK particularly by the work of Lewis Elton (e.g. Elton 1992). Unsurprisingly, perhaps, researchers drew heavily on the already existing conceptual and theoretical framework of constructivism. Although Piaget's and Vygotsky's views on constructivism differ in that the former gives primacy to individual cognitive processes and the latter to social and cultural processes, both believed that knowledge is constructed by the learner as s/he tries to make sense of experiences. This, they discovered, applied equally to adult learners as it did to the process of developing children's intellectual capacities (Richardson 1997).

So, if we accept that knowledge is constructed by the learner, how has the almost infinite knowledge as information so easily accessible via the internet affected the role of the university teacher? The traditional knowledge-transmission model of teaching becomes even more redundant. However, selecting what knowledge is to be included in the curriculum is still a legitimate concern and there is an ongoing academic and political discourse on priorities for inclusion within and across the subject disciplines.

The focus for us as teachers is to be creative in finding multiple ways of actively engaging the diverse student population in their learning. Modelling and teaching how to think critically are central to this aim.

Barnett has defined different types of critical thinking, pointing to a need for students to engage in the wider context of their education as a sort of critique in society (Barnett 1997). He asserts that higher education has become a world of 'supercomplexity' and rapid change, and that in this world of uncertainty and contestability, our frameworks for understanding ourselves and the circumstances in which we operate have had to become increasingly complex.

He perceives a gradual shift away from university teaching centred primarily upon critical thinking and cognitive development to include a wider concept of 'critical being' which incorporates ontological concerns (see Chapter 5). He explores ideas of critical self-reflection and considers how we as teachers may facilitate our learners in acquiring and sustaining this all-important *will* to learn (Barnett 2007).

The concept of cultivating a *will* to learn is not new. Steiner, an early twentieth-century philosopher and educationalist, founded an entire curriculum designed to awaken in children and young people a *will* to learn and to be eternally curious about life (Steiner 2005). The Steiner curriculum aims to balance the 'physical, behavioural, emotional, cognitive, social, and spiritual' aspects of the developing person, encouraging thinking that includes a creative as well as an analytic component (Woods et al. 2005). That holistic pedagogic ideas should now be incorporated into the discourse of higher education is indicative of a rapidly shifting landscape. Barnett and others (e.g. Perkins et al. 1993; Haggis 2003; Dall'Alba and Robyn 2007) have challenged the traditional approach to higher education where ontology has tended to be subordinated to epistemological concerns.

Acquiring knowledge and the development of higher cognitive skills, it is argued, is insufficient for twenty-first-century 'super-complex' life without also giving due consideration to the learner's commitment and existential involvement. In other words, personal aspects of self-identity such as culture, class, gender, mental health and well-being all play their part in how we approach life and learning. Maslow's (1943) hierarchy of human needs, still so loved as a motivational business scheme, illustrates how attention should be paid to *all* the needs if one hopes to operate in the top section of his pyramid and achieve or aspire to self-actualisation, where he claims high-level problem solving and creativity reside (see Chapter 5 for further discussion of this theme).

Facilitating student learning may feel a long way away from helping individuals in achieving self-actualisation. Indeed, it could be argued that this is not what you 'signed up for' as a lecturer. Be that as it may, it is undoubtedly the case that without having the basic physiological, social and economic needs reasonably satisfied, HE learning will be severely hampered as students are unlikely to focus their undivided attention on the task in hand.

While this may be self-evident to readers, it is patently not always understood or acted upon by new entrants to university. The increasing demands made on student support services is testament to the need for a more holistic approach to be taken – one in which we, as a learning community, consider how we encourage self-regulated learners and support in them what Barnett (2007) terms that all- important *will* to learn.

Learning as student engagement

Baron and Corbin (2012) argue that ideas of student engagement in the university context are often fragmented, contradictory and confused. They maintain that the student experience as a whole is the key to achieving engagement and assert that efforts to engage fully students cannot be successful until a 'whole-of-university' approach is adopted. Achieving a 'whole-of-university' approach is complex and fraught with difficulties, not least due to the different perceptions of key pedagogic issues between senior management and teaching staff. For example, in a study of the changing HE landscape carried out by Stevenson et al. (2014), the term 'teaching excellence', routinely employed in institutional marketing and used by senior managers, was frequently rejected or contested by some staff, while others claimed that 'teaching excellence' had become synonymous with 'student satisfaction' in ways that rendered both terms vague and ambiguous.

While we acknowledge there are compelling arguments for developing a 'whole-of-university' approach and support open dialogue to achieve this, we shall limit our focus here to student engagement in relation to our role as facilitators of their learning. What do *we* need to *know* and *do* in order to engage *all* our students and create inclusive learning environments? The question of students as full or engaged partners in learning will be the focus of Chapter 6.

The Higher Education Funding Council for England (HEFCE) is clear about the importance of inclusive learning communities:

> Widening access and improving participation in higher education are a crucial part of our mission. Our aim is to promote and provide the opportunity of successful participation in higher education to everyone who can benefit from it. This is vital for social justice and economic competitiveness.
>
> (HEFCE, n.d., http://www.hefce.ac.uk/whatwedo/wp/)

It has already been argued that teaching can never be innocent due to the cultural, psychological and political complexities of learning and how it may either function as an instrument to engender conformity or a desire to participate in the transformation of the world (e.g. Freire 1970). With this in mind, many attempts have been made to develop inclusive learning environments.

One such attempt is Universal Design for Learning (UDL) which offers a set of principles for curriculum development that give all individuals equal opportunities to learn (http://www.cast.org/udl/index.html). What this means to us as teachers and supporters of learning is adopting flexible approaches that can be customised and adjusted for individual needs.

UDL has as its goal 'to develop purposeful and motivated, resourceful and knowledgeable, and strategic and goal-directed learners'. Colleagues, especially in the humanities and arts, might wish to further include the notoriously hard to measure qualities which students may also develop in HE which include personal growth, self-identity and creativity. To explore further ideas about inclusion and how to create inclusive learning environments, readers might initially refer to Smith's (2011) annotated bibliography.

Activity 2.2

- With reference to your own discipline context, in what ways have you actively sought to establish an enabling/inclusive learning environment?
- In what ways have you been involved in seeking to embed an enabling/inclusive learning and teaching philosophy/strategy for your school/faculty or institution overall?

A theory, which is now used worldwide as a framework for good course design, teaching and assessment is the conceptualisation of outcomes-based learning developed from the concept of constructive alignment (Figure 2.1) (Biggs and Tang 2007).

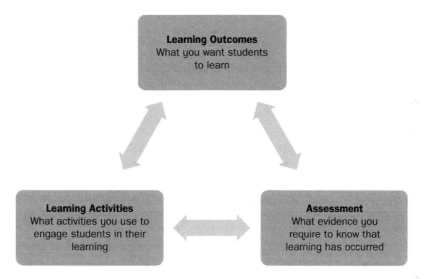

Figure 2.1 The three components in constructive alignment.
Source: after Biggs and Tang (2007).

Constructive alignment basically states that the intended learning outcomes, the learning activities and the assessment tasks in a course/programme must be properly aligned to facilitate the learner in constructing his or her knowledge and skills. Thus, the intended learning outcomes (what we want the learners to know) must be supported by appropriate use of learning activities (how we facilitate the learners in their learning) and the assessment tasks including the languages employed (how we ascertain what the learners have learnt). It is vitally important when we design our course/programme so that these three components are carefully considered and conceived so as to enhance student learning.

Good teaching sees 'motivation as an outcome of teaching, not as its precondition. Good teaching makes students want to engage with the tasks ... the learner has to *expect success*' (Biggs and Tang 2007: 57; original emphasis). For the inexperienced facilitator, this view of good teaching may seem daunting, especially when s/he is expected to motivate students in large mixed ability classes. The good news is that there is a growing body of online, freely available Open Educational Resources (OERs) with subject-specific activities, tasks, targeted reading, audio and visual materials, all specifically intended to engage students in their learning. These multitude resources are, however, insufficient to do the job on their own and there is still an important and highly skilled role for the teacher/facilitator to manage the learning environment to ensure that *all* students are able to engage with the work.

To help us understand the challenge we face as teachers aiming to engage *all* learners, let us use Biggs and Tang's archetype students, Robert and Susan. Susan is academically committed, bright, interested in her studies and wants to do well. When she attends lectures, she comes prepared with sound background knowledge, possibly some questions she wants answering and generally operates in an 'academic' way making her own connections by reflecting on what she encounters. Students like Susan take a *deep* approach to their learning, they virtually teach themselves and do not typically need much help from us (Biggs and Tang 2007: 9–11).

Robert finds himself at university *not* out of a driving curiosity about a particular subject but to obtain qualifications for a decent job. A few years ago he would not have considered going to university. He is less committed than Susan, possibly not as academically attuned and has little background of relevant knowledge. He basically wants to do whatever is necessary to pass and may consequently take a *surface* approach to his learning. Our challenge then is to teach and scaffold knowledge so that the Roberts learn more in the manner of the Susans and are encouraged to take a *deep* approach to their studies. The basic distinction between a deep and surface approach to learning and assessment is in the *intention* of the learner. In the former, the learner is aiming towards understanding, and in the latter s/he is aiming to reproduce material in a test or exam rather than actually understand it (see Marton and Saljo 1976; Ramsden 2003).

Biggs' SOLO taxonomy (Biggs and Tang 2007) describes levels of increasing complexity in a student's understanding of a subject, through five stages, and it is claimed to be applicable to any subject area. SOLO is an acronym for Structure of Observed Learning Outcomes (Figure 2.2).

At the *Pre-structural* stage, students are simply acquiring bits of unconnected information, which have no organisation and make no sense. At *Unistructural*, simple and obvious connections are made, but their significance is not grasped. At *Multi-structural*, a number of connections may be made, but the meta-connections between them are missed, as is their significance for the whole. The final two levels are those we should be aiming at in higher education. *Rational* level is where the student is now able to appreciate the significance of the parts in relation to the whole. At the fifth and final level, *Extended Abstract*, the student is making connections not only within the given subject area, but also beyond it, able to generalise and transfer the principles and ideas underlying the specific instance. Not all students get through all five stages, of course, and indeed not all teaching (and even less 'training') is designed to take them all the way (Biggs and Tang 2007).

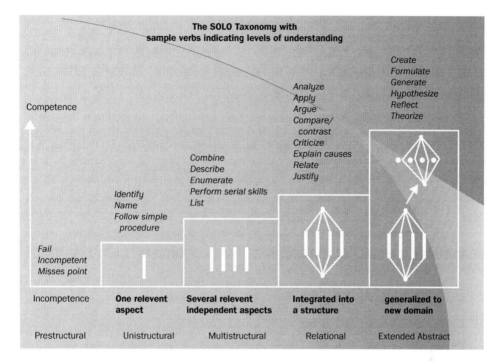

Figure 2.2 Biggs' SOLO Taxonomy.

Source: http://www.johnbiggs.com.au/academic/solo-taxonomy/ (used with permission of the author).

While Biggs' SOLO taxonomy focuses on students' cognitive development, there is a parallel movement known as the *Capability* approach which is concerned with higher education's role in human development and quality of life, particularly poverty reduction and equality (Walker 2006: 27–43). A recent study suggests that well-being among some students in higher education is lower than in the general population (HEA and HEPI 2014).

Individual human capabilities and the fostering of these capabilities through social arrangements, such as how we manage classroom discussions by openly acknowledging and attempting to redress power imbalances, now become central to creating a more just society. A starting point for some serious critical reflection as a professional teacher might be to consider that 'pedagogy is not neutral or "uncontaminated" by the institutional and social context in which it operates but acts as a complicated carrier for the relations of power and privilege' (Walker 2006: 39–40).

In seeking to establish an open, inclusive and democratic learning environment, Brookfield and Preskill (1999) advocate that students name and learn some dispositions of democratic discussion which they, as facilitators, also model. Though they admit to a mixed success, they claim that even the naming of the dispositions is useful in helping students become more collaborative and develop respectful communication.

They list the dispositions of hospitality (an atmosphere in which people feel invited to participate), participation, mindfulness (paying attention), humility, mutuality (trying to ensure that all participants benefit from the discussion), deliberation (a willingness of participants to discuss issues fully supported by evidence-based arguments and counter-arguments), appreciation, hope, and autonomy (Brookfield and Preskill 1999: 7–11).

Adding a relatively new and innovative dimension to inclusive and democratic learning environments is a move to incorporate spirituality, health and well-being into mainstream curricula (Marshall and Morris 2011). The draft module description outlines an approach which has benefits for CPD across subject disciplines both for the health of staff and to enable them to support the health and well-being of their students. The approach has been extensively trialled with staff and volunteers in a hospice environment.

Health, well-being and spirituality: a holistic approach to the health benefits of spirituality

Module overview

This module explores a holistic (Bloom 2001, 2005) approach to the theory and practice of the health benefits of spirituality. It is delivered via face-to-face lectures, experiential workshops and small group peer support meetings. Participants will be required to submit a portfolio containing a reflective log of their learning and one written assignment reflecting on their overall understanding of the connections between spirituality, health and well-being.

Aims

This module aims to enable participants to acquire knowledge of the biological, psychological and cultural factors that inform spirituality, health and well-being. Within a framework that is person-centred and experiential, participants will learn practical models and skills that can be used to support their own health and well-being and that of their colleagues, service users and service providers.

They will develop practical communication skills and techniques to become more effective care-givers and educators, maximising the opportunities to improve support and self-care in their work and life situations.

Module learning outcomes

Participants will develop the concepts and skills that enable them to do the following:

- communicate effectively about the cultural, political and scientific context of the links between health and spirituality;
- communicate effectively with people of all cultural backgrounds, of diverse faiths and no faith, about the benefits of spirituality to physical and psychological health;

- enable others such as colleagues and service users to explore, identify and develop their own best approach to self-care;
- practise, demonstrate and enable the core skills of:
  - meditative self-care;
  - values-driven self-development;
  - appropriate retreat, meditation and rest;
  - giving and receiving compassionate care.
- adopt caring practices that encourage autonomous self-care;
- evaluate and develop their own self-care for resilience, personal and professional development;
- reflect on and use feedback on their caring skills to develop future practice;
- reflect on and articulate the risks of spiritual concepts and practices in relation to mental health.

Mode of delivery

This module will be delivered through a series of workshops, consisting of lectures, practical exercises, periods of self-reflection, plenary and small group discussion. Learning will be collaborative with the module tutors both facilitating and modelling reflective participation.

During this module, participants will work through course materials and readings. Students will also be required to participate in small peer support groups, which can meet online or in person, and to log their experience of these meetings.

Participants will be observed during workshop sessions and formative peer and tutor feedback will be given.

Summative assessment

Students are required to submit a portfolio consisting of a reflective log of learning from each workshop session and peer group meetings. Students will also submit a written assignment of between 3,000 and 5,000 words.

- pre-requisite module: N/A
- 15 Level 7 CPD credits = 150 learning hours (30 tutor and peer-facilitated and 120 independent study).

© William Bloom 2014 http://www.williambloom.com/
events/soulution-140.htm

Since Schön's (1983) seminal text on the reflective practitioner, which looked at how a range of professionals gained the knowledge which underpins their theory and practice, the notion has become integral to many courses, particularly professional learning courses. Indeed, facilitating forms of reflective learning and striving to become reflective practitioners are an approach which has now gained wide recognition (e.g. Boud et al. 1985; Brockbank and McGill 1998; Clegg et al. 2002; Bryan and Green 2003; Grossman 2009; Brigden and Purcell 2013; Cowen 2013). And as we saw in Chapter 1, it is a key concept underpinning the UKPSF.

Learning how to be critically reflective about our experiences and our learning does not come naturally to some learners, as is evident from recurring online discussions on the subject within the Staff and Educational Development Association (SEDA 2014). It is, therefore, our role as teachers to help to scaffold for these learners a framework. The intention being to progress reflection from what often starts with some hazy notions of descriptions of experiences to a more analytical perspective, drawing on literature, on relevant theories and on personal experiences and examining the interplay between the different elements. Whichever framework may be employed for this purpose, we need to acknowledge the potential changing identities of the learners as they engage in ever more critical and reflective processes which may challenge some of their assumptions and beliefs.

Fostering student reflective capabilities simultaneously requires our own reflexive professional learning and is at the heart of the renewed academic professionalism associated with SoTL. Edward Said suggests that our professionalism should not be based on 'doing what one is supposed to do' but on asking 'why one does it, who benefits from it, how it can connect with a personal project and original thoughts' (Said 1994: 62). And as such, is therefore concerned equally with educational aims, processes and outcomes. It is also at the heart of the kinds of scholarly narratives that the HEA is encouraging us, as professional learning and teaching practitioners, to produce when claiming a HEA fellowship (see Chapter 8).

The process of reflective learning is dialectical; it looks inward at our thoughts and thought processes and outward at the situation under scrutiny. This interaction between the internal and external propels us towards further thought and action. The reflective dialogue may take place as a solo activity in our minds, perhaps subsequently recorded, or it may also be facilitated between pairs or within groups; it may use words or work in conjunction with embodied knowledge and other means of communication (Bryan and Green 2003).

Facilitating learners in this process continues to be one of the ongoing challenges for teachers. How we convey to students this meta thinking, or 'thinking about thinking', in which we consider the relationship between our thoughts, feelings and action in a particular context can also provide a real stimulus for innovatory curriculum design. The learning activities we devise thus become key to scaffolding the development of students' critical and meta thinking capacity.

At the centre of this reflective thinking lies the concept of 'critical thinking', but this is also a highly contested notion, and opinion among theorists is divided about whether critical thinking or ways of reasoning are universal or culture- and context-specific, and indeed what constitutes this critical thinking in the first place (Mason 2008). What is clear is that both critical thinking and reflection may be viewed in many different ways. The two examples, drawn from different disciplines each use direct prompts to get participants started on the critical reflection process.

Example 1 from a Post Graduate Learning and Teaching in Higher Education programme

In your reflective journal consider and address some of these questions as you progress through the programme:

- What does it mean to be a Critical Reflective Practitioner in your discipline area?
- What is the difference between critical reflection and 'just thinking about things'?
- Did you experience any uncomfortable moments in your learning?
- How are you feeling now?
- Was all the learning relevant to your needs?
- If you could change anything about your learning experience, what would it be?
- How might you begin to DO that?
- Do you feel there are any gaps in your understanding and can you remedy that?
- What do you need to do now? (Action Plan?)

Example 2 from a BSc (Hons) Nursing programme

- Describe events as you understood them.
- Describe your feelings about this event.
- What have you learned from this event?
- Given a similar situation in future, how would you behave and what support would you like?
- In what ways do the theories of psychology, sociology, biology, philosophy and nursing research underpin the situation you have witnessed?

Distinctions are also made within the pedagogic literature between reflection-*in*-action (at the time but drawing on past experience or learning) and reflection-*on*-action (after the event, reflection for the purpose of learning more). They each have their uses but it is no good, for example, expecting a drama student to reflect-*in*-action during a performance or s/he will probably forget her lines!

Argyris (1976) proposes double loop learning theory which is a form of reflective practice that helps to challenge and potentially to change underlying values and assumptions. The focus of the theory is on solving problems that are complex and ill-structured and which change as the problem-solving advances.

An important aspect of the theory is the distinction between an individual's espoused theory and their 'theory-in-use' (what they actually do); bringing these two into congruence is a primary concern of double loop learning. Typically, interaction with others is necessary to identify the conflict.

The double loop is a step-change in the *depth* of the reflection. Without it, you might still achieve some satisfactory results but at higher education level, it is necessary to be able to articulate not only what is achieved, but also *why* it was achieved in the chosen way. It could also flag up what might be done differently next time. Ideas such as these are now at the centre of many HE courses, particularly those that prepare students for entry to a range of professions, but they are also increasingly featuring on some of the more traditional academic courses, and, as we have already shown, they lie at the heart of what the HEA understands by adopting a scholarly approach to HE learning and teaching.

It is also worth noting that in developing critical and reflective thinkers, the teacher–student relationship as co-learners engaged in joint inquiry is further consolidated. That is, students with highly developed critical thinking skills directed towards their own learning are much less likely to accept didactic teaching, or a teacher-centred approach, as the main teaching strategy afforded them at university. We might also suggest here that the potential to see reflective practice not just as reflection on existing knowledge and practice, but also as a construction site for new knowledge, could qualify reflective practice for threshold concept status or troublesome knowledge (Meyer and Land 2006), that is, conceptual understanding which has the potential to take students (and ourselves as professional learners) to new and higher levels of understanding.

Another important dimension to these forms of active learning has been engaging students in dialogue with their own peers. And the 'flipped' or 'reversed' classroom is now advocated to maximise opportunities for active engagement with both peers and with tutors (e.g. Berrett 2012; Bishop and Verleger 2013). In this educational model, students are required to view videos or listen to podcasts of the lectures in their private study time and engage in active learning activities during their contact time with tutors. The merits of a 'flipped' classroom include the opportunity for students to view material wherever they choose prior to the session and to stop and restart the lecture as often as they like. Content can include recorded lectures, demonstration videos, adaptive quizzes, performances or anything the lecturer deems suitable. Class time can be used for higher-order questioning, discussion, experiments, group activities, role play and other active learning approaches.

The 'Goldfish bowl' model is an example of a highly flexible 'flipped classroom' method designed to actively engage students in problem solving. It works by selecting some participants to silently observe and then provide feedback on the working processes of their peers, as though watching them from outside the 'goldfish bowl'. It enables students to step outside the problem-solving activity to focus on group dynamics, and other collaborative processes while still keeping abreast of the task in hand. This model and other innovative methods to engage students in their learning were successfully employed in Colleges of Further Education decades before entering HE pedagogy.

The 'Goldfish bowl model' outlined as a generic vehicle for enhancing collaborative problem solving

Before the session

Set appropriate pre-reading, viewing, exercises or research for your topic to be actively explored through group discussion in the session (i.e. what you think they should know to engage intelligently with the subject matter).

Plan your task for discussion and write clear instructions for the outcome(s) you expect from the 'problem solving' discussion within a specified time

The task should be sufficiently complex so that there is not any possibility of a 'right answer' but rather a necessity to discuss and collaborate on different approaches to achieve your specified outcome(s).

Task setting might also entail writing a few key questions to get the discussion started; some guidelines on democratic discussion techniques; suggestions for electing a Chair, time keeper, note taker, etc.

Depending on what role you want for your observers, you might want to write them some instructions on what you would like them to focus on. It might be to provide feedback on the structure of the discussion and how this served/hindered the achievement of the task, or it might be to focus on the group processes (how participants engaged) and how well these served or hindered the achievement of the task. It could be both, or one student focusing on one task while the other focuses on group dynamics.

If you have ample time and wish to explore assessment issues, you can introduce a simple grading system. Only do this if you are prepared for some heated discussions and are confident to handle any or all aspects of assessments with your students!

During the session

Divide the class into groups of 7–15 students where each group has at least two observers. If there are multiple groups in one large space, organise into circles, as far apart as possible but with sufficient space for observers to circulate around the outside.

- Distribute the task sheet to all.
- Distribute the instruction sheet to observers.
- Start the exercise and say exactly how long groups have to complete the task.
- Circulate around the room with as little interference as possible and maybe give a 5-minute warning before the allocated time is up.

Observers giving feedback

Invite observers to give the group some feedback (according to the criteria you have devised for the exercise).

It can be helpful to request that all group members remain silent while receiving the feedback (no justifying, no explanations, etc.). Only after all observers have fed back, you may then open up discussions for anyone, including the tutor, to comment on what worked well, what might be done differently next time and how it felt to be observed etc.

As this model may initially require an element of 'teaching how to run productive group discussions', it is an ideal time to raise potential cultural differences and invite input from overseas students so that they may help to shape the group 'rules of engagement'.

The flipped classroom represents a unique combination of learning theories once thought to be incompatible – active, problem-based learning activities founded upon a constructivist ideology as advocated throughout this chapter, and instructional lectures derived from direct instruction methods founded upon behaviourist principles. There is considerable scope for teachers to offer creative alternatives to 'instructional lectures' as evidenced by the burgeoning industry designing OERs (Open Educational Resources).

Reports of student perceptions of the flipped classroom are somewhat mixed, but are generally positive overall (Bishop and Verleger 2013). Anecdotal evidence suggests that student learning is improved for the flipped compared to the traditional classroom. However, there is very little work investigating student learning outcomes objectively. Bishop and Verleger recommend that future work studies investigate the learning outcomes using controlled experimental or quasi-experimental design.

Activity 2.3

- With reference to your own discipline/subject context, in what ways have you sought to embed active and engaged forms of student learning in your teaching and learning regime?
- In what ways have you been involved in seeking to articulate a notion of student engagement to underpin your school/faculty or institution-wide learning and teaching strategy?

Assessment and feedback as forms of dialogue

As we have seen, assessment forms one of the three pillars of a constructively aligned curriculum:

> Assessment defines what students regard as important, how they spend their time and how they come to see themselves as students and as graduates. It is a major concern of those who learn, those who teach and those who are responsible for the development and accreditation of courses.
>
> (Knight 2001: http://www.heacademy.ac.uk/resources/
> detail/assessment/assessment_series)

Within the wider society, there is a discourse of assessment that historically has emphasised measurement and grade over opportunity and a political agenda that emphasises product over process. This discourse is mirrored in higher education by our concern with accounting and legitimising knowledge. Historically, as educators, we have, therefore, tended to delude ourselves in the belief that assessment has scientific reliability. While this may hold true for simplistic quantitative tests, the idea of precise and scientific reliability as applied across diverse HE practices is a nonsense and one which has rightly been challenged (Clegg and Bryan 2006: 216). How can an acting role, a musical performance or a portfolio of work be meaningfully summated in a single number?

A major shift in emphasis has occurred regarding the purposes of assessment in higher education. Where assessment used to be primarily concerned with the measurement of students' performance and consequent classification of award, i.e. assessment *of* learning, it now takes centre stage as a formative process and tool to enhance learning, i.e. assessment *for* learning. Much that has been written on Assessment for Learning (AfL) has been presented as fragmented or partial implying, for example, that formative feedback is *the* major driver of learning.

To address this fragmentation, Gibbs (2006) and others involved in the National Assessment Project Network, devised a conceptual framework outlining 11 conditions under which assessment supports learning. The framework is based on the findings from the student Assessment Experience Questionnaire (AEQ) (Gibbs and Simpson 2003) clustered under the headings used to structure the questionnaire. A summary of the 11 conditions appears below. It is included here as it offers a holistic approach to assessment in the form of a comprehensive guide which may be used as a check-list for anyone involved in curriculum design or who seeks to enhance his/her pedagogic practice through the promotion and application of AfL.

Underpinning the 11 conditions under which assessment promotes learning is a need for assessment activities, support and feedback to be powerful and integrated features of learning within the curriculum. For these activities to be valuable they need: (1) to enable students to fulfil the learning outcomes of their work; (2) to provide information on the ability and progress of the student in fulfilling the aims of their course; and (3) to relate closely to their academic development.

Eleven conditions under which assessment supports student learning

Quantity and distribution of student effort

1   *Assessed tasks capture sufficient study time and effort*. This condition concerns whether your students study sufficiently out of class or whether the assessment system allows them to get away with not studying very much at all. This is the 'time on task' principle linked to the insight that it is assessment, and not teaching, that captures student effort.

2   *These tasks distribute student effort evenly across topics and weeks*. This condition is concerned with whether students can 'question spot' and avoid much of the curriculum, or stop turning up to class after the last assignment is due in.

Quality and level of student effort

3   *These tasks engage students in productive learning activity*. This condition is partly about whether the assessment results in students taking a deep or surface approach and also about quality of engagement in general.

4   *Assessment communicates clear and high expectations to students.* This is partly about articulating explicit goals that students understand and can orient themselves towards, and partly about the level of perceived challenge.

The remaining conditions concern feedback.

Quantity and timing of feedback

5   *Sufficient feedback is provided, both often enough and in enough detail.*
6   *The feedback is provided quickly enough to be useful to students.*

Quality of feedback

7   *Feedback focuses on learning rather than on marks or students themselves.*
8   *Feedback is linked to the purpose of the assignment and to criteria.*
9   *Feedback is understandable to students, given their sophistication.*

Student response to feedback

10   Feedback is received by students and attended to.
11   Feedback is acted upon by students to improve their work or their learning.

See Gibbs (2006).

Assessment tasks may have diagnostic, formative or summative aspects which may determine *when* and *how* you use them in your teaching (QAA 2006):

- *diagnostic assessment* provides an indicator of a learner's aptitude and preparedness for a programme of study and identifies possible learning problems;
- *formative assessment* is designed to provide learners with feedback on progress and to feed forward to inform development;
- *summative assessment* provides a measure of achievement or failure made in respect of a learner's performance in relation to the intended learning outcomes of the programme of study.

So, having established the major role assessment plays in orientating all aspects of student learning, why are we advocating assessment and feedback as forms of dialogue?

We have already argued that dialogue is an essential aspect of social learning theory (Vygotsky 1978) and that students *construct* knowledge, rather than reproduce it. Self- and peer assessment are forms of dialogical engagement with assessment criteria. In applying methods of AfL, students are, therefore, *actively constructing knowledge* and *developing critical judgement*. Holistic models of AfL advocate assessment tasks which incorporate dialogue at their centre, thereby creating social and collaborative interactions between students and tutors, and between students and their peers.

AfL models draw on a social perspective of how people learn, and in particular on the work of Lave and Wenger (1991) in creating communities of practice. Lave and Wenger's social learning theory proposes that through dialogical engagement in communities of practice (in this case, *communities of learning*), student participation may at first be legitimately peripheral but that it increases gradually in engagement and complexity. Participation in the social group therefore becomes an *essential* part of the learning.

Social learning of this sort has much in common with the apprentice model in which the apprentice acquires skills, knowledge and 'ways of being' from senior practitioners, peers and others within the community. In higher education contexts, dialogical assessment is integral to pedagogic communities of practices which aim to foster engagement with academic knowledge and to encourage learners to develop their individual voices and discover their identities (Wenger 1998).

Active engagement in self- and peer assessment, just like critical reflection, does not come naturally to a majority of students. In fact, peer assessment is often vehemently resisted by students initially before they subsequently experience its multifarious benefits to learning (e.g. Stephanie et al. 2001; Smith et al. 2002).

One study which supports and extends previous research on students' perceptions of peer assessment identified the following dimensions as to why it is so frequently resisted as 'discomfort', 'difficult' and 'problems with implementation' (Stephanie et al. 2001). That it is uncomfortable and difficult to have to judge our peers should come as no surprise, and may indeed be an experience mirrored by some staff engaging in any sort of peer evaluation or appraisal scheme. Assessment is an emotive business and feelings of anxiety allied to self-esteem and feelings of 'not being good enough' are common to us all. When discussed and shared openly and honestly, thereby becoming normalised, these negative emotions lose some of their hold and may be considerably reduced.

As to students citing problems with implementation, this is again a common experience and one which has been addressed in the literature. It is widely acknowledged that for peer assessments to run smoothly, there may be a need for heavy 'front-loading' of effort devising appropriate tasks and preparing students to participate in activities which may be unfamiliar to many of them. Added to this is a need for regular practice so that all concerned become familiar and comfortable with the process (Bryan 2006: 151–5).

In the same study, students identified the following positive dimensions for engaging in peer assessment. These were: 'gained better understanding of marking'; 'productive' (including learning benefits and improved work); 'read others work'; and 'developed empathy' (with assessing staff); and 'motivation' (especially motivation to impress peers) (Stephanie et al. 2001).

The following example of peer assessment designed to enhance group learning, illustrates further some of the pedagogic benefits of dialogical assessment. Students were briefed to follow a step-by-step process: they received guidance and discussed positive ways to give and receive feedback; they devised their own criteria; and they engaged in structured post-performance debriefing. The following student comment is typical:

I was one of the ones who said how unfair it is not to get marked on how well we work together in our group projects but I had no idea how difficult it is to do it properly. I have learned so much from watching our group and having to articulate the grades I gave.

(Second-year Drama student, cited in Bryan 2006: 152)

Yet another benefit of dialogical feedback and assessment is how evaluative processes we may have used for many years are shared and may require justification or updating in the light of curricula change. Dialogical assessment can, therefore, be said to transform tacit into explicit knowledge, as the following student comments illustrate.

At first I couldn't see the point of deciding our own assessment criteria but having done so now on three separate occasions, I realise how it helped the whole group think and agree what was most important and should therefore carry most marks.

(PGCE Drama student, cited in Bryan 2006: 153)

Everyone knows the rules if you have to set the assessment [criteria] together so we don't waste time arguing when we're working without the tutor.

(First-year Jazz student, cited in Bryan 2006: 153)

The pedagogic arguments for applying methods of AfL are compelling. As designers of assessment and learning activities, we need to be mindful of the relationship of the assessment task to the context in which it is set. When the two are appropriately aligned, the assessment may be said to be 'authentic' (Birenbaum 2003; Gulikers et al. 2008).

To this we would reiterate the importance of regular practice so that self- and peer assessment simply become an integral part of our classroom and professional practice. Achieving effective dialogical assessment may well require us to 'teach' and, where necessary, model for students some fundamental principles and rules of engagement. Students will need us to provide ample opportunities where they may practise the 'art' of giving and receiving critical feedback. Only by repeated practice can we expect that their skill and collaborative participation in dialogical assessment processes will indeed increase to be able to encompass the inherent complexities of assessment (e.g. Lave and Wenger 1991; Lewis and Allan 2005; Bryan 2006).

There are numerous resources on assessment, many of which also offer case studies which may easily be emulated or amended for differing contexts (e.g. Schwartz and Webb 2002; Bryan and Clegg 2006; Black and Rust 2006; Bures et al. 2010; Sambell et al. 2012; http://www.heacademy.ac.uk/assessment; http://www.lancaster.ac.uk/palatine/AGP/index.htm).

Some key pedagogic benefits of engaging in dialogic methods of assessment include:

- development of vocabulary in the language of academic assessment (often described in student surveys as a complete mystery to them);
- development of evaluative skills including realistic self-assessment and recognition of high-quality work;

- introduction to the complexities inherent in all assessment – whether it is encountering positivistic principles of reliability and validity or having to contend with a more interpretivist approach to assessment, commonly applied in arts and design programmes;
- development of communities of learning in which tacit knowledge is transformed into explicit knowledge;
- inculcation of the belief that the learner is empowered to exert significant control of his/her learning so as to enhance individual and collaborative performance (self-regulated learner);
- inculcation of the belief that assessment processes need not be feared and are integral to achieving and demonstrating programme learning outcomes.

Activity 2.4

- With reference to your own discipline/subject-context, in what ways have you sought to embed a notion of assessment for learning in your teaching and learning regime?
- In what ways have you been involved in seeking to integrate assessment policy and practice into the learning and teaching regime/strategy for your school/faculty or institution overall?

Conclusion

This chapter has introduced some key pedagogic approaches aimed at enhancing student learning, and contextualised it within the broader history and development of the pedagogy of HE as a distinct discipline. Themes running throughout have illustrated a changing higher education landscape in which curricula are evolving and in which a, still relatively new, dimension to academic practice and academic professionalism is being advanced: a distinct scholarship of learning and teaching for HE, with its own (albeit contested) concepts, and principles. And which has a focus on HE pedagogy as a researchable subject, with a growing (albeit contested) evidence base. We take the view throughout this book that the contested nature of this emerging discipline is a healthy sign, and not evidence that it is weak or pre-paradigmatic (Kuhn [1962] 2012).

Academic practice in twenty-first-century Western universities also now clearly spans traditional subject-based research, leadership and management, and, increasingly, business functions too. These will be discussed in subsequent chapters, and specifically how they relate to learning and teaching. However, it would be remiss not to restate here in the conclusion of a chapter entitled *enhancing student learning*, the implicit need for us as professionals to continually enhance *our* learning, and particularly in partnership with our students. We hope that the way we introduced the UKPSF in Chapter 1 will act as an encouraging spur to use it to develop your own critically reflective narrative account concerning your current learning, teaching assessment regime. And, particularly if have you have not thought about this already, how that

narrative could become part of your own growing pedagogic research and/or scholarly profile, as an academic or someone who supports learning activities in UK HE. Chapter 3 explores in more detail some of the themes and issues related to this aspect of academic practice.

Gone are the days in which academics like Professor K.G. Reason, a fictitious character with whom you will become better acquainted in subsequent chapters, might proudly proclaim: 'My teaching is fine; I've done things like this for 30-plus years and heard no complaints from any students.' Or perhaps better, gone are the days when proclamations like this will go unchallenged, with colleagues increasingly demanding that such statements be accompanied by some scholarly evidence to support them.

Opinion Piece, Debate, Dear Lecturer, and Fellowship Application extracts

In the following opinion piece, Yaz El-Hakim reflects on his involvement in the Transforming the Experience of Students Through Assessment (TESTA) project and some of the important messages to have emerged from this. This is followed by a debate between Patrick Smith and Trevor Hussey, on one side, and David Gosling, on the other, on the uses and limitations of learning outcomes in higher education. To finish, Kate Riseley, a recent graduate from Canterbury Christ Church University, reflects on the chapter overall. This is followed by three extracts from successful HEA fellowship applicants who discuss some of the aspects of academic practice which feature in this chapter.

Opinion: Transforming the Experience of Students Through Assessment: a case study

Yaz El-Hakim

Since the National Student Survey (NSS) began to reveal that assessment and feedback were a key aspect of the learning process that needed further development (from the student satisfaction scores), it has become a central point of focus for institutions across the HE sector. Many projects were subsequently funded through a variety of bodies to enhance this aspect of the student learning experience. This led to the project, 'TESTA' (Transforming the Experience of Students Through Assessment) being funded by the Higher Education Academy, through the National Teaching Fellowship Scheme Project Strand.

The TESTA project team devised a methodology to be able to collect and triangulate data relating to the assessment and feedback experience of students, *in relation to their programmatic experience*. The three tools of the methodology were: an Audit, the Assessment Experience Questionnaire (Gibbs and Dunbar-Goddet 2007) and Focus Groups with students. These tools were then trialled at four Cathedral group universities: the University of Winchester, the University of Chichester, the University of Worcester and Bath Spa University. Key trends that became apparent from the data across the sector revealed that degree programmes in the UK were:

- Heavily biased towards the quantity of summative assessment over formative assessment.
- Creating unclear students, regarding the goals and standards expected by staff. This was mostly attributed to marker variation and perceived inconsistencies in marking practice against the criteria. Unique assessments were also dotted throughout the programmes creating anxiety in students who were unclear what would be expected due to no previous practice at such assessments.
- Ineffective in producing consistent student effort as effort did not seem to be distributed across academic years and the different modules within them; but rather, followed a peak and trough (Graham Gibbs' fondly named 'Alps') model of bunched assessments deadlines in the middle and at the end of each module/semester.
- Lacking in intra-programme awareness, specifically by members of programme teams, as to how their individual modules connected with the other modules within the programme. This meant a heavy bias in the types of assessments, as the module leaders set the assessment types in line with accepted institutional or subject norms, e.g. an essay and exam.
- Not mapping assessments across a programme in order for programme leaders to become clear on the amount, timing, variety and overlap of assessments. The audit process often led to logical and evidence-informed reflections and some ideas as to the types of changes against the literature alone.
- Giving inconsistent feedback, which students perceived to have limited use at the end (or later) of each module due to the next module being with a different academic, on a different topic and/or a different assessment type. Subsequently, there was a feeling that feedback from one module was not as transferable to others, as staff may have assumed.

More detailed findings and data are well documented (Jessop 2012; Jessop et al. 2014a, 2014b).

Some key reflections on TESTA so far

- *Formative assessment has played second fiddle to a burgeoning of summative assessments through the modularisation and massification of HE over the last 20 years*. Largely, the assessment experience of students has been an evolution to this point, with more modules being created and refined to include more summative assessment points, as staff believe that summative assessments drive students' efforts. Ironically, for staff looking to create learning environments that support critical, self-reflective, autonomous and mastery-focused students, a constant series of high stakes (counting to degree classifications) assessments are more likely to create dependent learners, who struggle to internalise standards tacitly held by individual staff and become more instrumental (Black and Wiliam 1998; Ryan and Deci 2000; Nicol and McFarlane-Dick 2006).

- *Modules appear to be the focal point for staff teaching them whereas programmes are the focal point for students studying them.* This point alludes to the need for staff to reflect upon how assessments could align across modules within programmes. This may also create greater awareness in the programme team about coherence and timings of assessments. This may afford more feedback from summative points to be used formatively within the year.
- *Programme teams are separated by workload, and create less 'quality time' or 'useful data' to reflect upon in order to enhance the programmatic experience for all.* For example, marking workshops where academics compare different marking practices and standards on an essay may allow for tacit understandings of criteria to be explained and shared.
- *That staff and programmes are willing to change (quite substantially at times) if the evidence for the change(s) is presented in a collegiate way that engenders the teams' autonomy, and is both useful and resonates with the team.* A weighting of assessment and feedback literature to support and guide innovations and changes being proposed or undertaken by the team has also created more confidence in some academic teams that may not have the same assessment and feedback literacy as central development units.

In summary, the useful, relevant and relatable data collected by TESTA (www.testa.ac.uk), which has led to collegiate programme team discussion, has been compelling to the institutions and staff within them. So much so, that the process has continued to spread, by largely word of mouth, to be used in over 50 universities in 2014, nationally and internationally (that we are aware of), and potentially transforming tens of thousands of students' experiences of assessment and feedback, hopefully for the better (as well as the experiences of assessment and feedback, for staff too).

Debate: the limits of learning outcomes

Patrick Smith and Trevor Hussey

Why is it that what so often starts as a perfectly reasonable idea eventually transmutes into an intellectual harness, complete with bearing rein? When first discussed, the suggestion that learning outcomes are preferable to learning objectives seemed reasonable, if hardly revolutionary. In the UK it was soon taken up, elaborated and eventually mandated by the Quality Assurance Agency (QAA 2007). In 2013, their Europe-wide use was reviewed positively in a conference in Thessaloniki (ECDVT 2013). Educators at all levels now appear obliged to use them.

In 2002, we published an article entitled 'The trouble with learning outcomes' in which we accepted that it is often a good idea for a teacher to make clear to themselves, and to their students, what learning is intended during a teaching session, but we argued that there are dangers if this becomes too formalised and rigid. In brief, learning outcomes can do educational harm and become a vehicle for an excessively bureaucratic accountability.

The educational harm can come about in several ways. First, there are situations in which precise and explicit learning outcomes are inappropriate or of little use. A teaching session, especially in higher education, can be designed as an exploration in which what is learned is unpredicted except at a very general level, even by the tutor. In many circumstances, sticking rigidly to stipulated learning outcomes can be stultifying: it can lure a teacher into ignoring or suppressing what learning emerges during a session, and deter students from pursuing personal lines of enquiry. Nothing encourages students more than when a skilled teacher picks up what emerges from a discussion, irrespective of whether it was one of the stipulated learning outcomes.

In other situations the tutor may have certain learning in mind but may not tell the students, and so employ a tactic of surprise. In situations where several groups of students are following up, say, a shared lecture, and are using a range of forms of interaction, from seminars to virtual learning environments and social media systems such as Facebook, Linked-in and Twitter, parity of coverage may be impossible and within weeks any intended learning outcomes, beyond the most general, become meaningless.

Second, learning outcomes can be excessively rigid. Consider the idea that they can be specified using precise 'descriptors', such that at one level the students will recall, repeat and describe, while at the next they will comprehend, understand, define and explain, and at the next they will evaluate, analyse, integrate, criticise etc. This is mistaken in any discipline and is ridiculous in some, such as philosophy and literature. What is meant by describing without comprehension? What is 'understanding' without some degree of evaluation? Can we know without comprehension? And so on. Can any subject, from primary to doctoral level, be taught in such a fractured way? Sit and watch an infant classroom for half an hour and you will find plenty of evidence of analysis in operation – analysis, that is, relative to their level of operation. Since Bruner's spiral curriculum we have recognised the importance of returning to a topic several times at different levels, each time gaining knowledge, understanding and critical awareness.

Third, the supposed clarity and precision of pre-specified learning outcomes is largely spurious and illusory. Would 'Students will be able to describe the structure and function of the mammalian heart' be adequately and positively confirmed by the answer 'It is a pump with four chambers that forces blood around the body'? Perhaps it would be among 12-year-olds but not at degree level. Learning outcomes appear precise only because the teacher and the students know roughly what is required at their level. What is expected from the students emerges during the course of learning: given by the level of the teaching materials, classroom discussion, feedback on coursework, and so on. Most learning is demonstrated by what students can do – 'knowledge how' – and this can rarely be captured precisely by verbal descriptions.

Fourth, learning outcomes, stipulated using the prescribed 'descriptors' will not capture many of the outcomes that the teacher most desires. Such statements as 'Students will develop a love of poetry' or 'Students will come to see the point of philosophy and enjoy it' describe outcomes that most good teachers of those subjects would value before all others, but they are unlikely to be accepted by an accrediting authority.

Finally, the extension of learning outcomes to cover the description of whole educational courses is very questionable. In designing modules, courses and degree programmes, teachers almost always begin by deciding on the content and suitable reading and teaching material, and teaching methods. To re-write this in terms of broad learning outcomes adds nothing to the documents except extra words. Courses, especially at university level, need to be flexible so as to accommodate contemporary events. Imagine sticking doggedly to the stipulated learning outcomes on an economics or banking course designed before 2008/9 (Mirowski 2013).

There is a real danger that the demand that teachers formulate precise learning outcomes, whether for each teaching session or whole courses, can be part of an oppressive bureaucratic regime designed for the benefit of managers. If the intended learning could be specified with the clarity and precision purported to belong to learning outcomes, a teacher's performance could be monitored by generic managers with no understanding of teaching. Although we have argued that such clarity and precision are illusory, that need not deter the façade being maintained out of managerial convenience.

There is a supreme irony in the fact that institutions whose concern is with learning and education, prove to be so comprehensively immune to the process of learning themselves. Of course, people coming into the teaching profession need guidance, and it makes sense to advise them to think clearly about what they want their students to learn, but this ought not to result in them wearing learning outcomes like a chastity belt, just in case they go astray.

Debate: A case for learning outcomes in HE

David Gosling

The distinctive feature of acts of teaching is that they are directed towards the achievement of learning – and not just any learning but learning of particular areas of knowledge, skills, and values. In this respect they are unlike conversations, requests, protests, prayers, performances, and other speech acts. In so far as these other speech acts include the intention to learn something, they are, in part, teaching acts. What is intended to be learnt may be more or less explicit, more or less articulated, more or less precise. Disciplines differ in the extent to which it is possible to articulate precisely what it is that students are expected to learn. But it does not follow that because the ends of teaching are difficult to specify that there are no ends. The ends remain even if they have not been articulated by the teacher.

When the intended ends of teaching have not been articulated, students must discover what they are. Placing the responsibility on students to discover what they are supposed to learn has been, and is, used as a means of discriminating between those students who 'get it' and those who don't. By refusing to articulate the ends of teaching, tutors engage in mystification while controlling the assessment process.

The act of assessment implicitly specifies the objects of learning (or at least those important enough to be assessed) – both by selecting what is assessed and how grades are allocated. Both these determinants are, in higher education, within the power of the teacher – even if the teacher's freedom is restricted by professional bodies. Of course, this is why students look at past papers to work out what they will be assessed on. However, this is a highly fallible process with a large element of guesswork involved. Pre-specified learning outcomes are intended to take this element of mystification and guesswork out of the process. The reasoning is that learning is more effective when it is focused.

It also helps teachers to design teaching programmes and individual teaching sessions. The process of thinking carefully about what students need to learn – rather than simply what content is being taught – helps the lecturer to think critically about the teaching, learning and assessment process. It encourages lecturers to design activities that will maximise relevant learning rather than leaving what students learn to chance or sometimes misguided guesswork. That is not to say that learning cannot emerge in unpredictable ways and be all the better for that, nevertheless, the core outcomes on which students will be assessed should be in the public realm rather than hidden and discoverable only through a secret ritual controlled only by the lecturer. Put simply, students have a right to know where their learning is heading and on what they will be assessed.

It has been argued that most lecturers pay no attention to learning outcomes once their courses have been approved, implying that the only purpose for writing them was to satisfy quality assurance officers. This may be right, but it does not show that learning outcomes have no other purpose than satisfying quality assurance protocols – only that their potential for sharpening-up the design of courses and assessment is not being recognised and used.

Lecturers are faced with a demand by university authorities to write learning outcomes without there being any discourse about the educational justification for an outcomes-based approach and the implications for course design. Furthermore, by making an outcomes-based approach a regulatory matter, all other legitimate forms of course design are ignored or devalued. In these circumstances, specifying learning outcomes becomes a technocratic chore, not an educational choice.

Much of the resistance to learning outcomes derives from lecturers' dislike of being accountable to quality assurance regimes and the implied loss of teacher autonomy. But teaching, within public institutions, should not be a private and secretive transaction between a lecturer and his/her students and should be available for scrutiny and monitoring. However, that scrutiny should not be overly obtrusive and be fit for purpose. Unfortunately quality assurance processes often become over-specified and rule-bound, where the emphasis on writing correctly formulated learning outcomes becomes a fetishistic replacement for real judgements about quality. The act of approving learning outcomes for a course does not assure the quality of the course nor does it guarantee that successful students have reached a pre-determined 'level' of learning. The quality of student learning is influenced by, but not determined by, their experience of the teaching they receive. The learning outcomes students actually achieve are significantly influenced by their own efforts, attitudes to and motivation for learning as well as the quality of the learning environment. The act of specifying learning outcomes is a useful tool in course design but is clearly not sufficient to ensure the quality of learning achieved.

Some of the opponents of learning outcomes believe that teaching should be more like a conversation where the learning achieved is unpredictable and they argue that clarity and explicitness in learning outcomes are 'largely spurious'. Furthermore, they argue that their use can be restrictive.

There are certainly dangers in an over-positivist approach. At best, learning outcomes are indicative of the threshold learning that students are required to have achieved in a subject at a specified level. Where credit accumulation is used to define qualifications, some statement of the thresholds are needed, but we should never fall into the trap of thinking that such statements offer a full and rich description of what any individual student has learned or what has been taught. The claim that learning outcomes are 'largely spurious' is based on a false expectation of the function they have in the teaching and learning process.

To escape the seemingly endless recurrence of the debate about learning outcomes, we require a more realistic understanding of their purpose, what they can achieve and their limitations. We need statements of learning outcomes that are useful to students and not simply written to meet the requirements of quality assurance processes, which often fail to assess quality and rarely give the assurance sought. The valuable debate we could have is not for or against learning outcomes, but about the many and varied ways of motivating and inspiring learning, within which the value of articulating learning outcomes may be fairly considered.

Dear Lecturer

On my state of becoming

Kate Riseley

University is a place full of possibilities. Sure, some students are there because society dictates that their chosen profession requires it, some because it's just what you do, some because their parents told them to be there, but imagine just being there because you want to learn.

I worked hard academically and personally to become ready for university. I had earned my place and no doubt my being there ticked a few widening participation boxes but none of that mattered to me. University suspends time; we go there, leaving the real world behind temporarily. It is a chance to discover who we are, to grow, to learn as Newman said 'to reach out towards truth, and to grasp it'. But we, as students, need to know more of this as we *begin* our studies.

Reading the draft of the chapter of this book made me think, hold on! It's all very well focusing on how teachers should teach, how about sharing with learners how and why we learn? Hearing about von Humboldt, Newman, Rogers was all new to me. Why don't we, as students, know this stuff? Armed with just this first chapter of this book my peers and I could have used our time so much more effectively. We could have actively engaged with our being and our learning rather than just accepting at the end that, apparently, we now have some transferable skills. I suppose I was one of the lucky ones, I was at university because I wanted to be. Okay, I might have sold it to my family under the guise of improving my employability (isn't it sad we have to justify learning) but really I just wanted to be there.

It's now six months since I finished my degree in English Literature. I loved my degree programme but I probably could have studied anything, I just wanted to be in the environment that encouraged learning. Being at university made me feel like royalty, I loved the automatic doors that literally opened for me as I walked towards them, this made me smile every day.

It was in this state of being that I could really learn, and interact with lecturers. I sought part-time work, I engaged with feedback, I did everything a student is supposed to do. Yes, my knowledge has grown, I am theoretically more employable but the thing I enjoyed most was walking towards those doors, acknowledging a little flutter in my tummy in case this was the one time they didn't open and then the euphoria as they swept majestically open, welcoming me to *be*.

As I write this, I am still reeling from the news this week (November 2014) from Education Secretary Nicky Morgan warning young people that choosing to study arts subjects at school could 'hold them back for the rest of their lives'. Hold them *back*! A true love of learning, anything, can only take you forward. To the me that was quietly be-ing on campus the only thing that really mattered were the boundless possibilities it created for me *be-coming*.

Extracts from successful HEA fellowship applications

Dr Orange (FHEA)

I am a strong believer in encouraging students to engage with their own learning by providing them with a traffic light card 10 minutes before the end of the lecture. On this piece of card they have three headings under which they must write: STOP: Which parts of the lecture you did not enjoy; START: Which parts of the lecture you would like improvements on and suggestions of how; CONTINUE: Which parts of the lecture you enjoyed and why. Lastly they would be asked to note down ... 'Are there any concepts you would like to be revisited next week?'

The students would then place the anonymised card in a box as they exit the lecture room. The answers to the questions would be placed onto the study space for students to read. The student feedback from the end of module evaluation forms has indicated that they enjoyed this form of interaction with the lecturer. With this style of interaction it is possible that any difficulties that students are having with their learning can be identified early on and I am able to evaluate the method of delivery and revise it as necessary. Students in particular enjoyed this method of providing feedback to the lecturer as some stated: 'I was able to let the lecturer know if I was stuck on something' [K5].

Dr Brown (SFHEA)

In my first post as Senior Lecturer, I continued to research the learning experience through internal research funding, and to explore the experiences of mature learners [K3] returning to education and wishing to enter the teaching profession. This pedagogic research and enquiry was embedded in my teaching which was from this point increasingly research-led and research-based [V3]. My methodology of choice was established by now, through my PhD and subsequent and parallel undertakings. Using my counselling skills and understanding of the therapeutic alliance, I used free associative narrative interviewing techniques (Hollway and Jefferson 2000) to gather biographic, rich data, wherein the lines of narrative could be traced and examined; the play of word and metaphor explored, and the speaker's hopes and plans for reparation (a psychosocial understanding of justice) could be traced.

Dr Blue (PFHEA)

One of the issues many students face in HE is being able to read the feedback they receive. Research indicates that speedy, constructive feedback can have a major impact on student learning (Gibbs and Simpson 2004). While typing feedback was strongly recommended, this tended not to happen and many said they lacked the typing skills. I decided to run a pilot on 'paperless' online marking. The use of the term 'paperless' was purposive, the focus was not on the technology but on sustainability and the student experience. The first year of the pilot was quite successful, but only a small number of 'early adopters' took part. After communicating the findings of the pilot I expanded this the following year, and persuaded the Dean to offer all staff taking part new equipment (large screens, connectable laptops) to encourage staff to try out the system. Student feedback was so good we decided to roll-out online marking across the faculty, making it the preferred option for any work that could be submitted to Turnitin. Sensitive to the resistance this decision would lead to, I initiated a major communication drive, including ten workshops in computer labs where staff were able to try out the system and ask questions. I led these workshops myself as they were an important part of the change process. I started each session by explaining the rationale for the move and the impact this would have on student learning. During that year, the knowledge I was able to bring to university committees led to a decision to move the entire university to online submission and feedback and my work enabled this to be implemented immediately.

3

The nature of academic time
John Lea

If the people judging the validity of my work are outside the institution which employs me, what's the point of me caring about my institution?

If I could get someone else to do my teaching, wouldn't that give me more time to do research and to publish?

I didn't become a professional in order to be line-managed, particularly by somebody who doesn't do any academic work.

Introduction

To whom or what do we owe our allegiance as academic practitioners? From the following list where would you place the emphasis?

1　Primarily, my allegiance is to my department.
2　Primarily, my allegiance is to my discipline or subject.
3　Primarily, my allegiance is to my institution.
4　Primarily, my allegiance is to my students.
5　Primarily, my allegiance is to my research and knowledge creation.
6　Primarily, my allegiance is to my teaching and knowledge dissemination.

If, like me, you were torn on these choices, you may have opted to say that allegiance is shared between all of them, and that they naturally overlap. You may also have felt that, while you would *like* to put the emphasis on one or two of these, there are reasons why, in practice, your allegiance has ended up coalescing around one or two of the others. Of course, you might also have said that your allegiance lies somewhere else entirely. This chapter looks at these questions from three angles. First, asking how these allegiances are formed and become part of our academic identities. Second, asking how teaching and learning might become a more integral part of everyone's academic identity. And, third, looking at the ways in which accountability and quality enhancement have become key features of our academic identities. The general theme of the chapter is to look critically at how we spend our time. Throughout the chapter we will also be hearing from two fictitious academic colleagues, Professor K.G. Reason and Dr M. Bracewell, who will be interjecting from time to time with their views.

The nature of academic identity

When I reflect on the staff development events I have attended over the years, there seem to be two broad purposes to them: either, there is an offer relating to institutional induction, that is, to learn something about 'how we do things round here', or, there is an offer as to how I might enhance one of my academic abilities, for example, how to be a better researcher, writer, or teacher. These two sets of broad purposes need not be in conflict, but because they are often run by different people, working for different departments, a different emphasis will be evident. At the extreme, institutional induction events often feature slide shows demonstrating the health of the institution, strategic targets for the institution, and include line management structure diagrams, and a corporate logo on each slide, whereas academic ability events tend to be more discursive, often speaking to discipline-based forms of peer review, national and international networks, and a sense of an academy beyond institutional walls, or an 'invisible college' (Halsey and Trow 1971). But do these emphases just reflect different aspects of our academic identities, or are they evidence of conflicting allegiances? Indeed, might we find evidence here of a battle between traditional forms of collegiality and more contemporary forms of corporatism (Fanghanel 2012), and continuing evidence of the general demise of academic rule or 'donnish dominion' (Halsey 1992)?

The notion of discipline (or subject-based) allegiance has been depicted as one comprising 'tribes and territories' (Becher 1989; Becher and Trowler 2001), where the conflict is not necessarily between allegiance to discipline vs. allegiance to institution, but a conflict between discipline boundaries, for example, between so-called hard and soft subjects, and between competing epistemological paradigms. This is also a question of 'how we do things round here', but here the induction is into how one's subject, discipline or department distinguishes itself from others; how discipline-based questions are raised and particular research methods employed, and how new knowledge is taught and disseminated (Kreber 2008). Within an institution this can create a 'balkanised' existence (Hargreaves 1994) for a particular department or subject, who pride themselves on their distinctive nature, and who might actively oppose themselves to other departments. On occasion, they might even view other departments or subjects as epistemologically weak or flawed in some way. These entrenched attitudes, particularly when presented as a pride in the validity and reliability of a subject's history of knowledge production and dissemination, can go on to create powerful discipline allegiances way beyond a particular institutional setting. This is what prompted Barnett's comment: '[T]he typical academic might know better and feel more connection with other researchers in his or her discipline on the other side of the world than with an academic in another discipline in the same university, even in the same building' (2012: 51).

Reconciling these academic conflicts may prove difficult and require careful management (which we will return to later), but equally, the conflicts might be overblown. For example, if I am granted a term's study leave in order to complete my ground-breaking discipline-based book, I may feel some guilt that I will be letting down my students, particularly those who have chosen my third year research-led module, for which I am known to be a leading figure in the field. But, looked at another way, on my return after Christmas, those students will now get the benefit of my new-found knowledge, and might learn first hand of my experiences of, say, interviewing a number of important political figures in the process of completing that book. Similarly, my university will now be able to enter my work in the forthcoming Research Excellence Framework (REF) exercise (REF 2012), which in turn may attract more research funds to my institution in the future. And, I may now be in a position to complete that application for a professorship, which requires that I demonstrate success in discipline-based knowledge production and dissemination. Here we see those conflicts begin to evaporate, because even though it is the university that grants me my professorship, it does so largely on my standing within those discipline-based networks. This makes universities complicated institutions because the environment in which a particular institution enhances its reputation is heavily dependent on activities which take place beyond its confines. Put crudely, academics need to get out more if their university is to thrive.

Another way to approach the question of academic identity is to borrow the sociological (Durkheimian) term 'organic solidarity', and consider the extent to which it is the differences between us all that actually hold us together. In this approach the combined effect of all the staff development activities is to enable us to find which aspects of academic identity we are best suited to, so that we then might excel by concentrating

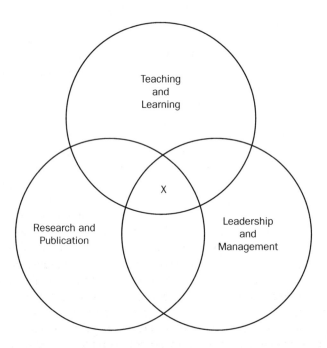

Figure 3.1 Dimensions of academic practice.

on enhancing those skills, while others concentrate on the other dimensions. Of course, this may occur of necessity rather than desire because it might be simply impossible to balance all aspects of academic activity in one career. But the net result is a division of labour, which should unite us rather than divide us. A simple depiction is given in Figure 3.1.

Depicting academic identities as a Venn diagram in Figure 3.1 offers the potential to consider the size and extent of any overlaps, indicating, for example, that it might be possible to balance excelling in teaching and learning with excelling in leadership and management, and so on. Indeed, these overlaps might speak to the existence of separate and distinct roles themselves. For example, excelling in teaching and learning is one thing, as is excelling in research and publication, but, equally, there may be a distinct role for those who are able to work successfully at developing a unique overlapping academic identity – maybe, in this case, as a pedagogic researcher. Equally, on the other side of the diagram there may be a particular set of skills required to be an effective academic programme leader, which is neither born of excellence in teaching and learning exclusively, nor wider leadership and management, but is a unique identity in its own right. To complete the diagram, there is an X in the middle, which might be interpreted as 'the X factor'– a unique individual who is able to combine aspects of all three areas of activity, or alternatively, X as a cross, indicating that universities are just too complicated for someone to be able to perform effectively in this way.

Relevant HEA project

Locke, W. (2014) Shifting academic careers: implications for enhancing professionalism in teaching and supported learning. Available at: www.heacademy.ac.uk/node/10079

A simpler way to look at academic identity would be to say that all the roles which could be identified in Figure 3.1 constitute the different dimensions of academic practice. Or that these are the core activities that help define a university as university. To go any further than that, that is, to look at which roles overlap; are complementary; or are in conflict with one another, can only be determined by looking at one particular institution, and then only at one point in its history. Or, to argue that one particular configuration is more in accord with the essence of what a university is, or is more likely to help a university thrive, will inevitability ignore the unique context of each institution. That said, those who have staked their careers on strong allegiances to their disciplines may quickly discover that a core feature of a successful academic identity is the ability to negotiate a somewhat split, ambivalent and culturally schizophrenic relationship with their employing institution, which might be summarised by challenging them on whether they think they work *at* or *for* an institution.

Prof. Reason: I'm glad this issue has been raised because I don't see why I should be embarrassed about saying that I work *at* this university not *for* it. I've been accused of being disloyal for saying that, but it's only ever said by those who don't really understand where this university's standing actually comes from. It's people like me that make this university what it is. It's because I publish in peer-reviewed international journals, and go on world conference tours, that this university appears in any league table. I should be respected for that. In fact, come to think of it, that Venn diagram could be simplified – if someone is not actively engaged in knowledge production, or actively supporting those people, they are not engaged in academic practice, and shouldn't even appear in the Venn diagram. They're the ones who are disloyal.

Dr Bracewell: I can see why you get angry about this, but we're not going to get very far by provoking a catfight. Look, someone's got to manage time, resources, and estate around here, and clearly that's not going to be you. Why not look at it from the division of labour perspective? If you're going on a world tour promoting your latest research, for goodness sake, someone's got to be looking after the shop, or what is it that you will be coming back to? And how about, instead of sending your apologies all the time, why not come along to some staff development and management events and explain your position, and help look for common ground? And what about the students? It's not just a question of putting a timetable together. What about the curriculum, including its learning, teaching and assessment regime? Are you saying that these activities are not part of academic practice?

Teaching and learning as academic practice

In the USA, in 1990, Ernest Boyer published what has became a seminal text for those who were seeking to raise the status of teaching and learning in higher education (Boyer 1990). The Dearing Report, published in 1997, was also instrumental in putting this debate on the policy agenda in the UK (Dearing 1997). But some of the underpinning issues in both texts – about undervaluing teaching and learning in the university – are not new and the point was made succinctly by Cardinal Newman over 150 years in his own now seminal text (or lecture notes as they were originally):

> [I]t [a university] is a place of *teaching* universal *knowledge*. This implies that its object is, on the one hand, intellectual, not moral, and, on the other, that it is the diffusion and extension of knowledge rather than the advancement. If its object were scientific and philosophical discovery, I do not see why a University should have students ...
>
> (Newman [1852] 1996: 3)

We might translate this statement provocatively to suggest that anyone can do research, and anywhere; it cannot and should not therefore be a defining characteristic of a university. But, outside of a university, how often do we see concerted attempts to bring together all that research and help students navigate through it all? Or, 'It's the university curriculum, stupid!' And there is a scholarship associated with it, but one which has, for several reasons, been undermined. For Boyer, the main reason lay in the gradual elevation of original research (or the scholarship of discovery, as he referred to it) as the most valued activity in the university. The effect of this has been clear; that even those academics who might wish to develop in other ways have been marshalled into believing that their status can only be significantly enhanced by success in this field of activity. As we saw at the beginning of Chapter 1 of this book, Boyer makes the point succinctly:

> What we urgently need today is a more inclusive view of what it means to be a scholar – a recognition that knowledge is acquired through research, through synthesis, through practice, and through teaching. We acknowledge that these four categories – the scholarship of discovery, of integration, of application, and of teaching – divide intellectual functions that are tied inseparably to each other.
>
> (Boyer 1990: 25)

Another way to look at this has been explored by Steve Fuller, who argues that this elevation of the research agenda in universities was, in part, brought about by making the PhD the required (and pinnacle) qualification to work in a university, which, in the process relegated the Master's qualification (Fuller 2013). This was a double-whammy, because the PhD qualification – aimed essentially at validating research ability – not only knocked the Master's qualification off its university employability perch, but also helped cement it as a mere stepping stone to a PhD, rather than as a qualification in its own right, and one originally conceived in pedagogical terms. Put simply, in the Bachelor's qualification, you prove you know your subject, and in the Master's qualification, you prove you can disseminate it.

Activity 3.1

- What strategies do you use to manage and integrate the various dimensions of your academic practice?
- In what ways do you actively seek to mentor/induct new members of staff into their various academic roles, and how do you help them to manage the demands of a varied academic identity?

In Figure 3.2, we see Boyer's four scholarships depicted, with multiple arrows to indicate the ways in which all four scholarships might begin to be connected and help form a more rounded scholar.

A key implication for Boyer of such a depiction is that an academic career should provide opportunities for academics to excel in one area, but also enable them to shift career path between them, and, importantly, that this should be welcomed and celebrated rather than frowned upon and viewed as evidence of a failed academic life. Indeed, each scholarship should be accorded equal status. These are all normative

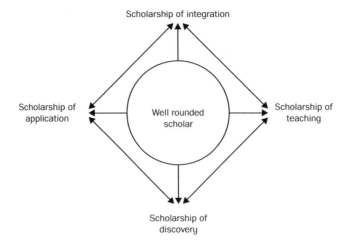

Figure 3.2 Boyer's (1990) four scholarships depicted as integrated practice.

statements, indicating not only that they are an ideal to be aspired to, but also that they might be courting controversy. For example, many academics might feel that though the balance has (perhaps) tipped too far in the direction of the scholarship of discovery, nonetheless activities associated with that scholarship do require the greatest effort and creativity, and that the others are – to some extent at least – parasitic upon that. Furthermore, there may be very practical reasons why excelling in one area alone is the only realistic option, for it may take many years to develop expertise in a particular scholarship, and could a department realistically afford to take a risk by allowing an excellent teacher to bid for a high profile research grant just because they have asked for a career shift? If nothing else, this speaks for a need to manage the career cycle of activities very carefully in a particular departmental context.

Equally, one might make a case for arguing that any of the other three scholarships could be viewed as the pinnacle activity, particularly if a university has an avowed mission in one direction, for example: 'this university is proud of its links with local industry and commerce and students coming here will be encouraged to use their knowledge in applied scholarly ways by working collaboratively with faculty members and local employers.' Here we see the scholarship of application being elevated, or what in the UK has become increasingly known as knowledge exchange. Indeed, many of the new higher education providers (including FE colleges) might argue that this is precisely the kind of higher education provision they are interested in offering. Some universities might also see little point in trying to compete with other more wealthy research-intensive universities, deciding instead to develop aspects of the scholarships of integration (including curriculum development) and of teaching, and become avowedly teaching-led universities. Boyer was counselling against such moves, and they would certainly appear to undermine the German Humboldtian tradition upon which many UK and US universities were founded, one where research and teaching take place in the same institution and feed off each other, and, importantly, ⸱⸱ely invite students to enjoin in scholarly endeavour:

> The relationship between teacher and learner is … completely different in higher
> education from what it is in schools. At the higher level, the teacher is not there for
> the sake of the student, both have their justification in the service of scholarship.
>
> (von Humboldt [1810] 1970, quoted by Elton 2008: 225)

That said, and particularly in a REF context, the sheer pressure to produce a high volume of original research may mean that the other scholarships simply have to take a
back seat, including in some cases teaching itself, let alone teaching underpinned by
scholarship, or co-joined forms of scholarship with students (see Chapter 6). Equally,
knowing that one's institution is not likely to fare well in a REF exercise overall (i.e. it
is unlikely to attract large sums of research money in the near future) might force a
senior management team to concentrate efforts in other directions, possibly to compete for funds associated with widening participation, which may have the subsequent
effect of academic practice having to be heavily skewed in the direction of proactively
supporting non-traditional learners or first generation entrants to university – in both
academic and non-academic ways (Thomas and Quinn 2006). To date, UK universities
have resisted the teaching-only designation, but in practice many may already see this
as their prime activity. Equally, some of the research-intensive universities in the UK
may feel quite comfortable in contemplating giving up on offering a full undergraduate
teaching programme, and concentrate instead on offering research-only post-graduate
degrees.

Clearly, the relationship between teaching and research (or nexus) is multi-
layered and offers many permutations (see Neumann 1992; Elton 2001; Brew 2006;
Healey and Jenkins 2009; and Kreber 2013, for detailed discussions of the various
dimensions to the research-teaching nexus). For example, for an academic to claim
that their teaching is underpinned by research might mean that they use their
subject-based research in their teaching, but it might also mean that their teaching (as
in pedagogical methods) is underpinned by research. In this regard, the former might
be referred to strictly as 'research-led teaching' (RLT) and the latter strictly as
'research informed teaching' (RIT), but there is no common usage of these terms.
There might also be a further distinction to be made between teaching being led and/or
informed by research, where in the former case the teacher has actually undertaken
the research (or collected the primary data) and in the latter they are informed of the
(secondary source) research of others. Clearly, the permutations can start growing
quickly, and with no strict agreement on the use of appropriate terms. This is further
complicated by those who distinguish between being *scholarly* about teaching and
learning and the *scholarship* of teaching and learning, where in the former case adopting a critically reflective approach to HE pedagogy is contrasted with 'going public'
on pedagogic research findings (Kreber 2013). And where, in the former case, peer
review is understood as internal to the institutional setting, and, in the latter, as external to that setting.

The question is also complicated by a consideration of whether simply *knowing*
about aspects of HE pedagogy will necessarily have a positive effect on student
learning, and, perhaps more controversially, whether bringing one's subject-based
research knowledge to the classroom will necessarily have a positive impact on student learning. Nonetheless, there seems to be something intuitively seductive about

wanting to claim that this must be true to some extent in both cases. Gibbs has put a lot of effort into exploring the former claim and Hattie and Marsh sought to unpack all the dimensions involved in the latter claim (Hattie and Marsh 1996; Gibbs 2010). And, at the risk of losing the wood for the trees in all this variable analysis, Lewis Elton has captured what seems to be at the heart of the matter (particularly if one is serious about student learning): 'A positive research and teaching link primarily depends on the nature of the students' learning experiences, resulting from appropriate teaching and learning processes, rather than on particular inputs or outcomes' (Elton 2001: 43).

Prof. Reason: This is getting far too complicated for me. I don't need any variable analysis to know some simple facts. I do my research, and I use that in my third year module, which was designed around my research findings, and the students benefit from me adding little golden nuggets each week, taken from my on-going research on the same subject. I will admit that giving these lectures does eat somewhat into my research time, but, generally speaking, I'm happy to deliver them. I also run a Master's module on research methods, which I unashamedly use to test student knowledge of those methods, which helps me decide who I should take on as PhD students. One of the privileges for those students then becomes the opportunity to teach my second year module as GTAs [Graduate Teaching Assistants]. That suits me and it suits them. You can call that a nexus if you want but I'd just say it's all common sense. Okay, I will also admit that occasionally I do deliver the odd first year lecture, mainly to tell the students about my second and third year modules. I don't see any point in doing much more, because a lot of them seem to fall asleep after about twenty minutes into the lecture.

Dr Bracewell: Well, I'm struggling to know where to begin on this one. Let's take those GTAs. Do they get any training in being a teacher? Do you at least observe them teaching? On second thoughts, probably not a good idea that you do that! And that Master's module sounds like a right bundle of fun! Don't they get a chance to actually do some research themselves? And those poor first years! Probably best you stay away all together on that front. Don't get me wrong, remember, I'm an active researcher in my subject, but I also do pedagogic research, often with my students, and I use the evidence from that research, particularly in my first year teaching. Yes, it's really important that they get a good grounding in the concepts and theories that underpin my discipline, but at the same time they need to develop good study and higher learning skills. My subject-based research just has to stay in the background for that context. And you know, you really are missing out on some fantastic opportunities for your students to become much more scholarly in their studies. It's ironic, because if your students were more like this by the time they came to your third year module, you'd probably find you wouldn't need to lecture at them so much, giving you and them time to work collaboratively on advancing knowledge in your field.

Dear Lecturer

On research-led teaching

Jenni Cannon

As a student, I definitely came across a few lecturers who clearly believed that their students' role was to be a passive recipient of their academic knowledge, and that the ability to impart cutting-edge research is the mark of a good teacher. To me, this missed the point of coming to university completely. I didn't want to be a sponge, soaking up information which I could regurgitate on cue on graduation! I wanted to be part of a discussion; for my teachers to give me the skills to assimilate and question what I was learning, in order to form my own views. I'm not saying research-led teaching isn't important, but I think it's naïve to believe that 'golden nuggets' of new knowledge allow your students to get the best out of you.

I felt I was much better served by the teachers who believed that production of knowledge was a collaborative and dynamic process that involved the students, our thoughts and our development as learners and future academics; as opposed to something that was done in a vacuum and then showed to us in its perfect, finished form.

Activity 3.2

- In what ways do you seek to use your research (and the research of others) in your teaching and learning regime?
- In what ways have you been involved in seeking to integrate the various forms of scholarly activity in a school/faculty or institution framework or to integrate separate strategies for research, learning and teaching, etc.?

Some of the issues being raised by Reason and Bracewell can be depicted in Figure 3.3 (Healey et al. 2014b). At the bottom of Figure 3.3, we see students learning *about* research methods, and academic staff engaging in research but not (for whatever reason) using it in their teaching. As we move up the diagram, we see students becoming more actively involved in doing some research themselves and academics actively using their research findings in the their teaching. But it could still be argued that the diagram is incomplete, because without the final slice of pie at the top, we would be missing the invitation to work more collaboratively with students on research projects, and ensuring that the learning and teaching and assessment regime itself is being researched (possibly also collaboratively with students). These types of activity would certainly seem to accord with von Humboldt's notion of staff and students both working in the service of scholarship, but also Boyer's vision of seeing scholarly activity more holistically (see Chapter 6).

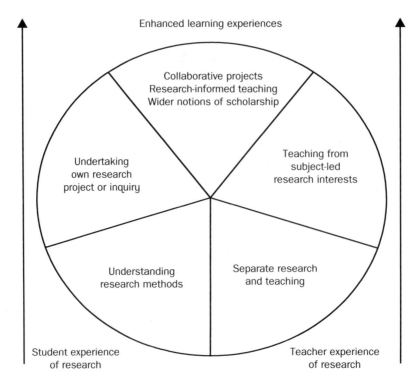

Enhanced learning experiences

Collaborative projects
Research-informed teaching
Wider notions of scholarship

Undertaking
own research
project or inquiry

Teaching from
subject-led
research interests

Understanding
research methods

Separate research
and teaching

Student experience
of research

Teacher experience
of research

Figure 3.3 Uniting staff and student activity.

The top slice of the pie chart in Figure 3.3 also opens up the possibility of incorporating more action research into an academic's scholarly profile – where the academic explores aspects of their own professional practice, and works more collaboratively with their research subjects (McKernan 1996, 2007: McNiff 2001, 2009). But, on the other hand, this type of research practice is not always considered to be true research activity, and may even damage an academic's career, particularly if they wish to excel in the field of original research, or the scholarship of discovery. Indeed, according to REF definitions of research, a lot of the scholarly activity in the top slice of the pie chart would not be admissible in a REF submission (REF 2012).

When the Higher Education Academy was established in 2004, one of its first tasks was to consult the sector on the proposal for a UKPSF (as it subsequently became known). As mentioned in Chapter 1 of this book, that proposal recognised 'that the scholarly nature of subject inquiry and knowledge creation, and a scholarly approach to pedagogy, together represent a uniquely embedded feature of support for student learning in universities and colleges' (HEA 2005). The following comment was also made at the same time: '[w]hile research endeavour and teaching endeavour are believed to be conceptually related in higher education, that relationship needs active management and explicit support since the pressures to split the two apart are powerful' (Atkins, quoted in Jenkins and Healey 2005). Placed alongside each other, both comments would appear to still have clear resonances ten years on.

Managing academic practice

The Dearing Report of 1997 not only spoke of the need to raise the profile of learning and teaching in UK HE, but also how this might be levered up by new forms of accountability. In some cases that accountability should be at the heart of every teaching session, that is, that students should always be clear about the purpose of a taught session and the nature of the learning that will be required of them. This, in essence, is a learning outcomes approach to teaching, and was discussed in Chapter 2. But what was also proposed was a series of wider checks, which collectively became known as the academic infrastructure for higher education (now subsumed under a wider Quality Code) (QAA 2011). This included: programme specifications, so prospective students would know in advance exactly what the nature of the learning experience would be on a particular course of study; subject benchmark statements, making it clear, in essence, what a degree subject needs to contain in order for it to carry that title; level descriptor statements, making it clear the nature of the skills required to be met at each year/level of study – from first year to PhD; and a series of other precepts, compliance with which would be taken as evidence that academic standards were being maintained, and, crucially, enable the standards of achievement in one institution to be compared with other institutions. The new Quality Code is not only more comprehensive but also now includes new sections relating explicitly to expectations about higher learning and teaching, student development and student engagement (Chapters B3, B4, B5).

Since 1997, in the UK, the guardian of this accountability regime has been the Quality Assurance Agency (QAA). This is not the place to chart the history of the QAA, suffice it to say that in its early days its main mechanism for calling institutions to account was a subject-by-subject review, conducted by a team of 'peer reviewers', which resulted in a written report and summary mark from 0–24 for each subject area, based on the reviewers' perceived maintenance of academic standards. This was changed to become a process of Institutional Audit (IA), administered on a five-year cycle in each university and centred on statements of confidence that the QAA reviewers had in a university overall. In the last couple of years all higher education institutions (including further education colleges and private providers with degree-awarding powers) have come under a new unified system of Higher Education Review (HER), along with a gradual movement in the direction of a risk-based approach to review – such as concerns about variance from the norm of statistical data compiled for the new Key Information Set (KIS) (HESA 2014), which in future might contain statistical data on the number of qualified teachers in a particular institution.

It is worth noting that teaching quality has been the focus of these reviews. The quality of research in UK universities was already being monitored and measured by a separate accountability exercise – the Research Assessment Exercise (RAE), the first of which was in 1986, and has been conducted every four years since then. This has been reformed to become the Research Excellence Framework (REF), with an enhanced emphasis on research impacts (see Chapter 7) (REF 2012); and the first results of which were published in December 2014. Again, this is not the place to chart the history of this exercise, but simply to note, particularly in the light of the previous discussion in this chapter of the book, there has been no concerted effort to bring both exercises together, or even consider – formally, in terms of national accountability – the results of one exercise in terms of the other. This may go some way in explaining the comment right at the beginning of this chapter, namely, that some allegiances may have been forced on us because of the *separate* need to perform well in these exercises. There are no brownie points – in terms of national accountability measures – in actively seeking to bring research and teaching together, and significantly, no brownie points for individuals or institutions, in considering the impact that research has on student learning (see Chapter 6).

Returning to our Venn diagram in Figure 3.1, and Atkins' comment about the need to carefully manage the relationship between research and teaching, the roles of the head of department or school (and those above that level) would appear to be crucial. For, not only do they need to keep one eye on the QAA, and one eye on the REF, but they also need to manage the aspirations of individual academics in what is often a large team of staff. And if Boyer's notion of a well-rounded scholar is taken seriously, the head may well find him or herself involved in a crusade, which may be supported in some quarters but not in others (including the senior management team). Heads may also feel personally torn between their own allegiance to the discipline and signing a management contract which commits them more to institutional allegiance.

More controversially perhaps, an ironic outcome of Dearing's demand for more accountability, which he clearly saw as an enhanced form of professionalism, has for many academics been experienced as a form of de-professionalisation; and a creeping perceived obsession not with managing but managerialism (Deem and Brehony 2005; Deem et al. 2008) - which might be defined as ensuring that all behaviour fits predetermined categorisation, or ensuring that action is performed in accordance with what is prescribed, and typified not by accountability but surveillance, not audit but compliance. Here we are talking more about managed academics rather than academic managers (Fanghanel 2012), and where, for example, being deemed 'research active' no longer means being involved generally in research, but ensuring that one's actions fit prescribed categories of behaviour; it is now 'managed activity' (e.g. having generated a certain amount of research money for the institution that employs you). In this scenario, managing professionals becomes an oxymoron, for why train to become a professional, the hallmark of which is to be accorded an autonomous status, when one is destined to become an academic worker, judged by meeting management targets often one has no say in?

Prof. Reason: At last, we've got to the point! I'm not an academic worker, accountable to a non-academic manager. This is a recipe for this place to go slowly down the proverbial pan. Universities are successful because they are able to recruit highly motivated academics, who are dedicated to the work of producing and disseminating new knowledge. The person who said that managing professionals is like herding cats was absolutely right, and we should learn that lesson, not try to turn cats into dogs. You simply can't manage academic life as if it was some kind of 9–5 job. No more than you can manage a classroom as if learning was some kind of tap you just turn on and off at will. In fact, if you did try to manage academic productivity, it would definitely go down! I get most of my good ideas at 2 in the morning, and sometimes I have a snooze in the afternoon, while the unproductive are all attending a management meeting. This place should consider itself lucky that it has such dedicated people working for it; not try to manage them into some kind of robotic monotony, where because you've met some made-up target you can then congratulate yourself. And come on, let's be honest, a manager is simply a failed academic. Given a choice, wouldn't you rather be teaching, researching and publishing? It's only people who are no good at those things who are managers, who then have to resort to messing around with performance indicators, or whatever they call them − it's what their performance indicates that's the real problem.

Dr Bracewell: Well, I'm glad I'm not your line manager! Whether you like it or not, this university is subject to audit and somebody's got to manage that process. And if somebody doesn't manage that well, there simply will be no space for you to do that ground-breaking work you wish to be left alone to do at 2 in the morning. We need some smart people with leadership and management skills keeping their eye on the ball when it comes to these matters, even if you are ungrateful and ungracious about that. Have you never heard of horizon scanning? I'll grant you that some managers are not particularly good at their jobs, but then neither are all academics. Are you seriously saying that academics shouldn't be called to account by their employing institutions? And, remember, your discipline doesn't pay your wages; this university does. My experience of working with my line manager, who is my Head of Department, is that we sit down each year, as a department, and discuss how we could enhance the reputation of the department; which research funds we might collectively target; which projects will be most manageable, particularly given our teaching commitments; and what will be the best division of labour between us all. That then forms the basis of my own plan for the year, including the balance between my teaching load and projected scholarly outputs, which my Head enables me to achieve through an individualised workload plan, upon which I will be appraised. We don't call them performance indicators, but that's essentially what these things are. For goodness sake, how else are you going to judge the quality of work − be that research, teaching, or anything else?

Activity 3.3

- In what ways do you engage with forms of peer review to identify any CPD needs, and how do you go about meeting those needs?
- What management and leadership principles and strategies underpin your appraisal and development of your colleagues?

Audit cultures also bring to the fore notions of gaming and performance (or perfor-mativity), as in ensuring that one complies with what is required but more through paying lip-service than any real or significant investment. This has been referred to as 'scripted communication' (Lea 2009) or 'ventriloquism' (see Macfarlane in the Opinion box on p. 73). And it also has the potential of shifting motivation to act in accordance with *winning* the game. For example, I might be persuaded that it would be better to have my work published in a peer-reviewed international academic journal, rather than a locally produced monograph even though my intended audience is much more likely to read the latter than the former. Here I may well come to see impact as defined by an 'impact measure', not a general idea that my research could have some benefits (Brown and Carraso 2013). But are these broader notions of benefit fast becoming rather quaint in the wider commercialisation of higher education, to which we are now accountable?

As with any business, survival depends on producing what the customer wants, and education is a commodity that customers can purchase from many sources on the open market. The commoditization of the research enterprise has transformed research knowledge into intellectual capital and intellectual property. This has been going on for decades. The commoditization of the teaching enterprise has just started, transforming courses into software, the activity of instruction itself into commercially viable proprietary products that can be owned and bought and sold in the market.

(Noble 1998, quoted in Birnbaum 2001: 92–3)

This quotation comes from an American context, leaving us in the UK to contemplate whether we have just been a bit slower to catch on or catch up. This also seems to demand of us that we consider carefully to whom or to what we are actually being made more accountable. To some academics, it may appear that they are being made more accountable to university managers, but in reality the managers themselves are also being made accountable to forms of academic capitalism (see Chapter 6).

Another significant way in which academics have been called to account in recent years in the UK is the National Student Survey (NSS), which has been running since 2005, but gaining in significance and impact on an annual basis, to such an extent that it is almost impossible (or very brave) for a UK university to ignore its results. The survey is administered annually by the independent marketing company Ipsos MORI, and the results are public knowledge. It is important to note that students access the survey directly through Ipsos MORI, implying that universities cannot refuse to take part. This is unlike the counterpart survey in the USA – the National Survey of Student Engage-ment (NSSE) – where individual universities pay the administering company in order to take part. The NSS is aimed at final year students who answer questions on a range of topics (currently 24 in total) where they rate their experience of being an undergraduate.

Not only are the results subject to detailed scrutiny by each university, who often employ specific people to undertake this work, but the survey itself has been the sub-ject of vociferous debate. Aside from the more epistemological considerations – about its reliability and validity as data – broader questions have also been raised about the value of a survey which seems to be more about how satisfied students are with their university experience, rather than how much their learning has been enhanced (Gibbs 2010). The point is a significant one, particularly for those who are interested in raising the scholarly profile of learning and teaching, because the data does not lend itself readily to taking steps to enhance learning. Indeed, being administered at the end of the third year, it offers no opportunity for students to enhance their own satisfaction, let alone their learning. Furthermore, many of the questions seemed to be more concerned with what the university has done for the student, rather than what the student has done for themselves. In which case, these questions could be argued to be out of kilter with a key purpose behind any undergraduate programme, that 'every student is enabled to develop as an independent learner' (QAA 2012, Chapter B3).

A somewhat ironic comparison may be made with the American survey – the National Survey of Student Engagement (NSSE) – ironic, because in a country well-known for its wish to keep the customer satisfied, the NSSE clearly attempts to measure the degree of the student's own engagement in their studies. Whereas the NSS asks students questions about whether teachers have been good at explaining things; whether they have received detailed comments on their work; and whether their courses are well organised and running smoothly, the NSSE asks questions like: how often have you come to class without completing readings or assignments?; how often have you worked with classmates outside of class to prepare assignments?; and have you participated in a community-based project as part of a regular course? It could be argued that neither survey is actually centred on measuring the amount of learning that has taken place, nor does either help students maximise learning gains, but the NSSE seems to be more in keeping with what is increasingly being considered to be at the heart of higher learning, namely, student engagement (Harper et al. 2008; Dunne and Owen 2013; Nygaard et al. 2013; Bryson 2014).

Relevant HEA projects

Buckley, A. (2013) Engagement for enhancement: report of a UK survey pilot. Available at: https://www.heacademy.ac.uk/sites/default/files/Engagement_for_enhancement_FINAL_0.pdf
Buckley, A. (2014) UK engagement survey 2014; the second pilot year. Available at:https://www.heacademy.ac.uk/sites/default/files/resources/UKES_report_2014_v2.pdf

The term 'student engagement' has become a pivotal term in explaining why some students do better at university than others. Whereas ability on entry (as measured by success in previous educational tests), and social background – including class, race, gender and other cultural factors – have long been understood as key variables in explaining academic success, and indeed, access to university itself, the more engaged a student is in their own learning and in the life of the university is now considered to be equally significant. And many universities have been able to report very positively on projects and initiatives aimed precisely at enhancing student engagement (Bryson 2014). Furthermore, some universities have been experimenting with the use of their own surveys which seek to measure the impact of these initiatives, and a national engagement survey may emerge on the back of that work. The work of Graham Gibbs in the past few years might also be taken as testimony to the importance of these developments (Gibbs 2010, 2012) because he is clear that students who are engaged in these ways are the ones who make the most learning gains.

More generally, for Gibbs, he is also clear that we do now have sufficient evidence on all the factors which are most likely to enhance learning, and it is high time, therefore, that we were all made accountable to that evidence, be that personally as individual academics who teach, or nationally, through, for example, QAA peer review processes. A somewhat alarming factor in that context is the attention being given to the number of class contact hours that students have with their teachers. Indeed, this is a KIS figure. It is alarming because a high figure is considered, by definition, a good one, but there is no real evidence that high-class contact enhances student learning. Indeed, if the aim of higher education is to produce an independent learner, one might claim that more time spent with teachers could well bring about the opposite. In reality, the relationship is a complicated one, and was well understood by Carl Rogers who claimed that a good facilitator of learning is one who takes students from a state of dependency to a state on autonomy, or freedom to learn (Rogers and Freiberg 1994). An HEA-commissioned project refers to the transitional stage as 'directed independent' learning, which sounds oxymoronic, but not if the whole process of learning is taken into account.

Relevant HEA project

Thomas, L. (forthcoming) Effective practice in the design of directed independent learning opportunities. Available at:https://www.heacademy.ac.uk/project/350

Activity 3.4

- What key evaluation tools underpin your evidence base for enhancing your teaching and learning regime?
- In what ways have you been actively involved in responding to, and enhancing, the quality assurance regime in your school/faculty or institution overall?

Other factors on Gibbs' hit list include the fact that small groups are qualitatively superior to large groups, so why therefore is this statistic not in the KIS? And there is some evidence now that qualified teachers are having a marked positive effect on student learning (Gibbs 2012). Indeed, qualified HE teacher status may well appear in the KIS in the future. But the key seems to be an overall environmental consideration – the concerted effort to create a learning environment which actually focus on maximising learning, without which, a small group might well turn out to be worse than a large group, and so on. The big lesson in terms of quality overall, however, seems to be the question of whether we will continue to be more interested in keeping the customer satisfied or will move in the direction of focusing more squarely on maximising learning. In this context perhaps, we should all be made accountable to the answers that students might give to these three questions at the end of their degree programmes: (1) Do you still need your teachers?; (2) Can you set your own learning outcomes?; and (3) Can you accurately mark your own work? (Lea 2012b).

Conclusion

Calling academics to account might be said to have heightened some of the tensions which exist in academic practice between allegiance to discipline and allegiance to institution. But some of those tensions also relate to the call to raise the status of teaching and learning, because this is often happening in contexts where research output is recognised as being not only where most of the status is for individuals, but also where most of the money is for institutions. Managers are also put in difficult positions here, because they may end up very often having to ensure that everything complies with the needs of the various quality measuring devices, and in the process annoy the very colleagues who are trying to produce the things which are in need of measurement. This can also become tribal, where academics start creating bulwarks around their work to prevent encroachment from what are perceived as unwarranted management directives. In this context, managers can quickly become overly managerial at the very point when it is their leadership that is most required. But some responsibility might also be laid at the door at the professoriate, requiring them to take a more active role in general academic leadership, rather just focusing on their discipline-based research (Macfarlane 2012).

Lombardi speaks of the American university as having an academic core and an administrative shell, and where the latter enables the former to operate (Lombardi 2013). Here, the word administration is used in the American sense to include all the activities associated with management and leadership. This balance is important, and if it becomes unhealthy the university will (in the end) suffer. This is very likely to happen when some of the entrepreneurial spirit of the administration – in seeing the university as a profit-making enterprise – clashes with some of the core principles of academic practice. Here, whereas a university may be a business, higher education is not, even if the university can profit from its academic activities. Leaders and managers are essential in ensuring that this balance remains a healthy one. And in this context, Lombardi reminds us that academics are primarily members of guilds and, in practice, actually work for those guilds. This is a unique feature of universities and just as academics need to be reminded that universities must remain economically viable, equally, administrators need to be reminded that the core activity on which the university rests largely takes place outside the walls of the institution: or, 'the national guild establishes the intellectual standards for their [academics'] work; the local university deals with their employment and work assignments' (Lombardi 2013: 2).

This scenario is complicated by the fact that there are many guilds, often operating with their own academic conventions, and notions of valid knowledge (see Chapter 5). To some extent this explains the kinds of balkanisation we often see, and also might explain why moves towards adoption of more generic professional standards and codes might be resisted. It is also complicated by the presence of students who will be invited by administrators to see themselves as belonging to the university, but by many academics as being inductees into particular subjects, disciplines, and even the guilds themselves. If nothing else, this contextualising of academic practice makes the question of academic freedom a very complicated one. Although it might be argued to be at the heart of what enables an academic to pursue knowledge (see Chapters 5 and 7), the duty one has to disseminate the results of those pursuits both to students within their employing institution, and within a prescribed framework of research excellence, may mean that notions of freedom and responsibility are one minute just two sides of one academic coin, but the next minute the means by which academic freedom is hopelessly compromised by incursive forms of accountability.

Academics and managers might also be considered to have a duty to each other. Rowland speaks of enquiry as representing the tension between contestation and compliance, and the need to remind managers of academic values rather than just reminding academics of their management responsibilities (Rowland 2006). Again, this needs a healthy balance, and a partnership approach, reminding us that managers and academics are both professional *colleagues*. And in this context, applying the word 'managerialist' to academic practice may just be a signal to both parties that something is wrong and in need of rebalancing: 'Educational management based on educational values is not managerialist' (Birnbaum 2001: 126), that is, it does not pretend that all decisions are simply technical ones. Birnbaum also reminds us at the same time that: 'Higher education does not need more good management techniques; it needs more good managers' (Birnbaum 2001: 239).

Some lessons may be very simple, such as recognising the need for individuals to *assimilate* change, and providing the space required for reflection, conversation, and interrogation of deeply held values (Kezar 2014), and a reminder that good ideas can still be badly managed and therefore fail to take hold (Fullan 2008). But we also need to recognise that those who have the strongest views about what a university is for – often those most involved in the 'production of knowledge' process – are much less likely to adopt a new and contagious idea; that contagion tends most to affect people without a place in that core process (Birnbaum 2001). Managing academics can also easily undermine their very professionalism, and, perhaps even worse, produce forms of 'contrived collegiality' (Hargreaves 1994) with an emphasis on team work, but only as the means for managers to have their decisions *appear* to have been the result of consultation.

Finally, and as Birnbaum consistently reminds us, universities are unlike most private companies in many ways, including the fact that, for many academics: 'production in higher education … is not the transformation of resources into tangible products; rather it is the transformation of resources into desired intangible qualities of human beings' (Bowen 1977, quoted in Birnbaum 2001: 228). And as the old cliché goes, when you only measure the easily measurable, you may well miss what is of true value. It is further complicated by the fact that universities are broad churches with contested notions of what they are for (see Chapter 6), in which case university leaders and managers might find their jobs a lot easier if only we could all 'come to some agreement on which way to aim the pointy end' (Seymour 1995, quoted in Birnbaum 2001: 99).

Opinion Piece, Debate, Dear Lecturer, and Fellowship Application extracts

In the following opinion piece, Bruce Macfarlane asks whether we need to radically reconsider the notion of academic allegiance. And in the debate, two of my senior colleagues, Chris Stevens and Ralph Norman, consider the question of whether academics should primarily see themselves as working *at* or *for* their employing universities. To finish, Kate Riseley, a recent graduate from Canterbury Christ Church University, reflects on the chapter overall. This is followed by three extracts from successful HEA fellowship applicants who discuss some of the aspects of academic practice which feature in this chapter.

Opinion: On academic identity

Bifurcation and ventriloquism in a performative age

Bruce Macfarlane

Primarily, my allegiance is to strive to tell the truth, without fear or favour. To me, and others (e.g. Watson 2007), this is what makes academic identity really special. Without this collective commitment to protect and promote academic freedom, we are little more than paid employees. I believe that this duty cuts across teaching and research functions which are too often bifurcated in models of academic life.

Most conceptions of academic identity also tend to exclude the service or academic citizenship role of the academic (Kennedy 1997; Macfarlane 2007). In reality, academics spend far more of their time doing things which are not directly related to either teaching or research. They spend time out of class giving feedback to a student, attend department meetings, review papers for journals, serve the community (such as being a school governor), or mentor a new colleague during a coffee break. This is the day-to-day stuff of academic life. It's not that glamorous but nonetheless essential to both the health of academe and wider society. This is service or academic citizenship as I prefer to call it (Macfarlane 2007). It is not just 'administration' or 'management'.

Sadly, service functions are increasingly marginalised by a performative culture obsessed by superficial measures of teaching and research quality – student evaluation scores, research grant income, citations, and so on. We should not forget that the things that are not audited, notably service activities, are often much more important than the ones which are. This performative culture also leads to a kind of ventriloquism: saying one thing but believing in another. We have all learnt to do this by espousing commitment to the language of performativity according to the audience or context (e.g. 'its important to evidence our key performance indicators') while quietly thinking the opposite (e.g. 'this is nonsense'). However, it is also rapidly corrupting academic life.

I can give an example of ventriloquism from my own practice. I was until recently an Associate Dean for Learning and Teaching and a professor of higher education at a research-intensive university. I took a new assistant professor (or junior lecturer) for a cup of coffee with my departmental mentor 'hat' on. Yes, it's the service role again! During our conversation, my new colleague asked me how they might balance teaching and research within their workload. My response was that far from balancing it, they should try to *imbalance* these roles as much as possible. My advice was:

> Teach as little as you can and build up your research profile. In terms of teaching, try to get as many doctoral students as you can. The workload formula is heavily stacked in favour of supervision. Otherwise, design your own specialisms and electives which suit your interests and expertise best. But, most importantly, get research grants and publish papers in ISI journals. This is what really counts if you want a successful academic career. Being able to teach is treated as a benchmark activity. It's not career-shaping like research.

For this conversation, as I told my colleague at the time, I was wearing my mentor's 'hat' and not that of the Associate Dean for Learning and Teaching – a clear example of ventriloquism!

In advising my new colleague I also knew that they were ambitious to develop a successful career as an international research academic rather than spend their life within a single institution. In understanding academic work and careers, I believe that there is an important distinction which operates here between 'locals' and 'cosmopolitans', originally made by the American sociologist Robert Merton in relation to organisational life (Merton 1947). 'Locals' are loyal to the organisation, knowledgeable about how it works, mainly relate to internal colleagues but have a limited skill set. Cosmopolitans, by contrast, have a wider set of professional skills but are less loyal and their identity is externally rather than internally focused.

This distinction illuminates the division between teaching-focused and organisationally loyal 'local academics', and research-oriented, mobile and more outwardly connected 'cosmopolitan academics', whose first point of commitment is their discipline rather than the institution they work in. This means that the university's particular mission is of less relevance to the cosmopolitan academic. In the academic labour market, what counts is your research profile. Other things, especially teaching experience, tend to be of secondary importance. On the other hand, someone who is content to stay in a single institution for their whole career may be able to forge a successful path by being a local, especially if it has policies that genuinely value good teaching rather than simply paying lip service to this commitment. Management roles also provide a route for academics as locals to thrive.

But what are we to make of those attempts to raise the profile of teaching and learning in higher education? The Dearing Report resulted in the widespread development of teaching programmes for new lecturers in UK universities and other initiatives linked to promoting 'teaching excellence'. Boyer's model has spawned the scholarship of teaching and learning (SOTL) movement which advocates more reward and recognition for those committed to pedagogic investigation and critical reflection on practice.

However, while the aims of the Dearing Report and the SOTL movement were well intentioned, I believe that their effects have been largely negative, even to the point of being counter-productive. This is because staking out teaching excellence and SOTL as rallying points only plays into the hands of those in powerful positions who define elite territory in academic life. This has led, for example, to 'pedagogic research' being cordoned off from 'subject research', lowering its status in the process. Institutional and national 'teaching excellence' schemes have been perceived as largely tokenistic and have had the effect of entrenching the divide between 'research' and 'teaching'. Meanwhile international survey data indicates that since the early 1990s, academics have less interest in teaching while an increasing proportion see research as their main focus (Locke 2008).

Where does this all leave us? Yes, there are now lots of ways in which modern academics are being 'called to account'. But academic identity has always been based on something more personally meaningful than fulfilling performative measures. At heart, this is about a generosity of time and spirit toward students rather than the pursuit of self-interest. While the lopsided nature of modern reward systems has begun to dangerously erode such commitments, they still remain the bedrock of the academic profession and need to be constantly reaffirmed if they are not to fall victim to the audit culture.

Debate: On academic allegiance

The importance of working for a university

Chris Stevens

It has become a cliché that, when academics are asked what they do for a living, they answer that they work *at* a university, not *for* a university. It has long been a fact of professional life that professions have dual responsibility both to their employer and to their profession, whether it be law, medicine or architecture. Academics, too, have a duty to the profession that underpins their academic area. It might, however, be suggested that academics see themselves, not as semi-autonomous professionals, but as independent scholars, whose venue of work is as irrelevant to their occupational status, as were the colonnades to the Lyceum of Athens, where Aristotle wended his peripatetic way. In this view, academics are given what amounts to a stipend by the state. It just happens to be remitted via a university, which extracts the task of teaching as a quid pro quo.

This caricature does not do academics justice. For every academic who takes the cynical view of students, there are very, very many more whose academic *raison d'être* is the creation of the best possible student experience. Working closely with academic colleagues and recognising that the university, at which they work, plays a fundamental role in providing resources, is essential to this. There is, nevertheless, more to the caricature than is comfortable. Academics do not, it might be suggested, feel at ease with the activities of the Higher Education Academy and institutional-based CPD, seeing themselves as academic subject specialists, rather than as practitioners of pedagogy. They expect to have their research ambitions supported, even if this means diluting teaching resources. They feel uncomfortable with peer observation, and a notion of learning goals. Some feel strongly that the whole idea of embedding employability skills in academic study is an assault on the liberal purpose of education. Indeed, the notion that the state, as the funder of higher education, can require universities and academics to meet social goals is often an anathema. We are still stuck in the Oxbridge model of independent intellectuals, delivering pure knowledge to those whose job aspirations come primarily from their social location rather than their higher education.

This model of universities, which was fully in place by the time that the Universities of Durham and London appeared in the early nineteenth century, has been remarkably resilient. The 'new universities', established in the large cities and towns in the late nineteenth century to support the industrial skills base of Victorian Britain, have since become 'old universities', indistinguishable in their academic ambitions from Oxford and Cambridge. The 'new universities' established in the 1960s, often predicated on different academic strategies, have joined them. Even the former polytechnics, which spent the first quarter century of their existence as vocational bodies under local authority control, now have more in common with the traditional model than their former selves. The abolition of the binary divide in 1992 privileged the three-year degree, in which skills and vocational development are squeezed into traditional academic structures. The development of foundation degrees after 2001 was intended to up-skill and re-skill the workforce. In reality, these too have been absorbed into the traditional system, extending, rather than revolutionising, vocational opportunities. Higher education is intrinsically linked to the English obsession with its own class structure. If nineteenth-century Oxford and Cambridge functioned as the intellectual finishing school of the gentry and high professions, the academic degree is still seen by many as the entry gate to the English middle classes. The academic that works *at* rather than *for* a university is perhaps still consciously or subconsciously the guardian of that entry gate.

Discussions about the role of the university often lead to the statement that it is the purpose of the university to produce and to share knowledge for knowledge sake. This, however, is to reify universities, suggesting that they have a preordained purpose, when, in reality, universities are social constructs, which need constantly to negotiate their goals with the society of which they are part. Nor should we, perhaps, speak of the role of universities, as if they were singular, with one definition. The university or universities sector might reasonably be seen as containing a number of different types of university, with different goals and different functions. What happened when the binary divide was abolished in 1992, and, at first, polytechnics, and, then, most institutions of higher education were given a university title, is itself contestable. On the one hand, it might be seen as an admission that a vast diversity of higher education institutions could rightly be called universities, whatever their mission. On the other hand, it has been taken to suggest that all institutions of higher education should demonstrate the 'protected characteristics', both real and imagined, of pre-1992 universities, rather than to populate the sector with different models of higher education. This latter view, which is probably the one that dominates, has led to debates as to what areas of study 'belong' in universities, whether some institutions fully deserve the title of university, and, consequently, whether there needs to be stronger regulation, and, if so, whether it should apply to the whole sector, and in doing so, could potentially damage world class institutions.

Underpinning such arguments are debates around university governance. Prior to 1992, university governance was based on trust, while the polytechnics were subject to the regulation of the Council for National Academic Awards, Her Majesty's Inspectors of Education and the Local Authority. The latter model went with the binary divide. Since 1992, UK governments have avoided regulation, but abandoned trust; while in 2010, the Coalition Government flirted with, but did not adopt, marketisation as a means of regulating higher education. The result, it might be suggested, has pleased no one, perhaps, least of all, those who pride themselves in working *at* rather than *for* universities.

Please note that this is a polemical piece, written for the purpose of argument, and represents neither the views of the author, nor of the university, for which and at which he works.

Debate: On academic allegiance

The importance of working at a university

Ralph Norman

Of course we work *in* higher education institutions, but do we work *for* them? What is the end goal of our activity: what are we aiming for?

It was once possible to answer such questions, as John Henry Newman did, with the argument that knowledge was its own end (Newman [1852] 1996). A decade or so later, Walter Pater made a somewhat analogous argument for poetry, encapsulated in the phrase, 'Art for art's sake'. Newman and Pater both justified what they did in non-utilitarian terms. This is no longer realistic. The idea that academic research is done for its own sake makes little sense in the socio-political environment known as the knowledge economy. Knowledge is now an economic good, used within the new socio-economic order. Knowledge is now an outcome, quantified and measured by managers, an objective by which performance is subjected to audit and measurement. According to the dogmas of managerialism, anyone working in this system who attempts to serve the interests of their discipline is now 'a problem'. They are described as 'just polishing stones or collecting footnotes', since they fail to relate their work 'to the needs of the whole' (Drucker 1989: 120). Management systems discourage any academic work which is done for its own sake, for in the knowledge economy, academic activity is directed towards the objectives of the strategic plan of the higher education institution.

Britain is now less a free market economy than a corporate market economy, run to serve the interests of corporate institutions. Warnings of the dangers of the presence of the business agenda in education have long been understood. The turn of the millennium saw a flurry of books on the corporate takeover of the planet. In *The Silent Takeover*, Noreena Hertz described how global corporations had become more powerful than national democracies and economies (Hertz 2001). She revealed ways in which 'internationalisation' actually represented an attempt to trump the demands of democratic politics. In *Captive State*, George Monbiot described the corporate takeover of the UK, and dedicated a chapter to the impact this had on universities. Monbiot argued that 'academic freedom' had been 'compromised by … funding arrangements' (2000: 284). In *No Logo*, Naomi Klein examined the situation in the USA, and warned of the 'branding of learning' in universities. She identified academic preoccupations with identity politics and postmodernism as a correlative of the corporate takeover of universities (Klein 2001). On the one hand, the 'politics of personal representation' had been 'co-opted by branding'. On the other, the 'postmodernist realization that truth itself is a construct … made it intellectually untenable for many academics to even participate in a political argument that would have "privileged" any one model of learning (public) over another (corporate)' (Klein 2001: 104–5). This was a good old Marxian criticism of identity politics and postmodernism, the sort of argument familiar from Terry Eagleton. Post-structuralism has its own economic ground in consumer capitalism: Foucault, Derrida and Lyotard had much to say about the collapse of meta-narratives, yet economics remained as the last grand narrative in their work, the secret servant of the corporations (Eagleton 1996; see also Mansfield 2003: 129–46).

People no longer blink at the use of the phrase 'knowledge economy'. Such language is derived from the teaching of the management guru, Peter Drucker. In 1969, he began to preach that, 'What matters is that knowledge has become the central "factor of production" in an advanced, developed economy' (Drucker 1969: 248). Drucker asserted: 'Education fuels the economy' (Drucker 1990: 236). He redefined knowledge to suit the needs of the managerial ideology.

Academia defines knowledge as what gets printed. But surely this is not knowledge, it is raw data. Knowledge is information that changes something or somebody – either by becoming grounds for action, or by making an individual (or an institution) capable of different or more effective action.

(Drucker 1990: 242)

The demands placed on academics for 'knowledge exchange' and 'research impact' are a direct result of Drucker's dogma. So, too, 'achievable, measurable learning outcomes' represent the application of Drucker's 'management by objectives' to the student experience. Druckerism affects just about everything the contemporary academic does. The unquestioning assumption of Druckerism by universities is astonishing. I suppose that universities have become a mechanism for the normalisation of managerialism in the minds of students and staff alike – a kind of surreptitious programming or indoctrination, through which, whatever the subject studied, the individual imbibes the basic *expectation* of being managed by objectives so that they can serve the corporations.

As the knowledge economy demands that academic work changes things, has 'impact', it is crucial that knowledge is transmitted – rather like an economic good – from one pair of hands to another. Information technology and learning technology are vital to this process of transmission (indeed, Drucker had much to say about the 'new learning technology') (Drucker 1990: 240f). But this same transmission also dissolves the boundaries of disciplines. In *The Age of Discontinuity*, Drucker expressed this view with a swipe at Newman:

> [There] is a symptom of the shift in the meaning of knowledge from an end in itself [Newman] to a resource, that is, a means to some result. What used to be knowledge is becoming information. What used to be technology is becoming knowledge. Knowledge as the central energy of a modern society exists altogether in application and when it is put to work. Work, however, cannot be defined in terms of disciplines. End results are interdisciplinary.

(Drucker 1969: 238)

Druckerism thus erodes disciplinarity. You may think of yourself as, for example, a creative film maker or playwright, but your managers will be measuring your performance with reference to your ability to move outside the sphere of your discipline. There can no longer be art for art's sake.

Should we put up with this? Can one attempt an *ethical* critique of the system? Drucker made some very questionable remarks on the subject of business ethics and prostitution. In 1994, he declared: 'Such things as the employment of call girls to entertain customers are not matters of ethics but matters of aesthetics' (Drucker [1974] 2011: 295). Is the world according to Peter Drucker the kind of place we want to live?

Critique was once 'a struggle against the absolute state' (Newman [1852] 1996: 76–91). Perhaps, then, *critical* academic work could now become an argument against the absolutism of managerialism, a struggle against working for the institution, and a recovery of art for art's sake.

Dear Lecturer

Be true to yourself

Kate Riseley

It seems to me that there is little difference between staff and students when it comes to mixed allegiances. It's just that the student list might look a little different:

1   Primarily my allegiance is to my subject.
2   Primarily my allegiance is to my proposed employment.
3   Primarily my allegiance is to my family's expectations.
4   Primarily my allegiance is to securing funding.
5   Primarily my allegiance is to attainment.

The key thing I learnt during my academic journey (which began with an access course and culminated by graduating with a degree in English Literature in June 2014) was the opportunity it provided me to demonstrate true allegiance to myself. Of course, by being at university, issues of employability, future funding and attainment were naturally being addressed. But, because I wouldn't get this chance again, every hour had to count; I simply could not get to the end and regret any decisions.

I took a module which examined both art and literature. I chose it for pure enjoyment, I knew nothing about art and thought it would be a nice alternative to words for a while. The first assignment brief suggested that it did not have to follow the normal guidelines. There was an approximate word count and grading criteria but how it was presented was up to me. Students were encouraged to maybe produce some artwork or include images within their essay, they could look at art, literature or both. Most students went into melt down, 'But how many words should I write?', 'If I put in an image will I be marked down?', 'Will I lose marks if I just write an essay?', 'If I don't get a first, I don't get the Master's bursary.'

I wrote my essay comparing Picasso's 'The Old Guitarist' and Wallace Stevens's poem 'The Man with the Blue Guitar' in traditional format. But then I printed it on blue fading sugar paper, just because I could, because it reflected the weight of the painting and poem in a way that shiny white copier paper couldn't. I did not care what mark the assignment gave me, I had thoroughly enjoyed its creation and my engagement with the module. That assignment also happened to return me my highest mark that term.

Primarily my allegiance is to myself and I urge academics to do the same. It's a risk, but one worth taking, because as the momentum of individuals becoming their true selves gathers, institutions will naturally and organically find their identity, and that identity will be real and authentic; whether it be primarily as a research institution or a teaching one, or one which comfortably embraces both.

Extracts from successful HEA fellowship applications

Mr Pink (SFHEA)

As an External Examiner, international co-ordinator and key member of staff with our faculty, my leadership roles have given me valuable insight into a wide range of L&T methodology. This has led me to continuously develop my areas of activity, core knowledge and professional values and bring valuable knowledge to my own courses. Our Faculty (Faculty of Art, Design and Architecture) relies on bringing in a large number of HPL staff alongside those on small fractions. This enables our courses to bring in a vital mix of preeminent practitioners to teach who are cognizant of up-to-date practice and developments within the creative industries. However, this can also result in having colleagues who are less knowledgeable about best pedagogic practice. Therefore, I have taken the mentoring of these staff seriously. I have initiated a thorough induction process that methodically goes through L&T and feedback essentials in a clear and succinct manner [K2, K3]. I have succeeded in creating systems both paper-based (thorough guidance notes in user-friendly terminology and diagrams of our systems) and one-to-one mentoring schemes [A2]. I believe that this thorough guidance has lent a significant contribution to our exemplary NSS scores [A3]. New and junior members of the team, teaching at any level, are personally and fastidiously guided through systems that can, at first, seem extremely complex or daunting [K3]. Under my management and coordination, these supervision processes have been rolled out to other members of staff throughout the faculty and have also been disseminated at university conferences and lectures at home and overseas [V4].

Ms White (PFHEA)

I consider leadership as something to be explored as a social process; as such, it is *how* I work with others to make sense of initiatives or issues that leads to action and, ultimately, success. This is not because my role does not allow for direct influence: it is more a result of appreciating the contributions of others, which can help to refocus a discussion and add alternative perspectives. For me, therefore, the most effective style of leadership is when it includes using my ability to work with others in a facilitative capacity. For this type of leadership to succeed, I need to encourage ownership of the problems or issues by those with whom I am working (Gastil 1997). If these become a responsibility of all those with a stake in the situation, with opportunities for them to share and participate, there is a higher likelihood that they will 'buy in' to the solution as they have been able to participate and add their insights. In turn, thinking through an issue and appropriate responses gives an incentive to act and to see an action through to its conclusion.

If a university is to be a true learning community, then opportunities to engage in reflection have to be available to all. These opportunities enrich the working environment tremendously and have a knock-on effect for the institution as a whole.

As Jarvis suggests: 'Reflective practice is more than thoughtful practice. It is that form of practice which seeks to problematise many situations of professional performance so that they can become potential learning situations and so that the practitioners can continue to learn, grow and develop in and through practice' (Jarvis 1992: 180).

Dr Blue (PFHEA)

As part of the management team within a matrix structure, I have to ensure that I influence and implement through engagement and rational argument rather than positional power. To this end, I immediately began a series of monthly 'Learning, Teaching & Assessment' (LTA) workshops for the faculty. I also brought in an external speaker from the QAA to the faculty annual LTA conference, to give the event a higher profile. I work on the basis of evidence-based and relevant information to persuade staff of the need for change (for example, including links to research). This is to ensure that staff understand the evidence and rationale behind change, feel they are being treated as academics, and minimize the perception that senior staff are remote from such research, they are then more likely to engage, increasing the chance of enhancing student learning (e.g. Bryman 2007).

4

The nature of academic space
Mike Neary and Helen Beetham

Why do we keep spending money on learning centres; why not just buy some more books for the library?

I'm not sure there's any point to seminars and workshops; students don't come prepared, so why not just lecture at them?

I'm not knocking VLEs but they only seem to work when they look and feel like Facebook, so what's the point?

This chapter focuses on inhabiting learning spaces. The first half, written by Mike Neary, focuses on physical spaces, and their potential to be experienced in liberating ways. The second half, written by Helen Beetham, focuses on virtual spaces, and particularly what it takes to create successful hybrid spaces – between the physical and the virtual.

Inhabiting learning spaces[1]

Mike Neary

Introduction

Over the last two decades, many universities have invested in eye-catching architecture aimed at attracting investors and business, as a way of transforming their institutions into marketing-driven 'brands'. In the process students now became 'customers', and providing a positive satisfying customer experience is a paramount preoccupation for university managers and a key instruction for architectural briefs (Glancey 2010).

In this chapter I want to challenge this phenomenon by looking at some university architecture designs based on very different ideals for higher education: not the 'business ontology' (Fisher 2009) of university managers, but alternative, more utopian ideals; and, in this way, to provide inspiration and motivation for current and future designs for teaching and learning spaces in higher education. Of particular interest is the relationship between material spaces and technology which, in the most extraordinary cases, have sought to meld not just the real with the virtual, but the physical, the emotional and the intellectual, to create dynamic patterns of student mobility, generating a more intimate relationship with our pedagogic environment, and which can counter the alienating effects of any consumerist-style models of building design.

I am basing my more utopian university of the future on ready-made visions and already-built university buildings, focusing, first, on campus universities in the 1960s, as well as designs for futuristic universities that were never built in the same period. I will supplement this with research I did at the University of Lincoln into academic involvement with the design of learning spaces, 2008–2010, as well as an account of a teaching space, The Reinvention Classroom, that I developed with colleagues and students at the University of Warwick in 2006. This discussion will then enable me to present six principles for the design of teaching and learning spaces.

But, first, I want to begin in another space, the John Henry Brookes Building, a new addition to Oxford Brookes University estate, opened in 2014, as an exemplar of contemporary university design.

The John Henry Brookes Building, Oxford Brookes University, Oxford

The John Henry Brookes Building stands in the centre of the Gipsy Hill Campus at the Oxford Brookes University. John Henry Brookes (1891–1975), after whom the building and the University are named, was a key figure in the development of higher and further education in Oxford. He was a compassionate and effective leader, as well as a talented artist and silversmith and a committed teacher of art (Addison 1979). Along with these abilities, Brookes was a conscientious objector, refusing to fight in World War I. Interestingly, the founding Director of Oxford Polytechnic, as Oxford Brookes was formerly known, Brian Lloyd (1920–2010), had also been a conscientious objector in World War II. The principled position taken by these two men demonstrates a profound anti-war sensibility by inspirational figures associated with this institution.

The building, constructed in the style of Hi-Tech Modernism, presents itself as 'a gateway' to the University. In its citation for selection as a candidate for the Stirling Prize, the University describes the building, somewhat blandly, as 'designed to meet the University's vision for a holistic approach to enhancing the student experience. Oxford Brookes' campus redevelopment provides an adaptable and flexible environment for a dynamic range of teaching and learning spaces' https://www.brookes.ac.uk/about-brookes/news/john-henry-brookes-building-judged-to-be-one-of-top-15-new-buildings-in-the-country/ (accessed 17 July 2014).

Despite its award-winning credentials, not all architectural critics are convinced, describing the façade as 'there's something of the glossy business/technology park about it', so that it resembles more of an 'office block' than a university. The effect is 'shiny and just a bit sterile at first glance' (Pearman 2014). Although once inside the building the same critic gushes with praise, describing the inside as 'remarkable', the social spaces a 'teeming mosh pit of what's called the Forum'. The Atrium has 'interesting things ramming into it from all sides' (Pearman 2014), including a lecture theatre 'hanging in the space', a walkway that works like 'a supercharged minstrel's gallery' and a physically accessible 'library without walls'. Interestingly, the teaching rooms, situated away from the central area, are described as 'more conventional'. But overall, this is an 'intelligent building' and more than an icon (Pearman 2014).

While the student experience is presented as being one of the main rationales for the building, students were not involved in the design:

> Certainly we had interaction with end users who were part of the Steering Group who were part of the process of understanding how the building was going to be made to work. I think, in truth, in terms of interaction with students, it has been fairly limited ... the reasons for that probably are the scale and programme of projects like this don't necessarily fit in with programmes in term of education programmes ... at times ... there could have been more of it [interaction], I suspect, in terms of that process, but in terms of end-users, there was good interaction with the client end side of things.
>
> (Richard Jobson, architect for the building. http://www.brookes.ac.uk/
> space-to-think/campuses/headington-campus/john-henry-brookes-
> building/build-talk-videos/build-talk-1/, accessed 26 December 2014)

Despite its claims, there is nothing exceptional about the John Henry Moore Building; it is an example of what Hatherley might describe as a pseudo-modernist building:

> That is, the Modernism of the icon, of the city academies [though he could just as well have said universities] where each fundamentally alike yet bespoke design embodying a vacuous aspirationalism [evident in its own Stirling statement]; a Modernism without the politics, without the utopianism, or without any conception of the polis; a Modernism that conceals rather than reveals its functions; Modernism as a shell.
>
> (Hatherley 2011: xxiv)

Also, in the words or another architectural critic, who in a further politicisation of Hi-Tech architecture describes this kind of building as an 'anaesthetized formal language ... a perfect complement to the hollowed out shell of social democracy' (Murphy 2012: 92).

In spite of the vacuousness of its self-description, these are not vacuous spaces, but have their origins in Fordist factories designed and built in the USA in the early part of the twentieth century: huge sheds 'more glass that structure ... vast impersonality ... the last word in architectural rationalism' (Wilkinson 2014: 207). It was in these massive structures where the new mass production automated labour processes were invented, based on the principles of clockwork scientific management and the logic of time and motion: the space-time of capitalist production (Wilkinson 2014). There is no pleasure in these factories, only an orgy of sado-masochism, where people might be made to love their pain through the injection of wages and consumerist fantasies (Wilkinson 2014). The industrial aesthetic that frames these structures was very influential for European Modernist architects, futuring buildings to cast a new process of production out of 'the white heat of technology' (Wilkinson 2014: 219). But, as we now know, this vision of the future was to appear always tantalisingly out of reach.

This short account of the emergence of a new university building could probably apply to many other similar buildings all around the UK. It speaks to a surface-like seduction, which underneath quickly reveals a more alienating core, particularly as a space for more intimate and democratic forms of pedagogy. So how might we do things differently, as designs for teaching and learning spaces, in a way that attempts to fully engage the challenges of the future? In what follows, I want to explore some buildings that self-consciously have attempted to create a futuristic university.

Activity 4.1

- In what ways have you been actively involved in extending teaching and learning space beyond timetabled classroom space?
- In what ways have you been involved in any campus design decisions and new builds and/or sought to ensure that students and academics are actively involved in any campus estates decisions?

University of the Streets (East London, 1962)

The 'University of the Streets', or the Fun Palace, as it was officially known, was to provide higher education as a form of play and entertainment for the local population of East London. The idea was developed in the early 1960s by Joan Littlewood (1914–2002), actor and communist activist, who combined her interest in education with avant-garde theatre based on the principles and practices of Bertolt Brecht and Russian Constructivism (Mathews 2005 and 2007); and Cedric Price (1934–2003), an anti-establishment architect and committed left-wing socialist (Mathews 2007: 15) with 'a rational, collaborative approach to design' (Mathews 2007: 21). The Fun Palace was not a building in any conventional sense, but a scaffolded-construction made up of prefabricated temporary structures, manipulated by a number of tower cranes: more like a shipyard than a building, within which indeterminacy was *the* design principle, with an instruction from Price that the building should not stand for more than ten years (Mathews 2007).

The design was based on thinking derived from the social sciences, in particular, Game Theory and Cybernetics, in a way that allowed for variation and real structural change. The structure was to respond to the recorded activity of its users, which would be converted into malleable data and algorithms to further develop the space, built initially as a series of zones: for research, film-making and scientific experimentation. The Fun Factory was to be an exemplar of anti-form and anti-function, where the structure found a way of articulating a vision of its users through a type of 'anticipatory design' (Mathews 2007: 41), or 'calculated uncertainty' (Mathews 2007: 41), that took into account cultural and social issues as well as aesthetics. The building was to be literally and figuratively alive (Colombino 2012).

This was not really a building at all, but a sort of 'interactive machine, a virtual architecture merging art and technology' (Mathews 2007: 13). The main issue for Price and Littlewood was not the aesthetics of the structure, but how to create a framework or armature on which a model for the improvement of the social world could be built, and in which 'an extraordinary interactive and cybernetic model of architecture would be arrayed' (Mathews 2005: 90).

This development of the building was preoccupied with the issue of work, and more particularly, the future of work in a society in which it was anticipated that work would be increasingly automated and workless. Work was the central issue for Littlewood and Price, i.e. the design for their futuristic universities was based on a vision of non-alienated human activity (Mathews 2005). The Fun Factory was designed in a way that would reclaim subjectivity through increased leisure.

The Fun Palace was never built, though a scaled-down version did appear as the *Interchange Project* in 1976 in North London. This structure was based on a steel frame that could be manipulated through the arrangement of ready made plug-in Porta-kabins, containers and other industrial artefacts, all imbued with 'the sense of potential for expansion and contraction' (Murphy 2012: 98). The structure was used for community activities and education until it was demolished in 2003 on Price's insistence (http://www.audacity.org/SM-26-11-07-02.htm).

Thinkbelt (The Potteries, 1965)

During the same period, the mid-1960s, Price worked on another building project based on a vision for the future of higher education. Left to himself, this solution was altogether more instrumental, though it had at its core ideas to reconsider the nature of work in the context of higher education. His plan was to create an environment that regenerated UK industry and technology to support the new 'white heat of technology' revolution (Hardingham and Rattenbury 2007). Thinkbelt, as the project was known, was not a university but 'a plan for advanced educational industry' (Hardingham and Rattenbury 2007: 13), against the notion of campus-style universities, of which the nearby Keele University was a prime example. Price considered Keele too detached from the local population and with almost no contact with local industry. Thinkbelt was meant to convert a post-industrial wasteland in the Potteries region into an education-technology park, in which not only would strong connections be made between industry and learning, but higher education would become its own industry. All of this would revitalise existing industries, e.g. ceramics, acting as a catalyst for further improvement in the local socio-economic environment and encourage enterprise so that, over time, all of the Potteries would be revolutionised.

This was a large site, more than one hundred square miles, across North Staffordshire, with space for 20,000 students. The site would be designed around the concept that 'cities can be made by learning' (*Architectural Design* 1966: 484, in Hardingham and Rattenbury 2007: 37), including housing and amenities that could be used by the local population, with space for up to 40,000 residents. The accommodation would be based on modular prefabricated housing of different types: *crate* – pressed steel containers in a 13-storey concrete frame; *sprawl* – timber-framed units built on a tray-like structure; *capsule* – fibreglass living spaces in a steel frame built primarily for single occupation, and *battery* – living units in a sealed environment with their own services enabling progressive expansion (Hardingham and Rattenbury 2007: 46).

Roughly triangular in shape, each vertex of the Thinkbelt site would contain a Transfer Area, promoting rapid mobility, with accommodation for staff and students as well as laboratories and workshops. These transportation links could be used by Faculties as sites of mobile learning, in train carriages and specially situated rail sidings as well as buses. The teaching accommodation would include self-teaching carrels, areas for fold-out decking and inflatable units for up to 30 students. Thinkbelt was to be built around a highly developed transport and electronic communications network, connected to national and international transportation links, including air travel, with the intention of creating a 'literate, skilled and highly mobile society' (Hardingham and Rattenbury 2007: 18). Anticipating Wikipedia and the Web, the pedagogy and teaching styles of this new institution would encourage students to make use of electronic communication equipment so as to create connected sites in an 'information store, which lets student develop their own patterns of study' (Hardingham and Rattenbury 2007: 18).

At the heart of the Thinkbelt design lay a reconceptualisation of time and the future of work. Students would be paid a salary, 'If people are doing a job society wants them to do, they must be paid for it' (Price, in *Architectural Design* 1966: 484, in Hardingham and Rattenbury 2007: 37). Professors at Thinkbelt would work part-time in industry and spend the rest of their working time at the Thinkbelt; but for Price, time was not just to be redistributed, rather it was to be distorted: Thinkbelt was designed to 'distort time … to devise not a new aesthetic, but to give an aesthetic quality to the ideas of indeterminacy' (Hardingham and Rattenbury 2007: 99); and through the extension of education time, what Price referred to as 'lifelong learning' before the term was commonly used: 'This is what education should do … to distort time in order to allow you more control and to bring benefit to yourself and by extension other people' (Hardingham and Rattenbury 2007: 99).

Taking these two university designs together, the Fun Palace and Thinkbelt, the key design principle was 'total invention and imagination' (Hardingham and Rattenbury 2007: 85), with designs that show 'absolutely no compromise' so as to 'create conditions hitherto thought impossible' as part of 'a continuous manifesto for education' (Hardingham and Rattenbury 2007: 11). Price's work consciously confronts university buildings designed in the way of Fordist factories and assembly line production, 'challenging the hegemony of this idea, with all its pseudo-functionalist and deterministic baggage' (Hardingham and Rattenbury 2007: 71), producing 'a very serious critique of what was becoming an imprisoned way of thinking about university building' (Hardingham and Rattenbury 2007: 71), as a sort of lightness made real by the removal of architecture (Hardingham and Rattenbury 2007: 107).

The campus university

There are other visionary architectural buildings on which we can draw inspiration, built as part of the expansion of higher education in the UK and around the world in the 1960s, characterised by their campus-style construction and location. The building of university campus(es) formed part of a 'utopianist mood' (Muthesius 2000: 1), or, at the very least, a commitment to 'social architecture' (Muthesius 2000: 282) that managed to convey both an idealistic and practical frame of mind (Muthesius 2000: 290), in what amounted to a form of 'New University Modernism' (Muthesius 2000: 2). What distinguishes these buildings in the UK is that they were:

> Not animated only by concerns for cost and utility … but also by less quantifiable considerations: beauty, visual drama and, above all, ideas of higher education, old and new … [as] art and machine … aimed to embody utopian principles and to facilitate their realization … to provide a place that gave memorable expression to a philosophy. If the talk was of revolution, of a bright start, tradition and memory continued to maintain a central presence.
>
> (Ossa-Richardson 2014: 131)

To focus on one campus: the University of York set out to be different. At York, there was much thought put into providing a collegiate system so that staff and students were in close proximity across different subject areas and disciplines, including the Arts and Science:

> The intention was to replace the anonymity of the mass lecture, the isolation of over-specialisation and the tyranny of end of course examinations with tutorials, multidisciplinary connections and novel, multiforms of continual assessment. At the heart would be colleges, places not just of learning and teaching but of residence and living … the core faith in college and community.
>
> (Smith and James 2008: 40)

The colleges would be made up of men and women, with public spaces for students, academics, porters and cleaners to 'stop and talk, eat and drink, or walk on' (Muthesius 2000: 135). The intention was to maintain connections with teaching, student life and residential living so that students 'spend much of their time in their own or another college' (Muthesius 2000: 134). The plan was to create a sense of community, applicable 'to life in a modern democracy', sharing an 'intellectual and emotional experience' (Muthesius 2000: 136–7). Andrew Derbyshire, the architect of the York campus, admitted to 'a socialism as incarnated in his buildings' (Ossa-Richardson 2014: 146). This was not simply utopian but a pragmatic way of achieving social economic and cultural regeneration (Muthesius 2000).

At York, the colleges were to be built in close proximity with connecting paths to stimulate interaction and effect encounters between staff and students from the Science and Arts buildings (Ossa-Richardson 2014: 136). The lake was crossed by 'delicate bridges' (Ossa-Richardson 2014: 148), settled within the campus so the buildings became part of the natural beauty of the landscape. Built away from the city, the campus provided a secluded space for private contemplation, more like a monastery with cloisters. There was a strong sense that buildings should encapsulate the nature of higher education even 'if the meaning was not articulated beyond philosophical abstractions as something between the emotional and the rational' (Ossa-Richardson 2014: 141) while at the same time infused with a new brutalism that was both futuristic and technological.

All of this was striving for an 'aesthetic language' for university architecture (Ossa-Richardson 2014: 142). Most notably as something that is characterised by a sense of 'incompleteness' (Ossa-Richardson 2014: 143), and of being open-ended, making a link between the design principles of Derbyshire, Price and Littlewood. All of this was reflected in the ease in which it is possible to get lost on campus, of creating a sense of never having arrived, encouraging 'mystery and disorientation' (Ossa-Richardson 2014: 152), i.e. a space for private and shared discovery, the opportunity to cultivate self-hood, so that one has to find oneself in the complex labyrinth (Ossa-Richardson 2014: 152).

Faced with the idealistic principles on which the design of York campus was based, the contemporary concept of 'student experience' becomes a much reduced way of thinking about what these architects and administrators had in mind when they were designing this university of the future. Now the issue is not so much about Utopia, but rather how to create an 'image' to enhance league table rankings (Muthesius 2000).

Learning Landscapes in Higher Education (Lincoln, 2010)

These visionary campus designs were mainly at the level of master planning and had less to say about how their visionary pedagogies for teaching and learning spaces might be manifest as part of the architectural design. Learning Landscapes in Higher Education, a research project carried out in the UK between 2008 and 2010, made a link between 'the idea of the university' and the precise character of learning and teaching spaces. It made the connection by encouraging a critical academic sensibility to inform classroom design, and how this could be expressed at the level of the campus: not only through the usual measures of *efficiency* and *effectiveness*, but, more demonstrably and architecturally, through the way in which the idea of the university is *expressed* (Neary et al. 2010).

The methodology for Learning Landscapes was enriched by grounding the empirical research in radical sociology and critical pedagogy, worked up as design principles and framed by a historically materialist and Marxist theory of the production of capitalist space (Lefebvre 1991). For Lefebvre, space is the outcome of the productive principle out of which societies are derived. In capitalist society, space is capitalised, by which he means space is given over to the logic of class struggle, imposed by the rationality of capitalist work – abstract labour: as factories measured in time and other clockwork forms of institutional life (Fordism), like prisons and schools and housework (Dalla Costa and James 1975). Lefebvre was interested in the way the rationality of factory time is resisted as counter-spaces, evident in the way capitalist space is colonised as public space, including, and in particular, the life of the street.

This Marxist interpretation of space was given a further radical twist in the Learning Landscapes Report (Neary et al. 2010), by an insistence that classroom design be imbued with the concept of gender. An example of gendered design was taken from the work of Virginia Woolf who, after having been excluded from a library at an Oxford College, argued that women should have a 'Room of One's Own' (Woolf 2008), and be supported financially so that they might write and study. She pursues this theme of design principles for university architecture in 'Three Guineas' (Woolf 2008) where she argues that higher education should be free from the principles of competition, acquisition and militarism that currently dominate research and teaching. In a speech to raise money for a new women's college, she anticipates the impermanence principle established by Price and Littlewood:

> Before you begin to rebuild your college, what is the aim of education, what kind of society, what kind of human being it should it seek to produce … the old education of the old college breeds neither a particular respect for liberty nor a particular hatred of war – it is clear that you must rebuild your college differently. It is young and poor; let it therefore take advantages of those qualities and be founded on poverty and youth. Obviously then it must be an experimental college. Let it be built on lines of its own. It must be built not of carved stone and stained glass, but some cheap, easily combustible material, which does not hoard dust and perpetuate traditions. Do not have chapels. Do not have museums and libraries with chained books and first editions under glass cages. Let the pictures and the books be new and always changing. Let it be decorated afresh by each generation, by their own hands. Cheaply.
>
> (Woolf 2008: 198–9)

As well as an appeal to gendered sensibilities, the Learning Landscapes Report (Neary et al. 2010), insisted that classroom design should reflect the design principle of anti-discrimination; taking its cue from bell hooks who, writing as a black feminist educationalist and activist, argues against all forms of educational discrimination; and how this must be negated by turning the classroom into a paradise:

> The academy is not a paradise. But learning is a place where paradise can be created. The classroom with all its limitations remains a location of possibility. In that field of possibility we have the opportunity to labor for freedom, to demand of ourselves and our comrades an openness of mind and heart that allows us to face reality even as we collectively imagine ways to move beyond boundaries, to transgress. This is education as the practice of freedom.
>
> (hooks 1994: 207)

Neary and Saunders (2011) further developed the theme of academic engagement in the design and development of teaching and learning spaces by arguing that classroom design could be informed by promoting a collective critical reflexivity among academics about the meaning and purpose of higher education: 'the idea of the university', and how this could be represented in architectural design of the pedagogical environment. This collective critical reflexivity should be informed by the academic literature so that universities might come to know their own institutional story and create their own radical history of the university, including its engagements with student protests and occupations (Neary 2012; Neary and Amsler 2012); and to use this as the basis on which they might confront the undermining logics of 'academic capitalism' (Slaughter and Rhoades 1994) and the pedagogy of debt (Williams 2006). They argued that academic input can be given greater academic credibility by making use of approaches to space and spatiality from across a range of academic disciplines, including Geography and Physics, as might be expected; but, also, and often with spectacular unexpected results, from less obvious disciplines, for example, English

Literature, following the example of Virginia Woolf, incorporating these poetic problematics into actual classroom design.

But what might all of this look like. Can we provide a concrete example?

Reinvention Classroom (University of Warwick, 2006)

The Reinvention Centre was a collaborative project between the University of Warwick and the University of Oxford Brookes from 2005–2010. Central to the project was the promotion of research activities for students as the organising principle of the undergraduate curriculum, and, in this way, for undergraduate students to become part of the academic project of universities. A key issue for the project was the design of teaching spaces to facilitate this radical proposal.

The Reinvention Classroom at the University of Warwick incorporates the principles and practices of radical sociology, critical pedagogy and Marxist theories of space, infusing the political aesthetics of fine art into classroom design. The space is an experiment as well as a work of art (Lambert 2011: 31, 42). The aim of the classroom was to create a space that would encourage collaboration between teachers and students for the production of knowledge and meaning. The room was designed by academics and students working with architects and Estates professionals and university administrators; it was opened in September 2006 (Lambert 2011: 35).

The Reinvention Classroom is situated in a remote site at the northern outer limits of the Warwick campus, housed in a detached building, co-habiting with a café and shop. It is rectangular in shape, 120 square metres of light and colour, stripped of all decoration – bare white walls with a blue floor covered in rubber stretched like a skin-membrane across the entire surface, primary coloured cube-shaped seats, round yellow oversized bean bags and long monochrome grey and black plastic benches. There are no tables and chairs. The space is lit by uplighters in the floor, halogen strips of electric light from the ceiling and sunlight streaming on sunny days through windows in the slanted roof. Polluted air from the nearby arterial road circulates through 'windcatcher' ventilators warmed by an under-floor heating system. The acoustics are sound-around. Along the wall at intervals are dance rails, melding the energy of the room with performance theatre and the critical sensibility of the fine arts.

The main artistic influences for the space are Purism and Neoplasticism: utopian art movements that emerged in the 1920s as a protest against the chaotic carnage of World War I. Purism, or Cubism without the decoration, is noted for its 'geometric forms and large areas of colour' as well as its 'cool and detached paint surfaces' and careful composite chromatic order. The space contains an exemplar of Purist design, Le Corbusier's chaise longue (1928) otherwise described as 'a relaxing machine' (Neary and Thody 2009). Neoplasticism is an extreme form of Purism, stripped bare to the barest elements of design with no recognisable figurative content. The artistic sensibility is reinforced by Liam Gillick's, 'Double Back Platform' (2001), fixed high up on one of the walls, made of plexi-glass and aluminium, 'the materials of McDonald's signs, and display cases in Prada, of aeroplanes and bullet-proof screens in banks, of really sexy nightclub floors and riot shields' (quoted in Neary and Thody 2009: 38). Not the kind of material or objects found in standard university classrooms.

Technology is ubiquitous. With no fixed projector or televisual screens there are no dominating lines of sight. The pure white walls act as a surface for images thrown from a mobile projector that can be rolled around the space. This lack of dominating focal point reflects the Cubist anti-perspectival sensibility (Berger [1965] 1998), with no pre-allocated point at which a teacher might stand to give a lecture: there is no Power-Point in the space, no space for teacher to dominate; each space needs to be negotiated and claimed (Rose 1993). All of this consolidating the utopian tendency of the room in which the space and, therefore, the future are something to be made and constructed: there is no ready-made. There is no fear of the future in this space: no 'future proofing' (Miller 2001). The future emerges out of the real world in which the present is grounded by the significance given to the floor which acts as a reality check for the whole room. The floor provides a sense of gravitas and gravity for the entire space. The floor is a surface for working on as well as walking on. The heated rubber provides an all-round feeling of warmth and comfort: as a site for social interaction, reminding us of the significance of the floor as a social space for other cultures, giving the room a racial and ethnic intelligence.

The space is not designed for any specific subject, all can be taught here to some extent. The room is uncomfortable and uncompromising. 'The Learning Mould is Smashed' (*The Independent*, January 2011), perhaps.

Parked outside the classroom is the Reinvention Bus, a jumbo transit van with spaces for 18 passengers, and disabled access. The bus is not just for driving students to Oxford Brookes and back, but to set up mobile teaching spaces on the M40. Although these mobile spaces were never established, without knowing about Price's ideas, the Reinvention Centre was reinventing Thinkbelt's commitment to mobile learning.

> **Activity 4.2**
>
> - In what ways have you been involved in working with students to negotiate teaching and learning spaces in order to help enhance learning?
> - In what ways have you been involved in any campus initiatives aimed at creating flexible and open-ended social and learning spaces for staff and students?

Six principles

Based on all the above, I suggest six principles to consider when creating university teaching and learning spaces of the future:

1 *Ground* – the space needs to be grounded theoretically in its own version of historical materialism; and, practically, to provide the room for social transformation or utopia, even. The floor should be fascinating, a surface for working on as well as walking on. Giving gravity and gravitas. While, at the same time, facilitate a lightness of being by the removal of anything that looks too much like architecture.

2 *Dynamic* – the space should promote movement and mobility, demonstrating learning and teaching is more than a mental activity, but requires physicality and

bodily functions – inter, intra and extra-mural, or Dance Dance Revolution. The spaces between classes can be transformed into learning events, as corridors, transporters, e.g. lifts and other vehicles, all in an environment that promotes walking as a philosophy and the root of *pedagogy*.

3 *Power* – the space should be democratic, with all arrangements to be negotiated and agreed. There is no locus of power or PowerPoint in the room, no space for teacher or student, and with all of the spaces designed for cooperation and collaboration. There should be Fun House mirrors on the walls to promote distortions of space and time and with that future possibilities.

4 *Open* – the space should be indeterminate and open-ended, as if it has yet to be complete. Sexy. Stretched like a membrane right up to its edges, except there are no edges, only the smooth curves of complexity. This is what we strive for: to be fully rounded. Sometimes we want it so bad it hurts, like an uncomfortable principle which should be reflected in the furniture.

5 *Play* – all work in the spaces should be kept to a minimum and only ever when it enriches life and pleasure. The space should contain the most labour-saving devices and work should be apportioned according to ability. An important part of play is learning to carry out activities that will enhance the life of the group using the space and our own lives as a sort of role-play area.

6 *Anti war* – the space should scream anti-war, recognising that violence can be 'divine' (Benjamin 1921) justified not as an absolute ethic, but as a sign of the injustice of the world, depending on each circumstance that cannot be pre-judged: as an excess of love, or 'Educative Power' (Benjamin 1921). The concept of educative power should be scrawled on the wall, as graffiti: *Learn, Learn, Learn – Teach, Teach, Teach* (after Žižek 2009).

Dear Lecturer

On inhabiting learning space

Sam Louis

Though there are some lecturers who can make a lecture interesting and interactive, many struggle and this just leads to everyone disengaging. With smartphones, laptops, netbooks and tablets, you guys are fighting a losing battle with what's left of our attention spans. If you are just going to stand at the front of a lecture theatre and read slides, cancel the lecture, put a recording online and use the time to increase the number of seminars.

With the re-cap service (whereby lectures are recorded, along with the projected presentation, and made available online), it is almost possible to completely do away with physically attending university at all, something that almost everyone I know has experimented with to some extent or another. But the end goal of technological advance is not to replace us (humans).

> Blogs and forums and VLEs can provide a great deal of support to a student's educational experience, but they cannot replace the value of being in a physical learning environment, face-to-face not only with a teacher, but also with other students. Without this multi-dimensional interaction, the chances of developing the later stages of Baxter Magolda's (1992) 'Ways of Knowing' are drastically reduced, because students are isolated in their learning. Technology should never replace interaction.

Inhabiting digital space

Helen Beetham

Introduction

There are two stories told about digital space. In one, it is continuous or contiguous with the space our bodies inhabit: a next-door room, or in the room with us, easily entered through the graphical interfaces that we have come to experience as windows. In the other, it is a radically alternative space where we can become someone other than ourselves, even realise new possibilities for human interaction. In education, the two stories are often told at the same time. So MOOCs (Massive Open Online Courses) are both spaces of a radically different educational experience – egalitarian, content-free, almost infinitely malleable to personal need – and shop windows for the traditional courses that participants can sign up to on the way out. Virtual worlds offer safe places to play, free from the real-world constraints of risk and resource, and where the trappings of embodied identity can in some ways be suspended, yet 'effective' only when their proximity to embodied life allows the lessons learned online to be transferred.

In this second part of the chapter, I explore the relationship between the physical and virtual landscapes of higher education. I ask how learning happens (differently) in virtual spaces, how they might be transformative, and what it means to be a teacher – and a learner – in institutions that increasingly have a foot in both worlds.

Academic space as hybrid space

Academic campuses are among the most virtualised places on the planet. Student status is largely achieved through access to and identity within institutional systems: registration, the library system and online subscriptions via Athens, the virtual learning environment (VLE), assessment and anti-plagiarism software and learner records. Increasingly universities are tracking learner behaviours in their online systems and using that data for rational planning, in some cases to offer learners personalised services and in others to subject students to surveillance in order to identify those 'at risk'. While students have always been subjected to various kinds of monitoring and control in the spaces of the university – not least in order to assess and accord them the grades which make sense of the whole experience – the capacity for surveillance is enhanced by the move towards a virtual campus.

Beyond its own systems, the university is a site of promiscuous access to digital networks and services which are used to perform academic work. This is regardless of whether specific services are commercially outsourced. Reliability and robustness of broadband are a ubiquitous issue of student concern: both students and staff now expect to have their personal media, social networks, information and collaborative opportunities at their fingertips. For a physical space of learning to exclude the virtual, digital devices would have to be banned (e.g. on hygiene grounds in a laboratory setting) or switched off (e.g. at the local request of a tutor) or inoperable (e.g. in a fieldwork setting out of broadband range). Otherwise the assumption is not only that learning in real spaces is penetrated with information and conversations from elsewhere, but that records of real learning events can be captured and removed to virtual space. So simultaneously with the virtualisation of institutional systems, the institutional space is becoming more porous to alternative networks and through them alternative ways of learning and contesting narratives (e.g. students 'testing' their lectures against an online textbook or Wikipedia).

So much is true of many institutions. In academic institutions specifically, digital technology is also reconfiguring core functions, purposes and values. Knowledge practice – how we come to know (individually and collectively), how we value what is known, even what it means to know (as core cognitive functions such as memory are shared with virtual agents and networks) – all these are changed profoundly. In every subject area, digital tools are shaping new methods and practices, while digital contexts are generating new theories and new forms of intellectual and creative expression. Virtual space has become a key forum for sharing academic ideas and for enacting academic identities.

And universities themselves supply most of the new technologies that afford these developments. Hall and Stahl (2012: 196) consider 'four emergent technologies [that] enable cognitive labourers to transcend physical barriers through virtual reality, and to consume their educational life-world in new ways'. The transformative technologies are of the moment and will change over time: what matters is the finding that all of the candidate technologies, and their capacity to transform education, have been 'catalysed by research inside the University' (Hall and Stahl 2012: 196). The same is true of Facebook and Twitter, the networked computer and the internet itself. So it should be no surprise that universities are leading the way in the development of hybrid spaces where real and virtual worlds intersect.

Activity 4.3

- How would you articulate the rationale behind any blended or hybrid approaches you have developed on a course/programme you teach or support learning on?
- How have you sought to enhance any wider technology-enhanced learning strategies which operate in your school/faculty, or institution, or beyond?

Meaning

Something that is obviously transacted between virtual and 'real' space is meaning. We encounter the virtual with the intention of making it meaningful, and we bring to it our identities as meaning-making subjects. Like other media – stories, paintings – virtual environments invite us to project ourselves in, to experience what we find as a context for action. It is this meaning-making stance that allows us to experience digital content as new ideas and creative forms; that allows us to experience the flow of data in time as events, cultural exchanges, identity work. Trainee pilots and fire fighters make this investment in the simulations they use for learning, otherwise we would be much less safe when we stepped onto a plane or found ourselves caught up in an emergency. Students make a similar investment when they encounter digital material that is relevant to their learning needs, or when they take part in online discussions and create digital materials for comment by others. We are used to making meaning through media, and virtual media are no different in kind.

Our stance towards virtual objects then is a generic stance towards human media, and an aspect of our complexly mediated social life. But we enter virtual space in *particularly* mediated ways. What we experience as an environment for action with tools for our use is in fact a series of data transactions: it is the interface that renders the data human-readable and humanly engaging, and the interface is designed by some people for use by others. Bayne (2008), in her visual analysis of virtual learning environments, argues that far from being neutral structures for content delivery, graphical interfaces serve to construct a particular pedagogic and organisational space. She asks:

> If the spatial organisation and visuality of the screen both represent and create a value system and an ontology, what social and pedagogical practices does the VLE interface reflect, inform and inscribe? What meanings does it produce? What version of pedagogy does it 'make visible', and what alternatives does it blind us to?
>
> (Bayne 2008: 397)

The same analysis of the power of designers over users and the same questions about how design makes some meanings/uses available over others can also be applied to the physical spaces of the institution, as Mike Neary has done in the first part of this chapter. We experience designed real-world environments as ready for occupation and use, when in fact they are carefully aligned with some uses and relationships and not with others. The lecture theatre is a case in point. In both kinds of space, the ideal user experiences her actions as natural and intentional rather than as systemically constrained ('lecture' or 'listen', 'post' or 'read'). In both cases, it is possible to make those preordained behaviours and meanings more visible and even to act against them. But in the real world we do at least have ongoing identity and capacity to act without the mediation of interfaces. By contrast with our experiences in the natural (non-designed) world, we can consciously bring to awareness the ways that designed environments and tools work on us. Virtual design provides none of these resources. Its processes become more invisible as they become more advanced, with transparency, nativity (e.g. through the use of gesture) and frictionless adoption of the explicit goals.

Neil Selwyn (2013) argues that technology is most invisible to the people who have the least resources to resist it and the greatest reason to distrust it. He cites Matthewman (2011): 'Ubiquity creates invisibility. McLuhan famously compared us to fish that fail to see our water. Under such circumstances, as Heidegger said, we are only likely to notice our technologies when they stop working as anticipated' (cited in Selwyn

2013: 3). One of our responsibilities as educators, then, must be to notice and make noticeable to others the ways in which meaning is constructed online, in virtual spaces and in the new digital media, and the ways in which digital tools work on us as well as the ways in which we can use them to fulfil our intentions in the world.

Relevant HEA project

Gordon, N. (2014) Flexible pedagogies: technology enhanced learning. Available at: https://www.heacademy.ac.uk/sites/default/files/resources/TEL_report_0.pdf

---

Feeling

In a recent keynote (Beetham 2014) I suggested that we should explore our feelings about living and working in virtual spaces. Acknowledging our vulnerability, boredom, isolation, frustration and compulsion – as well as our curiosity, excitement and professional interest – is important to our occupational health as well as our capacity to support students and colleagues. Like the meanings we make there, the feelings we have in and about digital environments are continuous with our embodied emotional life, but they have new qualities and resonances. In my keynote I cited interviews with students that suggest the virtual world presents particular emotional challenges. Many, for example, feel they need to disconnect from the distractions of social media to focus on academic work. Others are worried that the digital footprint they have already laid down, perhaps without realising it, may affect their reputation into the future, or they have had negative experiences online which make it difficult for them to participate freely. Virtual space leaves many learners feeling exposed. It blurs the boundaries between public and private, work and play, the classroom and the outside world. Although it can be rewarding for learners to participate in open communities of practice, or to produce digital artefacts for public access, or to contribute to online research – and all of these are sound strategies for helping them to thrive in the virtual world – it can also be very challenging to rehearse a tentative and emerging identity in a public setting.

Students may be wise to feel exposed in virtual spaces – even those under the aegis of the academic community. Recent research from the Pew Research Center (2014) shows that 4 in 10 online participants have suffered harassment,18 per cent have suffered serious harassment or abuse, and women are over-represented in both groups. Feelings of hatred and rage, lust and self-aggrandisement are expressed more openly online, and while the mediating interface seems to offer a licence to those forms of expression, it does not remove the negative feelings that arise in response. And women (online subjects identified as female) are particularly likely to be the targets. Participating online feels different if you are a woman. Particularly in academic spaces, it feels different if you are not English-speaking, not from the Global North, not from an elite educational culture or institution, not physically able, not digitally able, not a 'proper' (traditional) student or tenured academic.

As embodied subjects, we weave a continuous narrative about our experiences online and offline, and about the person we are when we act in those different spaces. How we deal with the affective fall-out of our virtual lives is important for how we cope as educators and is also something we can bring to the awareness of our students, ideally helping them to develop a wider repertoire of responses. We should celebrate the freedoms we experience online but not be afraid to speak out when we find digital spaces being colonised by values that are antithetical to educational (and human) development. As Bonnie Stewart has argued (Stewart 2014), we need to take care of each other in virtual spaces, recognising that they create new vulnerabilities as well as new life chances.

Bodies

The body and its physical location would seem definitively excluded from virtual space. This is, after all, the meaning of the real/virtual distinction. Bainbridge (2014) has recently argued that the separation of learning from the embodied self and from the physical (especially natural) world leaves learners without the 'holding' relationships that they need to experience genuinely transformational learning. Echoing my concerns in the previous chapter about feelings of isolation and compulsivity, he concludes that 'the reliance of humans on technology in learning environments can be considered a fetish' (Bainbridge 2014: 9). Undoubtedly the human body suffers when we live too much of our lives online – obesity, repetitive strain, sleep disorders and varieties of anxiety have been laid at its door.

But life online is hardly devoid of bodies, and not just pornographic bodies (the prevalence of porn is another important reason for dealing with issues of safety, vulnerability and ethical behaviour when inviting students to work in virtual spaces). Followers of the quantified life continually record their bodily functions and share the data with online groups, services and other virtual agents. While we are not yet mapping our students' biological data, we do encourage them to capture evidence of their learning activities. In doing so, they are not only building up a virtual profile of their embodied learning, but contributing to the enrichment of the physical environment with virtual traces: images uploaded to Google maps, video learning logs (vlogs) and data captured from fieldwork would be examples of this. GPS applications – widely used in the teaching of subjects allied to Geography – redefine our relationship with the physical world, making every location simultaneously a real place and a node in a global network of information (see e.g. Taylor and Dunne 2011). Virtual patients for the teaching of medicine and healthcare have been important drivers of technical development in learning technology. Virtual bodies at a lower level of visceral realism exist in a vast array of simulations, designed to support learning in the professions and social sciences. Inscribed into multiple virtual systems, learners have multiple online personae but very few that they do not mark with their bodily identity, whether that is through use of an avatar, a cartoon, the photo of a loved pet, or a recent selfie.

Of course, virtual space does allow for expression of identity in ways not marked by bodily difference – by gender, race, physical (dis)ability or appearance – and this can be used to serve an inclusivity agenda (Forman et al. 2011). The argument is a complex one. The issues that make it difficult for some people to identify as transgender, or disabled, or physically scarred might not be addressed if those markers can be erased, but that erasure also opens up a new space of communication in which entrenched ideas might begin to be challenged. The same is true of intercultural work in online spaces (Panichi et al. 2010). Some people find it easier to participate in learning spaces when their bodily identity is obscured, to add to the many people with physical impairments and other difficulties of physical access (remoteness, poverty, daytime commitments) who can only participate in educational opportunity through virtual means.

Finally, virtual space is brought into being through real-world labour and the consumption of real-world resources. Human bodies deliver our search results, whether they are mining rare earth elements, assembling iPads, or keeping Google's data centres supplied with power. Intersections of the material and the virtual world take many forms, and will be seen differently through the lenses of different disciplines. They are often a productive site of exploration for students who, like Heidegger's fish, can no longer see the virtual water they are swimming in except through the lens of a principled and deliberate critique.

Activity 4.4

- In what ways have you actively sought to incorporate the use of virtual space to provide for a more inclusive and/or engaged learning environment?
- Have you been involved in developing any strategies or policies aimed at guarding/guiding students when occupying virtual space?

Money

At this point I think it is worth taking a detour around the question of why virtual spaces are becoming such a significant aspect of the student learning experience. In the FE sector, a recent report commissioned by the Coalition Government recommends that courses should aim for a 50 per cent online component by 2017/18 (FELTAG 2013). While HE institutions are unlikely to recognise such an edict, there is no doubting the trend towards blended learning in 'traditional' courses, and online-only learning as a significant alternative market. The answer to this question, in obvious and less obvious ways, is money. (It is possible that money, as pure exchange or transaction value, works better in the digital world than the real one: the stateless, lawless, un-backed-by-any-central-bank bitcoin may prove this.)

In the obvious sense, aspects of online provision offer potential savings at a time of huge financial constraint. The savings are minimal if learning is understood as a human relationship, requiring dialogue, mutual understanding, support for personal developmental, collaborative opportunities, and modelling of new practices by more capable others. Then the main resource implications are human ones and can only be met by paying human beings for their time, expertise and attention. There may well be

environmental and cost savings if the offer is enacted virtually, but the really big savings are only made if learners can be convinced to minimise their expectation of human
interaction – especially with teachers – and to maximise their investment in content,
which can now be distributed virtually at very little cost.

Less obviously, students are online because money is online. They have been sold the
idea that higher education is a ticket to higher pay, and the higher paid jobs in our society
are predominantly virtual. (They may be 'virtual' in the sense of transitory and insecure,
but in this case I use 'virtual' to indicate the space in which the work takes place.) Our
current economic relations has been described as a mode of 'cognitive capitalism' under
which growth and profit depend on advances in our use of information and data, rather
than on trade and conquest or advances in production technologies, as under earlier
phases of capitalism (e.g. Fuchs 2011). This gives higher education a particular relationship with the digital, expressed by government as the need to supply 'skills' to the global
knowledge economy (BIS 2009). A study experience that neglected the virtual, then,
would neglect the very spaces in which graduates need to be productive (in their own and
the national interest) – neglect the very foundation and location of valuable work.

Unfortunately for UK graduates, the value of knowledge work in the developed
world is being undermined by advances in the higher education sectors of emerging
economies (Craig and Gunn 2010). As long ago as 2008 a TLRP report concluded that
'once [high value work is standardised], high-skill people in low-cost countries sud-
denly become an attractive option for multinationals … young people now investing
heavily in their education across the developed world may struggle to attain the comfortable jobs and careers to which they aspire' (Brown et al. 2008: 2). Virtual work is
more likely to involve live texting with irate customers from a distributed customer
services centre than managing a digital start-up. 'Skills' in the global knowledge economy cannot be confined to the technical: they must include resilience in the face of a
vast global redistribution of intellectual capital, as well as the capacity to thrive in
situations where the boundaries of work and personal life are blurring, and to undertake a constant project of self-upgrading to keep pace with technological change.

Just as not all virtual work is highly valuable or productive, not all productive
work is virtual. In fact, the continued existence of virtual space depends on material
infrastructure and real-world labour. This too is an issue that can be introduced to the
curriculum, depending on how the digital world intersects with the subject of study.
This is not to deny that most graduate employment demands virtual skills or that much
valuable work is cognitively based, but it does help to situate that work in a material
context of human needs and finite resources.

Utopia

A very different imagined future has also co-opted the virtual as a valuable space. Here
the virtual is figured as a democratic zone of infinite connectivity and interplay, where
inequalities are levelled and differences made less visible, oppressive laws have less
purchase, and oppressive organisations are less able to secure a hold. In some versions
of this utopia, the formal education sector is drastically reduced. Individuals engage in
ad hoc learning and interest groups gather evidence of their capabilities, and (if they
need to) seek confirmation via peer recommendation or open accreditation. Grades and

qualifications give way to rich representations of personal ability, and the institutions which have acted as gateways to high value employment become largely obsolete.

Once again, however, there is strong evidence to believe the opposite. Virtual participation in learning is higher among those who are already highly motivated and have high levels of educational capital. In fact, the more opportunities for real social advancement are available in virtual spaces, the more they are colonised by people who are already privileged (Hargittai 2008, 2010). Digital space is 'a class-structured, segmented, stratified social space' (Fuchs 2011: 346) and digital capital is just another benefit that can be deployed by the privileged to improve their advantages. Releasing open content from the global universities of the North, for example, even when this was done with the most egalitarian of intentions, has had mixed consequences for emerging sectors of higher education elsewhere and has led to concerns about digital colonialism (Amiel 2013). 'Open' learning may not even mean free access, and, where it does, it may not be accompanied by the kind of support that less advantaged learners need. In fact, while virtual space has given access to educational opportunity to many, and this is clearly a good thing, there is far less evidence that it can remedy inequalities of educational *outcome* or address inequities of a more systemic kind.

In the face of virtual alternatives, institutions of higher education have not disappeared. Instead they have diversified their offer to include virtual elements and become (particularly at the bottom of an increasingly stratified system) more reactive to the threat of competition from virtual providers, with the result that the more elite the institution, the more likely it is to sell the face-to-face, co-located campus experience as the gold standard.

As I outlined in the 'Bodies' chapter, utopian thinking also arises from the capacity to erase markers of difference and enter into relationships in 'the absence of contradictions and cross-purposes that haunt offline life' (Bauman 2000, cited in Selwyn 2013: 56). People have astonishing capacity to create new identities, new rules and new kinds of relationship, and there is no doubt that they are using online spaces to do so. Educators can create and contribute to these spaces, for example, by organising inter-cultural online exchanges. But this has to be done with a readiness to challenge preconceptions as well as celebrate differences, and to deal collectively with abuses of/in the virtual medium: trolling and bullying, the viral spread of images of violence and sexualised images, the tendency of self-selecting interest groups to reinforce their own prejudices rather than engaging in a meaningful way with different others.

We can, if we are wise, use to advantage those aspects of the virtual world that accord with our academic values: open exchange, peer review, collegiality and respect. But developments in digital technology are no substitute for political engagement with issues of equality and power, in the belief that entities such as 'the internet' or practices such as 'open sharing' necessarily entail more equal access to learning opportunities or more democratic institutions.

Conclusion

Virtual space is continuous but not identical with real-world space. As educators, we are particularly interested in how meanings, feelings and identities, social actions and economic values are transacted in digital space, and as I have tried to show, these transactions reproduce the inequalities, power dynamics and oppressive institutional practices of real-world space. Some aspects of virtual space disguise these continuities and make it difficult to adopt a critical stance. These include the radical separation of designers from end-users, the fact that actions are narrowly constrained but alternatives are literally unthinkable within the interface, and the 'natural' and 'frictionless' design ideal. All are good reasons why we should foster in our institutions, among our colleagues, and most importantly in our students, a critical approach to digital technologies and their uses. How we approach this will depend on our disciplinary resources, but we should be in no doubt that it will become more difficult for students to do this with their own resources, as they become more naturalised to living in a hybrid world.

Just like real-world spaces, virtual spaces can be co-opted against their original designs, or can be designed differently – collaboratively with students, for example, or in ways that are radically incomplete. And while real-world spaces can only be redesigned after much investment and long processes of consultation, in which radical ideas can easily be lost, virtual spaces are agile and reconfigurable. Personal learning environments, cloud services, community solutions and peer-to-peer networks are already deeply connected into the institutional infrastructure, introducing potential fault-lines and spaces of alternative play. Alongside virtual environments that reproduce an instrumental and managerial idea of the university, we can set alternative virtual spaces such as Coventry's Disruptive Media Lab or the Ragged University project and its various affiliates, online and physically located. Against the virtual pantechnicon we can imagine the hybrid university as a network of loosely affiliated spaces, some allowing for safe exploration and identity work ('walled gardens'), but with doors always opening onto other institutions and cultures, onto different ways of knowing, and onto an open landscape of knowledge in public use.

Opinion Piece, Debate, Dear Lecturer, and Fellowship Application extracts

In the following opinion piece, Wayne Barry reflects on his participation in two differently experienced online distance learning courses. This is followed by a debate on the merits of face-to-face learning compared with online learning, from two sisters who have had very different undergraduate learning experiences. To finish, Sam Louis, a recent graduate from Newcastle University, reflects on the chapter overall. This is followed by three extracts from successful HEA fellowship applicants who discuss some of the aspects of academic practice which feature in this chapter.

Opinion: On distance learning

Confessions of an online distance learning junkie

Wayne Barry

My first foray into the world of distance learning took place, for a brief spell, from 2004 to 2005. I enrolled myself onto a correspondence course on creative writing and had received, in the post, a thick, A4 ringed binder containing reams of papers and documents concerning the 'rules and regs' of the course, the course materials itself and the various assessment briefings. I had six assignments that would be posted to my tutor spreading over nine months. Around four to five weeks upon receipt of my assignment, my tutor would post back her feedback which would always be rich, critically friendly and very lengthy. I greeted my tutor's feedback with a mix of surprise and exhilaration as I had never received, previous or since, feedback with so much depth, coupled with words of supportive encouragement. But, in some ways this was just over-compensating for the severe lack of any kind of tutor communication.

I recognise that I do tend to be a solitary learner with a strong accent towards co-operative, rather than collaborative, learning, which, in part, is attributable to my hearing impairment. But this particular learning experience left me feeling crushingly isolated. Other than the postal communications I had no-one to share and express my ideas, fears, joys and frustrations with. So I would like to take the opportunity to reflect upon two very different online distance learning experiences that were mediated through synchronous and asynchronous technologies. One was formal (the Master's programme) and the other informal (the EDC MOOC). I would like to consider how these two very personal experiences have come to inform my own professional practice as an HE learning technologist.

Experience 1: an MSc in e-Learning

In 2006, I was appointed to the role of university learning technologist and in the following year, I enrolled myself onto the MSc in e-Learning (now rebadged as the MSc in Digital Education: http://online.education.ed.ac.uk/) at the University of Edinburgh. This is a very popular postgraduate course, which I took part-time, that attracts a great deal of national and international interest and is conducted over a distance and delivered totally online, which makes use of a number of virtual public and private spaces, such as the University of Edinburgh's virtual learning environment (VLE), discussion boards, blogs, wikis, instant messaging, immersive virtual worlds and social media. There were around 40 individuals from around the globe in my cohort and they brought with them rich and diverse experiences and biographies. We all shared a common passion for education and that technology was seen as a means to facilitate learning in ways that should motivate and engage students.

Some of my most rewarding and richest learning experiences have happened online through the Master's programme. However, it does raise some very real questions concerning the 'perceived' online presence, or embodiment (Blake 2002), of tutors, the engagement and motivation (extrinsic and intrinsic) of the students inside a space that is virtual, and working with peers who are temporally and culturally divergent. What works incredibly well for mature postgraduate students undertaking an online Master's course, at a distance, on e-Learning may not, necessarily, translate so well for campus-based undergraduates in their late teens who are used to predominately face-to-face interactions. Online learning has had a long track record of student dissatisfaction that has resulted in high student attrition rates. This neatly brings me to the second of my online distance learning experiences.

Experience 2: an e-Learning and Digital Cultures MOOC

In January 2013, I enrolled myself on to the e-Learning and Digital Cultures (EDC) MOOC (Massive Open Online Course: https://www.coursera.org/course/edc) that was being run by the University of Edinburgh using the Coursera platform. A number of the tutors who had taught on the MSc in e-Learning programme taught on this course as well. The course ran for five weeks and consisted of readings and short videos that formed the basis of 'thought experiments'. The students made use of the discussion board tool within Coursera as well as using third-party blogging tools and social media sites like Facebook and Twitter. The number of enrolments peaked to over 42,000 participants, but dropped down to just over 7,000 participants who were still active during the last seven days of the course (Knox 2014).

On this particular course, the tutors wanted an opportunity to research, experiment and participate 'in an emerging pedagogical mode' that was 'significantly under-theorised' where MOOCs were perceived as an 'uncomfortable territory' (Haywood 2012; Knox et al. 2012). One of the pedagogical theories that underpins MOOC technology is *connectivism* (Siemens 2005; Downes, 2005, 2012), which has been described as:

> [a] learning organization whereby there is not a body of knowledge to be transferred from educator to learner and where learning does not take place in a single environment; instead, knowledge is distributed across the Web, and people's engagement with it constitutes learning.
>
> (Kop 2011: 20)

However, the tutors found that 'MOOC pedagogy [was] not embedded in MOOC platforms, but [tended to be] negotiated and emergent' (Bayne and Ross 2014: 8). It soon became apparent within the discussion boards, blogs posts and tweets that a significant number of participants were struggling with a course that appeared to lack structure and 'scaffolding', where the tutors were decentralised, and there was an over-abundance (Weller 2011) of information and content that were leaving participants feeling very lost and overwhelmed. My previous experience on the Master's programme, my role as a learning technologist and being particularly confident with a range of virtual spaces meant that I had developed an acute 'critical filter' that allowed me to navigate and negotiate my way around this over-abundance of content and make strong connections with other participants on the course.

Informing practice

Being a student on these courses enabled me to experience the trials and tribulations that all students undergo when studying on their own, and being wholly dependent on technology working at critical points throughout the duration of the

programme. Students need significant 'hand-holding' and practically 24/7 technical support in courses dependent upon technology. Tutors need to factor in, during the first few weeks at the start of a programme, a level of socialisation and 'low-stakes activities' so that students become familiar with using the technology and are able to start to form a 'community of learners' (Wenger 2000). This was exactly what the tutors on the Master's programme had anticipated and done, loosely basing their approach upon Salmon's (2002) '5 stage model'. When the EDC MOOC was run for a second time, the tutors were at pains to ensure that there was sufficient structure and 'scaffolding' so that the students did not become overwhelmed with the nature of the tasks and activities.

From a tutor's perspective, there needs to be careful consideration and planning of content, activities (individual and group-based) and resources with opportunities to communicate and collaborate with peers and tutors. In addition, these online encounters need to be situated within authentic learning experiences that further develop a student's repertoire that is vital for working and learning in a digital age. These experiences have also strengthened my belief that academic staff should be working, in partnership, with their learning technologist to ensure that such opportunities are realised and problems are avoided.

Debate: Online vs face-to-face learning

My entirely face-to-face learning experience

Anna McCormick

I spent three years as an undergraduate at Cambridge University (2007–2010), studying English Literature. In that time, I spent countless hours in libraries poring over books and critical essays, hours in lecture halls alternating between taking copious amounts of notes and sitting back and absorbing the theatre of it all, hours in small classes with a few other students parsing texts and debating various points of detail and theory, and hours in one-to-one supervisions being challenged on my thinking and essays.

The majority of my learning and teaching was therefore experienced face to face, with a strong emphasis on dialogic teaching and Socratic questioning. Conspicuous by their absence perhaps were online teaching or essays and question sheets that were marked remotely and returned with a score.

Without question, the most challenging, stimulating and valuable elements of my study were found in the small classes and one-to-one supervisions. Cambridge University describes supervisions in this way:

> As well as helping you develop independent learning skills, supervisions enable you to explore course material in much greater depth than lectures allow, to gain

further insights into your subject, to clarify anything you're not clear about, to discuss your own work and ideas, and receive regular feedback.

They were focused on the primary paper each term and were delivered by a teacher who specialised in that area. Specific reading and focus areas were outlined by the supervisor and then frequently evolved over the course of the term to integrate the student's area of interest. In my experience, a question would be set with an accompanying reading list and I would produce an essay for my supervisor. The supervision then would use the essay as a springboard for a broader discussion of the topic, and also of how the thesis was structured and communicated. It allowed for the exploration of arguments and counter-arguments, coaching on essay technique and construction, prompting on wider reading, and often rigorous debate with an expert in a particular field. It is hard to imagine how so broad a spectrum of learning could be combined in any other format.

A crucial fact to highlight is that the impact of the face-to-face teaching was critically dependent on the quality of independent study done prior to the session: the pre-reading, the thought applied to the questions for discussion, the development of a line of enquiry and work done to support it. A tutorial couldn't be effective without the full engagement and preparation of both the teacher and the student – a lesson I rapidly learnt. There is no hiding in a one-to-one or small group environment, and it demands that you take ownership of your own learning and progress. However, it also allows for flexibility in study, whether that is to spend more time on an area that the student doesn't understand, or to create space for them to explore their own areas of interest.

As passionate as I am about the benefits of this mode of teaching, it is not without its complexities. Initially, the emphasis on discussion and questioning can be disorienting and more than a little daunting. Particularly if you are coming directly from school, where learning is highly directed and has clear parameters and marking criteria to structure your idea of what 'good' study is and what it isn't. With dialogic teaching and tutorials, the parameters are often redefined with each new supervisor and topic, which can result in a shifting view of what good looks like, and occasionally conflicting advice.

Linked to this, the tone and experience of small classes or supervisions are almost entirely determined by the teaching style and personality of the tutor and of other members of the class. Due to the emphasis on face-to-face teaching, this will in many cases have a significant impact on the student's learning experience – both for better and worse. Confidence also plays a key role in this learning environment. In order to participate in debate and to get the most from the teaching, you need to have the confidence to ask questions and to share your views and challenge those of others where appropriate. The environment actively encourages, and in fact demands, participation and it is a key way in which your progress and attainment are assessed. Therefore, individual discomfort with it could be stressful or intimidating, and ultimately impact how a student feels they are performing. However, the upside to this is that the environment created ensures that you will develop those skills over the course of your study, resetting your natural inclinations through practice.

Having left university and moved into work, what has come to the fore is this skillset that I developed almost unawares – a confidence in formulating and asking questions, regardless of my existing knowledge of a topic, and the appetite to explore the different facets of a situation. While the knowledge I acquired of Anglo-Saxon literature has not directly impacted my next steps and continued learning, the experience of and comfort with debate, challenge, and being set a broad area of inquiry from which to develop a thesis, definitely has.

Debate: Online vs face-to face learning

My largely online learning experience

Emily McCormick

I enrolled on a degree programme in a research-intensive university in 2012 that has a high level of online learning, both in terms of the content of the curriculum, and also in its delivery. The number of students enrolled on the programme and the nature of the subject matter mean that much of the teaching is delivered either in large lecture theatres or online. With the development of technology and the increasing inclusion of technology in degree programmes, online learning has become much more prevalent and widely accepted. The majority of degree programmes now have a large online presence including, but not limited to, online seminars, webinars, lectures and tests. Much of my experience of learning at university has been in this type of learning environment.

I have found some real advantages in this approach. Online resources can provide some much-needed structure to their independent learning as well as being much more convenient than attendance at large and often impersonal lectures, where it can sometimes be challenging for lecturers to teach one topic to many different people, and ensure that their content caters to, and engages, a large and diverse pool of learning needs and personality styles.

Online study is not limited to fixed schedules, it can be accessed at any time of the day or night and the student has much more control over the pace of their learning. Within a highly competitive and intellectual environment like university, with up to 200 students per lecture, there is often a fear of embarrassment or negative responses to what are viewed as 'interruptions' which may deter many students from asking questions or asking to revisit key points. Online learning may offer more opportunities to explore content and questions while studying independently as you are not required to keep pace with lecturers and other students, and can spend time understanding things which present barriers in getting to grips with certain aspects of a topic. This can be especially valuable for students who struggle with concentration, dyslexia or any other learning difficulty which may make it more difficult to keep up as slides can be revisited and audio or visual content can be replayed.

Progressing from the heavily supervised learning of school or college, university learning is supposed to be largely independent with lectures forming the skeleton of a student's wider learning. The internet is a great source of information with which to bolster lecture content, as exploring a topic on the internet can provide some thought-provoking alternatives. Though lecturers' teaching styles vary greatly, some still teach their opinion on a topic as gospel, rather than as simply one view of the content. Online learning may help a student to discover and explore many different viewpoints and theories, rather than just learning one specific perspective and being required to reiterate someone else's subjective opinion, which in turn can provide a better understanding of, and outlook on, a topic.

However, for some, the convenience of online learning can prove detrimental as with it can come the assumption that it is easier than traditional learning, when in reality it often takes much more self-discipline, motivation and better time management. The 'mandatory' nature of some lectures can provide some students with a much-needed push to remain engaged with their course materials, rather than putting it off or just giving up.

It is not only mandatory lectures that help to keep a student engaged, but also lecturers. Lecturers are selected to teach courses because of their extensive knowledge of and valuable insight into a certain topic or subject matter, for this reason alone, interaction with lecturers is extremely valuable in order to gain and develop a deeper understanding. I have often found that the passion of a lecturer who truly loves their subject can be infectious, providing a type of motivation that simply cannot be replicated 'screen-to-screen'. In a similar way, class discussions provide a very unique opportunity to learn in that they are organic and provide a fascinating insight into a topic by exploring many viewpoints and concepts that might otherwise never have been considered. The variety and diversity of students' backgrounds, cultures and opinions can prove an engaging and valuable resource.

Despite online learning sometimes being viewed as more convenient, face-to-face learning is often the most effective way of teaching one 'piece' of content to a large group of people, especially when it is particularly difficult or a key concept that needs to be understood as the springboard to move to a deeper understanding of or engagement with a topic. The potential for miscommunication or misunderstandings in general is much more prevalent online as many of the complexities of teaching are whittled down to simple written communication, or there can be so much information available that it is easy to feel overwhelmed and without direction, unless the learning activities are clearly thought through, carefully structured, and have specific aims.

Another challenge that I've found with online learning environments is that there can be limited opportunity for feedback, and for asking questions and discussion, especially when something has been particularly interesting, it can feel like a much more one-way relationship with information.

One of the aspects that is endangered if there is too much emphasis on online or self-directed learning is effective team building – one of the points of university is to prepare students for careers in their relevant field, in many cases this is not just the ability to absorb information but also to interact with other colleagues, work as a team, communicate effectively with others, disseminate your ideas in a way that influences or engages others, or lead a group. All of these skills must be learned, or at least developed, along with your subject knowledge base, within the context of your degree. If the balance between online/self-directed and face-to-face learning is not managed, these are the skills that can be at risk, as the university experience can provide invaluable opportunities and experiences to learn with and from others.

Dear Lecturer

Inhabiting and owning learning spaces

Sam Louis

Newcastle University is a continuous coagulation of architecture through the ages. As with many universities, the buildings range across period and style, from pre-1900 red brick grandeur to the ultramodern, dripping with shiny glass and vibrant colours. And while I loved the large, rolling desks in our library's noisy, flexible work-space, and the primary coloured furniture in the group work computer clusters, sometimes nothing made me sit down, shut up and work like vaulted ceilings, wood panelling and the hushed silence of the bookshelves.

Planning educational space to evolve with each generation is fantastic, but it should not be to the detriment of an academic tradition. To walk into a university and know that generations before you have sat here and learnt and worked, has an inspi-rational effect on people, and motivates you to learn, in much the same way as a new, vibrant, unrestrictive room can motivate you to stretch boundaries and create something of your own. The two must work in harmony and there should be access to both in the university of the future.

Likewise, the way in which a space is used changes as people interpret it differ-ently. I can't speak for how much student involvement there is at Newcastle in plan-ning new builds, but there is certainly a culture of student feedback on how they want to use the space there already is. During my three years, I saw the library become 24-hour use (as student sleeping patterns began to dictate usage times), and pop-up library space appeared around the campus to accommodate busy exam periods. Rooms in the student union could be hired out and put to whatever use was necessary, one minute hosting Socie-Tea tea parties and the next coming alive with the Circus Club.

A large part of student ownership and integration actually comes not from pro-viding dynamic, open, anti-war, play spaces (as Mike Neary suggests) but simply by being open to changing the uses of whatever you already have to accommodate student desire. I've done creative group work in dusty wooden-benched lecture theatres, with teams stretched across four rows, and had fascinating, teacher-centric lectures while sitting on bean bags and footstools. Space can be interpreted in whatever way you want, and it is the attitude and approach of the teacher that free or constrict, not the age or intention of the physical space.

The power of the brand and market investment in the university may long hold sway over architectural decisions, but the way in which you choose to inhabit and engage with the space can change in an instant.

Extracts from successful HEA fellowship applications

Mr Blonde (AFHEA)

For some academic staff, the virtual learning environment (VLE) presents a transitional stage of their teaching practice; for others, it can be quite transformational. The support, advice and guidance that I offer can be at a personal; programme; departmental; faculty and sometime institutional level [K1, K2, K4, K5, V3, V4]. Some of this support and guidance can be technical (i.e. how to insert a Turnitin assignment item into the VLE); pedagogical (i.e. how tutors support their students to make sense of the originality reports that are generated by Turnitin and how this relates to appropriate academic writing and understanding the issues around plagiarism); and strategic policy (i.e. advising the institution on best practices and procedures based upon current evidence-informed approaches and that of the wider higher education sector) [K1, K2, K4, K5, K6, V2, V3, V4].

Mr Blonde (AFHEA)

I have been supporting and guiding academic staff to avoid experiencing 'troublesome space' by working with them to think about, plan and develop learning activities that make best use of the physical spaces, mobile technologies and learning resources that are currently available (see Fisher, 2009) within the university's new learning and resources building [K1, K2, K3, K4, K5, V1, V2, V3]. Through this process they can begin to create dynamic and dialogic spaces that have the potential to support and sustain a scholarship of teaching and learning culture for them and their students (see Jenkins and Healey, 2005) [K2, K3, K5, K6, V1, V2, V3, V4]. The work and research that I have done in the new building and around learning spaces generally has informed my Master's dissertation [K1, K2, K3, K4, V3, V4]. Some of the findings taken from that have been used to develop support and guidance that has taken on many forms: one-to-one discussions, small group coaching and developing a practitioner's handbook and a leaflet of hints and tips on making successful use of learning spaces [K1, K2, K4, V1, V2, V3, V4]. Ultimately, I would like to see learning space design being offered as part of the University's PG Cert (HE) programme [K1, K2, K5, K6, V1, V2].

Dr Blue (PFHEA)

I have always avoided championing technology-enhanced learning for the sake of it, emphasising that technology should only be used with purpose and a clear understanding of the benefits (and weaknesses) of the tools – the focus should be on offering flexibility of 'place, pace & mode' (see Gordon 2014). When discussing TEL with staff and at an institutional level, I have emphasised the importance of purposive design of TEL and particularly with blended learning, ensuring clear planning which is then effectively communicated to students ensuring they understand their learning journey (e.g. Garrison and Vaughan 2008). These are the points I emphasise at university level in committees and in discussions, to ensure that this understanding is disseminated as widely as possible and I strongly believe this emphasis is influencing our approach across the institution.

Note

1 'Inhabiting learning spaces' first appeared in the paper, 'Making it with the university of the future: pleasure and pedagogy in higher and higher education', first presented at Trinity Laban Conservatoire of Music and Dance, as part of the Teaching and Learning Research Seminar Series, 19 November 2014.

5

The nature of academic knowledge

John Lea

You should see some of the stuff that's being taught at my place now; I mean, it's not proper knowledge, it's just political correctness gone mad!

I took this job to teach and research my subject, not to make people good citizens. I wouldn't say I was a good citizen, so what kind of role model could I be anyway?

It's all very well helping students to get jobs, but that's for the careers people, isn't it?

Introduction

What is the nature of higher education knowledge? In posing the question so starkly, it challenges us to consider not only whether there is something that underpins all the knowledge found in every course, department and discipline, but also whether, and in what ways, this knowledge differs from other types of knowledge. Another way of looking at this is to ask whether you think you could draw a line for your discipline (or subject area) between what counts and what does not when it comes to knowledge. You might approach this chapter as a challenge to see how clear that line remains as you read on.

In a classroom context, one way to begin to draw a knowledge demarcation line is to consider how you deal with student contributions, specifically, how you deal with unwelcome contributions. Or, put another way, what epistemological ground rules are at work in these situations? Like the car-parking attendant who guards the university campus against automotive interlopers, do you feel that you are holding a line by guarding against epistemological interlopers? One of my first recollections of experiencing some of these ground rules (I was unaware they were ground rules at the time) was the commentary from my lecturers in the margins of my first year undergraduate essays: '… is this just your opinion …?; where are the references to academic literature to support your claims …?; where's the evidence for this comment …?' Taken collectively, could this be read as a demand that I needed to earn my parking permit, which would then allow me to sit – legitimately – in the discipline-based seminar room?

This chapter might also be read as a footnote to Plato, specifically on the simile of the 'divided line', and how confident you feel about drawing your own disciple-based 'divided line' between what is true (epistemic) knowledge, and what is mere opinion (doxa) (Plato, circa 360 BC). This chapter addresses this question from three angles: (1) an exploration of the relationship between knowledge and purpose; (2) an exploration of the nature of the validity of higher education knowledge; and (3) an exploration of the relationship between some of the ontological and epistemological dimensions to higher education knowledge. In addition, Reason and Bracewell are back and will be adding their incisive commentary throughout.

Knowledge and the purpose of higher education

Ron Barnett and Kathy Coate distinguish three key purposes for higher education: (1) to produce a particular type of knower – with an emphasis on students' own engagement with knowledge; (2) to produce a particular type of actor – with an emphasis on being able to interpret one's own actions; and (3) to produce a particular type of being – with an emphasis on being able to resiliently work things out in a changing world (Barnett and Coate 2005: 48). These terms mirror traditional curriculum ideologies and curriculum models. In terms of ideologies: a form of classical humanism, emphasising what it is essential to know; a progressive humanism, emphasising individual self-development; and forms of social functionalism, emphasising the preparation for social and economic roles (Lawton 1983). In terms of curriculum models: a content model, emphasising what a learner needs to know; a process model, emphasising the process of learning itself; and an outcomes model, emphasising what the learning leads to.

These ideologies and models can also be linked to three broad theories of learning and Bloom's three learning domains: the cognitive, the affective, and the psychomotor (see, for example, Bloom 1956; Krathwohl et al. 1964; Biggs and Tang 2007). Specifically, learning theories which draw on cognitive processes, emphasising the mental acquisition of knowledge, as opposed to more humanistic approaches emphasising the value and meaning of knowledge to the knower, as opposed to those approaches drawing on variants of behaviourism, which emphasise what learners are able to demonstrate and do as a result of a learning process.

Clearly, we must resist the temptation to depict these ideologies, models, and theories in a three column table, because both the horizontal and vertical divided lines could simplify to the point of distortion, and mask the sometimes competing, sometimes complementary and sometimes unrelated relationships between the labelled boxes. But Barnett and Coate's three broad terms could feature in a Venn diagram (Figure 5.1).

If you were to use this Venn diagram to depict one of the courses you teach on, how would you draw it? What size would each of the circles need to be in relation to the others, in terms of where your course places its emphasis? How much overlap would there be between each circle, or would it be one, two or three separate circles? And how far do you think you could expand the middle overlap, or is it too much to expect one course to be able to achieve this (X as unique X factor, or no-go)? It is tempting to claim that an ideal course would indeed be one where the overlap between the three sets or circles is so great that they do all merge into one, but this is problematic for at least two

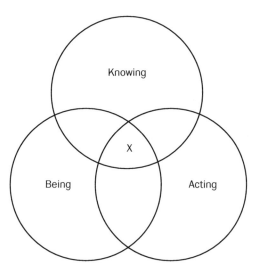

Figure 5.1 Dimensions of a Higher Education.

broad reasons. First, there is the 'horses for courses' question, that is, it may be highly desirable that a particular course only deals with one (or two) of the circles. And, second, even if a complete overlap is sought, it may still be desirable to distinguish between separate learning activities in order to enact, say, a knower or an actor, so that they could be subsequently merged, or that one needs to be considered the foundation for the other, and so on.

Prof. Reason: I can see where this is going so I'm going to throw down my yellow flag now. This is precisely where universities have gone wrong. If only we could just get back to the knowledge – generating it and disseminating it. One circle please, with the word 'knowledge' in the middle of it, in capital letters. It's just no business of a university what people do with it. I don't really care whether my students value the knowledge or whether it's going to make them better citizens, or more employable or whatever the latest jargon is. I'm not sure I even like the idea of a 'knower'; still sounds a bit too touchy-feely to me. Look, there's a clear distinction in philosophy between facts and values and we should remember that. My subject deals in the facts, that's my divided line. Do you think Einstein cared about whether people liked his equations, or that people would end up working in the armaments industry, using his equations to make atomic bombs? In the old days, you got your degree; you found a job; simple. I was employable because I had a degree not because I had employability skills, or that my university had taught me to be a good actor! And don't go telling me that it's more difficult these days because there are many more graduates now, because that just proves the point that we don't need as many graduates.

> *Dr Bracewell*: You're winding yourself up here, and it's clouding your judgement. You know full well that people learn best when they are enjoying it. Students need to feel comfortable about what they are learning, and, importantly, they need to know how to learn. That's not touchy-feely, that's just common sense, and it applies in a university as much as a primary school. And who doesn't ask themselves what the knowledge means to them? I would say that this question is crucial to higher learning. And it's no good bemoaning students wanting to get jobs. We have a duty to prepare people for life, and on top of that I do want our graduates to be good citizens. That's how societies improve, and I want to think our graduates will make a difference, in their local communities, and in their jobs. And let's get real here. Universities are judged on these things, and we can't afford to get left behind. You want fewer graduates? Well, you are going the right way to bring that about; unfortunately the drop in numbers will only be at this university, enabling others to benefit from our loss.

It is tempting to say that the emphasis on the 'being' and 'acting' sets in our Venn diagram reflect a recent turn in the articulation of purposes for universities, but it is too easy to find evidence to the contrary. For example, it would be difficult to claim that the colleges of the ancient Universities of Oxford and Cambridge have slowly – over centuries – expanded the being and acting sets at the expense of the knower set, for, if anything, the evidence points exactly in the opposite direction. Furthermore, though authors like Allan Bloom in the USA write convincingly about how Reason has been knocked off its perch in American universities by the unwarranted and misguided arrival of vocational and multicultural curricula (emphasising the acting and being sets at the expense of the knowing set), his appeal to put Reason back on its perch very quickly turns to ancient Greece, rather than any evidence drawn from the actual history of the development of many US and UK universities in the late nineteenth century (Bloom 1987). On that subject, it is not at all clear that the development of the so-called red brick universities in Victorian Britain were as a result of an appeal to Reason in the northern cities of the UK. Indeed, it is not clear either that ancient Greek intellectual thought would see it as desirable to demarcate knowing from being and acting, because it is surely in the combining of the three that a person is able to act wisely, and thereby prove that he is no idiot (in the Greek meaning of that word).

Other interesting Venn diagrams might be drawn from considering the following two quotations:

> Men are men before they are lawyers and if you make them capable and sensible men, they will make themselves capable and sensible lawyers ... what professional men should carry away with them from a University is not professional knowledge, but that which should direct the use of their professional knowledge, and bring the light of general culture to illuminate the technicalities of a special pursuit.

> (Mill 1867: 219)

[I]t [a university] is a place of *teaching* universal *knowledge*. This implies that its object is, on the one hand, intellectual, not moral, and, on the other, that it is the diffusion and extension of knowledge rather than the advancement. If its object were scientific and philosophical discovery, I do not see why a University should have students ...

(Newman [1852] 1996: 3)

Both are from around 150 years ago, but could easily have been written today. The first is addressing a perceived and unwarranted 'vocational turn'. And the second, which appeared in Chapter 3 to highlight the importance of teaching in the university, is used here to signal what has been called in recent times an unwarranted 'therapeutic turn', first, in the USA (Sykes 1992), then in the UK (Ecclestone and Hayes 2008). In the latter, it is no longer an unhelpful concern for the moral being, nor even the general well-being of a student, but a more dangerous casting of students as vulnerable, requiring their fragile egos to be positively massaged as a function of the educative process. Essentially, this is an infantilising agenda (Furedi 2004).

There seems to be two broad continua at work here. With regard to a 'vocational turn', there might be some distance between a university course which is specifically aimed at preparing students for a particular job (doctor, social worker, etc.), and a university course which has a graduate skills (or attributes) framework aimed at all students on all courses. And, on the therapeutic turn, there may be a huge distance between casting a student as a 'diminished self' (Ecclestone et al. 2005) in need of support to bolster a fragile ego, and providing opportunities for students to become 'unencumbered' selves (Barnett 2011a). And even if we could find clear evidence of both at work in universities and colleges, would it not be possible to unite these perspectives in a desire to heighten the sense that students should see themselves clearly as agents in their lives rather than as victims of circumstances? Or, to answer the question posed in that popular song by The Killers: 'Are we human or are we dancer?'; that is, are we free individuals or mere puppets?

Prof. Reason: Well, that all sounds very grand and noble, but I've been reading some of Frank Furedi's work and I'd certainly be happy to buy him a pint. We are infantilising our students. I mean, just look at the 'shit sandwich' we're supposed to use when giving feedback. How does it go, thank them for their essay – which they have no choice on – then say something positive, then make the critical comments – which is the only thing which really needs to be said – then say something positive again, even it if it's the worst thing you've ever read in your life. I mean. come on, what's this all about? As if students can't see through it anyway. Just give 'em the grade, that's all they want. I had to go to one of those staff development events a couple of years ago – last one I went to, I remember it well – where someone in the room suggested that we don't put 'fail' on a student assignment, we put 'needs development' and then tell them how to put it right. Seriously? I might as well just write the answer for them, it will save time all round. Come to think of it, why don't we just put 'needs development' on everything and just say it means 'pass'? I heard a rumour the other day that this place is thinking of having a learning and teaching ethics committee to whom we will have to submit lesson plans to check that we are dealing with sensitive subject matter correctly – yes, correctly is the right word – politically correctly. As if the research ethics committees aren't bad enough. What was it I saw, 'Be mindful when surveying students, or conducting interviews with them, so they are not harmed in the process.' Harmed by an interview? I'd like to harm the person who wrote that, then they'd know what harm really means.

Dr Bracewell: How wonderfully alarmist! I know that section in the ethics guidance document well, having conducted a number of interviews in the last year. You've paraphrased it in order to ridicule it. What it actually says is that we have a duty of care when conducting interviews, to ensure that interviewees, including our students, fully understand the nature and purpose of the exercise, and that they should be comfortable about that, and that there is mutual benefit to be gained by both parties. The word 'harm' applies to the process, that is, the potential for the interview not to generate valid, reliable and ethically sound knowledge. And anyway, it's guidance; you make everything sound like a diktat! Which is what people who rally against political correctness always do. And the same applies to the shit sandwich, as you eloquently put it. Are you seriously suggesting that we shouldn't be encouraging our students, prompting them on how to improve, and develop their study skills? You say you haven't been to a staff development event for the last two years; well, you've clearly missed out on some really useful conversations about feed forward rather than just feedback. Instead of reading Frank Furedi, I suggest you start reading something by Graham Gibbs. How about buying him a pint to thank him for over twenty years of evidence on what works in improving student learning? And number one on that list is probably the harmful effect of grading on learning. Sorry, I said that word harmful there.

Activity 5.1

- How would you articulate the principles that underpin the ways you support your students to achieve their academic goals?
- At school/faculty or institution-wide level, how have you been involved in seeking to establish an effective balance between rights and responsibilities when it comes to academic learning (for staff and students)?

The validity of higher education knowledge

The idea that we might be infantilising higher education students, turning seminars into a mirror of primary school 'circle time' (Ecclestone and Hayes 2008), raises the question of what exactly is meant by the word 'higher' in higher education. Returning to our original Venn diagram in Figure 5.1, what exactly might be meant by a higher knower; a higher being; and a higher actor? Or put another way, is there a 'divided line' above which we are clearly working at a higher level?

One way to look at this is to place Bloom's three learning domains above our original Venn sets, and ask to what extent we are moving students towards the high level skills in each of the domains. That is, to what extent is the learning enabling students to evaluate (and/or create) as knowers; to characterise (internalise and own) as beings; and to naturalise (as in second nature and/or originate) as actors. In turn, these higher level skills might be argued to be enactments of Maslow's original notion of self-actualisation (Figure 5.2), with its emphasis on the person as an agent or self-willed. In the language of Carl Rogers, the learner is 'free'; in the language of Barnett, the student is 'unencumbered; and in the language more commonly seen in higher education documentation today, we have the autonomous or independent learner. And, returning to the original idea of a completely overlapping three-set Venn diagram, we also have the possibility here of a university education being complete at the point where all three separate sets of activities come together in one person.

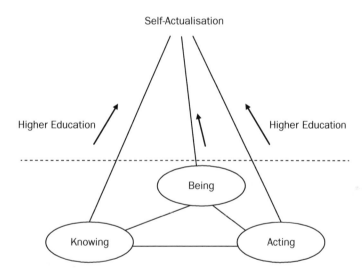

Figure 5.2 Higher education as an enactment of Maslow's self-actualisation.

In his book *Bringing Knowledge Back In*, Michael Young is particularly vexed by the question of vocational knowledge (Young 2008). Specifically, what is the status of experience gained from a work context that merits it being called knowledge, or, more precisely, what is the process of transformation required for these experiences to become real knowledge? Drawing particularly on the work of the sociologists Basil Bernstein (in the late twentieth century), and the work of Emile

Durkheim (in the early twentieth century), Young looks at how experiential forms of learning, gained in particular (often work) contexts (indeed, that it is context-tied) becomes elaborated – theorised, conceptualised – to become real, objective, knowledge. In the language of Durkheim, it passes from profane to sacred status, and, in the language of Bernstein, it desists from being horizontal in nature, and takes on elevated (vertical) status (Young 2008). This is another divided line which could be added to our previous diagram, requiring that our students deal strictly with this vertical knowledge, or, if they are to bring horizontal knowledge into the classroom, that they understand the process required to transform it into real knowledge.

Young's work is relevant to this chapter for two key reasons. First, it shifts debates about the difference between vocational and academic knowledge away from the value given to academic knowledge simply because it is academic (and favoured by the powerful upper middle classes in some lines of argument), and moves it towards a consideration of its conceptual underpinning, thereby providing it with an objective status. Bringing this question closer to the classroom, it also speaks to the need to consider the question of re-contextualisation, that is, the pedagogical interventions needed to enable students to effectively translate the work-based, experiential context into a conceptual one, and vice versa (see, for example, Eraut 2000; Young 2008; Hordern 2014; Simmons 2014). A vocational curriculum may need to be clearly and carefully articulated along these re-contextualising lines. This should also be extremely helpful in helping to determine what exactly is the higher element in that curriculum, or, in terms of Figure 5.1, what is it that takes the knowledge above the divided line?

The second reason why Young's work is important is because, for him, it stands as an important corrective to much of his earlier work which took the social construction of knowledge to mean that the value of classroom knowledge was, in reality, rooted not in questions of epistemology but political clout, that is, it was the knowledge deemed to be of value to those who had the wherewithal to get it onto the curriculum (Young 1971; Keddie 1974). In this debate the power of knowledge becomes the knowledge of the powerful, which the powerless are invited to invest in in order to gain the academic credentials to become socially mobile. In extreme versions of this debate, Shakespeare is on the curriculum not because his work has crossed an epistemological divided line in order to be deemed 'good', but simply because he is liked by those who have the power to put him onto the curriculum. To avoid this relativist (or Foucauldian) quagmire, Young challenges himself to establish a realist approach to knowledge, where, particularly with the help of Durkheim, he seeks the foundations for objective social knowledge. But there are also clear implications here for the humanities, in general, and the natural sciences.

This takes us to the heart of discipline-based epistemological debate, extending in the process some of the discussion about discipline allegiance covered in Chapter 3. One dimension to this debate is the demarcation line often drawn between natural science subjects and social science subjects, where in the former one finds the image of the scientist carefully listening to the voice of Nature (using an array of experimental equipment) in order to discover her (*sic*) secrets. To be contrasted to the social scientist who can only ever hope to approximate this exactitude, or give up altogether and satisfy themselves with perspectives rather than truths, or to seek understanding rather than explanation (verstehen vs. erklären, as Dilthey once described that contrast). But is this just a caricature of the differences, designed to defend different notions of valid knowledge, which in actual research practice are much closer on both sides? Durkheim certainly considered social facts to have as much weight as any other type of fact. And Einstein never claimed that he had discovered the truth, only that he had offered insight. Indeed, there are many people working in the world of quantum mechanics today who speak a language which would not be out of keeping on a Buddhist retreat.

These epistemological demarcation disputes are complicated by two other dimensions which are relevant to the themes of this chapter. First, the demarcation line between what are often referred to as the pure and applied subjects within disciplines (as in pure and applied physics, for example), and these apply equally across discipline boundaries (as in economics and business studies – where the weighting of pure and applied might be shuffled differently between them). Gibbons and colleagues speak of the applied subjects containing mode 2 knowledge (applied), as opposed to the mode 1 knowledge of the pure subjects (Gibbons et al. 1994). This distinction echoes that other contemporary distinction between hard and soft, but also the more ancient distinctions between the Trivium knowledge of the humanities and the Quadrivium knowledge of the sciences. But importantly, it also speaks to an increased need not for multi-disciplinary knowledge, but interdisciplinary knowledge – with an emphasis on *using* knowledge from many sources to problem solve, rather than just applying the knowledge gained from one discipline context (Trowler et al. 2014).

These distinctions have also been used to rethink the metaphor of 'tribes and territories' and the nature of discipline allegiance (see Chapter 3), prompting new metaphors, like 'oceans', which emphasise fluidity (Manathunga and Brew 2014) particularly for professional courses, which almost by definition, will have much closer links with workplaces (Trowler et al. 2014). Earlier, this also prompted Bernstein to speak of a distinction between 'singulars', 'regionals' and 'genericist' knowledge, that is, knowledge produced in insular fashion by a discipline community increasingly being overtaken by knowledge which is *brought* to the university, which in the process may then act as a de-professionalising force (Beck and Young 2005). These distinctions are important because not only might they provide different answers to the divided line questions, but also because the more applied the subjects are considered to be, the clearer it might be that the original Venn diagram would naturally have larger overlaps with the being and acting sets, particularly on those professional learning courses – where exercising professional judgements within vocational settings is paramount. Looking forward to Chapter 7, they might also help to explain why some subject areas seem more comfortable with the REF notion of research impact than others.

The second complicating dimension is more overtly pedagogical, and concerns the extent to which some of these epistemological disputes have spilled over into the ways that the subjects are taught, and whether, thereby, each subject area has its own very distinct subject pedagogy. There is something intuitively obvious about claiming that a mathematician would teach their subject differently from, say, an

English Literature teacher, but the challenge is how well the articulated distinction would stand up to critical scrutiny.

Relevant HEA project

Gunn, V. and Fisk, A. (2013) *Considering Teaching Excellence in Higher Education: 2007–2013: A Literature Review Since the CHERI Report 2007.* Available at: www.heacademy.ac.uk/sites/default/files/resources/TELR_final_acknowledgements.pdf

---

Prof. Reason: Well, I can certainly help out here. The further up the academic ladder you go, naturally, the more you will become involved in the dissemination of ideas. For example, presenting a paper at a conference as a PhD student is the best way I know of preparing that student for teaching that subject. But there's another important reason why we need to hold on to some discipline allegiance here, and that is to stop those staff development busybodies from imposing their useless generic teaching principles on us all. That's just a recipe to turn us all into school teachers, and even worse, robotic ones, using those ridiculous lesson plans with those even more ridiculous prescriptive boxes. Seriously, how would somebody who's never studied physics even begin to know how to teach it? As far as I'm concerned, this is just another form of unwarranted managerialism creeping into the university and we should resist it.

Dr Bracewell: Are you seriously trying to tell me that because a history teacher has been re-examining the causes of the Second World War, that they are, at the same time, involved in a re-examination of how to teach it? And could a physics teacher seriously claim that the methods they use to explore the movement of sub-atomic particles could be used to explore the nature of teacher–student interactions? There's another angle here as well, one which has clearly bypassed you, because, unlike me, you've never undertaken a teaching qualification. When I was doing my PG Cert (HE), it wasn't the teaching of generic learning principles that got everyone fired up, it was the chance to debate with colleagues from other disciplines. One of the best bits was where we had to defend our teaching and learning regimes. Under interrogation, it turned out most of us simply couldn't do it, other than to say that is how we do things in my discipline!

In summarising Reason and Bracewell's argument here, could we say that there are often some very sound political reasons for defending our teaching and learning regimes, but which can also act to hide some poor epistemological reasoning?

Dear Lecturer

On the nature of learning and knowledge as CPD

Kate Riseley

Who am I addressing in this short letter; surely not 'Lecturer', but 'Facilitator of Learning'? And in that respect we are surely not that different. While your specialist academic knowledge is no doubt greater than mine, the journey we walk is quite similar. Don't we both facilitate learning, our own and each other's and those we don't know? And don't we both strive to know more tomorrow than we do today?

Entering university, we leave the spoon-feeding of the education nursery and we arrive at the 'all you can eat' buffet. Everything is there for the taking and for the sharing. It is up to us to facilitate our own learning, to access the buffet and heap our plates. But we also facilitate each other's learning; as fellow students we communicate with each other, through the conversations unpacking the unfathomable theories and concepts. But I sometimes wonder what you are learning from your students. In what ways are we facilitating your learning? I also think my learning would be facilitated more by knowing more about how you facilitate your own learning.

Activity 5.2

- How would you articulate your discipline/subject's pedagogy, and how do you engage with forms of CPD to enhance aspects of your teaching and learning regime?
- In what ways have you been involved in establishing a regime of teaching and learning related professional development at school/faculty or institution level?

The question of whether epistemology is being used to mask the underlying political reasoning is at the heart of the American culture wars and the associated accusations of political correctness gone mad. These debates have been extremely heated, and many of them have taken place in universities, where they often revolved around those who want to keep politics out of the curriculum arguing against those who want the exact opposite. This politicisation was a key component in the sociology of curriculum knowledge in the 1960s and 1970s, but throughout the 1980s and 1990s (particularly in the United States), the debates spread to include the humanities and the natural sciences. For example, in English departments, vociferous debates took place between those who wanted to attack the so-called literary canon, as being little more than the works of 'dead, white, (mainly European) males'; in History departments, questions were asked about whether history as a discipline was quite literary history (i.e. narratives about the activities of men); and how history was being used as propaganda – both by those who wanted it to be used to celebrate, and by those who denigrate, aspects of cultural identity; and in the natural sciences, questions were being raised about the motivations of scientists in asking certain questions rather than others, and the influence of funding bodies on scientific research (see, for example, D'Souza 1992; Nash et al. 1997; Zimmerman 2002; Bok 2005, for critical discussions of these developments in American higher education).

For some authors, it was clear that this politicisation was at heart an attack on the Enlightenment, the idea of human reason shining its light to discover the truth, and embedded in the various disciplines which make up a typical university (Bloom 1987; Bronner 2004). However, those under attack were quick to defend themselves on the grounds that the Enlightenment was itself just a political project, full of ironies and contradictions, and a project which had simply elevated a particular approach to knowledge above all others (Choi and Murphy 1992). On this basis, those on this side of the culture wars invited university departments to adopt a more eclectic approach to knowledge, reflecting multiple axes of knowledge, and have them compete equally for curriculum space. It is here where we see talk of the post-modern university, one which invites the same critical approach to be taken to Enlightenment thought, as the latter took to religious thought. This also included an invitation to critically assess the extent to which aspects of discipline knowledge could be viewed (and possibly masqueraded) as revealed, discovered, or manufactured (Rorty 1989). For some, this also included an extended invitation to critically assess the role of theory in knowledge production: asking whether theoretical conceptualisation comes as a *result* of careful observation, or is *brought to* those observations (Patai and Corral 2005). And, once again, these invitations were sent across the board to all university disciplines, not just the social sciences.

Another way of approaching the role of theory was to consider the role of the researcher as 'detached observer' (of both animate subjects and inanimate objects). For, if it is impossible to view the world without some prior conceptualisation, it might equally be impossible to ask questions in the first place which are not value-laden in some way. For example, would disciplines have moved in different directions if different questions *had* been asked; if different bodies had been funding and disseminating the results; and, indeed if different people had been doing the research? These questions were at the heart of some of the most heated culture war debates in universities in the United States. For example, had more scientists been women, would scientific endeavour have looked different;? if more historians had been black or gay, would history books have looked different; and so on? These 'voice' perspectives were complicated by the extent to which black, female, queer (etc.) voices were viewed as being 'essentially' different (as in essentialism) or constructed (as a result of environmental influence) (Gilligan 1982; hooks 1996). If the latter, they were then open to critical deconstruction, but if the former, then the question is raised about whether only representatives of those groups can teach these subjects in university departments.

Prof. Reason: Whoa! Hold those horses right there! As a friend of mine in the USA said to me a while back, if we carry on like this, you'll have to be a rock in order to teach geology. This just goes to show how far we've gone in the wrong direction in higher education. The point about academic work is that it is, precisely, *academic*. What happened to being detached, not bringing emotional arguments to the table, speaking and writing in the third person? Has all this gone out of the window? Not that I have any desire personally to teach a feminist studies course, but are we really saying that this can only be taught by a feminist? Next thing will be that you have to prove you're gay in order to undertake a course on gay studies, or whatever they call it these days.

Dr Bracewell: Look, I'll grant you that it can sound a bit odd when it looks like some people are being excluded from teaching and studying on particular courses. But the intention is exactly the opposite. It's because certain voices have been lost to the academic world over the years that we need to take positive steps to bring them into the fold. Your argument would make more sense if we could prove that the mainstream subjects really were detached and objective. Are you sure that all History courses simply document the facts, and don't ever reflect the interests of those who've done the research? Are you really sure that those who teach Economics aren't mainly pro-capitalist, and those who teach Politics aren't mainly anti-capitalist? I'd be happy to wager some money on being right about this.

These questions are also extremely important when it comes to inclusivity. For, if the knowledge being taught is value-laden, particularly if it is viewed as a variation on the theme of 'dead, white, males', it is one thing to view access and mobility as an opportunity to engage with that knowledge, but quite another to view it as an opportunity to change the content of the curriculum to better reflect the values and culture of other groups; indeed, especially where lack of engagement by those groups might have been caused (in part at least) by being exposed to an alienating curriculum. This is also the starting part for the critical pedagogies associated with the work of Paulo Freire (see, for example, Freire 1970; Giroux 1981; hooks 1994; McLean 2008) the broad aim of which is to see the curriculum as a starting point to help people not just understand their circumstances, but also to challenge and change cycles of social disadvantage. Other variations of these radical pedagogies can be seen in the use of the classroom as a form of consciousness raising (which was originally popularised in feminist circles) and identity affirmation (which was originally popularised in anti-racist contexts). If we include in this list a desire to see research projects avowedly pursued because of their potential to enhance the lives of people living with disadvantage, discrimination and/or poverty, we can see how these 'knowledge as standpoint' perspectives might be equally embraced and denigrated by those on either side of the culture wars.

In stricter pedagogical terms, this division can also be summarised in the division between those who think it is more inclusive to support students to win a curriculum game which is heavily stacked against them, or to challenge the rules of that game, or, indeed, suggest that we should be playing another game altogether. For conservative authors like Allan Bloom and Dinesh D'Souza, this radical multi-cultural agenda in American universities was destined, in the end, to work against the very groups it was aimed at supporting (Bloom 1987; D'Souza 1992). For, not only would it produce minority enclaves in certain university departments, it would also mean that members of those groups would have to constantly defend themselves against the accusation that they got into university not based on merit but because they were members of those groups, and were there simply to advance that group's interests. This can only result, ultimately, in the pursuit of the 'particular' not the 'universal'; highlighting what separates us rather than what unites us.

Activity 5.3

- In what ways have you actively encouraged students from particular social groups, e.g. black, minority-ethnic (BME) to engage with, or change, the nature of the curriculum?
- In what ways have you been involved in institution-wide (and beyond) curriculum initiatives in order that it better serve a diverse range of students?

On the other side of that debate stand those who see 'merit' as a disguised euphemism for 'advantage', enabling students from privileged groups to be sponsored to achieve high marks on (so-called) standardised tests, and to view the curriculum as an objective authority, rather than, in reality, a political battleground (Fish 1994). This line of argument helped Fish gain his title as 'the grand wizard of political correctness' – of course, the title granted him by his Enlightenment opponents. In terms of our divided line, we might summarise this debate as an attempt by authors like Bloom to try to make it bolder (holding fast to what is objectively true), and by authors like Fish as an attempt to remove the line altogether (or perhaps better, to view it as a political line and not an epistemological one).

The ontological dimension in higher education knowledge

The culture wars discussion above has already encroached on the subject of this final theme; namely, the extent to which higher education knowledge should bring about the transformation of the person. For many on the conservative side of the previous debate, the worry was the extent to which this dimension had become so concerned with identity affirmation that it was not only overshadowing the disinterested pursuit of truth, but also beginning to question the very idea of knowledge as truth. While those on the progressive side of the debate wanted to emphasise that, at the heart of radical multiculturalism, there was, precisely, a critique of knowledge as truth, and it was not simply a moral crusade on behalf of the disadvantaged. Indeed, if there was a moral crusade, it rode on the back of that epistemological critique. Looked at in this way, a culture war can never be won because both sides have no common language to come together with.

One of the reasons why culture war debates are commonly associated with forms of political correctness is the progressive wing's conclusion that if notions of objectivity and truth are simply veils which are placed over what are, in reality, particular perspectives, then all knowledge must be, at heart, political. But one of the ways in which conservative thinkers were very successful in countering that line of argument was to accuse the progressives of demanding a slavish, self-righteous, pursuit of the interests of previously disadvantaged groups, that is, making it unquestionably the *correct* thing to do, and creating a 'dictatorship of virtue' (Bernstein 1994). This counter-argument has proved to be very successful in seeking to show how progressive groups have undermined, not pursued, the very forms of criticality one would expect to see in a university. This was the context in the culture war debates where progressives were accused of closing down free speech, by demanding that correct lines of thinking should not tolerate alternative lines of thought.

Prof. Reason: Aha! Is this the bit where I'm allowed to speak out against the green police who operate on campus? And what was that email I saw the other day that all degrees must have a module on sustainability and all students must take it. What business is it of mine or this university to tell students how to live their lives? It'll backfire anyway, because in two years time we'll all probably be told that smoking is good for us, and global warming is good, and so on. Or will that just become something else to ram down people's throats? It's bad enough being told that I don't have enough ethnic minority students on my courses, so what's next, how I'm supposed to address them and teach them? I've seen some of those speech codes that American universities have; it's laughable. Please don't tell me we are going to have one of them here!

Dr Bracewell: Actually, we do have a guidance document on the inclusive curriculum, which you've probably never looked at. It's not a speech code but it does have some great advice on developing intercultural literacy, including ways to support first generation entrants to university, and international students. You can ridicule this if you want, but a sense of belongingness is now well known to be a key feature in retaining students. And why wouldn't you want that? And you know full well that sustainability is not just a moralising agenda. I agree with you when it comes to some of the directives we have, but we are talking about the curriculum here, and any academic module on sustainability would cover a whole range of perspectives, including the importance of sustainable communication, and it would obviously include critiques and competing perspectives. You make it all sound like telling people off if they leave a light on, and you know full well it's much more than that.

There are a number of thorny issues here, though, because it might be one thing to teach values, as in ensuring someone's behaviour is in accord with a prescribed set of values (e.g. don't kick cats, because it's not nice), but quite another to develop an understanding of the conceptual frameworks that underpin ethical theory (e.g. having knowledge of, say, deontological and utilitarian theories). And it might be quite another again to avowedly claim that a student should be leaving university with a distinct sense of agency (as a particular type of being). And while this ontological dimension might be a very visible part of a mission statement for a college or university with a clear religious or political conviction, it is not so clear how this might be made manifest in other institutions. Indeed, echoing Professor Reason, whether it is any business of a university how its students might act beyond its walls (even within it) and certainly beyond graduation. For some, to even talk in this way is enough to demonstrate how far universities have strayed from their mission as knowledge generators and disseminators. But for others the question has become one of how exactly we prepare students for a world of: 'Fluidity, fuzziness, instability, fragility, unpredictability, indeterminacy, turbulence, changeability, contestability: these are some of the terms that mark out the world of the twenty-first century' (Barnett and Coate 2005: 53).

Relevant HEA project

Barnett, R. (2014) Conditions of flexibility. Available at: www.heacademy.ac.uk/conditions-flexibility-securing-more-responsive-higher-education-system

---

One way to look at this question is to consider Carl Rogers' notion of significant learning, and ask what it means to have learnt something which is not of any value. Here the very act of loving learning implies that it now occupies the heart not just the head (has entered the affective not just the cognitive domain). Furthermore, and returning to our 'higher' Venn diagram in Figure 5.2, we might also wish to say that our self-actualised student is not now just intelligent, but wise. It is in this context that we also speak of an ethical university, not just acting ethically as an 'organization' (or company, see Chapter 7), by for example, having a 'green' agenda, or having an explicit research ethics policy, but also in the ways that these impact on the curriculum. Here, the university continues in its mission of exploring the nature of truth claims (the epistemological dimension), but gives equal attention to the nature of human identity and the worthiness of the venture of the university itself (Nixon 2008). In terms of a Venn diagram, these last two elements will also impact (as overlap) on the epistemological dimension in demanding that we act truthfully (authentically, with integrity and conviction) in pursuing the truth, or advancing knowledge and understanding.

Activity 5.4

- In what ways have you actively sought to incorporate elements of self-development in your teaching and learning regime (e.g. students as virtuous citizens or ethically minded employees)?
- In what ways have you been involved in establishing an ethically based mission or strategy for your school/faculty, institution (and/or beyond)?

This elevation of the ontological dimension has several important strands. For example, psychoanalytically informed literature speaks of the need to help people deal with uncertainty (Frosh 1991) mixed with a reflexive social mood engendered by late or high modernity (Giddens 1991), where everything that was once solid now melts into air (Marx and Engels [1848] 2004), but which today increasingly includes the foundations for any knowledge claims. For Barnett, this makes it imperative that students learn to deal not just with the contestability of ideas but more profoundly with the 'supercomplex' nature of knowledge (Barnett 2000), and one which compels us to see human identity as always a 'becoming'; identity as an unfinished project. This is what we need to prepare our students for – that fuzziness and fluidity (Barnett and Coate 2005). Charles Bailey also once spoke of the need to see education as something which offers the potential to take a student away from the present and the particular, to be contrasted with training courses which act in the opposite direction (Bailey 1984). Here, employability is also as much a state of mind or set of dispositions, as a set of skills; not preparing students for a job, but helping them navigate an ever-changing job market; not being called to a vocation, but seeing work more like a series of self-development projects.

These ideas seem to follow logically from the notion of a student as unencumbered, for how are people to navigate all this uncertainty without a resilient sense of personal agency? Once again, we are back in the affective domain, using words prefixed with 'self': self-reliance; self-motivation; self-development, and so on. And here the notion of criticality, usually applied to the epistemological dimension, becomes *self*-criticality, and part of the ontological project of a university. As Sherman points out, this self-criticality is double-edged because it can result in the opening-up of horizons but also act as a reality check, by helping us to focus on what is 'structurated', to use Giddens' term (i.e. what are the structures which situate us) (Giddens 1984; Sherman 2003). Either way, it is this sociological imagination which enables us to see that things could be different but also what is needed to break free from the conventions which make us just one of the crowd (Riesman et al. [1950] 2001). This type of imagination also seems to be at the heart of management theories which encourage people to think 'outside of the box', as exemplified in the contemporary Theory U (Scharmer 2009).

Conclusion

Bill Readings speaks of 'the university in ruins' (Readings 1996). In part, this ruination has happened because of its pursuit of excellence – a vacuous quality term implying that if it meets its targets, then it congratulates itself on being excellent, but also because it has not been able to sufficiently defend itself against some of the implications of those culture war debates, leaving it without a clear purpose, and vulnerable to appropriation by a range of stakeholders. One way to rebuild it would be to take the Allan Bloom path and reinstate the role of Reason and all its implied Enlightenment baggage, but another way is to consider how the 'dissensus' engendered by the various epistemological disputes are themselves establishing a form of unity; the being as dissensus, or the university as a means to answer 'the question of being together' (Readings 1996: 20). Here the kinds of criticality commonly associated with university degrees form the foundations for students to become agents of community; diplomats and critical citizens; applying the skill of criticality to forge new relationships, partnerships, tolerance, and so on: 'It is to understand the obligation of community as one to which we are answerable but to which we cannot supply an answer' (Readings 1996: 187). In terms of our Venn diagram in Figure 5.1, this clearly helps to unite and overlap the sets, where the knower, being, and actor becomes a brokering agent in a world of dissensus; or a world where the epistemological and ontological dimensions are united, to form a wise citizen for the twenty-first century; one with the capabilities to transform the world (Maxwell 2008; Kreber 2013). Put simply, it is also a willingness to consider a situation from the perspective of someone different (Nussbaum 1997), and where teaching is primarily viewed as 'a matter of dialogue rather than the reproduction of a system of thought' (Delanty 2001:140).

This vision is not without its problems. It seems to demand that universities concern themselves squarely with notions of social justice; democracy, tolerance and even well-being. But these terms are themselves part of the dissensus for there is no universal understanding of their meaning, or general acceptance that they are, in themselves, good things. Why should I tolerate the intolerable, or will there always be a compromise? And what if I decide to live as a hermit after my university education; have I now failed my university, and even myself, by reneging on a civic duty? But the vision is significant, because it places centre stage the notion of a university not just as a special knowledge space, but also as a special civic space – where we present the evidence of our deliberations, but also learn to relate to each other (Nixon 2008).

The ontological dimension needs to be put under critical scrutiny. In the end, we may have to make a stand on it. For some, its elevation may have been enough to damage the role of the university as knowledge creator and disseminator, but for others, it may be viewed as a necessary rebalancing act between the epistemological and the ontological, or between knowledge and wisdom. And where the former helps us to understand and look critically at values, and the latter helps us to actually *value*. This question is not unrelated to the culture war debates, because not only might the disinterested pursuit of truth turn out to be a masquerade, but it might also produce a world of knowledge with no meaning – disenchanted knowledge, as Max Weber put it – or lifeless facts. The challenge now becomes to see wisdom as 'the capacity to realize (apprehend and create) what is of value in life, for oneself and others …'. (Maxwell 2012: 134), including a demand that we do not disassociate scientific and technological endeavour 'from a more fundamental concern with problems of living' (Maxwell 2012: 124).

Here, the cultivation of character (Bildung) also needs re-exploring, not as rational Enlightenment man (*sic*), but as a communicator in a world of uncertainty (Readings 1996) – not the aggregation of knowledge, but making it meaningful. Here, 'the university is a zone of mediation between knowledge as science (or academic knowledge) and cultural cognition' (Delanty 2001: 12–13). And where: 'the knowledge project should be ultimately judged by how students make a stand for what they believe to be a better world' (Harland and Pickering 2011: 27). Perhaps the simplest articulation is to take the notion of the craftsman as someone who does something *well* (Sennett 2008), and transpose that as an aspiration for all our graduates. For those worried by how much these ontological dimensions have undermined the epistemological one, the question might be asked as to the extent to which the epistemological drive to: render all knowledge as contingent; make everything an 'interim report' (Collini 2012), and pursue knowledge by critiquing knowledge (Barnett 2011a), might then be brought *to* the ontological dimension to form a complementary rather than a contradictory overlap.

Opinion Piece, Debate, Dear Lecturer, and Fellowship Application extracts

In the following opinion piece Ruth Lawton reflects on her role as an employability officer and the role generally of employability in the university curriculum. This is followed by a debate between Dennis Hayes and Celia Popovic, who take opposing positions on the nature of academic knowledge in the university and the extent to which it can be viewed as 'objective'. To finish, Dave Thomas, a recent graduate from Canterbury Christ Church University, reflects on the chapter overall. This is followed by three extracts from successful HEA fellowship applicants who discuss some of the aspects of academic practice which feature in this chapter.

Opinion: On employability

Why employability is so important

Ruth Lawton

When we talk about academic knowledge, we are usually talking about discipline knowledge – history, accounting, midwifery, architectural technology. But as academics in HE, we also have to have knowledge about other aspects of the student experience and outcome from HE. Our students don't just leave with a degree, we expect them to leave employable, and more than that – with graduate-level employment. Most graduate employers are not recruiting for a specific discipline (Prospects. ac.uk) instead they are recruiting for skills, qualities, attributes, behaviours, 'fit', and so on. And our graduates need to recognise, record, articulate, evidence and demonstrate that they match these employer requirements as well as their degree subject knowledge.

As an academic, it is asking a lot of you to know about all this! So, what *do* you know about graduate recruitment? And, do you even think it's your job to know this? And if it is someone else's job, who is that person and how do your students find him or her? Or, how does that person find your students?

My role at Birmingham City University is to facilitate embedding employability in the culture and curriculum of the university, thereby enhancing the career prospects of our students and graduates. When I first started trying to do this, about 15 years ago, it was a thankless task with enormous resistance from almost everyone, academic staff and senior management alike. Now I am welcomed everywhere and everyone is willing to explore and make changes to their practice where possible, but now new problems have arisen. The curriculum is under pressure from all sorts of stakeholders; the employability knowledge required to be effective in enhancing our students' prospects is also far more sophisticated and complex; and academic practitioners have so many things to balance alongside this agenda.

But let's be realistic. Surveys of students show that one of the reasons they are at university is for better job prospects and they expect us (we who teach them) to support them with that. And the fairest, most effective, and efficient way to do that is in your classroom via your curriculum.

If we ask students to engage with 'optional' activities (like going to see a careers adviser to discuss job/lifestyle options, career decision-making, researching themselves and researching employers, presenting themselves on paper, online and in person) then a small percentage will do that. The majority will not; this is the reality. The percentage who will take up the option are usually the ones who already stand out from the crowd – and who, I would argue, need that help the least.

So, whether you like it or not, it does seem to come down to you and your classroom, accompanied perhaps by a daunting feeling of 'but what do I know about employability?' But, actually, we all know a huge amount about employability. And I believe that embedding employability in your classroom and curriculum can start really effectively with your own reflection. How have you managed your own career so far? What has been your career history from Saturday/voluntary jobs as a teenager through to now? How did you get those jobs? When is the last time you formally applied for something? How did you get on?

As you read this, you may be actively thinking about (and perhaps daunted by) applying for a Fellowship of the HEA which is potentially a career step as – at the very least – it is now in the 'desirable' column on a person specification for many HE academic posts. It is also a political and strategic step for many of us. For example, your institution may be paying for your application to HEA but is it what *you* want? (i.e. what is your motivation for doing it?) These are the sort of issues that confront our graduates and they can lead to wider questions: do you know what makes you happy at work, gives you a feeling of achievement, and is a real strength? Do you know where you want to be in 1, 2, 5 years time?

How easy was it for you to answer those questions, and how easy do you think your students would find it? Would their answers be realistic (I am thinking about students who declare that in 2 years time they will be a chartered accountant; buyer for Next; and in 5 years they will be on TV replacing Alan Sugar)? In this context, have you ever considered that being engaged with your own career and employability is role modelling? That does not mean that your career has to be going swimmingly and you have answers for all of the above questions – successful people often claim that they learnt nothing from success, only failure. And how many of us have been happy to maintain the status quo because it is comfortable and easy? All of these things relate to managing our careers!

If you have not moved jobs recently, an HEA Fellowship application may be the first opportunity you've had for a while to think *actively* about your own CV. Indeed, sometimes we need these processes to recall very significant achievements that might otherwise get completely forgotten. And if you are finding it irksome, hard, revelatory, these are the very real professional knowledge spaces that your students could benefit enormously from knowing about.

But you do not have to know all the answers, there are resources you can call on and use, including careers advisers who can work *with* you and your students, and academic developers who can help you design your curriculum and assessment to support career management/employability. For example, I have a DUMP CV (Lawton 2011). DUMP stands for Don't Underestimate My Potential. This is my shoebox of everything I do/have done that I can dip into when needed. I haven't applied for a job since 2002 *but* I have had to provide a CV for funding applications, a biography for publishers and event organisers, and detailed accounts of how fabulous I am for fellowships with the HEA and SEDA. My DUMP CV is 8 pages long now – it includes publications, conference and workshop presentations, consulting … all sorts of weird and wonderful things (like being interviewed by Kerrang radio, taking part in a tweet chat) that might be lost, but might come in useful to make me stand out from the crowd in the context of perhaps just one application in the future.

After reading this, I hope that next time you talk to your students about professional life you talk with passion, conviction, and from (perhaps sometimes bitter) experience. And if you set aside some time in your classroom to invite in alumni, employers, recruiters, and careers advisers, that you don't see this as a 'bolt-on' to the curriculum to satisfy a management dictate, or to tick an employability box, but as a real opportunity to link academic knowledge meaningfully and authentically with professional knowledge.

Debate: On the nature of academic knowledge

Can knowledge be viewed as universal and objective?

Celia Popovic

My starting point is a firm 'no' – knowledge cannot be viewed as universal and objective. My response alone is a good example. I 'know' this answer, in that for me this is a truth and I believe I have evidence to support it – as I will show later. However, I also 'know' that others do not agree – and I can only assume they believe their position to be as true as I believe mine to be. So, no: this particular knowledge is not universal, and I'm sure it is not objective.

A while back, I took John Lea to task over his otherwise stylish and useful text '77 things to think about teaching and learning in higher education' – because aside from one image of bell hooks, all images used in this publication were of men and the vast majority of the references were to male writers. Is there evidence here of a long-running bias which has made the mainstream of literature about pedagogy appear exclusively male, and probably white, with English as a first language (which John, himself is part of)? And has this also had the effect of relegating my thoughts, or more accurately, those of my gender to the status of perspective, as opposed to 'knowledge'?

What is it about knowledge that is universal and objective? What knowledge are we privileging and who decides what counts? Were all writers before Jane Austen male? What about the playwright Aphra Benn? Are all classical composers men? What about Clara Schumann or Fanny Mendelssohn? In the sciences – who discovered DNA? Yes, we all know – Francis Crick, James Watson and Maurice Wilkins, according to those who hand out the prizes; but what about Rosalind Franklin? There are dozens of other examples in science alone where women's contributions are either ignored or attributed to men, often their supervisor or husband. So which version counts as 'knowledge'?

Who decided that we needed a slot for sports news at the end of radio or TV bulletins and the back pages of newspapers? Why not announcements on child rearing or health updates? Either of these would be of as much interest to some as knowing which group of players managed to kick a ball into a net more times than another group. Who decided we needed to hear a report on the stock exchange at least once a day? Why not current literacy rates or teenage pregnancy levels? Not all women would be interested in this either, and of course not all men are interested in sport: the point is that there are choices to be made and those with power and influence make the decisions.

In any account, the reporter, the writer, the commentator or the educator makes a choice. When the choice is repeated over and over again, and those making the choice are regarded by society as holding superior status (like a judge, a clergyman or an academic), those choices come to be seen as a fixed notion. But there is always a choice.

Who decides on the curriculum in a given subject? One teacher or a group of scholars select the elements that they think are key for this particular group of students at this particular level of their learning. Any such selection is arbitrary. But what about progression? Surely there are things we have to learn in order to understand the next step. Well, yes, I agree it is necessary to have an understanding of addition, for example, before you can understand multiplication. However, who decides that we need to learn multiplication or when we need to learn it? I am not suggesting we stop teaching basic maths to school children but I am using this as an analogy for most of the content of university courses. Who decided when I studied English and American Literature that I would be best served with nothing later than Dickens on the English syllabus and nothing earlier than Hawthorne on the American Studies? Medical students often complain about the overloading of the syllabus – why would a future psychiatrist need to memorize the name of every bone in the foot, when most non-foot medical specialists forget 90 per cent of the anatomy they learnt in medical school? Yet most medical schools emphasise and valorise anatomy as a basic element of knowledge needed by every prototype doctor.

Knowledge is not universal nor is it objective. What is fixed and known at one point, may prove to be contested or even faulty at another. We all know the tired example of Gallileo shocking his peers with the revelation that the earth revolves around the sun – an idea that is now considered fundamental. Knowledge is affected by politics (fundamental Christian Creationists, for example, or those who argue over the effect of climate change), by power (sports-keen men dominating the newsrooms), by fashion (research into breast cancer far surpasses research into any other type of cancer) and by opinion (Gove on the UK's National Curriculum).

I believe that knowledge is created by the learner, and that since each of us comes to learning with a unique set of experiences and prior knowledge, then each of us creates a new form of knowledge as a result of the experience. As teachers, we may be able to set boundaries around the focus of the study, but we can no more control what people do or do not learn than control their preferences. We can create the context and the opportunities. But what we can most usefully do is teach our students to question and to learn to live with uncertainty. To be able to analyse what is presented as fact and to be aware of multiple ways of viewing the world. To appreciate that we do not know everything and no one person can, nor that what is known now is static.

Debate: On the nature of academic knowledge

No more Mr Nice Don

Dennis Hayes

Many proposals for doctorates in education drafted by lecturers in education or teachers are about the 'perspectives' of managers, lecturers, teachers, students or pupils. Finished theses and education journal articles are filled with accounts of various 'perspectives' on any issue. Most will end up unread and gathering dust because their 'findings' are uninteresting. The reason is that people's 'perspectives', like their 'experiences', are just perspectives and experiences. They do not constitute knowledge nor does reporting them constitute a contribution to knowledge. What is needed, and what may well happen when these collections of 'perspectives' are in the dustbin of intellectual history, is a sociological study of why so much time was wasted on gathering perspectives over the last few decades. There is hint of a sociological explanation in a related example from the 1990s when there was a sudden surge in attitude surveys being conducted, particularly by government bodies. The reason was that traditional bodies that provided access to the views of ordinary people had collapsed. No longer did the trade unions, political parties or groups provide any collective understanding of what people thought or desired. The collapse of politics after the collapse of communism is the root explanation of the origins of the concern with individuals' viewpoints. Today, in what could be characterised as a 'post-political' era, there is little to constrain the spontaneous and continuous rise of this pointless perspectivism.

The existence of perspectivism in the academy is not the outcome of the triumph of influence of postmodernism, feminism or cultural studies. It can be explained in the same way. The collapse of politics allowed academics of a leftish persuasion to claim that their pet philosophy or subject had social force when in reality social forces allowed any ideas to gain a hearing in the academy. Perspectivism is one methodological expression of this intellectual anarchy. Although it can be labelled 'perspectivism', it is nothing more than a rattlebag of relativist views that have no philosophical foundation. Before discussing why relativism persists in a 'perpectivist' form, it is worth reminding non-philosophers that over two thousand years ago relativism was shown to be self-contradictory by Plato in the *Theaetetus* (s170–171). Protagoras in this dialogue is said to have argued in his book *The Truth* for a relativistic philosophy that held that what a person thinks is true, is true. Socrates points out a problem with this view. Some, if not all, people may think that Protagoras' philosophy is false. Given his relativistic position, Protagoras has to agree that what they say about his philosophy is true and that his views are false. He must therefore hold his own philosophy to be both true and false at the same time. Socrates concludes, after exposing this contradiction, that Protagoras' relativistic view is not true for anyone, including himself.

We can update that argument here and provide what are often called 'quick refutations' of relativism. Suppose someone believes that 'All opinions are equally valid' we can ask 'Is that statement true or is it an opinion?' Or if they say 'All truth is relative' we can ask 'Is that statement true or is it relative?' Any attempt to make a statement that expresses a relativist position will have the 'most exquisite feature' Socrates enjoyed pointing out (s171a); it will be self-contradictory and therefore *false!* This may seem to some a simplistic argument and conclusion. There are more complex philosophical positions. This is true but nothing follows from noting this fact. The existence of a difficult and complex philosophical tradition in which a battle is raged against relativism and in favour of realism, reason and truth says nothing in favour of relativism outside of philosophy.

Perspectivism persists in higher education and elsewhere because of what Allan Bloom perceptively and famously described as a psychological state of niceness. He characterised students as 'nice' and he said: 'I choose the word carefully' (1987: 82–3). Bloom felt that students, because times were good, had not been tested in class and other conflicts, and could not be expected to be particularly moral or noble. Their primary preoccupation was 'with themselves'. The same can be said of today's academics. They are 'nice' and I choose the word carefully. They are not particularly moral or noble and are primarily preoccupied with themselves. In higher education, everyone is nice, *too* nice. Bloom was describing what we would now refer to as a 'therapeutic ethos' in universities. Being nice and listening to everyone's opinions, perspectives or experiences seems nice in a therapeutic way.

But being at university is not equivalent to being on a non-judgemental therapist's couch. The university embodies the Enlightenment belief in the pursuit of truth through reason. Abandoning that belief is to abandon the academy.

Abandoning the struggle for truth in favour of listening to many voices has happened for many reasons. Institutionally, it makes life easier for managers if they are (unwitting) relativists and, therefore, never have to make judgements about the value of much of what they oversee. Down the hierarchy, lecturers don't have to judge one another or their students and a cosy relativistic consensus exists in the academy. Non-judgementalism makes life easy but it also seems 'empowering'. It means that you do not have to 'offend' anyone by challenging their religious, cultural or philosophical views.

If you take a perspectivist position you can flatter yourself that it allows minority voices to be heard. Allowing views to be heard without criticism is said to be empowering because 'powerful' academics will, by becoming perspectivists, no longer assert the power they have over students and other academics. That 'power' is the power of rigorous criticism.

To abandon this power in favour of flattering minorities by 'listening' to their voices is not empowering, it is deeply disempowering. It not only takes away the potential for anyone to use criticism to gain real knowledge and power but it strengthens the position of the truly powerful people outside of the academy. This is the consequence of the 'cultural relativism' that is today's most ubiquitous form of relativism. Like philosophical relativism, cultural relativism stands to fall through a quick refutation if it is stated, but it has an even more dangerous feature. If all voices are to be heard without criticism, it is not just the powerful voices of 'dominant' cultures that have no claim to truth or have any social or political force but the 'powerless' voices of minority cultures also can make no claim to truth or have any social or political force. Neither of them is 'true'. Cultural relativism leaves real power relations as they are. If you are interested in challenging real power, the condition for social and intellectual progress is to be part of the Enlightenment tradition and say what you believe is true, point out what you believe is false and get an argument going. That means academics have to abandon the intellectual laziness of being nice and return to their real role, which is, *criticism*.

Dear Lecturer

The real challenges of widening participation

Dave Thomas

Yes, widening participation initiatives have enabled students from disadvantaged backgrounds to access university education but the realignment of the university's curriculum to accommodate its increasingly multicultural cohorts is still very much a project in the making. And yes, while accepting that 'knowledge is liberating', in churning out 'knowledgeable' homogeneous graduates, are those graduates now devoid of personal cultural identity? Even worse, are we denigrating students' own habitus and (unwittingly perhaps) promoting a form of subservience, more along the lines of academic colonialism?

As a mature student of black and minority ethnic (BME) origin, I undertook an inclusive curriculum undergraduate project that allowed me to explore the formulation of academic knowledge. As I began, I couldn't help asking myself the obvious questions: 'Was this going to be another tokenistic, tick-box exercise?'; 'Was this going to change the established curriculum?'; 'Was the university ready to hear how BME students really think?' And who can provide me with answers to these questions? As my lecturer, could you? Or does it seem slightly uncomfortable? Unfortunately, widening participation comes with these thorny questions and responsibilities.

The Inclusive Curriculum survey raised many questions about the formulation of academic knowledge, particularly from BME students. Most students had no idea how their curriculum was formulated and didn't think they could influence this curriculum. Most students thought their curriculum was static, not encompassing or acknowledging their culture or context. One thing was very clear, that students didn't feel their curricula were contemporary and representative of their heritage and culture. Another key finding was that BME students were not informed of the statistics surrounding the academic attainment gap and felt this knowledge would have helped them to improve their academic engagement.

Most worrying perhaps is that students genuinely wanted to engage with the content of the curriculum but often felt accused of being colloquial in their thoughts when attempting to contextualise key concepts. Furthermore, some students thought the curriculum *was* somewhat Eurocentric and that lecturers inadvertently infantilised them by suppressing natural thoughts and ideas. BME students also felt that lecturers did not engage in enough dialogue with them and this itself could be enough to encourage their academic engagement. In conclusion, the students said that the chief barriers to their academic engagement were: (1) belonging to the university; (2) learning and teaching strategies; and (3) classroom culture.

I have since completed my undergraduate degree and have gained employment in HE in a student support role. This has provided me with the opportunity to work closely with academics. I have now concluded that there is no clear rationale for non-alignment of the curriculum to accommodate different social groups. But what stands out for me is that the lecturers who attempt to re-align their curriculum to accommodate different cultural/social groups are often seen as mavericks in some academic quarters. This is troubling because the wealth of experiential knowledge brought to the table by mature, BME, and under-represented students must surely be an asset in helping to create new knowledge, and for all students.

Some of the issues I speak about are quite small and could be resolved quickly, for example, are we doing enough to encourage students from under-represented groups to participate in curriculum development? But some of the issues remain huge, for example, the need to recognise that while academic learning is a commodity (and can be a means to a job market end) for marginalised and under-represented students, it can also be a destination, similar to the notion of self-actualisation. We must remember that students from under-represented social groups often turn to education for solace and liberation from their negative life events. And here the role of the curriculum in widening participation initiatives remains very much a project still in the making ...

Extracts from successful HEA fellowship applications

Dr Orange (FHEA)

Famous television series such as *CSI* and *Forensic Files* have inspired an increasing interest in forensic science; unfortunately they have also created a false high expectation and understanding of 'the science behind the crime' for students who pursue a degree in Forensics. In order to avoid the 'CSI effect' I have developed a range of problem solving activities which are based on adaptions of real crime cases (Bergslien 1998). After having the fundamental framework in place for each activity, I have been able to adapt it to align with the learning outcomes of students across different degree programmes in Forensics, Pharmaceutical Science and Pharmacy. Through this context-based learning approach I am encouraging students to build a deeper understanding of the interdisciplinary nature of their degree, an approach which will provide 'meaningful' learning for students (Gilbert 2006) [K1, V4].

For example, when teaching Forensic Science students the introduction to the case is through the use of photographs and police reports from a crime scene. The subsequent activity would then involve students developing their communication skills and organisation skills to explain how the crime scene would have been assessed, how the evidence would have been collected, and which evidence would require further laboratory analysis. From initial student feedback, in a consultation environment, it was apparent that students had enjoyed the crime scene aspect of the activities but felt they wanted more professional skills embedded within each activity, such as drawing sketches of the crime scene by using the electronic software Visio, a change that was implemented soon after.

Dr Brown (SFHEA)

My grasp of psychology and its various applications in such fields as health; mental health; education; community, cross-cultural and social work guided the design of the course content (within the parameters of the BPS and QAA standards [K6]) but also the learning activities [K2]. Special attention was given to debate, comparison and evaluation of theories, ethics and methods, in order to foster, from Level 4, skills of critical thinking so crucial in working with twenty-first-century psychology and its sometimes ill-considered applications [A1]. A wide range of audio visual resources [K4] were used as part of lectures and independent study, both to hold the interest of a new generation of university students glued to tablets and phones (use of both of which are allowed and even encouraged in lectures and workshops) and to access the contested and rapidly changing knowledge base of the different branches of psychology. Field visits, inter-university collaborative visits, visiting speakers, community partners and an online student collaboration with psychology peers at a large Indian university were all part of my aim of broadening the horizons and critical skills of a student group whose ethnic, age and diversity profile was more homogeneous than any I had encountered previously in my teaching career [K3; V1].

Mr Pink (SFHEA)

I have a strong belief that education should have a relevance to employability and am well aware that these issues are being actively discussed within the Higher Education Academy's Art Design Media (ADM) Subject Centre (Linda Ball's 2010 report, for example, *Future Directions For Employability Research In The Creative Industries*). Bringing outside industrial and creative collaborations to the students has a noticeable and tangible effect. In my experience, a targeted 'real' assignment acutely engages the learner transcending the typical classroom environment [A4]. It contextualises the learning and adds real power. I persuaded *Top Gear* magazine to bring a car into the studio for the students to review and draw. The results were outstanding, with a wide range of student work published. I persuaded the Royal Opera House to open up their rehearsals for students to observe and draw. The students were mesmerised by a totally different artistic context and produced artwork that reflected this. I persuaded Walker Books to host an evening for BA students at their Head Office so that a wide range of their staff from marketers, editors, writers, designers, even Managing Director could directly liaise with the students about their work. It was another example of a two-way process of mutual learning and inspiration. From this event alone, several students were mentored by the publisher and subsequently were published nationally and internationally. Articulate and motivated students graduate with real skills and industry acumen. These collaborations give them confidence and I am proud that they continue to innovate on graduation. They actually do what they have aspired to do. The course is proud of the high levels of student attainment and employment within the sector. They animate for the very best companies in the industry, Pixar and Aardman, illustrate for the *Guardian*, *The Times*, write and illustrate children's books. The list is extensive [V4].

6

Students as partners in learning

Mick Healey, Catherine Bovill and
Alan Jenkins

*I can understand postgraduates as researchers, but undergraduates; they
don't know enough about the subject or about research methods, do they?*

*I don't see how a student could effectively evaluate my teaching, what do they
know about higher education pedagogy?*

*This student voice idea is getting a bit out of hand; students will be running
the place soon.*

Introduction

We have often heard views expressed like those in the above statements by both new
and experienced lecturers. Whatever we think of these comments, they suggest that
engaging students as partners in learning is a hot issue in higher education. Although
not a new idea, it has come to the fore in the last few years and there have been many
events dedicated to discussing the range of complex issues raised by implementing
student partnership initiatives. Moreover, several books and reports have been published recently dedicated to the topic (e.g. Healey and Jenkins 2009; Werder and Otis
2010; Little 2011; Dunne and Zandstra 2011; Dunne and Owen 2013; Nygaard et al. 2013;
Bryson 2014; Cook-Sather et al. 2014; Healey et al. 2014a, 2014b). Politically the idea of
students as partners has also taken off recently within higher education. The UK government, for example, published a White Paper in 2011 entitled *Students at the Heart
of the System* (BIS 2011) and the following year the National Union of Students (NUS)
published: *A Manifesto for Partnership* (NUS 2012). In 2013, a Student Engagement
Partnership Unit was established by the Higher Education Funding Council for England
which is run by the NUS 'to help students and their associated representative bodies
become partners in the student experience' (HEFCE 2013).

In this chapter we want to explore a range of contexts where students can make a
valuable contribution as partners and to challenge you to think about circumstances
where working with students could benefit your teaching as well as their learning. This
was hinted at by Ramsden (2008) when he noted that:

There is abundant evidence that the most effective higher education environments are ones in which students are diligently involved as part of a community of learners. As part of this engagement, they work together with academics to enhance teaching, assure quality and maintain standards. In these contexts, they understand themselves as active partners with academic staff in a process of continual improvement of the learning experience.

(Ramsden 2008: 16)

Many staff are already quite good at listening to students' views through, for example, end-of-course evaluations and staff-student committees. However, we want to go beyond these conceptions of the student voice and examine situations where students act as co-creators, co-producers, and co-designers of knowledge and learning.

In this chapter we focus on three distinct but complementary areas where students may engage in partnership – as teachers, scholars and as change agents. Students may take on the role of teachers through peer-learning and assessment or through taking on responsibility for co-teaching with staff and other students; they may act as scholars through being involved in subject-based research and inquiry; and they may engage as change agents through undertaking scholarship of teaching and learning (SoTL) projects, co-designing the curriculum and acting as pedagogic mentors and consultants to staff. These three sets of activities are shown as overlapping circles in Figure 6.1 to reflect the interrelationships between them. For example, students undertaking SoTL are engaged both as scholars and as change agents. There is not an exhaustive set of ways in which students may be engaged as partners and other broader frameworks have been proposed (Healey et al. 2014a). Here we concentrate chiefly on students'

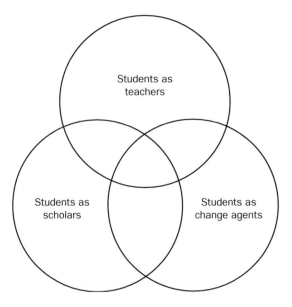

Figure 6.1 Areas of engagement in working with students as partners.

engagement as partners in learning and teaching within the formal curriculum, drawing on interesting practices internationally, but giving particular attention to the situation in the UK. The chapter is illustrated with mini-case studies of students as partners from a range of disciplines, institutions and countries, focusing for the most part at the course unit and programme levels.

The three roles we have chosen to concentrate upon are traditionally ones that are considered to belong to academic staff. We argue that students also have an important role to play in these areas. Inevitably as staff-student partnerships develop, some of the traditional identities of staff and students begin to break down and this raises issues of power and responsibility in higher education which we would like you to think about.

Relevant HEA project

Healey, M., Flint, A. and Harrington, K. (2014b) Engagement through partnership: students as partners in learning and teaching in higher education. Available at: https://www.heacademy.ac.uk/sites/default/files/resources/Engagement_through_partnership.pdf

---

The chapter contains many extracts from academics discussing how they have: involved students as teachers; reoriented students to adopt a scholarly approach to learning; and included students as change agents.

Students as teachers

Traditionally, academic staff design and implement most teaching activities in higher education, but as noted above, a range of approaches are becoming increasingly used that shift the traditional role boundaries between staff and students. These newer forms of relationship between students and teachers can lead to students taking on some tasks that might normally be considered to be the domain of the teacher. This is not about completely replacing your teaching role and expertise, which most people would see as an undesirable step, but rather it is about altering the roles of teacher and student and adapting the existing student–teacher relationship (Breen and Littlejohn 2000). Within these shifting boundaries, we are seeing increasing numbers of examples of students taking on teaching responsibilities, for example, students becoming involved in peer-learning and peer-assessment or students presenting disciplinary knowledge and concepts to their peers and teachers. These pedagogical approaches require a significant shift in the way that student and staff roles are conceptualised towards a more constructive, dialogue-based relationship between staff and students. Freire argues that 'through dialogue, the teacher-of-the-students and the students-of-the-teacher cease to exist and a new term emerges: teacher-student with students-teachers' (Freire 2003: 63).

One of the most common ways in which students take on the role of teacher is through peer-learning or peer-assisted learning. Frequently existing schemes involve senior students teaching junior students, such as at Kings College London, where their medical peer-teaching initiative involves fourth year students teaching clinical skills to third year students (KCL 2014), and at the University of Stirling in psychology, where fourth year undergraduates teach second year students statistics (Case study 1).

Case study 1: Final year students teach second-year students statistics in psychology at the University of Stirling, UK

Five to ten student tutors are recruited by asking for volunteers followed by a selection process that involves them doing practice lectures in front of a small group of staff and other fourth year students. The students are paid an hourly rate for the time they spend doing this, including preparation. In addition, they are encouraged to produce a report which they can use as credit in one of their final year modules. Two members of staff oversee the process and these meet weekly or twice weekly with the students for a few weeks before term begins and throughout the term. A key feature of this process is that each cohort of student tutors are invited to invent the module for themselves – to design all aspects of the teaching, given just the requirement that all learner students will have successfully completed a number of examples of the basic statistical tests. Student feedback for this process is highly positive and the external examiner is happy with the outcomes. The experience to date is that the students become adept at doing statistics quicker and more proficiently than under the more traditional lecturer model.

(Healey 2014; Roger Watt: r.j.watt@stir.ac.uk)

Other schemes involve senior students producing educational materials for junior students, such as at Loughborough University where senior students in mathematics produced worksheets on difficult topics for more junior students (Case study 2).

Case study 2: Four students who had completed their second year of a maths degree at Loughborough University, UK, were employed as interns to redesign materials for use in two second year courses

Fuelled by concerns about student engagement and performance in second year maths, students and staff collaborated to rethink and redesign materials specifically to help new second year students understand concepts that many students found difficult. The materials included handouts on difficult topics and video screen-casts of theory and examples. Two of the interns also acted as peer-assisted learning leaders, contributing to sessions where the more senior students taught the second years about troublesome concepts using the materials they had devised. The second year students developed a deeper understanding of the topics covered and the student interns and teachers described an increased confidence in their own maths ability.

(Duah and Croft 2011); Cook-Sather et al. 2014)

Here's another example of senior students designing online materials to teach more junior students in a geography degree in Ireland (Case study 3).

Case study 3: Programme co-ordinators redesign a first year geography curriculum in collaboration with students at University College Dublin, Ireland

The first year of the geography degree usually enrols about 400 students each year. The co-ordinators advertised for four third-year students who were paid to design a new virtual learning environment based on case studies covering important themes for first-year geography, such as migration and the coffee trade. They then produced written, audio and video resources within the virtual learning environment that first-year students could interact with and use to support their learning. These case studies prompted discussion among small groups of students online and in class. The third-year students then collaborated with the programme co-ordinators to identify examples of good student work that could be used as the basis for teaching sessions, thereby supporting use of the current students' work as an integral part of the curriculum.

(Bovill et al. 2011; Bovill 2014; Healey 2014)

A common concern that you might be thinking about is whether senior students teaching knowledge and skills to other students, are expert enough to teach others and whether the quality of the teaching will suffer. Interestingly, there is evidence that many students prefer the relative approachability of their peer colleagues when compared with staff and in fact often learn as much, if not more, than from staff teaching (Tolsgaard et al. 2007). There is also evidence of the enhanced understanding and confidence demonstrated by peer-teachers from having to teach knowledge and skills to peers (Krych et al. 2005). Indeed, the deeper exploration and investigation of a subject that are needed in order to teach something to someone else ensures that there are strong links between the role of student as teacher and student as scholar. It is commonly accepted that teaching a subject requires a deeper level of understanding of the subject being taught. Inviting students to teach other students offers them an opportunity to develop more nuanced and complex understandings of disciplinary knowledge and methodologies as well as enhancing their ability to communicate knowledge, concepts and skills to others – and all of this has significant potential benefits for students in their future career (Ross and Cameron 2007).

Another common format in which students take responsibility for teaching their peers, as well as the tutor, is in tutorials and journal clubs. In these settings it is not uncommon for students to take responsibility for teaching others about the findings from a relevant research article. Similarly where a problem-based learning approach is adopted, students often take responsibility for investigating concepts that they then share and teach other group members about. At this point you might be thinking what many academics think, which is how to ensure students complete required readings or tasks related to tutorials. There are some useful examples of ways in which staff tackle this challenge. One formal technique which holds promise is the use of the 'jigsaw classroom' approach. A technique first presented by Aronson (1978), it involves small group work where each group member is assigned part of a topic to learn about in order to teach the rest of the group. So the members of the group move to interim expert groups who focus on each topic before all returning to their original groups to be able to have all the pieces of the 'topic jigsaw' to fit together. More recently, Honeychurch (2012) has adopted this approach with philosophy students, using wikis as a way of gathering together knowledge in the interim expert groups.

An alternative approach taken by some staff to ensure students take more responsibility for reading and co-constructing discussions in tutorials is through the use of 'doughnut rounds' (Fleiszer et al. 1997). This technique does not require passing cakes around in class, though this might contribute to student engagement in tutorials. The 'doughnut round' refers to an approach where students have responsibility for formulating questions about the selected reading. They then have to be prepared to ask each other the questions they have about the reading in the tutorial. The round involves one student asking another student one of their questions, and after the chosen student has attempted to either answer the question or engage with some of the relevant areas of discussion raised by the question, the responder then has the chance to ask a different student one of their questions, and so on around the group. As we began to see above, the jigsaw classroom and the doughnut round re-envisage students as active collaborators, co-teachers and scholars. Reconceptualising the relationship between students and teachers tends to lead students to exceed staff expectations and to adopt collaborative responsibility for learning and teaching with staff (Bovill 2014; Cook-Sather et al. 2014).

Peer-assessment could be considered to be another form of peer teaching, in the sense that assessment is often accepted to be part of the teacher's role. However, using Freire's conceptualisation above, if we consider students to have the potential to be teachers and for teachers to be learners, then this opens the assessment process to collaboration with students. You might think that assessment is a controversial area over which students can collaborate, where assessment involves judging whether a student has achieved particular learning outcomes or competencies – a key quality measure in higher education. Students are one set of actors who have the potential to judge assessment outcomes, but crucially, they are often unaware of the desired learning outcomes and marking criteria (Orsmond 2004). So there is enormous potential for students to learn through peer-assessment processes (Healey et al. 2014a). We often talk of the importance of students being able to judge their own and others' performance against criteria, and peer-assessment can be a very useful way for students to learn to do this. Peer-assessment can be a key element of an ongoing learning process rather than an end point focused on measuring performance.

Where students are involved in grading and providing feedback to other students on their work, initially students often feel uncomfortable with the notion of sitting in judgement on their peers. However, there are many benefits from dialogue between students and staff about marking criteria and the importance of being able to judge the quality of work against criteria. With practice and time, students can become skilled and insightful in their judgements and comments. Some students will remain uncomfortable with this idea of taking on the teacher's role of judging someone else's work, and this may explain why in many cases peer-assessment is used predominantly for formative assessments that do not count towards final grades. Whether peer-assessment takes place in formative or summative assessment, it is sometimes revealing to see how much the tutor's marks are worth in comparison to the students' marks. For example, if you are thinking of involving students in peer assessment, consider the following scenario: in a class of 10 students, the students will be assessed on a presentation and the nine peers in the room will provide a mark and so will the one tutor. In this scenario, will the peers' marks count for 90 per cent of the mark and tutor's mark count for 10 per cent, or will the tutor's mark make up 50 per cent of the mark and the peers' marks make up 50 per cent, or will the tutor's mark count for 80 per cent and the peers' marks count for 20 per cent? In each of these possible marking schemes, you will communicate to students a relative value that is being placed on their judgements in comparison to the tutor's judgement.

Self-assessment provides an opportunity for students to gain enhanced insights into their own performance against criteria. Despite what many of us would think, in a study by Boud and Falchicov (1989), they found that there was no evidence that self-assessment consistently led to over- or under-estimating of performance. Falchicov and Boud (1989) found that explicit criteria led to more accurate self-assessment, as did involving students in creating marking criteria. Orsmond (2004: 20) argues that:

> Achieving empowerment for students in assessment processes demands their involvement with the assessment marking criteria. Although desirable, it is not always possible to have students involved in criteria construction. However, the onus is on the tutor to ensure that students have a good working understanding of the criteria.

Peer- and self-assessment may also be used for redistributing group marks between team members. For example, these approaches have been used to capture various group processes, such as the quality of group members' contributions to developing ideas, collecting and analysing data, preparing the presentation and writing and editing the final report. These are all activities which realistically only the group members know enough about to be able to make an accurate judgement on their peers' performances (Healey and Addis 2004). It is important not only for students to be involved in dialogue about the criteria, but also to be involved in dialogue about assessment feedback (Rust et al. 2005). Combining self-assessment with the tutor's assessment, Deeley describes the concept of co-assessment that involves discussion about performance and feedback (Case study 4).

Case study 4: Co-assessment of a summative oral presentation on a service learning course at the University of Glasgow, UK

Drawing together the benefits of students' self-assessment with tutor assessment of summative work in a service learning course, the tutor aims to maximise collaboration and co-ownership of the assessment process. The students self-assessed their own oral presentation and the tutor also assessed the presentation. Both students and tutor awarded a provisional mark and wrote reflective feedback comments about the performance. There were eight students studying the course and the tutor then met with each student individually to discuss the marks and feedback and to agree a mark. However, in this work, Deeley (2014) does note the potential difficulties that might arise in trying to use this model with larger classes. She also acknowledges and discusses the importance of maintaining safeguards within a summative assessment process. Deeley (2014: 39) argues that 'co-assessment requires the student and teacher to reach a mutually agreed appropriate grade for the assignment through discussion and negotiation which must be supported by evidence and reasoned argument'.

(Deeley 2014)

Activity 6.1

- In what ways have you sought to incorporate the notion of students as teachers in your teaching and learning regime?
- Have you been involved in articulating a notion of student as teacher in a strategy or philosophy to underpin the work of your school/faculty, or institution (or beyond)?

Students as scholars

At best teaching and research are very loosely coupled ... the fundamental issue is what we wish the relationship to be, and we need to devise policies to enhance this wish ... (and that to better ensure effective teaching research links) *we need to increase the skills of staff to teach emphasising the construction of knowledge by students.*

(Hattie and Marsh 1996: 529, 533–4, emphasis added)

What makes teaching in higher education distinctive from school-level learning? This question was asked by von Humboldt in 1810, and has been raised throughout this book. Our view – in keeping with von Humboldt – is that in higher education students need to be made aware of the contested nature of knowledge; the conditions under which knowledge is discovered and manufactured; and that higher education is as much concerned with what is *not* known, as what *is* known. Baxter Magolda, who has researched student intellectual development in higher education, argues that:

University curricula need to support student and citizen development from *absolute knowing* [where] students view knowledge as certain; their role is to obtain it from authorities [to] *contextual knowing* [where] students believe that knowledge is constructed in a context based on judgement of evidence; their role is to exchange and compare perspectives, think through problems, and integrate and apply knowledge.

(Baxter Magolda 1992: 75)

As teachers, then, our role is to bring students into the nature of scholarly knowledge in our discipline, the issues that discipline focuses on, and the research methods it uses to explore that knowledge. Here is how a researcher on ocean waves sees the role of a teacher in higher education:

Science is a conversation. The conversation has been in progress for a long time … science resembles the babble at a very large reception … The participants in the conversation have sorted themselves into groups, and sub groups, each dominated by a few brilliant conversationalists who set the subject and tone. Some scientists wander from group to group, while others remain fixed. Some groups talk about similar things, and occasionally snaps of conversation pass from one group to another. You have arrived in the middle of a party…. *My job is to catch you up on the conversation and show you how to find your way to the bar.*

(Kinsman 1965: 9, emphasis added)

As we bring our students into these disciplinary worlds of contested knowledge, key issues include helping students understand and contest the nature, connections and boundaries between 'scholarship' and 'research'. Practically we have to consider how to introduce higher education students into knowledge complexity and then how to ensure there is a coherent progression through their courses to develop that understanding.

Consider the following case studies that in our view exemplify how this can be achieved in the opening weeks of year one curricula. What ideas do they give you to adapt to your disciplinary and departmental contexts? To what extent do they show students entering into the worlds of scholarship and research in their discipline? To what extent do they support students in becoming partners in their learning?

Case study 5: Psychology students research students' quality of life at York St John University, UK

First-year psychology students at York St John University undertook an eight-week project in which they collected data from themselves and other students using short inventories and a biographical questionnaire in order to research topics related to students' quality of life. This project provided students with the opportunity to collect 'live' data, contribute to a developing database, select data for analysis and write up findings. The topics available for selection by students were linked to the research interests of the lecturer.

(http://www.heacademy.ac.uk/resources/detail/
subjects/psychology/Akhurst-case-study)

Case study 6: Undergraduate research begins at induction at University of Gloucestershire, UK

At the University of Gloucestershire, students undertake discipline-based inquiry projects during induction week. This involves them working in small groups to collect information from the library and in the field, analyse it, present it to tutors in novel ways and receive formative feedback. A wide range of projects have been undertaken over the years. For example, the human geographers and the sociologists have researched the experience of Gloucester residents of the 'Great Flood of 2007'. The biologists and the psychologists investigated how primates communicate at Bristol Zoo; while the English students investigated trees and poetry and visited Westonbirt Arboretum where, stimulated by the environment, they sent each other haiku poems.

(http://insight.glos.ac.uk/tli/resources/toolkit/wal/
sustainable/Pages/ActiveLearningInduction.aspx)

We can see from these case studies that:

- staff are central in shaping the curriculum both in content and in the process of learning in ways that are supportive of students entering disciplinary communities of practice;
- students are central as inquirers, actively shaping their understanding but in a context where that provisional understanding is made public and subject to critique by their peers and staff;
- the 'research' methodologies are largely determined by the staff but are being made explicit to students;
- the 'knowledge' that the students 'create' is not new knowledge, and indeed it may be uncertain as to its validity, but the students are on a journey – and this is but an introduction.

As students progress through the curricula, teachers need to make more explicit the forms of scholarship and research in their discipline and the research methods of inquiry. One contested area for both students and staff in this journey is the extent to which such learning can be described as 'research'. For some, research is clearly that knowledge which is new to the discipline and the academy. To others, while what the student produces and learns may not be new, it is new to them and more significantly shifts their understanding of the contested complexity of knowledge in their discipline. At what point do students see themselves as partners with 'fellow' students and perhaps more critically *see themselves* as partners with us as staff? At what point do we as staff see students as partners in *our* learning? Returning to some of the themes discussed in Chapter 2, a key issue for staff and students is to consider carefully the relationships between 'research' and 'scholarship'. Some may see clear distinctions between 'research' and 'scholarship', as can be seen in the UK Research Excellence Framework (REF 2012). We see these as both partly distinct; for example, in that with research the focus is more on creating new knowledge, but also as highly blurred in that in some disciplines, particularly the humanities, much research is *re*-search and research and scholarship overlap.

For staff who espouse this conception of the interconnections between research, scholarship and teaching in higher education, it is common to refer to the holistic view of academic practice proposed by Ernest Boyer, and summarised in the quotation we began this book with:

> What we urgently need today is a more inclusive view of what it means to be a scholar – a recognition that knowledge is acquired through research, through synthesis, through practice, and through teaching. We acknowledge that these four categories – the scholarships of discovery, of integration, of application, and of teaching – divide intellectual functions that are tied inseparably to each other.
>
> (Boyer 1990: 25)

Table 6.1 takes Boyer's categories and shows how they can guide us to bringing students into these higher education practices.

Table 6.1 Examples of ways in which learners may engage with Boyer's four scholarships.

Types of scholarship	Illustrative example of ways of engaging learners
Scholarship of discovery	Engage in inquiry-based learning; undergraduate research and consultancy projects; co-research projects with staff.
Scholarship of integration	Engage in integrating material from different sources, including across disciplines; integrate life and work experience with academic studies; reflect on implications of studies for personal development.
Scholarship of application/ engagement	Engage with local, national, and international community service projects; volunteering; knowledge exchange projects; apply knowledge and skills in work-based placements.
Scholarship of teaching and learning	Engage in mentoring; peer support and assessment; collaborative group work; learners as explicit partners in educational development and inquiry.

Source: Healey et al. (2014b: 56).

In developing your ability to bring students into the worlds of research and scholarship, the following framework in Table 6.2 and Figure 6.2, which builds on the international research on the student and staff experience of teaching-research relations, will help you in designing courses.

Table 6.2 The nature of research and inquiry by students.

Research-led: learning about current research in the discipline

Here the curriculum focus is to ensure that what students learn clearly reflects current and ongoing research in their discipline. This may include research done by staff teaching them.

Research-oriented: developing research skills and techniques

Here the focus is on developing students' knowledge of and ability to carry out the research methodologies and methods appropriate to their discipline(s).

Research-based: undertaking research and inquiry

Here the curriculum focus is on ensuring that as much as possible the student learns in research and or inquiry mode (i.e. the students become producers of knowledge not just consumers). The strongest curricula form of this is in special undergraduate programmes for selected students, but such research and inquiry may also be mainstreamed for all or many students.

Research-tutored: engaging in research discussions

Here the focus is on students and staff critically discussing research in the discipline as, for example, in many seminar-based courses.

Source: Healey et al. (2014a: 17).

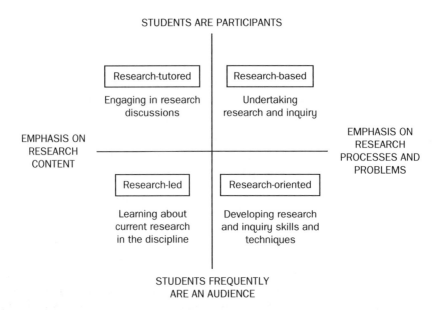

Figure 6.2 The nature of research and inquiry.
Source: Healey and Jenkins (2009: 7).

Clearly these approaches are not independent and we consider all approaches with a research or scholarship focus to be valuable – though our emphasis is on supporting students to be involved fully with staff and other students in undertaking research and inquiry. But you will need to decide which combination of these approaches to use in the contexts in which you work.

Dear Lecturer

On students as scholars

Martha Canfield

I have recently been working as a student intern on a research project called 'Re-imagining Attainment for All' (RAFA), looking at the gap between attainment and progression rates of students from Black Minority Ethnic groups. The main focus of RAFA was on encouraging transparency with regards to the process of assessment.

As a BME student myself, the chance of working closely with members of staff offered a great opportunity to show the set of skills that we students have. Especially, where these skills represent the social and cultural context we come from, and where we aim to apply all the knowledge that we seek to gain in our university programme of studying.

My main responsibility in this project was to facilitate the communication between students involved in the project and members of staff. I recruited and worked with students from different ethnic groups and departments of my university, as well as encouraging them to take part and engage in a debate about their experiences regarding assessment with members of academic staff in several workshops.

The experience of working in the RAFA project showed me that very often academics forget their practice can reach its full potential by simply boosting communication with students, promoting a dialogue that welcomes different perspectives and positions and thereby contributing to the success of BME students.

The four approaches discussed above will need to be adapted to the particular discipline in which you teach and the department and institution where you work. Examples of curriculum design which exemplify these approaches are given in the following case studies.

Case study 7: Research-led – Introducing students to academic staff research: Department of Geography, University College London (UCL), UK

All year one students in Geography at UCL do an assignment as part of a compulsory 'Writing and Analysis in Geography' course, in which students interview a member of academic staff about their research.

- Each first year tutorial group is allocated a member of academic staff who is not their tutor.
- Tutorial groups are given three representative pieces of writing by the member of staff along with a copy of their CV, and a date is arranged for the interview.
- Before the interview, students read these materials and develop an interview schedule.
- On the basis of their reading and the interview, each student individually writes a 1500 word report on: (1) the objectives of the interviewee's research; (2) how that research relates to their earlier studies; and (3) how the interviewee's research relates to his or her teaching, other interests and geography as a whole.

(Dwyer 2001; Cosgrove 1981; accounts of two interviews:
http://gees.pbworks.com/w/page/10115571/
UCL%20students%20interview%20their%20lecturers)

Case study 8: Research-orientated – Asking questions in plant biology at the Australian National University, Canberra, Australia

A practical exercise designed for a level two course involves students: making observations in a botanical garden; coming up with ten questions each (e.g. why do eucalyptus leaves dangle?); sharing one of these questions with another group of students; coming up as a group with hypotheses based on the question (e.g. eucalyptus trees in arid environments have leaves that dangle at steeper angles than those in wet environments); thinking of ways of testing the hypothesis; and writing up individually ten questions and one hypothesis as a 750-word mini-proposal for a research project.

Case study 9: Research-based – History students contribute research findings to a website at the University of Victoria, Canada

History 481: Micro History and the Internet; the main activity is primary archival research on various aspects of life in Victoria, British Columbia, from 1843 to 1900. Initial subject activities include orientation to the historical archives in Victoria and basic website creation skills. Students work in small groups on a research project and the final research 'product' of the subject is a website, not a standard research paper.

(http://www.victoriasvictoria.ca/; http://en.wikipedia.org/wiki/
Digital_history;http://web.uvic.ca/~jlutz/courses/hist481/index.html)

Case study 10: Research-tutored – Involving first-year English students in the international research community at University of Gloucestershire, UK

At the University of Gloucestershire, Arran Stibbe enables students to take on the identity of a researcher from the start of their time at university. In Sociolinguistics and Ecolinguistics, a first year module, the students have an opportunity to share *their* insights with the wider research community. The research community in turn has something to gain from student contributions because students can critically analyse aspects of their language and culture that others have yet to examine. The approach works best when students are becoming critically aware of texts that they are familiar with, rather than struggling to understand new genres understood better by the lecturer than students. The students are encouraged to take part in the international research community through working with the Language & Ecology Research Forum – the main international forum for research in ecolinguistics. The website contains a mixed collection of articles, some of which are by students and some by researchers.

(http://www.ecoling.net/articles; http://www.english.heacademy.ac.uk/
explore/publications/casestudies/sustain/ecolinguistics.php)

We have deliberately focused here on examples of engaging students as scholars early in their courses as it is already common in the UK and some other countries for final year students to undertake research projects. We do, however, believe that it is timely to rethink the forms that final year projects and dissertations take and introduce a wider range of choices (Healey et al. 2013).

Students as change agents

In addition to the two roles we have outlined so far – student as teacher and student as scholar – practitioners and researchers have started speaking about 'students as change agents'. A change agent refers to an individual with the freedom and motivation to be able to make decisions with the potential to alter and transform something. This implies a radical shift in the way many students relate to learning and teaching and also to the ways they relate to teachers and other learners. Often, students are passive recipients of teaching rather than active contributors and collaborators within the learning process. Re-envisaging students as change agents in learning and teaching begins to recognise that students have valuable views, ideas and experiences that they bring to learning and teaching. Where students gain agency over their learning experiences they also tend to become more engaged in the learning process (Mann 2001). Where students have agency over learning and teaching, this can lead to transformed learning and teaching. So what does this mean in practice?

Describing their work at the University of Exeter (Case study 11), Dunne argues:

There is a subtle, but extremely important, difference between an institution that 'listens' to students and responds accordingly, and an institution that gives students the opportunity to explore areas that they believe to be significant, to recommend solutions and to bring about the required changes….'students as change agents' explicitly supports a view of the student as 'active collaborator' and 'co-producer', with the potential for transformation.

(Dunne and Zandstra 2011: 4)

Case study 11: Students as partners shape and lead their own educational experiences through the 'students as change agents' initiative at the University of Exeter, UK

The University of Exeter has been running a 'Students as Change Agents' initiative since 2008. Students are invited to undertake small-scale research projects to investigate areas of concern in learning and teaching that have been identified within formal staff-student liaison committees. Students work in partnership with staff to use the research results to take action to improve the learning experience. Ultimately the aim is to enhance students' experiences of higher education. Projects have been diverse and have included research with a focus on assessment and feedback, technology, peer tutoring, seminar provision, academic writing and sustainability. Outcomes have included reports, student-led conferences, student-led writing skills seminars, a buddy system, peer tutoring and study guides. The initiative uses an action research methodology to underpin the research studies, and consistent with this research approach is the emphasis on change as an integral part of the research process. So students have agency within the research process, but also within the action planning and change processes that are an integral part of this model. Students therefore have an active role and an investment in changes made to learning and teaching within the institution affecting their own and their peers' learning experiences.

(Dunne and Zandstra 2011; Sandover et al. 2012)

At the University of Exeter, colleagues and students speak overtly of 'students as change agents', but in the university or college where you work, this may not be a familiar phrase. In some settings students are described as collaborating in the 'scholarship of teaching and learning' (SoTL). As has been discussed in previous chapters, SoTL is defined in many ways by different authors, but one useful definition for us here comes from Martin et al. (1998), who state that:

The scholarship of teaching involves three essential and integrated elements: engagement with the scholarly contributions of others on teaching and learning; reflection on one's own teaching practice and the learning of students within the context of a particular discipline; and communication and dissemination of aspects of practice and theoretical ideas about teaching and learning in general and teaching and learning within the discipline.

(Martin et al. 1998, cited in Healey 2003)

Hence when students are engaged in SoTL they are researching and inquiring into student learning, whereas when they are researching and inquiring into their subject, we have referred to them in this chapter as scholars. Clearly many of the same skills are required to undertake both activities and this demonstrates the overlapping nature of the roles we outlined at the beginning of the chapter.

Where students are involved in SoTL, we create opportunities for students to act as change agents in improving the quality of teaching and student learning. Most definitions of SoTL position students as the subjects of our research or the recipients of the changes we make. In higher education, often the term 'student voice' has been used to refer to the importance of gathering feedback from students in higher education (see, for example, Campbell et al. 2009), where really students feeding back on evaluation forms could be considered to be only the very first step in student voices being heard. In contrast, the research literature about student voice in schools-based education has often been far more overtly political and critical of the lack of student agency in decisions affecting students' own learning experience (Bragg 2007; Fielding 2004). By engaging students as active participants and partners in SoTL, we provide opportunities for much greater student engagement and empowerment than is provided by traditional models of gathering student feedback. Involving students as partners in SoTL acknowledges the unique knowledge, skills and experiences our diverse learners bring to higher education, and the key role students can contribute as co-constructors and co-creators of learning and teaching.

Case study 12: Students are co-inquirers in SoTL at Western Washington University, USA

Students and staff at Western Washington University collaborate to integrate the students' voice into institutional initiatives for enhancing learning. Each year, staff and students come together in the 'Teaching-Learning Academy' (TLA) on a bi-weekly basis to develop significant questions about learning and teaching that they intend to investigate during the year. Over the year the group develops the significant question, undertakes a survey to discover existing collective knowledge in the group about the question. Then others are invited into the study. The results are collectively analysed before developing a plan of action based on new understandings.

(Western Washington University (n. d.); Healey 2014)

Many universities in the UK are starting to involve students in SoTL projects even where they may not refer to SoTL explicitly. A couple of the more well-known examples of student involvement in SoTL are outlined briefly here (see also Healey et al. (2014a) for further details).

Case study 13: Students undertake SoTL within the 'Student as Producer' programme at the University of Lincoln, UK

The 'Student as Producer' programme at the University of Lincoln aims to use critical social theory to re-envisage the possibilities of higher education. The institution supports a range of student-led research and teaching initiatives and aims to make strong links between research and teaching rather than using pre-defined learning outcomes. One of the key aims is to shift students from being seen as the subjects of learning to being active producers of learning. Neary (2010: 8) argues that 'Student as Producer, and the revolutionary pedagogical practice which it promotes, is designed to interrupt the current consensual discourse about teaching and learning in higher education.'

(Neary 2010, 2014c)

Another institution that has encouraged students to become active partners in SoTL initiatives for a number of years is Birmingham City University (BCU). BCU has run their 'academic partners' initiative since 1998.

Case study 14: 'Students as academic partners' at Birmingham City University, UK

This partnership between the Students' Union and the University originally focused on partnership projects where students were employed to help staff and students research and implement changes to improve courses. However, as institutional support has grown, the scheme has evolved to include a student academic mentoring programme, cross-departmental initiatives and a 'student jobs on campus' service through which students can engage meaningfully with the work of the University.

(Nygaard et al. 2013)

Often these collaborative SoTL projects involve individual or small groups of students. Yet there are other SoTL projects that involve whole cohorts of students such as the collaborative evaluation project Bovill et al. (2010) undertook at Queen Margaret University, Edinburgh, involving all of the 21 students studying an educational research module. In this work, the whole cohort of students was involved in designing, implementing, analysing and collating the evaluation of the module. A subset of the student cohort chose to set up a working group after the end of the module to disseminate the lessons from this work in a journal article and conference presentation. We do acknowledge that it is likely to be more challenging to involve the whole cohort of students in SoTL if you are teaching and researching with larger classes, but it is not impossible.

Some institutions have set up schemes where students act as consultants to staff to discuss and enhance teaching and learning approaches. In this work, students are not only scholars and potential change agents, but the focus on investigating and changing teaching, places students as advisors to teaching and as partners in teaching. One of the most well-established models of students working as pedagogical consultants comes from Bryn Mawr College (Case study 15).

Case study 15: Students act as pedagogical consultants at Bryn Mawr College, Pennsylvania, USA

The Students as Learners and Teachers (SaLT) programme aims to support students and staff to create opportunities for critical and constructive dialogue where they can explore questions about learning and teaching with the aim of affirming, improving and developing classroom practices. The broader aims are to ensure that this critical and constructive dialogue between staff and students about learning and teaching becomes an embedded part of institutional culture and practice. The consultant's role includes making weekly visits to their staff partner's classroom, where they take observation notes focused on learning and teaching issues previously identified by the staff member. Student consultants meet weekly with their partners to discuss their observations and explore one another's perspectives on what takes place in the classroom as well as broader learning and teaching issues. The consultants are supported by participating in weekly one-hour discussions with the Director of the programme and other consultants.

(Cook-Sather et al. 2014)

Students also act as change agents through co-creating or co-designing curricula. Students and staff co-creating curricula is not a new idea, but it is one which, in common with conceptions of 'student voice', has perhaps gained more momentum within school education than in higher education (Bovill 2013). For the sake of this discussion if we combine some of the definitions of curriculum outlined by Fraser and Bosanquet (2006) and take curriculum to be the structure, content and processes of a unit of study, as well as the learning experience of students, then co-creation of curricula can involve students in a broad range of initiatives to co-design elements of learning and teaching. Some initiatives involve students acting as change agents focused on curriculum content, such as Ignacio Canales' work at the University of St Andrews, where he invited students to decide the content of the later parts of his Entrepreneurship and Business Planning course so they could ensure these sessions were focused on content that would help them to be able to complete their group entrepreneurship projects (Cook-Sather et al. 2014).

There are relatively fewer examples of students becoming involved in curriculum planning processes in a more integrated way with student and staff collaboration from the start of planning a whole curriculum. Indeed, Manchester Metropolitan University made a range of enhancements involving students as partners in curriculum design, but acknowledged the difficulties of sustaining student involvement in the design process (MMU 2013). At Elon University, in the USA, students have been involved in curriculum design teams since 2005 (Case study 16).

Case study 16: Students act as co-creators of course design at Elon University, North Carolina, USA

All the teams work slightly differently, but typically a team includes one or two staff and between two to six undergraduate students and one academic developer from the University's Center for the Advancement of Teaching and Learning. Teams usually meet every week for between one to three months, which is important for building trust and ensuring students realise their views are being taken seriously. In one team, the students were involved in choosing a new text book for the course, and when they realised that their negative reviews of some of the possible books were not objected to by staff, it was a key moment for students in sensing that their views were considered legitimate contributions to constructive educational discussions

(Mihans et al. 2008; Bovill 2014; Cook-Sather et al. 2014)

In our broad definition of curricula, based on Fraser and Bosanquet's definitions we included the students' learning experiences. This is a wide net that captures a large set of learning and teaching elements. For example, some students are involved in co-designing assessments, such as through designing their own essay title, or choosing between several possible assessment methods (Cook-Sather et al. 2014; O'Neill 2011). And here we see a natural overlap between students as change agents and students as teachers and indeed, this is another element where there is overlap generally between the partnership roles that students can adopt. What is clear is that student involvement in designing elements of both the formative and summative assessment process acknowledges that not only is assessment a key motivator for students (and staff) in higher education, but assessment also has value as an opportunity for learning, not just the measurement of what has been learned – or what we have come to know as assessment *for* learning (Sambell et al. 2012), and as discussed in Chapter 2. We mentioned earlier also that some students are designing their own learning outcomes, and this can have a significant impact on their learning experiences (Orsmond 2004) and therefore can be a meaningful way in which students can contribute to designing their own curricula, and in the process become more engaged, and independent learners.

Activity 6.2

- How have you been actively encouraging students to work with you on the design and planning of your taught sessions and their learning activities?
- How have you sought to invite students to become consultants and project steering group members for major change initiatives in your school/faculty, or institution (and beyond)?

Conclusion

We began this chapter with some statements we often hear from colleagues who express some scepticism about engaging students as partners in learning. We hope we have challenged these views in the ideas and examples we have discussed. There is growing evidence of the benefits of co-creating learning and teaching, whether through students being teachers, scholars or change agents. Many of the benefits appear to be shared by students and staff in terms of an increased level of engagement with learning and teaching; enhanced learning and teaching practices; and an enhanced meta-cognitive understanding of learning and teaching processes (Bovill et al. 2011; Cook-Sather et al. 2014). These benefits are likely to be due in part to opening up the messy processes of learning and teaching and curriculum design to scrutiny by both students and staff, but also to acknowledging the benefits of students and teachers entering into more collaborative relationships where multiple perspectives are valued. In order to develop meaningful collaborative relationships between students and staff, it is crucial to enhance dialogue about learning and teaching. The development of partnership learning communities may be a fruitful way forward in this area (Healey et al. 2014a).

Clearly we are enthusiastic about the potential of this agenda to change the nature of teaching and learning in higher education and we hope that some of you will be inspired to try out some of the ideas we have presented in your own academic practices. Individual staff can make a great difference to the learning experience of students. Consider some small-scale initiatives if you are new to the idea of working in partnership with students, and try to find colleagues in your own or other disciplines who have tried working in partnership with students and who might be able to offer advice and support (Cook-Sather et al. 2014). However, to move this agenda forward, conducive departmental and institutional strategies and structures need to be put in place and it is to some of these that we turn in conclusion.

While individual staff have the 'power' to bring students into their courses as teachers, scholars and change agents, for student partnership to become embedded through the curriculum, high-level leadership and support is needed. Thus, Case study 7: Introducing students to academic staff research at the Department of Geography, University College London, involves all academic staff and reflects strong departmental leadership. Case studies 6: Undergraduate research at induction at University of Gloucestershire and 11: The students as change agents' initiative at the University of Exeter, also require strong leadership and funding at institutional and departmental levels.

Departmental and institutional leaders can develop and embed initiatives that support student partnership approaches through:

- conferences, academic seminars and papers setting out a scholarly vision that shows the importance of such initiatives;
- deciding which initiatives and principles need to be embedded across the institution for all students and which should focus on particular groups of students;
- targeted funding; for example, Miami University, Ohio, supported initiatives in large year one courses to develop an overall vision of the 'student as scholar' (Hodge et al. 2011);

- ensuring that departmental and institutional strategies explicitly support student partnership approaches to curricular design and provide mechanisms through quality assurance and enhancement for ensuring their embedding and effectiveness;
- building into such initiatives strategies that embed and develop student leadership as well as staff leadership;
- researching the impact of student partnership initiatives in ways that also support the vision of students as teachers, scholars and change agents;
- ensuring that policies and practice for staff appraisal and promotion acknowledge and reward staff-student partnerships.

Further discussion and examples of departmental and institutional strategies to promote students as partners may be found in Jenkins and Healey (2005); Jenkins et al. (2007); Healey and Jenkins (2009); Cook-Sather et al. (2014) and Healey et al. (2014a).

Our vision for the future is that it should be the norm, not the exception, that students are engaged as partners in learning as teachers, scholars and change agents and that co-creating, co-designing, co-researching and co-learning should be common practice between students and staff across higher education. Having read this chapter, we leave you to consider how far you share this vision.

We hope that the ideas discussed in this chapter will have stimulated you to talk with your students about ways in which they may become partners in learning and teaching. One of the lessons we have learned is that students often bring fresh ideas of what research into learning and teaching needs to be done. Student and staff perspectives often differ and ideas for research will be richer for including ideas from both students and staff. Together you may find that you can quite quickly design and implement collaborative (often action) research ideas on a whole range of themes (for which your students might also be able to earn some HE credits). For example:

- implementing peer and self-assessment of group work projects;
- giving credit for students to develop teaching resources;
- arranging for first-year students to undertake a short inquiry project as part of induction;
- enabling dissertation students to undertake a wider range of types of project;
- thinking through how progression can be built into research and inquiry projects across your programme;
- employing students as pedagogical consultants;
- engaging students in SoTL projects to enhance the learning and teaching in their courses;
- inviting students to co-design courses, assessments and learning outcomes.

Students as partners is a rapidly growing area of interest in higher education. Some reviews which will give you a good coverage of the subject include: Cook-Sather et al.

(2014), Dunne and Owen (2013), and Healey et al. (2014a). For students as scholars, you will find a comprehensive discussion of the topic and an international collection of case studies in Healey and Jenkins (2009), Healey et al. (2013), Healey et al. (2014b), and Jenkins et al. (2007). To keep up to date with new developments, see the regularly updated resources at: www.mickhealey.co.uk/resources and the Students as Partners pages of the HEA website: www.heacademy.ac.uk/students-as-partners.

Activity 6.3

- In what ways have you been active in seeking to enable students to be involved in co-developing their own modules/course and or learning outcomes?
- How have you been actively seeking to involve students at committee/ strategy/QA level within your school/faculty, or institution (or beyond)?

Opinion Piece, Debate, Dear Lecturer, and Fellowship Application extracts

In the following opinion piece, Colin Bryson reflects on his involvement in student engagement projects and the creation of the RAISE network (Researching, Advancing and Inspiring Student Engagement). And in the debate, Frank Furedi and Mike Neary examine the authority of the HE teacher in the light of the increased involvement of students as partners in learning. To finish, Sam Louis, a recent graduate from Newcastle University, reflects on the chapter overall. This is followed by three extracts from successful HEA fellowship applicants who discuss some of the aspects of academic practice which feature in this chapter.

Opinion: On Researching, Advancing and Inspiring Student Engagement (RAISE)

Engaging students for transformation: ways forward

Colin Bryson

It came as a bit of a surprise to me this year to realise that it has been 40 years since I began my own journey in Higher Education as an undergraduate studying Mathematical Physics; a choice I soon regretted! That journey has had many twists and turns, and ups and downs but it's been a privilege to work as an educator in one guise or other for 35 years. Initially my understanding of learning and teaching (L&T) was limited and naïve but working with more experienced colleagues who were generous with their advice helped, but also made me realise how important community was, a safe place where I could take some risks, trying out innovations and learning from times when things did not go so well. I participated in a large number of events, and many of these have been of the nature of exemplars of good practice and innovation. I started to realise that the educational process was more important than the content.

However, the real breakthrough in my thinking was when I was charged with increasing independent learning across a large school – I will gloss over the senior management thinking behind this initiative! I was wary about this idea and decided to ask the students. So working with Len Hand, we conducted focus groups across a broad range of students. Really for the first time, I listened properly to the student's voices – it was a revelation. What the students talked about was their engagement – or rather lack of it – with their course and wider experience. Back in 2003, almost nobody in the UK was really aware about student engagement, with few if any studies and little scholarship about this. Our first dissemination to a wider audience was at the SEDA conference in 2005 where we received a lot of interest and an invitation to publish the paper (Bryson and Hand 2007). We got a lot of encouragement from colleagues and the HEA and embarked on a much deeper, longitudinal study over a four-year period.

Around this time the notion of student engagement really started to catch on, and the three of us (we had been joined by Christine Hardy) were much in demand to give seminars and workshops about this topic. As our scholarship of the issues and ideas increased, we became aware of a large body of existing work in the rest of the world, where there had been considerable interest, and research, in student engagement for much longer. I was fortunate enough to present at conferences abroad and have direct discussions with leading experts which helped to shape my ideas and refine my understanding. Our longitudinal study was just unfolding and we focused on transitions into HE. I went to the 2009 European First Year Conference and met a group of enthusiastic colleagues. It was here that the Researching, Advancing and Inspiring Student Engagement network was born. It did not have a name at that time (it was my 16-year-old daughter who created that), but it was just an idea. A few months later, four of us met to plan a first meeting and, in May 2010, we held a one-day symposium in Nottingham with the ambitious agenda of developing a definition and conceptual framework for student engagement, as well as a basis for how our network could operate. We created the website (http://raise-network.ning.com/) and held the first conference in 2011. The following year, the network became an organisation with a formal constitution and officers. We have continued with two-day annual conferences. These have now grown in scale as has RAISE. At the time of writing there were over 700 members from 15 countries. In 2013, special interest groups (SIGS) were created and this is already leading to a rather larger number of events to add to the conference and seminars RAISE has held. A particular feature of RAISE is the direct involvement of current students. They contribute to, and participate in all the events, e.g. 40 per cent of the conference delegates in 2014 were students, mainly undergraduates.

Based on the outcomes of my own and other studies, and discussion with RAISE members, I have produced a definition of engagement and, after considerable reflection, decided that there is no single conceptual framework that applies to this complex, multi-construct (Bryson 2014). I contend that student engagement (SE) underpins, not only a good student experience, but transformative learning and developing a sense of, and achieving 'graduateness'. These are the true purposes of higher education. Therefore, we, as educators, should put SE at the heart of everything we do.

I moved to a different post in 2008, and took over a combined degree where the students studied multiple subjects. Their engagement with the course and critical social domain, was low, in large part because their sense of identity and belonging was weak – much to their frustration. I was able to introduce a holistic SE strategy and have worked very much in partnership in students to do that. That has seemed to create a rather better student experience and many students who demonstrate *strong* engagement. I believe that the partnership approach has been the catalyst for these students to feel that they can take risks and move outside their comfort zones. I am researching the 'how' of this at the moment and how to enhance this across diverse students and contexts.

The HE sector now seems to have embraced student engagement in large measure, in policy and in practice. This has ratcheted up the general quality of the student experience. I am less sure that more than a handful of students are developing the type of deep and strong engagement that leads to transformation and really gaining all they can – 'becoming' (Fromm, 1977). Therefore, I believe that our goal should be to foster that through revitalising the curriculum and building partnership learning communities (Healey et al. 2014a). It is a very challenging goal but even trying to move towards that is so worthwhile for both students and staff.

Debate: On the authority of the HE teacher

Academic authority in higher education

Frank Furedi

Learning in any educational environment requires trust in the authority of the teacher. Learning, within the sphere of higher education requires that students rely on the integrity and the authority of their teacher. Though university students are expected to be independent learners and ideally engaged in an interactive partnership with academics, education still sometimes requires a leap of faith which people only undertake if they trust and accept the authority of the educator.

Authority is a difficult concept and is often wrongly confused with authoritarian behaviour. Often authority is also one-sidedly interpreted as the role and influence exerted by an individual who is 'in authority', that is officially designated as in charge of a classroom or institution. However, being in authority does not mean possessing the capacity to behave authoritatively and to exercise authority. Authority always rests on a moral foundation and its claim to influence, respect or esteem is far more fundamental than the formal power associated with an office or position. Historically, the term authority, which derives from the Roman word *auctoritas*, was associated with that of the author, as possessing both the capacity to initiate and provide a foundation for knowledge.

In higher education the authority of scholars is founded on their capacity to personify and lend meaning to a particular academic initiative. In a university environment the exercise of this authority is contingent on the nature of the relationship between the academic teacher and the student. Authority is used to facilitate the act of initiating students into the subject. It is the academic who draws up reading lists and course plans. Although students may legitimately attempt to influence the course content, in the end, it requires the authoritative voice of the academic to initiate and give direction to the work of undergraduates.

Ideally, undergraduate students swiftly develop into active participants in their course work, develop a capacity for independent learning and in many cases cultivate a genuine academic partnership with their teacher. Integral to this partnership is the right to contest and question the views of teachers. In such circumstances the authority of an academic can never sit on its laurels but will face the scrutiny of students. In ideal circumstances the criticisms and questions directed at academics will be answered in a manner that strengthens their claim to authority. In instances where the authority of the academic is not upheld, responsibility for the future of a course is placed on the shoulders of students. This unreasonable burden may disrupt the learning of the undergraduates concerned.

In recent years, the professional authority of academics has been undermined – not by questioning students but by the external pressure to formalise and rationalise university life. The growing focus on auditing academic performance and rationalising course content and assessment is motivated by the assumption that, left to their devices, academics will exercise their authority inefficiently if not irresponsibly. One important legacy of the introduction of the auditing culture has been the diminishing importance attached to professional judgement. The de-authorisation of academic judgement risks turning relationships between teachers and students into a technical affair.

In a world of online marking, pre-determined learning outcomes, externally constructed templates and auditing, teaching loses some of its moral force. Promoted as instruments of democratisation and inclusion, these technical changes are often cast in a non-hierarchical form of providing greater scope for the students' voice and the students' experience. However, in practice, these apparently democratic innovations represents a shift from the exercise of authority into unaccountable forms of control.

In the twenty-first-century university, discipline is increasingly perceived as a technical accomplishment. Its focus is on managerial techniques rather than on gaining the identification of students with the aims of their course. Indeed, the techniques of managerial control that are used in the classroom have little to do with education and its aims. Most disturbingly, through its emphasis and reliance on technical manipulation, it avoids a morally informed dialogue between academic and pupil. And as Basil Bernstein reminds us in another context – despite its rejection of hierarchical principles of authority, in practice, the reliance on managerial control is arguably more authoritarian than the open exercise of authority.

For Bernstein, the apparently non-hierarchical educational practices do not do away with control and hierarchy but render it invisible. He argues that invisible pedagogy establishes control through psychological techniques. He describes these as an 'implicit hierarchy', which is one where 'power is masked or hidden by devices of communication' (Bernstein 2003: 67).

The adoption of an invisible pedagogy has encouraged the colonisation of the university by a variety of new administrators and experts. Once an academic's authority became a subject of ambiguity and negotiation, the status and the autonomy of the profession became compromised. Ambivalence about the moral authority of the teacher has led to the introduction of what Foucault characterised as moral techniques – testing, measuring, surveillance and league tables follow. The proliferation of these moral techniques indicates that their introduction is likely to acquire a life of its own. In such circumstances the judgement of the academic teacher is trumped by the verdict of the league table or the opinion survey that purports to convey the sentiments of students. However, the authority vested in the outside authority lacks moral depth and serves to distract academic life from the pursuit of objectives integral to itself.

Trust in education has both an institutional and individual dimension. It presupposes confidence in the institution of education and specifically in the academic profession. For this confidence to be converted into active trust, students need to believe in their lecturers' integrity and capacity to educate them. Trust is based on a subjective assessment of the character and personality of the individual academic. It is through a subjective relation of trust that authority ceases to be a formal or official designation and acquires its moral force. Authority which in general gives meaning to power in the context of classroom offers academics the moral force to inspire belief.

Debate: On the authority of the HE teacher

Student as producer: authority and authorship in authoritarian times

Mike Neary

Higher education is not against academic authority; but is *contra* to academic authoritarianism: teaching based on a deficiency model of student capacities, or teaching which sees its prime role to transmit knowledge. Academic authoritarianism inflects teaching with over-explanation, leaving little space for critical intelligence to emerge.

Academic authoritarianism is antithetical to higher education, where students learn methods and methodologies, including theoretical understandings, to discover the world for themselves; and, in the process, create new knowledge and meaning. Higher education is saturated with content, presented to students for repurposing inside and outside of the curriculum. Higher education is full of explanation, but its explanations are non-dogmatic, open to the possibility of other explainings which may be counter-intuitive and contradictory.

Authority resides in higher education as the academic, who represents the subject discipline, and in the student, whose independent and collective intelligence has yet to be realised. Both student and teacher, each in their own way, have an important contribution to make to the production of knowledge and meaning, as well as understanding and representing the world to itself and to others.

This approach to teaching and learning in higher education is derived from the question: what are universities for? The first modern European university, the University of Berlin, founded in 1812, was conceived as a liberal humanist institution against the dogmatic scholastic medieval university, so that knowledge would now be created at the level of society, as a general encyclopaedia, to resolve the contradiction between knowledge for its own sake and instrumental (vocational) learning. The pedagogical principle on which this vision was based was the connection of research and teaching, with seminars replacing lectures as the main form of teaching. Students were to be directly involved in the speculative thinking of their tutors, in a Socratic dialogue, without strictly planned courses and curricula. Students should work in research communities with time for thinking and without any practical obligations.

This philosophical and idealistic purpose of this kind of knowledge production was undermined by the student revolts in 1968 in Paris, France, and around the world. These student revolts challenged not only the elitism of knowledge production, but the nature of knowledge itself. In this moment students became more than students, revealing the catastrophe of the liberal humanist project through a recovery of revolutionary theory, e.g., Marxism, Feminism, and practical political campaigns, e.g., Anti-war and Free love, in a movement of resistance where research became something that anyone can do. This movement of resistance is still being played out in student agitation and repressed by an increasingly authoritarian-militarised-violent Police-State. An important aspect of the student revolt was the introduction of the independent student research project as a central feature of higher education.

The University of Berlin in 1812 and the student uprisings of 1968 were grounded in the same problematic: the relationship between research and teaching. This is the key to higher education and remains its central preoccupation. In the current context, the relationship between research and teaching is dysfunctional, with each activity working against the other.

This dysfunctionality is exemplified in British universities by two main strategies for the regulation of academic life: the National Student Survey, which measures teaching quality, and the Research Excellence Framework, which assesses the quality of academic research. While each policy instrument has been subject to devastating academic review, taken together, they represent the bifurcation of the distinguishing foundational feature of higher education: the connection between teaching and research. This disconnection is framed around a narrow instrumental purpose for higher education, based on the promotion of students as consumers, students as proto-employees and the pedagogy of debt. This emphasis on a market-based approach to higher education is occurring at a time when the market-based model for debt-driven social development is in crisis, following the Great Crash of 2008.

Student as Producer is an attempt to reconsider the core purpose of higher education by reconnecting its central features, research and teaching, as a model of curriculum development. Student as Producer has been the organising principle for teaching and learning at the University of Lincoln since 2010 across all subjects and all course levels.

Academics at Lincoln are challenged and invited to consider the consequences of introducing research-based teaching to their own pedagogic practice: this means including research and research-like activities as a fundamental aspect of student learning, involving students in the design and delivery of teaching, setting out the learning environment to support research-based teaching through classroom design and learning technologies, and to develop curriculum activities whereby students can create the future: encouraging students to see themselves as subjects rather than as object of history.

In a recent project evaluation, students and staff at Lincoln were very positive about Student as Producer: students see the benefits of research-based teaching for their learning, earning and living. Staff acknowledged the institutional support to develop participatory and engaged approaches to higher education, with a recognition of the dynamic creative tension between Student as Producer and the market-friendly imperative of higher education policy. Student as Producer has been taken up and adopted by other universities and is at the heart of current initiatives to present Student as Partners across the sector.

While the success of Student as Producer is very encouraging, it is important to remember its radical credentials. Student as Producer has traces of the progressive idealists who founded the University of Berlin, to establish knowledge at the level of society, but is more grounded in the revolutionary politics of May '68, when the authority for knowledge production is based on a collaboration between academics, students and workers grounded in the challenges of everyday life.

The slogan 'Student as Producer', is based on a paper, 'Author as Producer', written by Walter Benjamin (1892–1940), the Marxist social theorist, and delivered to the Society of Anti-Fascists in Paris in 1934. The question for the paper was, how do radical intellectuals act in a moment of crisis? Benjamin's solution was to transform the social relations of production, based on human needs and capacities rather than profit, to ensure that intellectual workers see themselves as the subjects of history, able to recognise themselves in a world of their own design. While the circumstances of our current predicament are different from the 1930s, there are enough similarities to be very concerned about the future. While the future cannot be future-proofed or guaranteed, an important corrective against the Police-State and other forms of authoritarianism is that our students have the capacity to claim authority and authorship for their own lives and the social world which has yet to be made.

Dear Lecturer

On letting me be responsible for my learning

Sam Louis

Having had the opportunity to take part in a module where student and teacher were 'partners' in co-designing the structure and syllabus for the year, I can honestly say was one of the most stressful, confusing and alienating experiences I have ever undertaken. And by far the most rewarding.

A rough module outline was presented at the beginning of the year, within which we had the freedom to propose how we wanted to be assessed, when the assessments should be, how much they should be worth to our overall grade, almost everything was malleable. With three staff members and 20-odd students, this led to an awful lot of discussion and deliberation. Throughout the beginning of the year I consistently had little to no idea what was expected of me, what I was meant to do, how I was meant to do it or if I was even vaguely on the right track. Without being spoon-fed objectives and criteria, I was drowning, incapacitated by fear of making a wrong move. It was long since the halfway point of the module had passed before I began to realise that I just had to take responsibility and decide for myself. I was forced to engage with the material and with the syllabus, and determine what it was that I wanted from the module, and, by association, from HE itself. It made me realise how little thought or research I had put into the modules I chose, aside from the content provided. I just expected to turn up and be provided with material for learning, without ever contemplating what I wanted to gain or improve by taking the module.

I worked harder, and for longer on this module than almost any other I have taken because of the learning curve you had to tackle before you even started your work, and consequently I produced some of the work that I am most proud of. I understood more and grew far more than at any other point in my university career and it completely opened up my other courses, as I started to look at them from a far broader standpoint and see the possibilities each held as an opportunity to learn, explore and experiment.

I don't think that all modules should be jointly managed, and I also think that student participation in such schemes should be gradually introduced as the student progresses through HE. It is very difficult to be thrown in the deep end of qualifying marking criteria and assessment objectives and make any sense of what to do, without just resorting to form and suggesting exactly what you did on another module. But if gradually introduced, with increasing levels of control and participation given to students over the course of their studies, I think that it is a fantastically worthwhile undertaking. Why? Because you become aware of your own individual self-development and the need to take responsibility for it. More importantly, you become truly integrated in your learning. Not with the university through a team or society, but with your own personal process of learning, as you start to question and figure out the nature of your personal project, and to properly answer the question of why you have come to university.

Extracts from successful HEA fellowship applications

Dr Orange (FHEA)

I have designed formative simulated crime scene practicals which allow students to gain compulsory professional skills, such as communication, time management, documentation and organisation skills. Students are placed into small groups and are provided with details of a crime that has been committed within the forensic house. After having had the opportunity to assign their roles within the group, they would then set about to collect, preserve, document and package evidence from the simulated crime scene. Within this co-operative learning environment (Brown and Ciuffetelli 2009), students are encouraged to feedback to the rest of the group by filling in a proforma at the end of the session detailing how each evidence type was processed. They would then present to the rest of the group how they went about completing tasks within their specific role, and, more importantly, they would be able to reflect back on their actions individually and jointly as a group (Weinberger, et al. 2007).

I have found that using a proforma alone does not necessarily make the students feel that they have gained any immediate feedback from the lecturer, so I devote some time to questioning students about what they have recorded on their proforma and asking them for explanations. I have found that students do enjoy this form of assessment; however, they have commented that they would prefer to get direct feedback whilst they are carrying out the practical. Realistically they cannot be continuously disturbed with feedback, so I decided to film students while they are completing the practical within their group. This is a tool which has already been used in other disciplines to facilitate learning (Nilsen and Baerheim 2005). This way the students can view back the footage, carry out self-assessment using a proforma and then this can be discussed with the lecturer at the end of the session. Students will need to consent to being filmed as part of the ethical approval process, and if they are happy for the footage to be used for other purposes, then there is potential

to use it at university open days and to encourage college students to consider a career within forensic science [K5, K4, V1, V2].

Ms White (PFHEA)

I consider the students co-producers in their learning (McCulloch 2009) and design the curriculum to be sufficiently fluid to enable them to develop their voice (Barnett and Coate 2005). I continue to refine my pedagogic practices, so that the students experience vibrant and challenging learning and I try to develop their critical literacy by providing reflective space for them to question their context and assumptions (Andreotti 2006). I vary the format of each session, including small group work, an element of whole-group input, the opportunity to visit schools and see the theory in the actual setting, practical activities to illustrate experiential learning, concepts such as leadership and work with elements including interactive dialogue sheets, podcasts and film. My module evaluations comment positively on the range of teaching strategies I use, my enthusiasm for the topic and for teaching, and students feel that their contributions are valued, forming an integral and important component. I include group tutorials part-way through the module to support students to begin their assignments, and individual tutorials to discuss work on a one-to-one basis. I have introduced a personalised feedback strategy, whereby the students choose whether they would like face-to-face feedback, audio feedback, written feedback via coversheets or emailed feedback. Student evaluations suggest that this initiative has been positively received.

Dr Blue (PFHEA)

It is because of my strong views on the need to link staff and student engagement that I launched the faculty 'teaching' prize when I became Associate Dean. This prize is awarded to the top four staff in the faculty, based on student votes. The students are asked to say a few words to support their vote and this feedback is sent to staff who receive votes, to encourage them to continue good practice. This also helps us to assess which aspects of their teaching and learning students most appreciate across the faculty. Both staff and students are very engaged in this process, and this is further enhanced by my decision to award the official prizes at the graduation ceremonies, including a quote or two from the students. We display the winners on the screens in the Business School on a regular basis, to reinforce the importance of excellence in teaching. The major strategic aim of this initiative was to enhance the profile of teaching in the faculty, and as a vehicle to share good practice. NSS scores have increased on many programmes, particularly in the Business School, though I fully appreciate that this will be due to multiple factors I do believe that emphasising the importance of teaching has helped.

7

The landscape of higher education

John Lea

Some of the places delivering higher education these days, you couldn't call them universities, could you?

Well, we've got to pass everyone these days; look at the money they're paying, and they'll only complain if they fail, won't they?

Some of the courses we've got here now; I mean, really, we're just a training institute now, aren't we?

Introduction

What are universities for? Asking the question so starkly is revealing on many levels. First, surely, it is obvious what they are for, but if they do many things, maybe the question is really asking whether there is one core activity which unites all those things. Second, maybe the question implies the need to reconsider what universities do, that is, that they should be doing something else; that they have somehow lost their way. And third, perhaps the question is badly phrased because the word 'university' implies a place – a set of buildings – and is that inference a helpful one? This chapter deals with these questions, with the aim of prompting debate and reflection on our roles as academic practitioners in helping to shape the present and future landscape of higher education provision and its role in society.

The chapter has an obvious structure: a look at the past and what can be learnt from that; a look at the present reform agenda and some of its implications; and a look at the future in order to assess the direction of travel. As with all the previous chapters, the main focus will be on the role of teaching and learning in the changing landscape of higher education and the ways that we are both shaped by, and able to shape, that landscape. For the last time we will also meet up with Professor K.G. Reason and Dr M. Bracewell, who will be offering their views on what is presented.

A (very) short history of UK universities

To start, here is a short quiz, which requires you to resist the obvious temptation to look up the answers as you go:

1   By 1335, how many universities were there in England?

2   By 1835, how many universities were there in England?

3   By 1860, how many universities were there in the UK?

4   By 1963, how many universities were there in the UK?

5   By 1992, how many universities were there in the UK?

6   By 2010, how many universities were there in the UK?

7   What percentage of UK 18-year-olds went to university in 1975 (roughly)?

8   What percentage of UK 18–30-year-olds were expected to go to university in 2010?

Unless you are an expert on the history of universities, you might be quite surprised by how far out your answers are. When I did some checking (including on that well-known website) I discovered that the answer to the first one (not that surprisingly) was two – Oxford (circa 1167) and Cambridge (circa 1209). But much more surprisingly (to me anyway) was that 500 years later there only seemed to be three more universities – The University of Manchester (circa 1826), the University of Durham (circa 1832), and the colleges making up the University of London (established between 1826 and 1836). And it's not at all clear that any of these would in any way resemble the institutions we know today. If we then jump forward a few decades, and include the other parts of the UK, we still only get less than a dozen institutions using a university title, including, in Scotland: St Andrews (circa 1411), Glasgow (circa 1450), Aberdeen (circa 1494), and Edinburgh (circa 1583); and then, in Ireland, Belfast (circa 1845). Colleges making up the University of Wales were established throughout the nineteenth century. Jump again 100 years to 1963 and that figure has only just doubled – if we exclude those being built at the time (see below), and jump again to 1992 and it's still only doubled one more time – leaving the UK with still fewer than 50 universities (if each college of the Universities of London and Wales are disaggregated, the number grows by another dozen or so).

The years referred to in questions 4, 5 and 6 were chosen to correspond with three important reform documents. The 1963 Robbins Report spoke of the importance of public investment in building new (latterly called glass-plated) universities – including, for example, what became the Universities of Kent, Warwick, and York – to complement those ancient ones mentioned above and the newer civic (or red brick) universities which had been built in the Victorian period – including, for example, Leeds, Birmingham, and Sheffield (Robbins Report 1963). The 1992 Further and Higher Education Act which abolished the binary divide between universities and polytechnics, allowing all higher education institutions (HEIs) to apply for university status, and abolished the University Grants Committee (UGC) – which had funded universities – and established in its place new competitive funding bodies for each of the UK nations, to which all universities (old and new) would be able to apply for funds (DFE 1992). And 2010 saw the publication of the Browne Report (Browne Review of HE 2010), subsequently followed by the Government White Paper (BIS White Paper 2011), which not only recommended a fundamentally new way of funding teaching and learning in universities (primarily through full cost student fees) but also encouraged new providers to apply for degree-awarding powers – including private providers and further education colleges.

Depending on which definition of a university is used (i.e. those strictly with university in their title or all HEIs), the answer to question 7 can vary between around 115 to 170 institutions. But the point I wish to make here is that it was only after 1992 that the growth of universities in the UK could be considered to have started to become exponential. Indeed, if we take the higher figure from 1992 (around 60) and compare it with the lowest figure from 2014 (115) the number of universities has still only just doubled again. Of course, the time period in which the doubling is occurring is shrinking considerably (down to 20 odd years, from the 500 years of the first comparison), and this is how we have arrived at the total figure for HEIs we now have (which I am guessing is closer to the figure that many people might have considered to be the case for 100 years ago).

Another way to consider the nature of the growth pattern is to look at the percentage of full-time students attending universities. In the mid-1970s it was roughly 10–13 per cent (of 18–24-year-olds), up from around 8 per cent at the time of the Robbins Report in 1963. Which, when compared with the (then) Prime Minister Tony Blair's pronouncement in 1999 of a commitment to having a participation rate of 50 per cent by 2010, it points to the fact that a radical revolution was beginning to replace a quiet evolution, notwithstanding the astute observation at the time that: 'Although British higher education is (quantitatively) mass, it is still (qualitatively) elite' (Scott 2003), and the subtle change in the definition of participation rate. As it turned out, the newly defined participation rate (18–30-year-olds with an experience of higher education) never actually hit 50 per cent but it has been consistently over 40 per cent for the last ten years or so, which is more than enough to qualify for the label of a 'mass' system of higher education, which Martin Trow defined as a participation rate between 15 per cent and 50 per cent – below and above those figures being 'elite' and 'universal' respectively (Trow 2010).

Prof. Reason: This is all very well, but somebody has got to stand up at some point and ask the politically incorrect question of why we need 50 per cent of the population to go to the university. Before you know it, you'll need a degree to be a plumber. And if you work in a university, it's plain to those who are honest enough to admit it, that standards are falling. How can 50 per cent of the population achieve the standard that 10 per cent were achieving only a generation ago? It just doesn't make sense. And even worse, it's no secret any more that lecturers are being put under pressure to mark student work leniently. And why? Because departments can't afford to lose students; because universities want to advertise the number of 2:1s that students achieve; and individual lecturers just write kind things on student assignments because they think they should be either massaging their fragile egos, or they don't want to have to deal with student complaints. Widening participation is a farce and I just don't understand why more people don't speak out against it.

Dr Bracewell: Why do you seem to have no empathy with those students whom you must know have come to university as non-traditional learners or as first generation entrants? Are you really against giving people opportunities? It's not their fault they don't have the cultural capital that the privileged 10 per cent have always had. And I'll tell you the real reason why the number of 2:1s has risen, it's because university teachers are now more than ever much more mindful about how they support student learning, and they don't want to lose students they know could excel if they tailored that support to fit their circumstances. And what you call 'kind' feedback in reality is simply comments aimed at helping students do better in the next assignment. And anyway, what's to be gained by not being kind? The real problem is not widening participation, but why people like yourself want to defend, perhaps unwittingly, social class privilege and elitism and then associate learner support with some kind of misplaced therapy for the masses, or just plain cheating – and there's just no real evidence to support either claim.

However you define participation in higher education (for example, whether you just include achieving an honours degree in a traditional university, or extend it to include, say, dropping out of an HND course in a further education college), it is clear that participation rates have grown enormously. Indeed, there are now as many students studying on higher education courses in further education colleges as there were studying throughout the whole of higher education provision at the time of the Robbins Report. But increasing participation is not the same as widening participation and because of that we now have detailed data on, for example, the changing social class, gender, race and ethnic, age, and disability profile of students in all universities and on particular courses (available for view on an annual basis from the Higher Education Statistical Agency (HESA) website).

Prof. Reason: I must follow up here with another important politically incorrect point. It's one thing to monitor these variables, it's quite another to deliberately act on them. If we want to maintain standards, surely we must only let students into university based on their ability – as measured by their A Level results. And while it's lovely to see lots of students from different backgrounds on campus, it's surely up to the students to decide where to study, not for us to try and engineer a particular type of student profile. That's just a sure-fire route to political correctness gone mad, and as we've seen in the United States, it will inevitably result in some high flying students complaining that their places have been taken by other less able students just because their faces fit the type of profile that the university wants.

Dr Bracewell: Now you're bordering on being offensive, and demonstrating just how completely out of touch you are. For a start, why are you still stuck on the idea of an A Level grade being the gold standard? There are many different ways in which students can demonstrate their abilities and their readiness to benefit from higher education. And all students benefit from a wide student profile on campus. Indeed, the whole place will be enriched because of the mix of students. Students learn from each other as much as what they are taught by lecturers. Indeed, lecturers like you might learn a thing or two if you just listened once in a while! How do you think the curriculum is going to be enhanced if each generation of students is just the same as the previous generation, which then just goes on to produce the same-looking professoriate?

Activity 7.1

- In what ways have you been involved in actively monitoring the student profile on the courses/programmes you teach and/or support learning?
- What strategies have you been involved in which has sought to change the student profile of your faculty/school, or institution (and/or beyond)?

But are students today actually entering very different types of intuitions compared with students even one generation ago? The answer is complicated in part by the increasing numbers and the changing profile of the students – which varies from institution to institution and course to course. But also by the fact that some of the institutions didn't exist as higher education providers one generation ago, and some of them may be providing a very particular type of higher education, for example, technical vocational HE on a foundation degree (which didn't exist as a qualification a generation ago).

Furthermore, one of the implications of establishing the new funding councils in 1992 was to shift funding in the direction of universities meeting specific targets in order to receive their funding. This enabled successive governments to dangle carrots and sticks at universities in order to engineer not just a wider student profile, but also to provide particular types of courses (ones which are vocationally more relevant, for example). These social engineering projects were given a new twist in the 2011 White Paper which, in the interests of putting students at the heart of the system, now require universities to supply annual data for a Key Information Set (KIS), which includes, for example, data on the percentage of their graduates in employment (HESA 2014). The combined effect of these changes has been to erode the ability of universities to decide – autonomously – the nature of their provision and their student profile. Or perhaps more accurately, if they wish to continue to act completely autonomously, it has put pressure on them to seek alternative sources of funding, and/or risk losing the confidence of regulatory agencies, and/or potentially risk losing students to rival universities.

The previous two paragraphs highlight that there have been both endogenous and exogenous factors at work over the past twenty years or so. In some cases, where for example, a particular institution wanted to widen its student profile anyway, the relevant carrots and sticks could be seen as complementary. But some of the forces have been viewed as antagonistic or contradictory. For example, Stefan Collini has been vociferous in defending the liberal tradition in universities (specifically the humanities), which he sees as being undermined by the biggest social engineering project of the State, namely, to see universities primarily as engines of economic growth, ignoring in the process the role of knowledge as a public good, aimed at widening and deepening understanding and valuing that knowledge for its own sake (Collini 2012). And, in a more overtly political context, we might also say that there is an important difference here between *really* useful knowledge (Johnson 1979) and *merely* useful knowledge, the former being aimed at enabling disadvantaged groups to understand their circumstances so that they could then change them, rather than just being accommodated to them. Clearly, what it means for higher education to be experienced as *transformative* has multiple meanings and dimensions.

Dear Lecturer

On HE as transformative

Diane Locke

I am a single mother, 43 years old, with two children, studying a full-time degree course in Youth and Community Work. When I came to university, I nursed anxiety from my schooldays. The labels and assumptions people had of me back then were still present within me. We had tasks to do, group work, presentations and speaking to the group about our values, which for me was difficult. I could not see at the beginning of the course where I could find any value from my past life.

Through transitions and perseverance I was able to dissect my past life, transferring it into positive attributes and a framework that I could use to enhance my understanding. With this new vision I became me again, but reawakened, with eyes that could see new things, that in the past I was too blind or scared to see. I can feel my strength without egoistical tendencies, and at the same time I recognise my limits and weakness. My ability to make mistakes and to learn from them, without anxiety, has been crucial in this development.

I struggled with the language of academia. I feel uncomfortable quoting theories and speaking rhetoric, yet when I write it flows fluidly. This is because I have learnt that I value who I am, where I have emerged from and what I represent for my community. That the way I speak and talk is entwined with every piece of flesh and bone in my existence of class and gender.

So here I am, now, in my third year and thinking 'how the hell did this happen?' and wondering whether the person who writes this way is even me any more. But then I speak and I realise all is not lost, she is still here and now she has learnt what her voice can achieve, she does not want to go back into the silent shadows of her previous existence.

In the 1990s, Ron Barnett in the UK, and Bill Readings in the USA both questioned whether universities, largely of their own accord, had lost their way, requiring a reconsideration of what exactly was their way, and what might be the way forward. These questions were prompted not so much by the narrower political and economic agendas of successive governments, but by wider social and cultural movements, including, particularly, post-modern ideas which questioned some of the ontological and epistemological foundations on which universities had traditionally established themselves, chiefly, the notion of rational, autonomous individuals using human reason to shine a light on the discovery of truth, and the enhancement of humanity (Kant [1784] 2009). (Some of these issues were discussed in Chapter 5 and we will return to them again at the end of this chapter.)

The current reform agenda

Given the very positive way in which many colleges and universities have embraced the idea of students as partners in learning (see Chapter 6), one might have expected the idea of placing students at the heart of the system to be a natural complement. In reality, it has provoked enormous debate and discussion, the essence of which might be summarised in the contrast between the student as producer and the student as consumer of knowledge. For Neary and Winn (2009), the idea of a student as a consumer of knowledge is completely at odds with the idea of a university as a place where students and staff work cooperatively and collaboratively on producing knowledge. As we saw in Chapter 3, this is also in keeping with the idea of the university as espoused by von Humboldt:

> The relationship between teacher and learner is ... completely different in higher education from what it is in schools. At the higher level, the teacher is not there for the sake of the student, both have their justification in the service of scholarship.
> (von Humboldt [1810] 1970, quoted by Elton 2008: 225)

This notion has also been axial throughout all the previous parts of this book. Here the idea of 'schooling' speaks to that strictly pedagogical relationship between teacher and pupil, where the former is the font of wisdom demanding that the latter sits at his or her feet. Indeed, the very architecture of the university lecture theatre cements this in the mind of the former school pupil as soon as they enter the university. And this is what prompted von Humboldt to further comment that we should see the seminar room rather than the lecture theatre as the axial knowledge context for a university (see Chapter 4 in particular).

But in what ways does the current reform agenda actually undermine these ideas? Although the 2011 White Paper contained a number of significant reforms, the headline-grabbing 'university students to pay £9,000 annual fees from September 2012' was the one whose implications have been most discussed. In reality, colleges and universities can charge up to that figure – there being several triggers at work in deciding on a lower figure, and, of course, this is very much an English reform. But the key point was that students (in England at least) would (in essence and for most courses) now be paying the full tuition cost for their degrees. For some commentators, this has been enough to prompt the claim that even if students didn't see themselves as consumers before, that this would certainly focus their minds on what exactly they would be purchasing with that money. Added to that, if we look at the Key Information Set (KIS), we can see that a number of its components concern the purchase price of goods and services associated with being at college or university (HESA 2014). Furthermore, the implied association that more contact teaching hours is a positive thing may well heighten the sense that it is what students receive from teachers which is at the heart of the university experience, not what they, themselves, invest in their studies. Further evidence of this mindset might also be gleaned from the National Student Survey (NSS) questions, the majority of which are about what teachers have done for students and not how students have engaged in their own learning (see Chapter 3).

> The full list of NSS questions is available here: http://www.thestudentsurvey.com/content/nss2012_questionnaire_english.pdf (accessed 19 Nov. 2014).

But does this mean that the idea of consumerism is somehow anathema to the whole notion of being a student at university? Clearly, unless student accommodation is going to run as a kind of workers' co-operative, and the university bookshop is going to give away all its books, and the coffee shop is to provide free coffee, we will continue to see forms of 'commodification' on campus – where a good or service will be bought in exchange for money. Furthermore, if competition for high achieving students continues, we will surely see a mirroring of the student service arms race often spoken about in the USA, where institutions 'gild' their campuses in the hope that prospective students will be seduced by all the bling on offer. But it could also be argued that these developments are as much to do with wider social forces than just the activities of university estates managers. In this context, George Ritzer has written about the need for universities to positively embrace the idea that they are 'cathedrals of consumption', or perhaps better, take steps to become more 'spectacularly irrational' for fear that they will become hopelessly out of touch with these broader trends, and thereby possibly lose all credibility with young people as places to be seen (Ritzer 2001).

> *Prof. Reason*: This is all very well, and I can buy some of this (excuse my pun). But I'm really not sure that I want my department to resemble the local shopping mall, and I really don't see anything wrong with first years hanging on every word spoken in the lecture theatre – after all, we are the font of all wisdom, on our subjects, at least. But I do rather like this idea of students being prepared for the seminars and actually contributing something. How many times has a seminar just turned into another one of my lectures? Come to think of it, it's every one of them.

Dr Bracewell: Well, I want to look at this from a different angle. How do you know that your students are actually enjoying their lectures and learning something in them? And if they're not, maybe that explains why they don't do anything in your seminars? All contact time with students should be aimed at enhancing their learning and I'm not seeing any evidence from you that you are really that interested in that. And when you say 'shopping mall', I think you're just being deliberately facetious. There really isn't anything wrong with making the campus look more appealing. Creating café-style social spaces is actually good for learning. And, anyway, if that's what students want, that's what we should provide.

Activity 7.2

- In what ways have you been involved in extending learning beyond the classroom and making use of social space?
- In what ways have you been involved in seeking to balance the need to provide an appealing campus environment for students while maintaining some of the more traditional academic conventions?

The reforms which followed the Browne Report in 2010 may have heightened the sense of students being consumers of educational products, but the broader notion of universities and colleges competing for those students in an educational marketplace has been felt for some considerable time. Indeed, in countries like the United States, it might be argued to have been a core feature of higher education provision since the inception of each institution. In the UK, the idea that public service provision would be more efficient if provided in the marketplace was given its most significant ideological and legislative backing with the election of Margaret Thatcher as prime minister in 1979. And the two key political and economic pillars of Thatcherism have had clear effects on the university sector in the UK. The first of these emphasised how State control of the production and distribution of goods and services was the road to bureaucratic inefficiency and waste (and ultimately a road to serfdom) (Hayek 1944), and the second emphasised that individuals know best how to spend their own money (and that people should be free to choose) (Friedman and Friedman 1980). The added dimension was the general distrust at the time (particularly among Conservative government ministers) of public sector professionals, who seemed to be more concerned with their own welfare than that of their clients and therefore needed to be called to heel through more transparent forms of accountability (overseen, as it turned out, by State-backed quangos and watchdogs).

Aside from the direct cuts to university funding (recouped to some extent by the subsequent Labour administrations, headed by Tony Blair), the broad effects on universities of these reforms was a curtailment of the universities to act as autonomous bodies, and to seek State funding based on their own decisions about its need. At no point in this period was any decision taken to actually privatise universities (only the University of Buckingham was considered a completely private institution), in which case the term 'marketisation' became a blanket term to indicate the general direction in the movement of reform. For example, the funding councils established in 1992, along with ending the binary divide between universities and polytechnics, created a distinct sense that universities were now seriously competing for funds. The establishment of the RAE in 1986 and the QAA in 1997 also created clear mechanisms of public accountability, along with the subsequent channelling of funds to those who were kite-marked as market leaders on the basis of success in those processes.

One broader trend, which has been bolstered by the revisions to the original RAE in becoming the REF, has been to cement the heightened sense that the knowledge being generated through research activity is itself a commodity (Holmwood 2011). There are two distinct ways in which this particular trend is being felt. First, the idea of knowledge having an impact by being 'near market'; that is, not blue skies thinking, but a marketable innovation. And, second, that these 'knowledge products' be viewed as having the potential to be a much-needed source of income for a university. Here, the university is no longer an incubator of ideas, but a supplier of products; no longer working *with* companies, it is a company itself, protecting its copyright, and attempting to profit from its patented products. It might also be argued that 'generating impact' is actually quite a long way from the idea of the 'curious mind', and, as we saw in Chapter 3, the latter is beginning to sound rather quaint as a consequence. They also resonate with Marx's depiction of capitalism in Volume I of *Das Kapital*; that is, you know that capitalism has taken hold when money has become the purpose of exchange and not just the means of exchange (i.e. C-M-C –commodity-money-commodity – becomes M-C-M – money-commodity-more money) (Marx [1867] 1974).

Do these reforms have obvious impacts for learning and teaching? Clearly, they do. For if teaching and learning are to be led by subject-based research and informed by pedagogic research, what are we sharing with our students and asking them to become part of? Perhaps this is, quite literally, a *production* process; where students are learning about how to turn knowledge to economic use; no longer knowledge for its own sake, but 'commodified knowledge'. And is this now the key lesson we are teaching, that is, academic capitalism, with an emphasis on knowledge not just as private property, but also as profitable property? Here we see a stark contrast between the university as a marketplace of ideas, and as a marketplace of commodities. But whether we feel we may have overstepped the mark here must surely depend on how we answered that original question on what we believe universities are for.

Relevant HEA project

Tomlinson, M. (2014) Exploring the impacts of policy changes on student approaches and attitudes to learning in contemporary higher education: implications for student learning engagement. Available at: https://www.heacademy.ac.uk/sites/default/files/resources/Exploring_the_impact_of_policy_changes_student_experience.pdf

Prof. Reason: Well, I can see how all this marketisation would work for the Business School, they all think like that over there anyway. As far as I can see, they are not asking their students to be critical of capitalism, but how to embrace it, and make it work for them. But what about poor old Higgins in biology, slaving over his microscope looking at the sex lives of newts for the last twenty years? What's he got to sell? And old Jenkins in English, busily being vexed by the use of metaphor, or was it simile – never did know the difference. And this is surely the end of all the Marxists round here. On second thoughts, maybe that's no bad thing.

Dr Bracewell: I see your point, but whether we like it or not, this university has been put in this marketplace and we've got to make the most of it. And let's be honest, some of that research our colleagues have been doing, it's surely self-indulgent? What about that guy in History who seems to have been working on the biography of that local Victorian philanthropist for what seems like the last twenty years? Does anyone actually read those journal articles he writes every time he comes across another notebook? And surely it's a good thing if a student produces something that can be sold while they're at university? That's money in the bank for them, and isn't that going to increase their employability when they leave university?

Activity 7.3

- In what ways have you been active in incorporating or resisting the notion of knowledge as product in your teaching and learning regime?
- In what ways have you been involved in seeking to balance the need to create an environment in which knowledge could be pursued for its own sake as well as become intellectual property, with commercial potential?

When I was studying Economics as an undergraduate I remember being told that no matter what ideological perspective you bring to the notion of a free market, there will always be two key issues at play: first, what you leave a marketplace with will be heavily dependent on what you bring to that marketplace (importantly, more money), and the fiercer the competition is between the suppliers in that marketplace, the more likely you will see: corners being cut; secrecy and espionage; and exaggerated claims about the benefits of the products. In reality, it does matter what ideological perspective you bring to the table, because those from the right are usually very quick to claim that it is the very competition (in the end) which will drive out the unscrupulous, while those on the left will be very quick to claim that it is those who know that they will definitely benefit from a free market who will be its keenest advocates.

In the case of a higher education marketplace we have seen these tendencies play themselves out in interesting ways. Brown and Carasso are succinct in their summary:

'We have moved a long way from the notion of universities as expert providers of specialised services. The vision now is of a market in which consumers with the right information will (and should) determine what is provided' (Brown and Carasso 2013: 117). And Andrew McGettigan expresses his disquiet concerning the outcome; that we are facing the prospect of 'a polarised sector featuring a handful of selective universities (privatised to all intents and purposes) and a selection of cheap degree shops offering cut-price value for money' (McGettigan 2013: 10). Put crudely, the middle classes get what they always got, and the working classes get something else entirely. But is this unfair on some of the new private providers, including further education colleges, who may be providing something which entirely suits the needs of their prospective students (Simmons and Lea 2013)? These students, for example, may not be in a position to access a traditional campus university experience; and may expressly wish to pursue a higher vocational curriculum tied to the local job market; and may even wish to disassociate themselves entirely from what might be perceived as the bourgeois lifestyle validation exercise which takes place annually in the so-called elite universities.

Relevant HEA project

Healey, M., Jenkins, A. and Lea, J. (2014c) *Developing Research-Based Curricula In College-Based Higher Education*. York: HEA. Available at: http://www.heacademy.ac.uk/resources/detail/heinfe/Developing_research-based_curricula_in_CBHE (accessed 19 Nov. 2014).

In the United States Arum and Roksa (2011) have claimed that many universities have been able to position themselves in the marketplace in very understandable but equally very troubling ways. Using a Weberian form of 'social closure' theory, which might be summarised as requiring us not confuse the middle-class rush to educate their children as a newfound love of knowledge, but rather as a means to secure their social status, modern American society has (unwittingly perhaps) produced a pact which suits all the key stakeholders. In essence, parents are happy to send their children to elite universities, paying very high fees in the process, not because these students will receive a good education, but because it will secure them the credentials to access higher professional roles in society.

These 'well-heeled' students very rarely question the teaching and learning regime, because it suits them to go unchallenged in their academic activities, and it also suits many of the academics because it leaves them free to pursue the activities which are most likely to bring them status and kudos (i.e. research). Everyone is colluding in a game, from which each key stakeholder, ironically perhaps, gains; signing up to what George Kuh has called 'a disengagement contract', all the while knowing that 'Students are allocated to occupational positions based on their credentials' (Arum and Roksa

2011: 125), the gaining of which has little to do with investment in actual learning activities, a point which Gibbs also makes in his UK-based publication (Gibbs 2010). What students actually benefit from is the reputation of the university and the social capital networks they gain access to, not the teaching and learning regime. This seems to be a long way from the idea of students as consumers even of knowledge, let alone the idea of knowledge in the making, or student as producer.

The (near) future

If, as neo-liberals believe, the key watchword of quality is competition, and this ideology prevails, we can expect to see many more UK education providers being encouraged to seek degree-awarding powers (TDAP) in the near future, and possibly 'university' title. We might also expect to see greater variance in the fees that students will be paying to the institutions in this new higher education marketplace. That said, and at the time of writing this, the fact that all the traditional universities have ended up charging the full £9,000 fee, and the fact that current estimates indicate that the government is unlikely to save any money in switching the fee burden to students, it is very likely for some time that this market will not remain free from government manipulation, including the possibility that the £9,000 fee cap will itself be either raised or reduced, or even removed altogether, depending on the political colour of future governments.

But what of the broader trends we are seeing in UK higher education? For example, have these marketising forces begun to create particular and distinct types of organisational structures for UK universities and other HEIs? Ron Barnett speaks of the corporate university as the most obvious manifestation of the responses to these forces (Barnett 2011b). That is, the university which projects itself as a branded enterprise; its logo being the symbol of that quality. Here, its employees – including the academic practitioners – must pledge a distinct allegiance to this brand for it to work. Universities here are clearly not places that academics work at, but for; no longer allegiance to discipline here, or the 'invisible college', but a managed environment, in which each plays their part in meeting the strategic mission of the institution, requiring both a bureaucracy and a management structure through which this can be enacted.

But Barnett also speaks of a 'liquid university' (after Bauman 2000), which would seem to be at odds with the attempts of a corporate university to clearly demarcate itself and find its market niche (Barnett 2011b). For what if the university or college needs to strike alliances with other providers or other types of knowledge-based organisations? In a world where time and space are compressed (Harvey 1990) and knowledge is 'supercomplex' (Barnett 2000), with lots of axes of knowledge and information centres all equally competing on a global scale (often with instant electronic access), can highly bureaucratised institutions be nimble enough to survive that dynamic landscape? Hargreaves once spoke of the need for educational organisations to view themselves more as 'moving mosaics' (Hargreaves 1994) and this metaphor seems to chime well with a slightly more restricted notion of liquidity. Either way, unless a university or college has carved out such a distinct niche for itself and/or has established the educational equivalent of a patent on that provision, the immediate future would appear to be one where partnership managers begin to play increasingly important roles in the landscape of higher education.

Returning to some of the issues raised in Chapter 5, could it also be argued that the most important niche is one for the concept of the University itself, and one that Plato conceived for his Academy; that a love of wisdom is a necessary function for a healthy society if not a wealthy one? Or in terms of an organic conception of social order, the pursuit of wealth, while needing to be unfettered for its practitioners, needs a wider check, from those who must themselves in turn be unfettered in their pursuit of wisdom. This makes universities not only very special places, but also carves out for them the role of 'national social conscience', and as guardians of the sustainability of the social order as a whole, and which seems to require of its academics that they act with integrity and authenticity (see, for example, Nixon 2008; Macfarlane 2012; Kreber 2013). And which might be summarised as a demand they seek the truth, truthfully, that is, by being true to themselves.

In today's universities this 'social conscience' function could be (in part at least) exercised by the public intellectual, the academic who takes a perspective precisely at variance with strictly economic or political perspectives. Or in the case of students, it speaks to the need to see wider and deeper questions of sustainability being at the heart of citizenship. This may also spill over into a concern that questions of social justice are not side-lined in the pursuit of profitability. The university in these conceptions acts to prick the conscience of the nation, and it may need to be actively supported and defended in order to be able to exercise this function. Here, the notion of 'walking in the groves of academia' or 'living in an ivory tower' should be seen much more positively, rather than as derogatory swipes aimed at people who don't live in the 'real world'. And it may also require that academics act in this way, within their own organisations. For example, sometimes speaking out against, or just reminding, the bureaucratic, corporate and entrepreneurial elements in a university when there is a danger of overstepping the mark. It is in this context that Kavanagh speaks of the academic as the 'fool'; the person who disturbs the status quo; who, through ridicule or irony, prompts a questioning of the taken for granted; the person who sees the joke and reminds others of it. But this playful side is not destructive – 'the fool as playmaker extraordinaire is central to [the] continual process of institutional re-creation through which an institution breathes, lives and renews itself' (Kavanagh 2012: 108).

Conclusion

This brings us back once more to our original question, concerning what universities are for. All these developments seem to be pushing some people into answering that question in new ways, but send others on a mission to rediscover and re-emphasise some of the more traditional answers. At the polar extremes the answers seem to revolve around those people willing to embrace the neo-liberal political agenda which underpins many of these new developments – a world where private individuals and markets form the nexus of activity, and become the guardians of quality (if nobody wants to buy your product, the consequences are obvious) – and those who wish to counter that with the older (in reality, both ideologies are as old as each other) liberal educational creed, which emphasises the value of pursuing knowledge for its own sake, allied to a republican creed, which emphasises the value of other (non-market) social bonds, ties, and communities. Put simply, are universities to be viewed as private companies, marketing private goods, or as public institutions, serving a social good?

These debates are also complicated by epistemological allegiances. Are universities upholders of the Enlightenment project, comprising academics engaged in the disinterested pursuit of truth, discovering what is universal to humanity, or has post-modernity so infiltrated the landscape, that truth is just perspective, and where what is particular is just as valued as what is universal? At the extremes of this debate seems to be a deep desire to see the university as a special place, contrasted with a kind of (sometimes, hopeless) nihilism where there is nothing unique for the university to uphold so nothing of value is lost in it going in whatever direction it chooses.

These are all polar extreme arguments and the reality for most of us working in universities may well involve a much more pragmatic search for answers. Maybe a liberal creed could still subsist within a broader neo-liberal agenda? Surely a course can engender the love of a subject (an intrinsic factor), as well as provide opportunities to enhance employability (an extrinsic factor)? I choose this example to open up the notion of drawing not hard lines set in concrete, but softer ones, in sand. For example, at what point does the demand that research be judged to have had impact by being near market, actually begin to compromise or start to undermine the blue skies thinking which often sparks insight, or that sense of being guided by wherever the research takes one? And at what point does a student's request that she be allowed to start up her own company as her third year project begin to compromise the conceptual framework which underpins the course she has signed up to? If nothing else, we can see from this last example that the idea of student as producer or students as scholars can quickly get complicated by these market reforms, because different academic practitioners may bring to the classroom very different notions of what it means to be scholarly (and what is meant by scholarly output).

Of course, these are not just individual decisions, for at what point does the Head of Knowledge Exchange at a university suggest to an academic colleague that they might consider some 'gardening leave' before they decide to publish the results of a research project which would surely undermine the credibility of a local company – particularly where this local company has an intern partnership arrangement with the university? And at what point does a highly prestigious university decide to roll back a lucrative MOOC for fear that it is undermining its own credibility as an institution which attracts high achieving (and rich) students to its campus? These examples, at both individual and institutional level, point to a need to carefully negotiate our relationship with the market, and particularly the broader notion of academic capitalism. Some of this discussion can be summarised in a final Venn diagram (Figure 7.1) which highlights three of the key dimensions in the discussion, and asks what are we to make of the overlapping areas (particularly, once again, the X in the middle)?

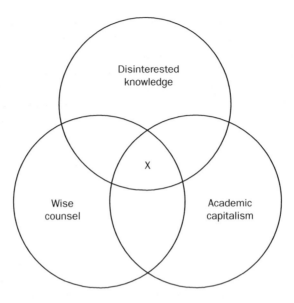

Figure 7.1 The role and purpose of HEIs as a Venn Diagram.

- In what ways do you engage with the question of what higher education is for with students and within your learning and teaching regime in general?
- Have you been involved in seeking to articulate a mission statement or set of core principles for a higher education institution or HE in general?

In Figure 7.1 we see the traditional notion of academics pursuing knowledge in whatever direction it takes them – without vested interest – but this now is being increasingly overlapped with a notion of academics practising and teaching forms of wise counsel, for example, asking 'Is this a direction in which we truly wish to be going?' And this notion also finds itself overlapping with questions of what will be the economic gain or return on the investment in particular forms of knowledge, for example, the possibility of claiming intellectual copyright on a research output.

Perhaps the overlaps here might best be described as compromises rather than true overlaps. These compromises might also be viewed as examples of pragmatism, which may require very active management, and where one of the biggest challenges may be the need for universities to embrace many aspects of the market in order to survive, financially, *while at the same time* embracing a clear sense that the university is both a socially responsible organisation, and a place which provides for a purer form of knowledge pursuit and love of subject (if not completely pure). That responsibility might be made manifest in its desire to help produce socially responsible citizens of its students, along with an *avowed* sense of pride in its role as social conscience for the nation. And, on the knowledge side, it may need to become more active in protecting its role as a repository for the more conceptual knowledge, for fear of some of the consequences of pursing a headlong embrace of applied knowledge. For, in the words of the old Joni Mitchell song: 'You don't know what you've got 'til it's gone.'

Another way of looking at this issue is to reconsider Robert Merton's four key norms for scientific practice and extend them to become principles for all academic practice; namely – universalism, communism (as in communal), disinterestedness and scepticism, or, in summary, knowledge first, through collective effort (Merton 1942). And for each of us to ask ourselves whether we believe in them still, and if we do, whether we can draw a line for each, beyond which we would have a duty to call our universities to account, for fear that that crossing those lines could undermine the very nature and purpose of a university's pursuit of knowledge. For example, at what point does commercially exploitable knowledge start to undermine the free dissemination of ideas? And can we draw a workable line between claiming intellectual copyright and commercial copyright?

But to exercise any of these roles, the university and its academics may well have to demand a degree of autonomy from the demands of the State's various social engineering projects, and also monitor carefully their own partnership relationships they might have with large private corporate bodies. For those opponents of the marketisation of higher education, this might be taken as all the evidence that is needed to argue that we should return the university to its public place, funded entirely by the public purse, and have it afforded that original high degree of professional trust in exercising its research and teaching responsibilities. Or is this line of thinking now simply too idealistic, given the dominance of the neo-liberal political agenda (particularly in England), but also because of the broader social and economic forces at work in a globalised marketplace of higher education provision, which has already firmly embedded commodified notions of what is meant by a 'knowledge economy'?

Prof. Reason: Well Marlan, this seems to make us small fish in a rather large pond, and it also looks like it's the end of our contributions. We don't seem to have agreed on much, but I've enjoyed the exchanges. Now, I'm off to prepare for the Geography degree field trip. I love these trips, where everyone bonds for a short period away from the campus. This year I'm taking some third years to Croatia.

Dr Bracewell: It's been great fun engaging with you Karen, and we mustn't forget that we can make a difference to how our university positions itself in this global market. And you know what, I think we might have just found something we agree on – the value of field trips! Later on this year I will be taking some of my engineering students on a tour of Brunel's projects around Britain. One of the things I've been working on recently is an assessment tool which measures their value for students.

Prof. Reason: Now, don't go spoiling it again, just as we were getting on!

Dr Bracewell: I think it's time to say good night and good luck and over and out!

Opinion Piece, Debate, Dear Lecturer, and Fellowship Application extracts

In the following opinion piece, Jonathan Eaton looks at the role and growth of college-based higher education (CBHE). And in the debate Patrick Ainley, followed by Ted Tapper and David Palfreyman, take contrary positions on aspects of the marketisation of higher education. To finish, Sam Louis, a recent graduate from Newcastle University, reflects on the chapter overall. This is followed by three extracts from successful HEA fellowship applicants who discuss some of the aspects of academic practice which feature in this chapter.

Opinion: On College-Based Higher Education (CBHE)

Teaching in college-based higher education

Jonathan Eaton

Colleges play a significant role within the national higher education landscape; with around 8 per cent of HE students in the United Kingdom currently taught within the college sector (Parry et al., 2012). Traditionally delivering higher qualifications with a focus on vocational skills, college-based higher education (CBHE) displays a student profile distinct from that of many universities. CBHE students are more likely to be aged over 25, originate from areas with traditionally low rates of participation in HE or to be enrolled on part-time courses (HEFCE 2006).

The CBHE sector is remarkably heterogeneous with providers ranging in size from a handful of HE students to those with cohorts of over 3000. Colleges offer a diverse HE provision, including both undergraduate and postgraduate courses. Foundation Degrees, with a pronounced vocational emphasis and opportunities for work-based learning, are particularly common. Students graduating with Foundation Degrees may choose to enter employment or progress on to a Bachelor's top-up programme offered by CBHE providers or universities. Most CBHE provision is validated or franchised by a university partner. The nature of the relationship between validating university and partner college is highly variable with some, but by no means all, including collaborative staff development opportunities and access to research networks.

In recent years, four CBHE providers have secured Foundation Degree Awarding Powers (FDAP) in their own right. A number of larger CBHE institutions aspire to Taught Degree Awarding Power (TDAP) status, which would allow them to validate full undergraduate and taught postgraduate programmes. The review process for such applications, overseen by the QAA, involves considerable scrutiny of the qualifications, experience and knowledge of CBHE teaching staff (QAA 2013c). It can be argued that the award of FDAP and TDAP status to suitable providers will stimulate colleges to further contribute to regional economic growth without the need to convince a validating university, sometimes located outside of the region, of the need for a specific area of provision in response to local skills needs.

Delivering FE and HE courses within the same institution can prove challenging, particularly in terms of nurturing a distinct sense of 'HEness' (Simmons and Lea 2013). By their very nature, colleges support a diverse student body, from students on basic access courses to those potentially studying on postgraduate programmes. While some institutions have physically separated their HE delivery environment from FE spaces, this is often not possible, particularly when access to physical resources in the form of workshops, studios or real work environments is required. Lecturers may be called upon to deliver both FE and HE programmes, which can prove challenging in adapting to different academic levels and quality assurance systems. Teaching observations conducted to assess pedagogic competence can prove problematic, particularly when Ofsted criteria are applied to a HE environment. Some institutions have contextualised observation criteria which embrace HE delivery in an appropriate manner. Yet the link to FE can prove valuable in terms of raising the standard of teaching and learning, as most CBHE staff are required to hold a teaching qualification. It may be significant that, of the top 20 institutions identified in the 2014 National Student Survey, 12 were CBHE providers. Colleges are increasingly embracing the UK PSF through accredited staff development programmes or individual applications, and the Higher Education Academy currently has a sizeable CBHE membership at an institutional level.

Ensuring a sense of 'HEness' inevitably requires evidenced engagement with research and scholarly activity. The lack of CBHE access to RCUK funding inevitably has an impact on the time allocated for teaching staff to undertake scholarly activity. The nature of scholarship within the CBHE sector is a matter of considerable debate, particularly within institutions aspiring to FDAP or TDAP status. Scholarly activity within a college environment may take a number of forms which are distinct from, but nevertheless to be equally valued as, the traditional nature of research recognised by universities. This includes the activities of teaching staff with dual identities as academics and professional practitioners. It can be argued that the latter is particularly important within a vocational HE environment. The nature of the CBHE student body should also be recognised as a fruitful source for scholarly activity, particularly through part-time learners sponsored by their employers and the deep engagement with industry which many students enjoy during their programmes of study. A recent Higher Education Academy report provided a number of case studies of student partnership in the context of research and scholarly activity within the CBHE sector (Healey et al. 2014c).

In an increasingly complex HE ecosystem inhabited by universities, colleges and alternative providers, CBHE providers have a distinct role to play in delivering vocational HE provision which drives local and regional economic growth. This is particularly the case in large urban areas which host a number of HE providers, where colleges can utilise their deep sense of place as opposed to the global out-look of ambitious research-intensive universities. Newcastle College, for example, has around 3000 HE students within a city which also hosts large Russell Group and post-1992 universities. College HE provision focuses on vocational programmes which respond to industry trends and meets the needs of local and regional employ-ers. FDAP status allows the college to shape Foundation Degrees which avoid overt competition with local HEIs through the development of niche provision, with an emphasis on technical skills and employability. For this reason, the HE staffing pro-file of the college is also distinct with a greater focus on industry engagement and technical expertise than doctorates and publications. This expertise has been rec-ognised through collaborative initiatives with local HEIs, including an award-winning subsea project involving Newcastle University and sector employers.

The nature of CBHE teaching defies easy categorisation, owing to the pro-foundly heterogeneous nature of the sector. Larger providers increasingly play a role akin to polytechnics through higher technical education and applied research. Smaller providers may offer niche programmes which address specific local skills gaps or widen participation in HE within under-represented areas. With a rich heri-tage of public education and industry engagement, the professionalism of CBHE staff cannot be doubted. While teaching in CBHE can prove challenging, it should be recognised as a valuable addition to the wider HE sector.

Debate: On marketisation in HE

Meanwhile, beyond the city walls ...

Patrick Ainley

In the long view from New College, the 2010 funding changes to English higher edu-cation are only the latest accretions to the evolving model of the university that has grown down the ages to absorb more narrowly defined vocational training under its academic aegis. Supposedly, this enables more students to obtain jobs, increases the size of HEIs, thanks to enhanced funding, and possibly also benefits politicians and funding agencies with the feeling that 'this still reasonably generously funded sector of society is finally about to make a more substantial contribution to the ben-efit of the wider society' (as Ted Tapper and David Palfreyman write in THE 9 Oct. 2014). However, crucial for them is that the academy remains in control of its own goals.

Yet, 'academic freedom' – officially abolished with loss of tenure in 1988 – is constrained, on the one hand, by the corporate management of semi-privatised uni-versities; on the other, by government demands for 'research impact' as another state subsidy to private corporations. In the two antique universities, however, it is preserved in the form of medieval guild democracy, adding to the self-importance of those there who feel that all is for the best in this best of all possible worlds.

It isn't! Unlike Labour, which havered over reducing fees to £6,000, the Conservatives made no General Election comment on fees but would like to raise the current £9,000 cap they only agreed as a compromise with the Lib Dems. Oxbridge and a few other 'top' universities would then charge more, possibly forsaking state support and leaving state universities that cannot compete on price to collapse into virtual learning centres. Other 'efficiencies' would further unravel institutions, including 'mergers' or take-overs, buy-outs and buy-ins, fragmenting what is left of a once more or less coherent HE system.

But then, while all save the two Real Russells compete for fee-bearing students, these two restrict their numbers to increase demand, thus maintaining their staff's time for research and so further raising their reputations. Meanwhile, they invest in bursaries and other widening participation efforts not only to cover their backs but to 'skim the cream' of state school applicants. Thus, they preside over and benefit from the current situation in which (with few exceptions) the older the university, the posher, younger, whiter and proportionately more male its students.

This academically selective system's close connection to the private schools, symbolised by Cameron and crew, is integral to UKanian flummery. It tests mainly literary abilities as proxies for more or less expensively acquired cultural capital. Even in the sciences, burgeoning into academico-medical complexes in hock to Big Pharma, where enrolment is less related to social origin though not to gender, as Bourdieu and Passeron noted, 'the teaching of culture ... implicitly presupposes a body of knowledge, skills, and, above all, modes of expression which constitute the heritage of the cultivated classes'.

So what students know is less important than how they say it, while they learn less but pay more to run up a down-escalator of rising debt for devalued qualifications. Yet they cram (sic) in, desperate to secure semi-professional employment even while it is proletarianised by corporate management and further reduced by automation, deskilling and outsourcing. Meanwhile, the other half of 18+ year olds (adults have long gone!) are fobbed off with promises of 'apprenticeships' equivalent to subsidised job placements or internships for non-graduates. This divisive system of social control threatens to revert to bi- or tri-partite divisions – this time at tertiary level – supported by genetic ideologies of so-called 'intelligence'.

Instead, HE might recover itself in connection with FE by replacing market-driven expansion with regional partnerships to end competition between universities, colleges and private providers. An expectation of, and entitlement to, free local/regional adult further and higher continuing education would then follow from a general schooling, just as it still does (just) for US High School graduates; especially with more students living at home, as in other European countries. This should be the aim, even if not everyone wants to go to HE immediately – including many who are already there! Vocational considerations could then balance personal interest with progressive taxation defraying costs of cutting fees so that anyone (graduate or not) who earns more pays more.

Rediscovering the purpose of higher study within and across disciplines includes the relation of such study to an academic vocation dedicated to learning critically from the past and with research and scholarship enabling change in the future. Undergraduate participation in that continuing cultural conversation can restore a sense many have lost of what higher education is supposed to be about.

Debate: On marketisation in HE

The marketisation of English higher education

Ted Tapper and David Palfreyman

It is important to remember that the critical driver of change from an English system of higher education that was overwhelmingly publicly funded to one which is ever-more privately funded was the increasing parsimony of public funding. If higher education institutions were not to become bankrupt with the attendant loss of faculty, termination of courses and even institutional closure, it was critical for them to find alternative sources of funding. In effect, institutional well-being could only be guaranteed though increasing private funding, of which a critical early (and continuing) source was the fees paid by overseas students. While one may make a strong critique of the failure of government policy to recognise through taxpayer funding the importance of higher education to sustain and enhance the national welfare, the actual saviour has turned out to be the availability of market resources (though it remains to be seen whether the UK/EU undergraduate tuition fees now at £9000 p.a. will be allowed to increase in line with the inflation of university costs).

Moreover, it is difficult not to sympathise with the direction of government policy. In the context of financial stringency, governments have to make tough decisions as to where their priorities lie. It is clear that politically the National Health Service has a more sheltered position than higher education, as also schools and pensions. It is simply that, in the context of an ageing population and a programme of prolonged austerity/deficit-reduction, this is a political and economic inevitability – indeed, given that for much of its history, English higher education has been elitist in terms of its social composition, conservative with respect to serving the needs of society, and academically narrow, this direction of government policy was to be expected. Perhaps the funding crisis is of our own making in that HE has not, as an 'industry', been noted for the sort of innovation and productivity gains found in other areas of economic activity, both private-sector and public-sector, that has driven cost reduction and price competition.

Critically, the pressures of the market are, however, regulated by the state rather than risk the disruption within the context of a completely free HE market of potential market failure, and also given the state's duty as the provider of consumer protection. This regulation takes different forms: the instigation of inter-institutional competition to secure state funding (note the research assessment exercises), the control of student numbers (now in fact to be uncapped) and of tuition fees (perhaps in due course also to be relaxed if not uncapped), and the burgeoning of quality control mechanisms. Indeed, there is the possibility of the state-regulated market becoming such an intrusive means of state control (even compared to the days of state block-grant funding of HE) that many of the current opponents of marketisation may start to wish for less state guidance and a less encumbered market – though, as has been noted, the state through its enactment of consumer protection law, as well as competition law, will always have a duty to see that the HE market is operating efficiently and effectively in the student-consumers' interest in that the marketplace should engender innovation in HE provision and also competition on tuition fee pricing.

The state needs to fulfil its duty as the provider of consumer protection by requiring higher education institutions to demonstrate precisely how they arrive at their fee levels. Second, it needs to explore ways in which students should be able to question the academic standards of the courses they have been taught, for this should not be a matter that is determined solely within the academy by academic procedures. Third, the arrangements for repaying loans must be revised to ensure that student loans do not become an undue burden upon the Exchequer, and thus the taxpayer at large. But there is no doubt that the marketisation of higher education has arrived. But what has yet to be determined is its precise *modus operandi*.

Dear Lecturer

There are no substitutes for enthusiasm, energy and passion

Sam Louis

A return to the teacher-centric ways of 100 years ago would likely not serve the current generation of students particularly well. They are preparing for a world that expects them to be versed in buzz-speak and action words, where CEO's are 24 years old and Silicon Valley is a business mecca of t-shirts and flip-flops. The marketplace, despite its faults and impurities, cannot be ignored. This does not, however, spell the end for the disinterested pursuit of interesting phenomena and pure truths, because it is exactly this that leads to one of the most marketable, valuable qualities a student can take from higher education. Enthusiasm.

The notion that lecturers (and consequently students) are becoming divorced from exploring intellectual curiosities and are instead being led by fund-influenced, marketable avenues of research, or 'employability-approved' curricula, is both sad and counterintuitive. Having just finished my degree and spent 6 months in various internships, assessment centres and job interviews, one of the biggest influences on how your application progresses is your level of enthusiasm. Your energy. Your passion for the company, or for what they do, or what you do, or even what you used to do. Passionate interest is learned and infectious, once you get it about one thing, it can spread to other areas of your life, and other people around you, and I believe one of the best places to catch it is higher education.

Spending time around people who have dedicated their lives to their passion is how I caught that passion for learning; that 'will to learn' which Ron Barnett speaks of, and which allows you to develop to the later stages of Baxter-Magolda's 'ways of knowing'. With this, I trust that I will manage okay wherever I might end up, because if you can learn, you can adapt. Consequently, I believe that the duty and aim of a university lecturer should be to inspire and ignite energy in their graduates, which they can only do if they pursue and convey their own passions and personality.

If universities were solely for the generation and dissemination of knowledge, blindly ingested by students, then it might as well all be online. If you gain nothing but a spoon-fed, rote learned understanding of texts, then as 'Good' Will Hunting remarks, you've spent an awful lot of money on an 'education you could'a got for a dollar fifty in late charges at the public library' (*Good Will Hunting* 1997). Lecturers do need to fight to retain their 'ivory towers', and in turn their passion for academic life, so that they might pass that passion on to the next generation, and prepare them for whatever life may bring.

Extracts from successful HEA fellowship applications

Dr Orange (FHEA)

Student engagement is placed at the heart of the student retention and success model developed by Thomas (2012), who also commented that 'The process of engaging students should begin early and extend throughout the student life cycle. It is essential that engagement begins early with institutional outreach interventions and that it extends throughout the process of preparing for and entering HE.' I am involved in the process of creating awareness of HE through outreach activities and student recruitment open days. I am a believer that student engagement begins before students have entered into Kingston University, and with this in mind I was determined to improve the open day experience through designing interactive hands-on activities that promote the school's courses and relate them to the wider world. The activities included analysis of the chemical constituents of pain killers and the natural sources of major drug types. The visitors were provided with a questionnaire to leave feedback on their experience from the open day, and the results when analysed indicated that the visitors had an excellent experience and many visitors commented that the activities provided them with a greater understanding of what each degree entailed and it provided them with additional information that they were not aware of before. This experience has made me understand the importance of engaging with students from very early on; from the first instance they enter the university premises, and when possible through tailor-made outreach activities [K3, K4, K5, V1, V2].

Dr Brown (SFHEA)

There is no part of my present-day practice in HE that does not carry the memory trace of my work in community settings with some of society's most disadvantaged groups. My research in mental health settings is one of the enduring links between my HE practice and my community foothold, a link which also nourishes my approach to ethics in research; research-led teaching [V3] and indeed, the employability agenda which is often the spearhead for encouraging students into volunteering and placement roles. In this memory trace there is the continued belief that 'outreach' as performed by 'higher' education, is often a form of *noblesse oblige* rather than a relationship between peers striving for symmetric power relations (Webster and Buglass 2005; Sagan et al. 2010). This informs and guides the way I work with community 'partners' – attempting to 'use' them less as placement, 'community engagement' and WP opportunities, and engaging with them, rather, in collaborative exploration of possible joint research and ways in which they might benefit from my and the university expertise and resources [V2], while I and my students benefit from theirs [A4].

Ms White (PFHEA)

Learning and Teaching conferences can enable one of the primary purposes of academic development: 'informed debate about learning, teaching, assessment, curriculum design, and the goals of higher education' (Gosling 2001). However, as well as showcasing best practice and providing a forum for informed debate, I want the conference to stand out as an exciting and vibrant event and also to respond to delegates' feedback and suggestions. Two years ago I introduced a student panel, enabling colleagues to hear directly from students about learning at the university. This has led to some departments adopting panels in departmental boards. Last year I included a LectureMeet, where colleagues shared ideas on teaching and learning in an 'unconference' format. This was the first time that this had been done for higher education. The short presentations were broadcast to audiences beyond the university via WebEx, enabling virtual presentations from other HEIs and our good practice was shared across the sector. This event proved highly popular, attracting contributions from colleagues who do not usually engage in learning and teaching events, thus raising the profile of learning and teaching in harder-to-reach areas of the university.

8

Conclusion
Raising the profile of learning and teaching, being reflective and scholarly, and becoming a Fellow of the Higher Education Academy

Nigel Purcell[1] and John Lea

Introduction: SoTL and its discontents

The previous six chapters have looked at how learning and teaching in HE relate to different aspects of academic practice. In some cases the links were straightforward (as in Chapters 2 and 6), in others (particularly Chapter 7) they may have been less obvious. In all cases, attempts were also made to look at how those links might be enhanced in order to better integrate the different dimensions of academic practice with learning and teaching, while at the same time acknowledging their contested nature. Sometimes this contestation related to the concepts and principles which underpin higher education pedagogy as a distinct discipline (indeed, whether there is such a thing), and sometimes the contestation related to much wider questions concerning the very purposes and aims of higher education.

Another key thread running throughout the book has been a consideration of what it actually means to raise the profile of learning and teaching in higher education. For some, this is a straightforward issue, and would involve removing 'original research' or the 'scholarship of discovery' (as Boyer referred to it) from its elevated perch. But scratch below the surface of that issue and things turn out to be far from straightforward. For example, even though there may be many academics who would be keen to knock original research of its perch, all the while that the most cherished rewards and recognitions continue to relate to original research, it may just have to be a case of needs must. Allied to this, there will be those who believe that the most fundamental and hardest task in academic life *is* to produce original research, and therefore it simply wouldn't be right to seek to raise the profile of one aspect of academic practice by mounting an unwarranted attack on another. Or, in its most derogatory formulation: those who can't do research have to teach (and those who can't do either have to manage).

Boyer's (1990) re-visioning of these issues was carefully constructed so as not to denigrate but integrate as much as possible, and in holistic manner, the widest range of academic practice and grant all aspects a scholarship status (i.e. the scholarships of discovery; of application; of integration; and of teaching). Naturally, this leaves wide open the question of whether management, leadership and administration might also be accorded scholarly status, but his concern at that level was to ensure that as many academics as possible got to pursue the widest range of scholarly activities in their careers, and that this would need careful management.

His work was also key in raising the issue as what exactly constitutes a *scholarship* of teaching. For some, it was enough just to label 'discovery' and 'teaching' in the same way, because in doing so it put into focus the similarities between anyone who undertakes a systematic understanding of something – problematising, collecting data, analysing results, and asking epistemological questions about the reliability and validity of the knowledge which has been generated. In this sense, pedagogy *is* a discipline like any other. But in the case of *HE* pedagogy, it also put the epistemological cat among the pigeons by raising questions about whether practitioners (as in action research) are actually involved in true research, or just reflecting on practice, and/or whether practitioners are best placed to be researchers (i.e. they are not detached observers). While it might be easy to counter those claims by asking questions about whether any researcher is ever truly detached from their work, this was enough for some to claim that if this type of action research *is* research, it is surely of inferior status (in research-intensive universities particularly).

Even among those who were keen to distance themselves from these ranking debates, questions remained about whether scholarship and research are the same thing, and particularly whether engaging in critical reflection on and in practice would be enough to raise the profile of learning and teaching. Put simply, if practice improves next Monday morning – based on reflection about what happened last Monday morning – and particularly if students learn more next Monday compared with last Monday, does the 'research' status of the enterprise really matter? Or, what works will do for me! But, for others, there is still an important stepping stone between these classroom experiments and the *scholarship* of teaching and learning, for the latter must involve a clear sense that one has 'gone public' – and been subject to peer review and scrutiny, and become part of academic community (if not wider public) debate.

The focus for the rest of this conclusion is on practical advice in putting together an application to become a fellow of the HEA. We hope that the content of the previous chapters has helped to some extent in providing sufficient food for thought in beginning this process, but we also hope that the refocus in this first part of this conclusion – on how teaching and learning might be related to the other aspects of academic practice in many different ways, and that being scholarly about teaching and learning also has multiple dimensions and meanings – that both will act as stimuli in helping to put together a personally meaningful and individualised narrative account of your involvement in learning and teaching in higher education in the UK. One very simple and practical exercise to help begin that process might be to review the Venn diagrams which were presented in Chapters 3, 5, 6 and 7, and consider the extent to which they could be effectively combined to become one diagram encompassing all aspects of your academic practice (or what would need to be put in place before this could happen).

The HEA Fellowship Scheme: direct route or accredited provision?

The HEA provides two routes to fellowship: (https://www.heacademy.ac.uk/professional-recognition).The first route is by making an application directly to the HEA. The second route is via accredited provision (https://www.heacademy.ac.uk/consultancyservices/accreditation).

On the second route, the HEA delegates to those subscribing institutions with accredited provision the autonomy to award the fellowships. Depending on where you work, you may have the choice of either applying directly to the HEA or of applying through your own institution via their accredited provision. If you undertake HE work related to teaching and supporting learning, but do not work for an institution, both routes may still be available to you by approaching an accredited institution (a complete list is available on the HEA website) or simply consulting with the HEA about the direct route. (Whichever route you are pursuing, you should of course ensure that you have read the relevant guidance and accessed any support available under the relevant scheme.)

Some accredited institutions offer a taught route to Associate Fellowship or Fellowship status, usually in the form of credit-bearing PG Certificate HE courses (collectively known as PG Certs). The advantage of these courses is that you are given substantial formalised support to develop your knowledge and practice and this is especially beneficial if you are new to HE teaching and supporting learning. However, it does involve a substantial commitment to assignment and course work. But this route is well worth considering if you are aiming for Associate Fellowship or Fellowship status, and if your institution provides this option. On successful completion, you will also be awarded a teaching qualification as well as a fellowship, and, in some cases, some Master's level HE credits (level 7).

It is normal for more experienced staff to register for a non-taught route to fellowship (be that directly with the HEA, or through an institution-accredited scheme), and this is usually the only option for those seeking senior or principal fellowship status. If you are still unsure as to which fellowship category you think you should be aiming for, you may wish to look again at the introductory chapter of this book before you read on, and or/check the relevant pages of the HEA website.

Beginning your application

Naturally, you can approach making an application (whether via the HEA direct route or via accredited provision) in a variety of ways. At one extreme, it might be treated as a mere hoop jumping or tick-box exercise, even though doing so will obviously reduce the intrinsic value of the process. At the other extreme, it might be treated as part of an ongoing action research project and in the process become a contribution to the scholarship of teaching and learning – particularly if you 'go public' with the findings of that research. For most, however, it will probably lie somewhere between the two, experienced as a developmental exercise, and result in a critically reflective narrative account of the role that learning and teaching play in your academic practice.

It is worth pausing at this point to reflect further on the reasons for submitting an application and acknowledge any feelings which it may invoke – particularly those of trepidation. If you wish to make an application purely for the intrinsic reward to be gained from engaging in such a scholarly exercise, and/or you relish the opportunity to critically reflect on how your current academic practice is able to enhance student learning, any feelings of trepidation might simply be triggered by the desire to do well, accompanied by some healthy self-doubt as to whether you are worthy. On the other hand, if you are making an application simply because it has been mandated by your institution, coupled with a fear that you might not get a job at another HEI without the recognition, some of your feelings of trepidation may border on resentment about the process.

We think it is important to both interrogate the reasons and acknowledge those feelings. Indeed, engaging with both aspects could end up featuring in your narrative account. And, as Ruth Lawton pointed out in the opinion piece which accompanied Chapter 5, making an application for fellowship status is not dissimilar (as a process) to what the vast majority of our students are facing on a regular basis as they apply for jobs, internships and higher degrees (often for the first time). In this respect, the application process could also become a teaching and learning tool.

It is also important to acknowledge that an application may take some time, and in looking at the various descriptors (D1–D4), you may well decide that you should be working *towards* an application, rather than making one immediately. In this regard, no institution should be putting pressure on you to complete an application within a strict period. To do so would clearly undermine the developmental nature of the process. On the other hand, we also need to be honest with ourselves and recognise how easy it is to let the 'day job' and other activities become the excuse as to why we haven't engaged with the process.

Lastly, we think it is important to acknowledge the genuine fear which can accompany an application, particularly if you are a senior and/or experienced member of staff – that feeling that the process will expose you in some way. In this regard, we all (including mentors and assessors) have a duty to acknowledge and work through these natural anxieties. Indeed, one way to measure the developmental nature of the whole process could be to consider how you feel your own institution is able to acknowledge and work with you on these fears and anxieties.

Putting together an application

The following suggestions are drawn partially from material developed for HEA-provided workshops and designed by consultants to support staff in making their fellowship applications (in all categories). However, they could equally apply if you are simply reviewing your current practice in order to plan personal development, or are engaging in 'remaining in good standing' exercises. Naturally, the suggestions are generic in nature and apply to the process of constructing a coherent narrative account of your practice, not to the specific requirements of any particular scheme. In the case of the HEA direct route scheme, for example, it has a different template for each category of fellowship and you will need to structure and order your narrative accordingly. The same will apply for any of the many accredited schemes.

1 Make it personal

Your application is a personal claim relating to how you have engaged with teaching and supporting learning in your professional context. It is a narrative describing and analysing your professional practice and thus it is generally best expressed in the first person. We appreciate that a lot of academic work demands third person writing, and particularly in certain disciplines, and therefore this narrative style may be easier for some. Acknowledging this, your own narrative may well end up as a combination of first and third person writing, but it is worth reflecting on whether what you are saying might have sounded better (more engaging, more authentic, more meaningful) in the first person. Writing in this way should also make it easier to acknowledge your personal and subjective responses to your experiences.

2 Make it individual

Of course, much of your work will be in a collaborative, team context, but in an application it is essential to identify your own contributions to team efforts. This is particularly important when it comes to committee work, because it is very easy to talk about the work of a committee, without serious consideration of why you sit on that committee, and the impact you have had – personally – on that committee's work. Individualising your application in this way should also help generally in heightening the sense of the impact that you have had on a range of professional practice – be that at course/module level, programme/degree level, department or school level, faculty or institution-wide, and/or sector/(inter)national level (according to fellowship category).

3 Make it reflective

It is essential that your claim is not only descriptive, but is also thoughtful and reflective. This should follow naturally from points (1) and (2). You need to explain not only what you have done, but also how and why you did it, as well as what were the outcomes, impacts, and changes – if any – that followed. And if things didn't go as well as you envisaged, what lessons you learned from that. It is tempting to miss those bits out of an application, for fear that they will read like failures, but actually they can be important springboards into new action, and thereby constitute forms of continuing professional development.

4 Make it scholarly

As we have seen throughout this book, the term 'scholarly' is a problematic one, in having a variety of meanings. Our practical advice here is to consider which of those meanings have the potential to strengthen your application in the most authentic ways. For example, your professional practice might be underpinned by some key pedagogical concepts or ideas. When referring to these, we suggest either seeking to move from particular examples to the underpinning principle, or, moving from a statement of a key principle or value to examples of how you have applied it. In a nutshell, try to avoid simply stating principles without illustrating them, or simply describing aspects of practice without commenting on it. But you might also have engaged in your own research and scholarship relating to learning and teaching in your discipline context, and you should obviously refer to this as a contribution to the scholarship of teaching and learning (SoTL).

In both examples above, your practice is 'orientated' to, or 'informed' by, research and scholarship – in the first case, by the work of others, and in the second, by your own work. But, do be careful with your own subject or discipline-based research, because the key here is to speak to how that research informs your teaching and learning regime (or a strategy related to teaching and learning). Finally, pedagogic research literature, especially in your own discipline, is of course potentially very valuable, but, if used, you should be mindful to refer to it in a context of how it has influenced your specific practices.

To illustrate the many ways in which your application might be deemed to be scholarly, here is Mr Pink, from previous chapters, reflecting on how his practice is underpinned both by the research of others but also by his own reflection on his practice.

Mr Pink (SFHEA)

My pedagogic practice is contextualised by research into a range of contemporary practitioners and learning and teaching theorists [A5]. Design theorists, such as Naylor and Ball (Naylor 2005: 17) have given me incentive to expand the parameters of my subject area, bringing three-dimensional possibilities into a discipline previously seen as paper- or screen-based. I have a strong belief that my students' work, and for that matter my own practice, has not only been contextualised but also has to be forward facing and expansive. It should begin through self-reflection but also through experimentation referring to Donald Schön's concept of discovery 'in action'. According to Schön, 'discovery in action', is intrinsic to reflection in action (Schön 1983: 140) or as Fulton-Suri puts it in her introduction to *Design Research Through Practice* to 'think to build and build to think' and bridge 'the gap between understanding and making, and between theoretical and actual solutions' (Fulton-Suri 2011) This linkage and the theory behind are one of my core values in extending the creative potential of my students.

---

5 Make it evidence-based

This follows naturally from making your application scholarly, but can also include other aspects. For example, in demonstrating impact, you might find yourself having to resort to making your own evaluative claim about that impact. This is where some evidence drawn from other sources can be extremely helpful. For example, you might have some statistical evidence you could draw on to indicate that your interventions have improved 'results'. Or you may have some qualitative evidence in the form of personal testimony from individuals who have commented positively on your inventions. In addition, you might consider using evidence from engagement in your institution's peer review and/or peer observation of teaching processes. Indeed, if you are thinking about making an application in the future, you might consider how you could incorporate anticipated evidence from engagement in these processes. One of the key characteristics expected of an HEA fellow in any of the categories is that their practice is based on evidence of its effectiveness and is modified and adapted in the light of this evidence. Demonstrating that your practice is informed by a range of evidence can enormously strengthen your application, and don't forget that it doesn't always have to be positive. Remember, all evaluative evidence can be used as a springboard for new actions and interventions.

6 Make it aligned (with the UKPSF)

In your application the UKPSF acts as a benchmark in judging whether you should be awarded a fellowship. As we saw in Chapter 1, it is very much up to the individual (subject to any institutional interpretations) how they use the UKPSF in that benchmarking process. The first thing to do is to consider carefully the type of engagement with the UKPSF that the category of fellowship you are aiming for demands (e.g. for Senior and Principal Fellowship your leadership of learning and teaching should be to the fore). Second, you need to consider how you will demonstrate that engagement against the three dimensions of practice. A simple way to do this is to mark up each paragraph or section in your application with coded references to the individual elements of the three dimensions (i.e. A1–A6; K1–K6; V1–V4). Leaving these references in your final application is often very helpful to an assessor of your application. It can also act as a quick aide-mémoire to you, in checking that your engagement stretches equally (more or less) across all the elements and dimensions. On that score, there is evidence from HEA assessors that the Values tend to get the least attention in applications.

7 Make it current and sufficient

These last two aspects are very much based on personal judgement but can be useful in reviewing your own application before it is submitted. Currency refers quite simply to how up to date your application is. For example, to what extent do you think you have relied on evidence drawn from a long time ago? This might be evidence of the effectiveness of your own interventions but also evidence drawn from pedagogic literature and research. Clearly, this evidence may be highly significant, but is it balanced against more recent evidence? In checking for sufficiency, you might ask yourself whether you would be happy with the application if you were assessing it. For example, if you are new to HE teaching, do you think you have demonstrated sufficient evidence from across the range of the areas of activity; or, if you are aiming for a Principal Fellowship, do you think you have provided a good range of examples of impact at institution level and/or influence at (inter)national level? Finally, ask yourself, honestly, whether there are sections where you feel you might have just paid lip service to engagement with an element or dimension of practice. In which case you might want to consider strengthening this aspect of engagement or delaying the application until you feel your engagement would be more genuine or authentic.

In all cases it is probably worth having a colleague read through your application (particularly if they are already a fellow) to give you some constructive feedback before you formally submit it.

Developmental activities

If you are just beginning to think about making an application, you might consider joining, or forming, a learning set. A learning set need be no more than an agreement among a group of colleagues to meet/engage regularly for a set period to have their ideas/work critically scrutinised. An initial exploratory meeting can establish the ground rules, which may need to be renegotiated as time progresses. For the purposes of compiling evidence for an HEA fellowship application, participants might agree to share and scrutinise each other's pedagogic ideas and practice, and offer scholarly-focused suggestions, using the UKPSF as guidance.

Experimentation with learning sets indicates that reflective learning is more likely to be productive if it is focused and consistent. If undertaken in groups, it is also likely to encourage a deeper understanding of the issues particularly if individuals are receptive to wider peer review. And on a practical level, the necessity of meeting/engaging regularly with colleagues can help to defeat the procrastination which comes with busy working lives (Revans 2011).

We offer the following practical guidance on working with learning sets:

1   The group can be any size, but practice indicates that 6–10 is probably an ideal size.

2   The lifespan of the group can be any length, but practice indicates that too short and too long can be unproductive – suggest 2–3 months as an ideal.

3   The group must commit morally to the validity of the exercise, i.e. recognise the duty to meet/engage, and offer up – in equal measure – honest reflections on one's own practice and probing/constructive reflections on colleagues' work.

4   Learning sets can be ideal environments for honing listening skills, and practising Socratic questioning techniques – helping colleagues to answer their own questions.

5   The group might benefit from a designated facilitator, but a member of the group could take on this role.

6   A fundamental ground rule is that the group/set should be collegial in nature and understood as a safe and secure environment for critical reflection on professional practice (i.e. what is said in the set, stays in the set).

The following types of questions might also be useful in starting a learning set meeting:

•   In what ways have I worked /could I work with academic colleagues/professional services/students to experiment/innovate with pedagogical ideas?

•   In what ways have changes I have made to pedagogic practice had a positive impact, and how could I enhance that?

•   How have I been involved in shaping/implementing university/national policies, strategies or initiatives? (e.g. inclusion and diversity, TEL, etc.)

•   In what ways is my teaching, learning and assessment regime informed by pedagogical research/evidence?

•   In what ways is my subject-based research able to lead/inform my teaching?

•   In what ways could my professional practice forge new links within the wider teaching-research nexus?

The three following diagrams (Figures 8.1–8.3) might also be useful in prompting reflection in preparation for making a fellowship application. In the first one we see a variation on the many versions of David Kolb's learning cycle (Kolb 1984) (Figure 8.1).

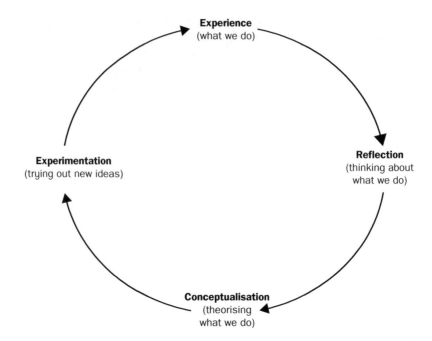

Figure 8.1 A Learning cycle (after Kolb).

In Figure 8.2, we see the three dimensions of practice in the UKPSF depicted as a triangle, aimed at encouraging us to make links between them as we reflect on practice (e.g. I operate with an assessment regime (an activity) which is informed by how students learn (knowledge-led), but is also underpinned by a desire to widen participation in HE (values-driven).

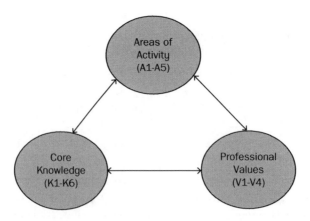

Figure 8.2 The UKPSF Dimensions of Practice triangle.

In the final one, Figure 8.3, we see a simple depiction aimed at encouraging reflection on our motivations for action: what I did, why I did it, and the impact it had.

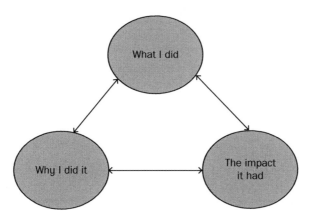

Figure 8.3 A continuing professional development triangle.

In all these figures there is an inbuilt assumption – depicted by the arrows – that the process of reflection is ongoing, and multifaceted. For example, in Figure 8.3, the impact may have been small, or even adverse, which might then initiate a new engagement with the process.

Examples of reflective writing in narrative accounts

Throughout the book we have used extracts from some successful fellowship applications. In this final chapter we use a few more, this time to illustrate some of the points we have been making in this conclusion, and also (hopefully) as an encouraging spur to help you begin your own narrative account.

Reflective writing for an associate or fellowship application

Here we see a university lecturer working in a practice-orientated science discipline. In the first example she is addressing 'A2 Teach and/or support learning' by reflecting on some revision and drop-in sessions she has been running.

When I first started teaching at postgraduate level, the students asked me if it was possible for me to arrange extra revision sessions on specific topics. This was because many of the learners were struggling with the new terminology that they were being introduced to [V1, V2]. As a result of this, I facilitated extra revision sessions and this is now a practice that I incorporate into each module [K5]. The revision and drop-in sessions provide students with the opportunity to ask me questions, to revise topics that they may be struggling with, or to come to talk to me to receive informal feedback on their progress. I let students know that I am happy to meet with them in individually or in groups to help them learn. Recently, a student missed a class and so I arranged a time that suited us both to teach her how to apply stature estimation equations [V1, V2].

Here, the applicant provides a very brief description of her engagement followed by an explanation of why she adopted these particular strategies. And note the use of the personal pronoun. Throughout the account she also maps to the UKPSF with a particular emphasis on the often-neglected values that underpin her work.

In the second example she is addressing 'A1 Design and plan learning activities', discussing the importance of active learning strategies.

> I incorporate a range of learning activities to help the students engage with the topics that they are learning. It is widely acknowledged in the teaching literature that students often learn best through completing practical activities and through discovering new information for themselves, to facilitate this, I incorporate activities into my classes at all levels.
>
> For example, to encourage students to think critically. I have also often incorporated articles and videos from popular media into my classes and then compared these to the academic research that they are based on [K4]. I encourage students to ask questions, and to participate in discussions and debates in tutorials and seminar groups.

Note again the personal nature of the account and also the allusion to the findings of the literature – on the value of active learning. A specific reference might have been useful here but was not essential. The point is sufficiently widely accepted to justify simply stating it. She then goes on to elaborate on the methods employed, interspersing the examples with the rationale for them and her own individual approach. Although not all explicitly mapped in this chapter, a number of core knowledge and professional value elements are covered (e.g. K3, V1–V2).

In the third extract, again addressing 'A2 Teach and/or support learning', she is discussing how she approaches tutorial and seminar work.

> I have designed and delivered tutorials to undergraduate and postgraduate students. The students are encouraged to talk, engage and interact in the workshops and tutorials, and there are activities built into these sessions. At undergraduate level, I have asked the students to work in groups to read an article and them to present back to the class the main argument or theory outlined in the piece of writing. This aids students in developing their critical thinking and their oral communication skills. It is clear from the student feedback that this technique is an approach that is popular with students.

Notice here the mixture of description with reflective elements, such as how she relates to the students. She might have underpinned her application with more detailed references to pedagogic ideas and principles, and the evidence base for judging effectiveness could have been more formal and drawn on wider sources, but, on both counts, the application is thoughtful and reflective.

Reflective writing for a Senior Fellow Application

At first glance, the differences between Associate/Fellowship and Senior Fellowship do not seem to be that great. It looks as though it is just the addition of the seventh descriptor element (relating to supporting colleagues). But, in addition to that additional descriptor element, the Fellowship (D2) preamble starts with 'Demonstrates a *broad* understanding of effective approaches to teaching and learning support ...' whereas the Senior Fellowship (D3) preamble starts with 'Demonstrates a *thorough* understanding ...' (emphases added). So, a Senior Fellow is typically expected to have a much deeper engagement with aspects of the scholarship of learning and teaching and to be able to provide a deeper and more comprehensive rationale for his/her practice.

Strong Senior Fellow applications will therefore provide evidence of support to enable others to teach and support learning more effectively, and will be underpinned by a much deeper understanding of the other six descriptor elements (than that required for an Associate/Fellow). In a nutshell, it is the difference between being able to perform a particular role yourself, and the additional insight and understanding required to explain how that role might be performed and enhanced in others, and being able to provide evidence of the design and implementation of effective strategies to support others in performing that role.

For example, in the following extract from a Senior Fellow applicant referring to teaching in a university on a gender studies module, the interaction between theory and practice is expertly explored in a narrative which combines a practical example (described in the preceding paragraph) with clearly stated values and a strong core knowledge base.

> I wanted part-time students to make the leap from 'learning facts' to 'understanding concepts' (Ramsden 2003: 45). I needed to do this in a way that was inclusive and accessible. I was aware that it was important to balance accessible content with Dearing's recommendation for a universal standard of theoretical depth (Dearing 1997; Randall 2000). I noted these marginalised students offered personal insight on complex ideologies. When allowed to reflect, the class discussion would lead to a rich dialogue that clearly enhanced the group's understanding. I was trying to facilitate the cognitive link between 'knowing' what is learned in the classroom and 'being' that is their lived experience (Fontana 1988: 279). My goal was for students to reach some depth of academic knowledge (Gardner 1993) from personal experience [A1, A2, A3, A4, K1, V1, V2, V4].

Note again the personal nature of the account and the applicant's own motivations and also the explicit statement of values 'I needed to do this in a way that was inclusive and accessible.' Interestingly, the mapping list at the end of the application doesn't seem to do justice to the full breadth of Core Knowledge displayed in this extract. An assessor would nonetheless give credit for the other relevant Core Knowledge elements even though they had not been specifically listed. Not all Senior Fellow applications would show such a deep theoretical foundation for their practice but ideally they should all have this kind of reflective commentary.

In this second example from the same applicant, the stress is primarily on the support of other staff (D3.7).

My work with part-time tutors inspired active support for part-time disabled student support staff. I oversaw the review of the recruitment, selection, training, and ongoing evaluation of these staff. I brought practices into line with employment legislation and university policy while streamlining administrative process. My key change was to train these staff not just in what they were doing but why they were doing it. I gave the key address during training; I offered an ethical, political and informative account of the need for the support work. I wanted to get away from the reductive legal model (we make adjustments because of the DDA) and move toward a more motivating ethical argument (to enable every student to reach her/his potential; it is the right thing to do). The disability service employed up to 90 such staff, who supported approximately 1500 students over each academic year. The effectiveness of this review was measured in the increased efficiency of the service: there were fewer queries, complaints and confusion and improved feedback from supported-students at the annual independent review of the service [D3vii; D4iii].

Notice how the applicant has clearly stated and briefly explained her staff support role thus addressing the crucial D31.7 element and then gone on to explore her goals and her ethical stance. She concludes by mentioning how the effectiveness of this initiative was measured in terms of increased efficiency of service. She could have easily added some mapping to V1 and V2 if she had wished.

Reflective writing for a Principal Fellow application

The key difference between a Senior and Principal lies in the focus on leadership and specifically *strategic* leadership. The preamble states that a Principal Fellow should be able to demonstrate, '… a sustained record of effective strategic leadership in academic practice and academic development as a key contribution to high quality student learning'. So a Principal Fellow is typically expected to have a strong engagement with the strategic leadership typically at institutional or at national/international levels. And again, underpinned by a thorough understanding of HE pedagogy.

In the example below taken from a strong Principal Fellow application, the applicant is explaining the source of his deep commitment to widening participation and inclusive practice.

Throughout my academic career I have always championed the causes of widening participation and inclusive practice, and this is evidenced in my academic writing as well as my professional practice. My mother was from a Romany gypsy family and my father from a mining family, and both left school at the age of thirteen. I grew up in a home with no books, and I was expected to work from the age of fourteen. These experiences have profoundly shaped my outlook on the role of education and from two distinct directions. First, a strong belief in the power of education to transport oneself from 'the present and the particular' (Bailey 1984), but also, second, an equally strong belief in the importance of the curriculum reflecting the authentic aspirations of individuals, not just as a means to accommodate them into prescribed and pre-existing roles and practices. To this end, all my work is informed by the transformative possibilities engendered by forms of critical pedagogy (McLean 2008) [V4].

Note that the experience referred to dates back to the applicant's childhood and yet is clearly and unarguably relevant to his current practice and so is appropriate to include. Note also that the focus is on the applicant's values and that this is carefully related to examples taken from relevant pedagogic literature.

In the second extract, the applicant refers to the second of two internal papers he produced for the university's senior management team outlining suggestions for strategic initiatives.

The second paper took a more ambitious position, outlining how the university might rise to the challenge of placing students at the heart of the system, by championing the notion of students as co-producers of knowledge rather than just its consumers. The starting point was Neary and Winn's chapter in Bell et al. (2009) which drew on the history of this notion from von Humboldt through Vygotsky to Freire. Specifically I outlined how the notion of 'student as producer' could become an umbrella for a range of learning and teaching initiatives at the university. To this end, throughout 2012 and 2013 I have been presenting a series of such cases for change ...

Note the broad strategic scope of the paper he has produced, and how he refers to relevant literature and national policy agendas. He clearly identifies his own role, using 'I' throughout. And then he concludes by showing how he is taking it forward.

Finally, the same applicant talks about his national standing established while sitting on national committees, specifically on the impact he has had on policy initiatives aimed at vocational higher education in UK colleges.

[This] included consultancy and lobbying work with ministers, civil servants, and the various bodies charged with overseeing the development of the professionalisation agenda laid out in the *Equipping Our Teachers* document (DfES 2004). This experience was invaluable in developing my communication and lobbying skills, and in helping to fully understand the mechanisms through which education reform is administered in the UK. I also provided oral and written evidence for the Skills Commission inquiry into teacher training in vocational education, chaired by Sir Mike Tomlinson (Skills Commission 2011) [V4].

Again, we see the impact that the applicant has had in a personal capacity. He might have said more about what exactly he presented to the Skills Commission, but his evidence claim here seems more related to the CPD opportunity this work presented to him. Note again, the reference to the values component in the UKPSF.

Conclusion

Twenty-five years on from Boyer's (1990) publication – which started many people re-exploring ways to raise the profile of learning and teaching in HE – we hope we have clearly demonstrated (throughout this book) why and how this has proved to be tricky. Significantly, while concerted efforts have been made (including by the HEA) to raise the scholarly profile of teaching and learning, the tensions to pull teaching apart from research are perhaps even greater today than they were even twenty-five years ago. And even among those who oppose these trends, all the while that the big money, status, and kudos remains with research, the pressure to acquiesce is strong.

Furthermore, all the while that the QAA and the REF continue to be administered by separate bodies, and the desire to formally measure the impact of research on student learning remains weak, we may continue to find much of the impetus behind Boyer's work being dampened considerably by academic conventions which seem to exert themselves in equal measure from both outside and inside academe. That said, many universities in the UK are now moving steadily in the direction of creating distinct learning and teaching pathways to readerships and professorships, criteria for which are drawing on a much wider evidence base than traditional subject-based research output.

Many of us are also finding that there are interesting history lessons to be heeded in re-exploring the past – particularly in the work of prominent figures, most notably von Humboldt ([1810] 1970) and Newman ([1852] 1996). In their work we see a central role for *students* in developing forms of scholarship co-joined with academics (von Humboldt) and the central importance of the curriculum and the dissemination of new knowledge (Newman). If nothing else, this indicates that the battle for the very soul of the university is very much a contested one, and answering that question about what universities are for is not just a simple matter of reading from an original manuscript or blueprint. We can also see here that there is another question, which is not so much one of elevating the status of learning and teaching, but rather one of *returning* it to being a naturally integrated and holistic part of academic practice.

Throughout this book we have also seen many references to what it means to be engaged with *higher* education – that students will increasingly find themselves grappling not with textbook knowledge, but knowledge which is challenging the textbook; grappling with knowledge not at the core of the discipline but on the edge; knowledge in the making; and which reflexively looks at the conditions under which that knowledge was discovered or manufactured. Here, referring again to von Humboldt, we see that higher education is much more concerned with what is not known, than what is known. Recognising this, and armed with the appropriate curriculum design principles (see Chapter 6), it should then be possible to meaningfully (re) co-join the learning activities of students with staff, or as Healey and Jenkins put it, to 'enable students to learn in ways that parallel or reflect the ways academic staff themselves approach research and learn in their disciplines or professional area' (2009: 28).

Finally, we hope that we have provided you with sufficient stimulus throughout this book to encourage you to put together a thoughtful and coherent account of your engagement with issues relating to learning and teaching in HE, and how this can form the foundation for your application to become a fellow of the HEA (in whatever category). We also hope that the way we have presented the UKPSF will also be helpful in this regard; not as a competency model which grants you a licence to practice, but as an opportunity to interrogate the various dimensions of academic practice and how they might be better related to, and integrated with, learning and teaching, in the expectation of enhancing higher learning.

Relevant HEA project

The Staff and Education Development Association (2013) *Measuring the Impact of the UK Professional Standards Framework for Teaching and Supporting Learning (UKPSF)* www.heacademy.ac.uk/ukpsf-impact-study

As a final activity you may wish to consult and interrogate the Transport Map in Appendix 3 and ask yourself which of the key concepts (or stations) have the most influence on your practice. Only the concepts and stations which are discussed in the book appear on the map, and you may feel strongly that there are some that are missing or misplaced geographically. The map is accompanied by a glossary which briefly defines each concept. The map is available as a free download from the address at the foot of the map.

We finish this conclusion with one more opinion piece, which demonstrates how the notion of 'sustainability' both can and should be (for the author) the central axis around which all aspects of HE academic practice are holistically integrated.

Opinion: On sustainability

If not education for sustainable development, then what for?

Katja Hallenberg

Why do we work in higher education? What is the point of the classes we teach, the courses we design, the assessments we set and mark? What, in fact, is the purpose of our home institution? An easy answer will have us scurrying to learning outcomes, subject benchmarks, university strategies and perhaps even government policy. But I have never known an academic who settles for an easy answer. For most of us, I believe, such questions evoke deeper consideration of the very purpose of our discipline, and of higher education in general. Such existential crises are important, prompting us to question and change our thinking, actions, ourselves. Indeed, trans-formational learning (e.g. Mezirow 2009) would deem this as the *raison d'être of higher education.*

But it is important that we consider the direction of that transformation, for our students, universities, ourselves and the higher education sector as a whole. In their 2005 book Barnett and Coate refer to the responsibility of HE curriculum to address the 'challenges of a changing world'. Six years later, Barnett (2011) puts the case for an explicitly values-based model of an 'ecological university' that does its utmost to enhance global well-being (as measured in more than just economic terms) and develop the world in positive ways.

Such discussion reflects a wider call for Education for Sustainable Development (ESD), the United Nations' Decade (2005–2014), which has just drawn to a close (see Jones et al. 2010, for an overview). It placed particular responsibility on universities regarding research, learning, leadership and curricula development to facilitate ESD and its underlying values of human rights, social and economic justice, intergenerational responsibility, protection and restoration of ecosystems, respect for cultural diversity and commitment to peace (UNESCO 2004). Sustainability/sustainable development form the meta-narrative of our time (Scoffham and Kemp 2014) and should arguably also do so for education, shaping and driving its purpose and activities.

ESD requires pedagogic approaches that are interdisciplinary, holistic, embedded, values-driven, critical, problem-solving, participatory and authentic (i.e. relevant to real-world issues and experiences), that incorporate multiple perspectives, acknowledge and use prior skills and knowledge, and promote learning opportunities beyond the traditional curriculum (UNESCO 2004; HEA/QAA 2014). Encouraging critical reflection is crucial, both in terms of providing space for exploration, discussion and reflection of sustainability issues (Cotton and Winter 2010) and clarifying, challenging and de- and reconstructing our own values (UNESCO 2002). Specific teaching and learning methods that facilitate the above include, for example, use of stimuli and case studies, simulation/role-playing, problem-based learning, and experiential projects including service-learning (Cotton and Winter 2010).

No easy option, then, but possible, and very rewarding. I have been involved in ESD for several years, starting with the Manchester Leadership Programme (http://www.mlp.manchester.ac.uk/) focused on addressing twenty-first-century problems in the context of sustainability and ethical leadership. After moving to Canterbury Christ Church University I sought to introduce something similar within my own discipline. The end result was a module 'Criminology for a Just Society' (CfJS), developed with a support from the university's sustainability team and planned in collaboration with the students who helped shape the content, structure and assessment. This was done to facilitate a collaborative, more democratic learning environment, creating a sense of ownership and personal responsibility, important not just for ESD but learning in general.

The module aims to develop a broad and nuanced understanding of sustainability and criminology's potential to further it within the framework of environmental, social, cultural and economic justice. The four themes are addressed with an interdisciplinary focus, using readings and guest speakers from other disciplines and outside academia in order to encourage 'big picture' thinking. A big part of the module is service/action learning as students are expected to complete a minimum of 40 hours of volunteering which is closely linked to the assessment. This includes a reflective blog which solicits reflection-on- and in-action (Schön 1983) of the volunteering experiences, and allows students to make links between theory and practice.

CfJS is currently in its pilot year, running with a very small group of students, so it is too early to make any definite statements regarding its impact but the experience has so far been positive. Students are highly motivated, actively participating in the sessions and volunteering placements, and based on reflective blogs and class discussions appear to find the module both challenging and enjoyable. For me, CfJS is one of the most rewarding aspects of my practice. It is not only intellectually and pedagogically stimulating, but also aligned with my personal values and ethics, providing a clear sense of 'making a difference'. Modules that explicitly address sustainability have both strategic and symbolic value, signalling the importance and providing examples and catalysts, particularly in disciplines and departments where sustainability considerations have not previously been addressed (McGoshan and Martin 2014). They can create ripples that reach far, forming a part of a bottom-up, grassroots approach to facilitating a wider and deeper transformation (Scoffham and Kemp 2014).

Such a wholesale reorientation of core higher education systems, structures, practices and institutional cultures (Sterling 2004; UNESCO 2009) is crucial, because – to return to the questions raised at the start – if not Education for Sustainable Development, then what for? While the governmental *Zeitgeist* considers economic prosperity and employment as the key drivers of higher education, it is important to remember how both depend on the continued sustainability of resources and societies that support them. The other side of the argument highlights education as both the means and the end, emphasising the importance of creating new knowledge and pushing the boundaries of understanding. But is it not that very knowledge that has revealed the critical situation the world is facing? How to respond to that, or to choose not to respond, therefore becomes a dilemma higher education must engage with. Indeed, one can make a case for sustainability precisely to ensure the continuity of our ability to devote time and people to the pursuit of knowledge. After all, to put the point in its crudest terms, without a sustainable future, there will not be steady land or stable society to build any ivory towers on.

While it is important to question what counts as success in education, or in the world (Barnett and Coate 2005), I believe it is more important for the higher education to ask what counts as success *for* the world? Engaging with that would move beyond individualistic dispositions that view higher education and students as separate from the world they live in, highlighting how the success of the former is *dependent* on the success of the latter.

Note

1 Throughout this chapter Nigel Purcell writes in a personal capacity and not as a representative of the Higher Education Academy.

Glossary of Key Terms/Stations (see Transport Map)

Academic Capitalism: term often used to describe the process by which goods and services which were once outside the 'commodification' (see separate entry) process have now become potential sources of profit for universities and colleges, e.g. intellectual copyright being exploited for the purposes of income generation, and research projects being judged according to their profitability.

Academic Citizenship: term sometimes used to refer to the (perhaps undervalued) activities that academics routinely engage with in service to the academic community. For example, offering support and mentoring for new colleagues and students; undertaking external examining duties and/or reviews for other universities; reviewing book proposals and joining a journal editorial board.

Academic Freedom: broad term, often used when referring to the protection afforded academics as employees to speak freely and critically on controversial subjects, and the unwritten research code allowing research endeavour to be governed by the direction that the research takes the researcher. In practice, often used to mark its limits, and in drawing a line between freedom and responsibility.

Academic Guilds: term used to highlight that many academic disciplines operate like professional bodies – generating their own academic standards and conventions – and which academics (effectively or actually) join, and which may result in strong allegiance, possibly in contrast to, or even sometimes in tension with, their employing institution. Balancing allegiances is perhaps a unique feature of academic careers.

Academic Partners: broad term useful in asking questions about the extent to which students could be considered peers. For example, at what point might we speak of students being involved in the same types of discussions that academics routinely have with each other? The term also speaks to a contrast between students being involved in the decision-making process as opposed to just listening to their views.

Accountability: term applied to the increasingly explicit requirement to account for the use of time and resource. Often used positively when the process is a form of 'peer review', or unmediated by third parties (e.g. direct staff/student liaison). Often used negatively when third parties become proxies, and the exercise is perceived as controlling and de-professionalising, and unlikely to result in enhanced performance.

Accreditation for Prior Learning: APL; usually divided between APCL and APEL, where the former refers to previous certificated learning (essentially existing qualifications) and the latter to experiential learning (from appropriate experience). Usually requires evidence of having already met the learning outcomes for a course, and thereby achieve exemption or advanced standing on that course.

Action Research: approach to research which emphasises the role of the professional practitioner using research tools to solve professional problems, and which often treats the research participants as collaborators (often students) in the research process rather than as just respondents (see particularly the work of Jean McNiff). Sometimes accorded a low research status by non-users.

Active Learning: blanket term often used to highlight a contrast between active engagement in learning and passive acquisition of knowledge. Can imply active as in workshop style learning, but also more broadly to imply the active processing of the more cognitive and reflective learning activities, where meaning is constructed by the student, in the process of learning (see Deep Learning and Constructivism).

Anti-Authoritarian Classroom: a term which speaks to a contrast between teachers as authority figures and as *authoritarian* figures – in the latter, dictating the classroom rather than facilitating learning. More controversial when this process is perceived as undermining the subject expertise of the teacher. Has links with Student as Producer, Wilhelm von Humboldt and Carl Rogers (see separate entries).

Anticipatory Design: an architectural term implying the need for buildings to be able to accommodate multiple (possibly future) uses. Can be adapted as a curriculum design principle to think about how a range of students might be able to engage with learning resources (including virtual ones). Has links with Universal Design for Learning (UDL) (see separate entry).

Assessment for Learning: broad term used to distinguish between assessment practices which focus on what students are expected to do in their assignments and on feedback which concentrates on what they actually did, as opposed to a focus on what will enable learning, and develop learning between assignments. The term is often linked with notions of developmental feedback and feed-forward.

Audit Cultures: term referring to the growth of (particularly) external and (mostly) State-backed auditing of professional and organisational activities. Largely negative in connotation, emphasising the incursive and high-stakes nature of the exercises, thereby distorting forms of authentic professional behaviour, and rooted in a lack of trust in public-sector service oriented professionals (see Thatcherism).

Business Ontology: term which refers to the increasing amount of university estates which are being given over to eye-catching buildings, but which are celebrated more for their architectural design principles, than their effectiveness in enhancing learning and teaching. Could also be understood more literally to imply that the buildings look more like corporate buildings than traditional university ones.

Calculated Uncertainty: term which refers to ways in which space is able to combine aspects of e.g. technology and art, which while delineating a set space also helps facilitate creative subversions and new imaginative ways of being, acting and thinking. Has connections with post-modern ideas and with Max Weber – embracing uncertainty rather than engineering it away, for fear of creating a disenchanted world.

Campus Gilding: term which refers to the ways that college and universities are increasingly investing in eye-catching architecture and services which relate more to the social side of university life rather than the strictly academic, in the hope that it will be attractive to students, and guide their decision to study in one institution as opposed to another.

Capability: a term which reflects a move away from an emphasis on the more cognitive aspects of learning traditionally associated with higher education, and a move in the direction of education enhancing human development and quality of life. Questions of social justice and social inequality might also be to the fore. It has links with Critical Pedagogy and the Ecological University (see separate entries).

Capitalised Space: term associated with the Marxist writer Henri Lefebvre, which speaks of the way that space in capitalist societies comes to reflect and reproduce the logic and needs of capitalist work relations, e.g. maintaining social class divisions. It invites a consideration of how these ideas can infiltrate university estates thereby curtailing more utopian, subversive, and countervailing ways of being.

Cardinal Newman: John Henry Newman, whose series of lectures delivered in Dublin in 1852, have become seminal in defending the primary intellectual (not moral) function of universities, emphasising the teaching and dissemination of Universal knowledge. Now collectively known as *The Idea of a University.*

Carl Rogers: the psychotherapist who applied many clinical ideas to educational practice, particularly highlighting the importance of personal growth and the affective domain. He also inspired many teachers to concern themselves less with their own ability to teach and to concentrate more on what enhances learning – particularly promoting the idea of autonomous student learning.

CBHE: College-Based Higher Education, as a term it speaks to the growth of higher education outside of designated universities, and particularly its distinctive nature, and contribution to 'widening participation' (see separate entry). For example, CBHE often serves local 'non-traditional' students and local employers, often with a more obvious vocational portfolio of courses compared with some traditional universities.

Co-Assessment: term used to describe the process where teachers and students *together* agree the appropriate mark or grade for a piece of work. The process might begin by each party separating marking (and as a piece of self-assessment for the student) but then both parties negotiating together the final mark or grade. It mirrors the second marking approach more traditionally associated with teacher marking.

Collegiality: broad term used to refer to the democratic principle at work amongst academic colleagues, affording each an equal status and stake in decision-making. Sometimes used to highlight 'academic rule' or 'donnish dominion' (Halsey 1992) as opposed to rule by managers. In practice, often used to contrast a collegiate ethos with forms of Corporatism (see separate entry).

Collegiate Architecture: term which implies that space can be designed to reflect forms of Collegiality (see separate entry) and in opposition to forms of Corporatism (see separate entry), with its implied management hierarchies. Examples might be found in spaces which are open to all, and/or where designated staff and student spaces are in close proximity, creating a sense of community and democracy.

Commodification: term that refers to the way in which educational services are increasingly becoming saleable products. Relates to Karl Marx's idea of a contradiction between something having use-value (i.e. being useful), but at the same time having exchange-value (i.e. being saleable) and which is the stronger force. Generally derogatory in tone, but can also reflect an economic realism.

Communities of Learning: term associated with the work of Jean Lave and Etienne Wenger, along with 'communities of practice'. Commonly used when discussing the ways that 'novice' learners are inducted into ways of being and acting within a professional and/or discipline-based community, including using the appropriate methods and approaches to knowledge which are conventional in that community.

Constructive Alignment: term associated with John Biggs, specifying the need to produce explicit and transparent links between learning outcomes, and learning, teaching and assessment strategies (to create a virtuous triangle) (Biggs and Tang 2007). Sometimes referred to as a learning outcomes approach, designed to enable students to meet or demonstrate the stated learning outcomes.

Constructivism: a broad term with sociological implications about the social construction of identity, but in educational circles more often associated with the work of Jean Piaget and Lev Vygotsky. Commonly used when considering the way that students make sense of new knowledge and their need to assimilate it with their existing knowledge. It has connections with Scaffolding (see separate entry).

Contestability: term which can be used to highlight the importance of high order analytic skills (see Learning Taxonomies), enabling students to recognise and deal with the contested nature of knowledge, particularly when working at the limits of a discipline's knowledge base. Could also be linked to higher education being about what is not known rather than what is known (see Wilhelm von Humboldt).

Contrived Collegiality: term associated with work of Hargreaves (1994), to highlight a form of management behaviour which promotes outwardly an image of collegiality and collective decision-making, but only when the outcomes of the decision-making process are in accord with prescribed management outcomes. Can be contrasted with other forms of teacher culture, e.g. 'balkanised' (see Subject Allegiance).

Corporatism: broad term referring to organisational structures which usually have a strict management hierarchy, an emphasis on economic accountability and require explicit allegiance from employees to organisational goals. Often used in a derogatory manner by academics when they see these developments encroaching on Academic Freedom and allegiance to Academic Guilds (see separate entries).

Critical Pedagogy: term commonly associated with the work of Paulo Freire, in highlighting the need for the curriculum to help (particularly) disadvantaged groups not only understand their circumstances, but to be educated such that they could act to change those circumstance. Term continues to be key for authors such as Henry Giroux and bell hooks in the USA and Monica McLean and Mike Neary in the UK.

Cultural Cognition: or cultural literacy or cultural citizenship (Delanty 2001), terms designed to raise awareness of the need for students to leave university not just with a set of traditional cognitive and practical skills, but also an ability to understand and apply forms of cultural awareness. The terms speak not just to the need to understand cultural difference but also to communicate effectively across cultures.

Culture of Compliance: blanket term used to describe organisational behaviour where there is an emphasis on complying with prescribed rules and procedures. In some circles the term is used positively but in academic professional circles it is more often used in derogatory ways to indicate forms of de-professionalisation, particularly where once decision-makers have increasingly become rule followers.

Curriculum Ideologies: broad term used to convey the idea that the curriculum can have multiple and/or broad aims. Generally: to develop the person; to prepare people for social roles; and/or develop understanding and knowledge. In practice a particular curriculum is likely to combine elements of these, which speaks to the need to articulate how these aims will be enacted and the relationship between them.

Dead White Males: colloquial term to highlight how much of the university curriculum is taken up with the ideas of a narrow cross section of the population (and usually from Western societies). The term is often used in conjunction with the concept of Euro-Centrism to highlight a bias away from ideas embedded in other cultures and societies, to create an impression of Western Civilisation *as* civilisation.

Deep Learning: term originally attributed to Marton and Saljo (1976), and as a contrast term with surface learning, where the latter emphasises recall of information and description of concepts and principles, as opposed to the deeper skills of attributing meaning, contextualisation, and application. Has links with Active Learning and Engaged Learning (see separate entries).

Digital Colonialism: term used by Amiel (2013) with reference particularly to MOOCs (massive online open courses), which while being open and democratic, when run by Northern/Western universities might also have, perhaps hidden, colonial connotations. Has links with Widening Participation (see separate entry) in asking whether new forms of digital learning are just serving those already well represented.

Dis-engagement Contract: term associated with George Kuh, which speaks to the way that it is possible for students to go through university or college essentially disengaged from their studies, but still leave with the appropriate qualifications. This may happen when students are not stretched and/or when students learn how to be strategic in minimising the effort they need to exert (Arum and Roksa 2011).

Disinterested Knowledge: term often used when describing the nature of academic knowledge production (as in original research and discovery); that it is pursued without vested interest and directed by the results of the research findings, rather than the values of the researcher, or the interests of other stakeholders, e.g. employing institutions or funders (see Standpoint Knowledge as a contrast term).

Dissensus: term associated with Readings (1996), to imply the need for universities to produce students who can successfully negotiate not consensus, but operate effectively in a world of dissensus. The term speaks to the idea that reaching a consensus is not always the best outcome, and that the ability to negotiate disagreement would be a better axial principle for universities.

Diversity: broad term which speaks to the pedagogical implications of widening the student profile (e.g. a broader mix of social class and minority representation). Often used in discussions about what kinds of support minority groups need to access and engage better with the curriculum, and/or whether the curriculum content needs to change to reflect a wider cross section of Voice Perspectives (see separate entry).

Divided Line: term used by Plato in *The Republic* to distinguish knowledge as Universal truth (episteme) from orthodoxies (doxa) and opinion, and that it is the pursuit of the former which should occupy the minds of the philosophers in his academy. Continues to hold sway in curriculum ideologies which emphasise the disinterested pursuit of truth as a core principle for teaching and research.

Doughnut Round: colloquial term for a teaching and learning strategy designed to encourage students to become more actively engaged with reading material. Students are asked to formulate questions for other students about some selected reading for a class or seminar. It becomes a 'round' because each responder then gets the chance to ask another student their question and so on.

Ecological University: a term which refers to the idea of a university's principles and practices being grounded in notions of Sustainability (see separate entry), Well-being, and interconnectedness. For example, this might be made manifest in an active monitoring of an institution's research output and partnership working to ensure they are in accord with these principles.

Employability: term often linked with Vocationalism (see separate entry), but one which implies a broader underpinning of the curriculum (and wider student experience) with a range of skills and attributes which would make a student more generally employable. Can be used in derogatory manner to imply unwarranted vocational drift, but also as valuable in articulating discipline-based graduateness.

Engaged Learning: broad term which refers to learning activities which require the active engagement of students in order to complete them. Has obvious links with Student Engagement (see separate entry), but can also be used to distinguish between engagements which are closely linked to gaining university level credit, and the wider engagement of students in all aspects of university or college life.

Enlightenment: term often used to explain the nature of knowledge and understanding in the 'modern' era. Literally it speaks of illuminating; discovering the truth for oneself through reason and empirical methods rather than waiting for it to be revealed through religious faith, or believing in fate, or traditional authority. Often critiqued by post-modern thinkers who claim that it too requires a form of faith.

Ernest Boyer: his seminal work on *Scholarship Reconsidered* (1990) is often viewed as the step change text in promoting the Scholarship of Teaching and Learning (SOTL) (see separate entry). The text was also instrumental in promoted a more rounded and holistic approach to scholarship – including discovery (original research), application, integration, and teaching – and equalising esteem between them.

Ethical University: broad term implying a need for universities to ground their activities more in ethical principles. This might also manifest itself in organisational practices (e.g. choice of business partnerships and/or resource purchases) but also as embedded in research and in the curriculum (e.g. ethical principles for research practices and/or an emphasis on, e.g., notions of social justice in course content).

Flipped Classroom: colloquial term used to summarise a pedagogical approach where students come to the classroom after having engaged with various learning resources and then proceed to teach (or share) with their peers and teachers what they have learnt. Associated with a questioning of the value of lectures and elevation of the seminar as being more important for learning (see Wilhelm von Humboldt).

Gaming: term used to highlight a contrast between the desire to enhance practice and a desire to perform well in audit exercises, particularly where the latter has little effect on the former, and/or where an organisation is more motivated by the latter than the former. Tends to be most evident when the stakes are high for an organisation in terms of the potential to drop down an audit-related league table.

Going Public: term used to distinguish between being critically reflective about teaching and learning – possibly through engagement in institution-based peer review exercises – and disseminating the results as publicly available published research – subjecting those results to wider peer review and public scrutiny and debate (see Kreber 2013).

Goldfish Bowl: a term which describes an approach where students observe (without intervention) a group of their peers at work on a learning task, and then provide feedback. Tried and trusted as an approach in helping students focus on the nature of the learning (not just what was being learnt). It has obvious connections with the notion of a Flipped Classroom and Active Learning (see separate entries).

Hybrid Learning: term which speaks to the ways that by combining aspects of traditional face-to face with aspects of on-line learning that combination creates its own unique form of learning, with implications for curriculum design and pedagogy. Can be linked with 'blended learning', but with a focus perhaps more on the uniqueness of the pedagogical result rather than the nature of what is blended.

Impact Measures: term relating to the need to provide explicit evidence of the effect of professional interventions. Has particularly significance because of the explicit need to demonstrate the impact of research as a mark of its quality (REF 2012). For some, this could distort the motivation for engaging in research, along with Pa narrow definition of impact – emphasising Performativity (see separate entry).

Inclusion: broad term with multiple level meanings. Can refer to general social inclusion, with links to belongingness, Widening Participation and Diversity (see separate entries). Closer to the curriculum it is often used to signal not the readiness of a student to learn, but the readiness of the institution to enable that student to learn. Has added implications when considering Online Self (see separate entry).

Indeterminacy: term popular with post-modern thinkers to imply that rational calculation often has unintended and ironic consequences. In terms of learning space the term implies that that this should be embraced rather than denigrated; implying that a more playful and creative inhabiting of space is both liberating and in keeping with forms of Critical Pedagogy (see separate entry).

Infantilisation: term associated with the work of Frank Furedi, implying that there has been a gradual movement in higher education, away from ideas of Self-Actualisation (see separate entry) towards students being treated as vulnerable and in need of constant support. It might be seen in the unwarranted and over cautious desire to ensure that the educative process is not harming students.

Jigsaw Classroom: colloquial term first used by Aronson (1978) to explain a teaching and learning strategy where small groups of students work together on one aspect of a topic, and then teach it to the rest of the group, who have also been assigned different aspects of the same topic. Each piece in this jigsaw then becomes part of the process of piecing together the bigger picture.

Knowledge Economy: term used to describe an economy which is increasingly dependent on Knowledge Products (see separate entry) and on the knowledge of its workforce. Sometimes viewed in a derogatory way because of its potential to corrupt a more traditional view of knowledge – that it should be loved for its own sake, or for general public good, rather than just for its potential to drive the economy.

Knowledge Products: term used to describe the process by which knowledge becomes an essential ingredient in product creation, in particular where a product has a knowledge component at its core. The term might apply to the perceived need for students to see this as essential to their Employability (see separate entry), but also, where academics are invited to see the output of their research in these terms.

Learning Taxonomies: term which refers to the classification and ranking of skills in various learning domains. Popularised by Bloom (1956) and colleagues for the cognitive, followed by the affective and psychomotor domains. Refined several times since then, for example, in the SOLO taxonomy (Biggs and Tang 2007). Often used when writing learning outcomes to help specify appropriate skill-related verbs.

Lecturing: a term which summarises the traditional didactic approach to delivering content to a (often very large) group of students from behind a pedestal in a designated lecture theatre, set up with fixed rows of seating. A resilient method of teaching that has survived countless attacks on its merits as a means to enable or enhance student learning. In practice, can be highly interactive.

Liberal Tradition: term used to describe educational pedagogies and knowledge production processes which are rooted in the idea of loving and pursing knowledge for its own sake. Often used when countering the claim that knowledge should be pursued for the extrinsic purposes of, for example, wealth creation, or that subjects should be studied in order to prepare students for jobs and future social roles.

Liquid University: term associated with Ron Barnett, after 'liquid modernity' (Bauman 2000). It speaks to the idea of universities and colleges having less fixed boundaries, working and forming collaborative partnerships, which might be short term and/or global in scale, reflecting a contraction of time and space in modern life. Might also require more entrepreneurial rather than bureaucratic modes of operation.

Managerialism: term used to describe management practices which emphasise the need for employee behaviour and activities to be in accord with what has been prescribed. Can be used to distinguish between active people management and bureaucratic compliance. Generally unpopular among academics when they perceive that their professionalism is being undermined by intrusive management.

Marketisation: a broad term often used to describe not markets per se, but the process of exerting market forces on goods and services which have been traditionally protected from these forces. Terms like 'regulated market' or 'social market' also indicate this process, for example, as applied to attempts to increase the competition between educational providers for State funds and resources.

Massification: term which refers to the growth of student numbers in universities and colleges, particularly when it results in the need to restructure educational practice to accommodate the growth (e.g. larger teaching groups). It also has a technical definition, where 'mass' means that 15–50 per cent of an age-cohort are in higher education (below 15 per cent means 'elite', and above 50 per cent means 'universal') (Trow 2010).

Mindfulness: a term which relates to a soft skill or attribute of teacher presence in the classroom. It speaks to an ability to be aware of an audience and work to enhance warmth and connectedness. Also often connected to the wider notions of contemplative learning, affective learning domain, and balancing the more cognitive and rational aspects of learning (see Capability and Well-Being).

Mode 2 Knowledge: term associated with Gibbons and colleagues (1994), which speaks to the way in which universities are increasingly validating courses, and developing knowledge bases which are inter and trans-disciplinary and have closer applied links with the world of work and professions, particularly when compared with the more traditional, more insular, university-based disciplines (Mode 1 Knowledge).

Near Market: term often used to describe a motivation when conducting research where marketable products are likely to be an outcome. Often used in a derogatory way to distinguish this motivation from 'blue skies' thinking, or the pursuit of Disinterested Knowledge (see separate entry). Can be used positively in an applied research context and or as a colloquial Impact Measure term (see separate entry).

Neo-liberalism: a political philosophy which emphasises the role of private individuals and companies being motivated by their own actions in the consumption and production of goods and services, provided in free markets, and unfettered by State regulation or interference. Often used to contrast with those who value the role of the State and the wider community in providing access to societal resources.

Objective Knowledge: term often used to contrast curriculum knowledge from subjective opinion. Sometimes used to describe the nature of academic knowledge – as being beyond anecdote and personal testimony – as rooted in systematic study, using agreed research tools (often, discipline-based). Sometimes used in a derogatory manner to ask whether knowledge could ever be completely objective.

Online Learning: broad term which speaks to the way that more learning and teaching is happening in Virtual Space (see separate entry), and the implications of that. Commonly used when speaking of distance learning software packages and MOOCs (massive online open courses), where the learning is open to anyone, anywhere, and happens entirely online.

Online Self: term which speaks to the ways that individuals develop aspects of their learner (and wider) identity in Virtual Space (see separate entry). Has a troubling connotation when implying that this self may not be a true self, but also has an inclusive connotation by enabling students to engage with learning in ways they might feel more comfortable with (see Inclusion).

Open-Ended Architecture: blanket term which can be used to summarise the opposition between university buildings and space which dictate how they should be used, and the possibilities for more liberatory forms of learning when there is the possibility for flexible negotiations of space by all users, at all times, and into the future.

Peer Assessment: broad term used when a student's peer group is involved in the assessment and feedback process. Commonly used in group work where each group gives feedback to the other groups. Often used in a 'peer assisted learning' (PAL) initiative where senior students give advice on assignments to junior students. Can also be useful in helping students become more familiar with grading criteria.

Peer Learning: broad term relating to all the ways in which students might learn from each other, rather than just from their teachers. This might be, for example, informally outside formal class time; as directed by teachers within formal class contact time; and/or as part of a 'peer-assisted learning' (PAL) scheme. Increasingly, it also refers to students acting as (formal or informal) assessors of their peer's work.

Performance Indicators: similar to Impact Measures (see separate entry), but with emphasis on the construction of the measures themselves. Used positively in corporate circles to help strengthen organisational allegiance, but also used negatively when academics perceive the indicators to be constraints on creative thinking, and as examples of Managerialism (see separate entry).

Performativity: term sometimes used in sociological circles to highlight the social construction of aspects of human identity, but more commonly used in educational theory to refer to behaviours which are in accord with what has been prescribed by institutional custom and practice, but are engaged with or enacted in an inauthentic manner, and often perceived as a form of de-professionalisation.

Private University: term relating to a university or college which has no primary funding from the public purse. In effect, there is no clear boundary between a Public University (see separate entry) and a private one, because both in practice can attract funds from similar sources. Often linked to privatisation, and a perceived need to be less dependent on the public purse for accessing income and resources.

Problem-Based Learning: broad term relating to learning and teaching strategies which focus on setting problems (either real or simulated) which students, either individually or in groups, set about solving. Its rationale is often linked to the merits of Active learning and encouraging Deep Learning (see separate entries), but also because it mirrors the type of learning more likely to be encountered in a work place.

Public University: a university (or college) which is funded (primarily or entirely) by the public purse, and/or serves the public good rather than acting for private gain. It is also often linked with a desire to see knowledge pursued for its own (intrinsic) sake (see Liberal Tradition), rather than for what it might (extrinsically) lead to. Used by supporters as a positive contrast term with Private University (see separate entry).

Realist Epistemology: term used to promote the idea that certain methods of enquiry will enable us to understand the world (social and/or natural) as it *is*, rather than as a collection of ideas, perspectives, or interpretations. The latter may leave us with no basis to decide what enters a curriculum, other than the wherewithal of those who have the power/influence to get their perspectives heard (Young 2008).

Really Useful Knowledge: a contrast term used to distinguish between the emancipatory learning which will enable people to change their social circumstances (e.g. poverty and social disadvantage) and 'merely useful knowledge' which has the effect of leaving those circumstances untouched. It has connections with Critical Pedagogy and Transformative Learning (see separate entries).

Recontextualisation: term sometimes used to articulate the relationship between theory and practice in a discipline-based or Work-based Learning (see separate entry) course. The term speaks to the two-way process of generating theory from practice, and vice versa, and the need for all knowledge to be re-contextualised as it moves from context to context.

Reflective Practice: broad term popularised by the work of Donald Schön, which focused on the ways that professionals learn by reflecting in and on their work. Can be linked with 'grounded theory' and the ability to generate concepts and theories from practice rather than vice versa, and when considering how reflection can be a construction site for knowledge, not just the process of thinking about knowledge.

Reinvention Room: literally a room at the University of Warwick, but as a term it speaks to the perceived need for teaching and learning spaces to become more flexibly available to a wide range of users. Conceptually it speaks of a need to be able to break free from the dictating influence of fixed furniture and fittings, and of the learning potential in having to negotiate the space each time it is entered and used.

Research-Based Learning: term popularised by Healey and Jenkins (2009), to distinguish it from Research-Tutored, Research-Orientated and Research-Led Learning (see separate entries). The term is designed to emphasise the participatory and process-driven nature of student involvement in research and inquiry, specifically where they undertake their own research projects as part of their degree programme.

Research-Led Learning: term popularised by Healey and Jenkins (2009), to distinguish it from Research-Tutored, Research-Oriented and Research-Based Learning (see separate entries). The term is designed to emphasise the perhaps more passive and content-driven nature of student involvement in research and inquiry, specifically where they learn about current research within a discipline.

Research-Oriented Learning: term popularised by Healey and Jenkins (2009), to distinguish it from Research-Tutored, Research-Based and Research-Led Learning (see separate entries). The term is designed to emphasise the perhaps more passive but process-driven nature of student involvement in research and inquiry, specifically where students develop research and inquiry skills and techniques.

Research-Tutored Learning: term popularised by Healey and Jenkins (2009), to distinguish it from Research-Based, Research-Oriented and Research-Led Learning (see separate entries). The term is designed to emphasise the participatory and content-driven nature of student involvement in research and inquiry, specifically where they are actively involved in discussions about research and inquiry.

Resilience: term which speaks to a general attribute associated with successful learning. Can be linked to attribution theory, which ask questions about to whom or what do people attribute their successes and failures. Resilient learners tend not to be fatalistic, have a strong Will to Learn (see separate entry) and a strong sense of personal agency.

Scaffolding: term associated with the work of Lev Vygotsky, but coined by Jean Bruner. It speaks to the ways that students build from what they already know and through this can be enabled to reach higher and more independent forms of learning. Has connections with Constructive Alignment and Learning Taxonomies (see separate entries) and the writing of effective learning outcomes.

Scripted Communication: term used to highlight how professionals are often required to 'learn their lines' to ensure a positive outcome in a review or inspection exercise. Often motivated by a desire to look good rather than be good, or to 'toe the party line' for fear of the consequences of not doing so. The term has an obvious ironic connotation in academic professional circles (Lea 2009).

Self-Actualisation: term associated with the work of Abraham Maslow, used as the pinnacle term in his hierarchy of needs. The hierarchy demands that the lower needs are met, which then enable the enactment of self-actualisation. The term has links with autonomous learning (see Carl Rogers) and Unencumbered Self (see separate entry), implying that self-direction and self-will are key to higher learning.

Self-Assessment: broad term used when there is an emphasis on students assessing their own work. This might include constructing their own assignments, but more usually refers to the monitoring of their own progress, and/or marking their own work, possibly in a joint manner with their teachers. Often used as a pedagogical tool to help students become familiar with grading criteria.

Self-Criticality: term used to highlight not just the ability to think critically about a subject, but also to think self-critically, that is, evaluate aspects of one's own identity, and attachment to certain ideas, and their foundation in character formation. The term is likely to feature in courses which concentrate on self-development and personal growth (see Carl Rogers) and/or Reflective Practice (see separate entries).

Significant Learning: term associated with Carl Rogers (see separate entry), highlighting the need for knowledge to have significant meaning for a student in terms of its affect on self-development. Can be used as a contrast term against the cognitive learning of abstract principles, and behavioural acquisition of psychomotor skills, particularly where both have little prospect of guiding personal growth.

SOTL: the scholarship of teaching and learning; term highlighting the importance of teaching and learning methods being underpinned and informed by the research and scholarly evidence for their effectiveness. For some, an emphasis was placed on Action Research (see separate entry). For others, reflecting on practice and the further need for Going Public (see separate entry) on the findings was emphasised.

Standpoint Knowledge: term which speaks to research and knowledge which is avowedly in the interests of certain social groups or political causes. Sometimes used as a contrast with Disinterested Knowledge (see separate entry), highlighting how the latter can disguise its own vested interests. And sometimes used to promote identity affirmation amongst exploited or underrepresented social groups.

Student as Active Collaborator: blanket term which refers to the multiple ways in which students might take a more active role in the life and work of their university or college. The term speaks to moving away from listening to the student voice, and moving more towards seeing students as active partners, possibly working more as Student as Teacher, as Scholar and/or as Change Agent (see separate entries).

Student as Change Agent: broad term relating to the ways that students might get more actively involved in the organisational life and work of a university or college. Does not imply need for particular forms of change, with potential for tension between students who view HE knowledge as intrinsically valuable compared with those who hold more utilitarian notions (e.g. as a means to get a high status job).

Student as Co-Creator: a term which refers to the ways in which students might begin to see learning as a contribution to knowledge production. Has obvious links with Student as Producer (see separate entry), but in the use of the prefix 'co' it might point to the types of activities where students are supported to make a step in this direction; possibly working alongside, or as junior members of research teams.

Student as Co-Designer: a useful term to highlight the ways in which students might get more involved in understanding and enacting curriculum design principles. This might involve students sitting as advisers on course validation events, and/or working in partnership with staff on designing a course or module (e.g. its Constructive Alignment – see separate entry), which they will then subsequently undertake.

Student as Consultant: a term which is useful in highlighting a mirroring of the types of consultancy work that academics routinely undertake – as advisors, experts, and reviewers. For example, students might advise university committees by presenting evidence from the student experience, or they might advise staff team meetings, particularly on their experience of, and research evidence on, learning and teaching.

Student as Producer: term associated today with the work of Mike Neary at the University of Lincoln. It speaks to a contrast between students as passive consumers of knowledge or as active contributors to the production of knowledge, by being engaged in a range of scholarly and research activities. Has many historical links with, e.g. Critical Pedagogy and Wilhelm von Humboldt (see separate entries).

Student as Scholar: broad term relating to all the ways that students (particularly undergraduates) might take a more scholarly approach in their learning. At one extreme it might involve students actually publishing a piece of work, but might also mean undertaking a small-scale research project; and/or using an evidence-based approach to solving a problem within a discipline context or beyond.

Student as Teacher: broad term summarising all the ways in which students might act in a teaching capacity, for example, as part of a group presentation or poster presentation for their peer group, or taking responsibility for explaining concepts and ideas to their peer group and teachers. Recognised as a way to promote Active Learning, Deep Learning, and Engaged Learning (see separate entries).

Student-Centred Learning: blanket term used to summarise approaches which place the student at the centre of the planning and enactment of learning. Commonly seen in notions of the Flipped Classroom, Active Learning, Engaged Learning, Deep Learning and in the application of the principles of 'constructive alignment' and has connections with the work of Carl Rogers (see separate entries).

Student Engagement: blanket term used to describe myriad ways in which students might be more actively involved in student life. Has obvious connections with Engaged Learning (see separate entry) but can also be used to distinguish engagement which is relating to formal learning, from broader notions, e.g. acting as mentors to other students; and/or engaging in outreach and community projects.

Student Surveys: blanket term used to refer to the growing evidence base on the nature of the student experience of higher education, as documented in the results of large scale social surveys, e.g. the National Student Survey (NSS) in the UK and the National Survey of Student Engagement (NSSE) in the US. Questions have been raised about their reliability and validity, and their distortion of academic behaviours.

Subject Allegiances: term used variously to highlight the central importance of subject knowledge in the teaching of a subject; the importance of being versed in its conceptual language; and/or that this is best foundation for preparation to teach a subject. This can create 'balkanised' (Hargreaves 1994) divisions between subject-based departments (see also Tribes and Territories and Subject Pedagogies).

Subject Pedagogies: term used to recognise the ways that different subjects are taught, and related to that, how new teachers are prepared for their teaching roles within their disciplines. The term raises the question of whether these pedagogies are simply conventional or rooted in deeper epistemological considerations, and the link between this and the way a subject develops it knowledge base.

Super-complexity: term associated with Barnett (2000), highlighting not just the complexity brought about by the sheer amount of knowledge and information currently available, but also the multiple epistemological axes for knowledge production, and the need to be critically aware of the conditions of its production – requiring a heightened sense of reflexivity among students.

Sustainability: term which can apply equally to the practices of a university or college overall (see Ecological University) but also how its principles are embedded in the curriculum. For students it might be defined as a need to promote the idea of environmentally responsible citizenship. For an organisation it could include active monitoring of new builds to ensure they use renewable energy and building sources.

Teaching-Research Nexus: broad term used to highlight the multiple relations or permutations between teaching and research in higher education. For example, teaching led by the research interests of the teacher; teaching informed by the results of pedagogic research; teaching which seeks to develop the research capabilities of students, etc. (see Neumann 1992).

Technological Fetishism: term used by Bainbridge (2014) which speaks to the way the use of technology in learning can dominate discussions of its pedagogical appropriateness and ability to enhance learning. The term 'fetish' implies that the real object of desire has been substituted for another, and/or that substituted object has been granted a misplaced power and status.

Technology-Enhanced Learning: (TEL); a broad term which refers to the ways in which technology is used to enhance the learning and teaching process. In practice is most commonly used in curriculum design discussions, when asking the question of how the technology is being used pedagogically – as a tool of teaching and learning rather than just focusing on the functions of the technology itself.

TESTA: Transforming the Experience of Students Through Assessment; a national project based at the University of Winchester, enabling teams to evaluate their courses by taking a bird's eye view from a student's perspective. Results indicate that the emphasis on individual modules can have adverse effects for students, e.g. in the bunching of assignments and repeated meeting of learning outcomes.

Thatcherism: term used to describe the monetarist (see Friedman and Friedman 1980) free market policies of the UK governments led by Margaret Thatcher in the 1980s. Thatcherism, as a term, was also a way of linking those economic policies with wider social and political ideas. In universities and colleges this was particularly felt in the perceived need for public-sector professionals to be called to account (see Audit Culture).

Therapeutic Turn: term useful in implying that higher education is increasingly concerning itself with the well-being of students and eroding its true purpose. First popularised in the USA by Sykes (1992), who spoke of students being encouraged to see themselves as victims of circumstances, and in the UK by Ecclestone and Hayes (2008), who spoke of students being cast as 'diminished selves'.

Threshold Concepts: term associated with work of Meyer and Land (2006) which speaks to those discipline-based concepts and ideas which are often 'troublesome' for students, but once grasped can lead to significant subsequent learning. Can also be adapted to refer to wider, more generic concepts and ideas, like the notion of 'reflective practice' (see separate entry).

Transformative Learning: term often used to describe learning which has a profound effect on the learner. For example, learning which makes a significant contribution to personal growth, or provides significant opportunities for students to bring about changes in their personal circumstances or life chances. It can be linked to 'critical pedagogy' (see separate entry).

Tribes and Territories: term associated with Becher (1989) to indicate how universities are typified by distinct discipline-based research allegiances, which help to cement strong in-group and out-group behaviour. The term continues to be reworked by Paul Trowler – see Becher and Trowler (2001) and Trowler et al. (2014).

Tutor Embodiment: term which speaks to ways that learning is supported by the on-line presence of tutors. This might require careful consideration in supporting those who are not so-called 'digital natives' – with the technologies as much as the learning – but also has wider implications when seeking to support the development of a student's Online Self (see separate entry).

Unencumbered-Self: term associated with Ron Barnett, used to highlight the importance of education in forging a distinct sense of agency for a student, in stark contrast to forms of dependency (which they may start their education with). It could be connected with forms of Critical Pedagogy (see separate entry), with an emphasis on students being confident about their ability to enact social change.

Universal Design for Learning: term popularised by the Center for Applied Special Technology (CAST) in the USA, which utilises the architectural principle of universal design of buildings (consider potential users of a building not just the immediate client group) and asking teachers to consider the multiple ways in which students might be able to access and engage with teaching and learning activities and resources.

Universal Knowledge: term used to imply that some knowledge is not just 'objective' (see separate entry) but applies in all circumstances and at all times. For some, such knowledge has *a priori* status (i.e. is beyond experience and not liable to contradiction by empirical evidence). Can be used in derogatory manner to imply that a claim is being made to Universality in order to close down debate (Fish 1994).

University as Social Conscience: term which speaks to a special defining characteristic of universities as offering a space to reflect on the efficacy of social, political or economic trends and developments. Academics themselves may also need to be accorded a special status within their own institutions to exercise this function when calling their own institution to account.

Ventriloquism: term used to highlight situations in which professionals will say one thing but mean another. Particularly prevalent in situations requiring acts of

Performativity (see separate entry) and 'scripted communication' (see separate entry). Also used to highlight a bifurcated existence, i.e. the process of splitting into two parts.

Virtual Pantechnicon: from the term Panopticon – the ability to be able to see everything from 360 degrees, with obvious implications of surveillance, control, and imprisonment for those who are being observed. The adapted term implies that Virtual Space (see separate entry) may be experienced in this way, for example, by tracking the movements of students in virtual learning environments.

Virtual Space: blanket term often used to heighten awareness of the pedagogical implications of learning and interaction taking place in virtual learning environments (VLEs), and how they are inhabited and experienced. Sometimes involves debate about the competing nature of various platforms (e.g. Facebook vs. Blackboard VLE) and the issues around expanding virtual space and reducing physical space.

Vocationalism: broad term used to convey the idea of courses being primarily a preparation for work. Sometimes used to make a contrast between training and education, but also used when highlighting disconnects with employers' needs. Often used in a derogatory manner to imply that academic courses are drifting from their original purpose to pursue knowledge for its own sake (see Liberal Tradition).

Voice Perspectives: term used variously to highlight the distant nature of some voices and ideas in higher education. Also used in some circles to promote the idea of knowledge as perspective, philosophical relativism, and/or post-modern ideas, making the claim that truth is actually the ideas of the powerful masquerading as truth. Has some connections with Dead White Males (see separate entry).

Well-being: term used to support a move away from an emphasis on the cognitive, rational, and atomistic aspects of knowledge in many courses, and towards a more holistic and balanced approach, particularly including more spiritual and contemplative dimensions (Bloom 2005). Has positive connections with Capability and negative ones with an unwarranted Therapeutic Turn (see separate entries).

Widening Participation: term that refers to the ways that universities and colleges have been seeking to widen access to, and participation in, HE. Often used as a contrast term from *increasing* participation, and as a check on whether reforms aren't simply giving more opportunities to social groups who were already well represented. Often used alongside 'non-traditional learner' and 'first-generation entrant'.

Wilhelm von Humboldt: German philosopher, whose memorandum on the establishment of the University of Berlin in 1810 is often quoted when highlighting some of essential qualities of *higher* education – the combining of research and teaching; the importance of seminars rather than lectures; an emphasis on what we don't know rather than what we do; and enjoining students in scholarly endeavours.

Will to Learn: term commonly associated with Barnett (2007). It speaks more to the ontological aspects of being a student (as opposed to the strictly epistemological), seeking to identify that disposition, that sense of agency, which propels a student forward, in seeing learning as part of the project of 'becoming' as well as just being. It has connections with Self-Criticality (sees separate entry).

Wise Counsel: term which speaks to the ability of students to make measured decisions which are not just knowledge based but more widely rooted in the benefits they are likely to bring. The term also speaks to academic decision-making being ethically based and resting on an ability to *evaluate* factual and/or scientific knowledge, particularly *so-called* Disinterested Knowledge (see separate entry).

Work-Based Learning: broad term relating to the ways that learning either takes place in a work setting, or is integrated into that work setting. Has implications for discussing the multiple relationships between theory and practice, the role of placement learning (common on professional learning courses) and/or conceptualising Recontextualisation (see separate entry) in curriculum terms.

Appendix 1: UKPSF dimensions of practice and elements

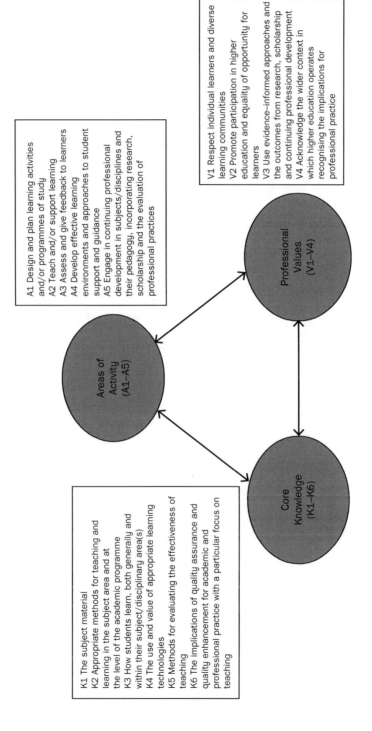

A1 Design and plan learning activities and/or programmes of study
A2 Teach and/or support learning
A3 Assess and give feedback to learners
A4 Develop effective learning environments and approaches to student support and guidance
A5 Engage in continuing professional development in subjects/disciplines and their pedagogy, incorporating research, scholarship and the evaluation of professional practices

Areas of Activity (A1–A5)

Professional Values (V1–V4)

Core Knowledge (K1–K6)

V1 Respect individual learners and diverse learning communities
V2 Promote participation in higher education and equality of opportunity for learners
V3 Use evidence–informed approaches and the outcomes from research, scholarship and continuing professional development
V4 Acknowledge the wider context in which higher education operates recognising the implications for professional practice

K1 The subject material
K2 Appropriate methods for teaching and learning in the subject area and at the level of the academic programme
K3 How students learn, both generally and within their subject/disciplinary area(s)
K4 The use and value of appropriate learning technologies
K5 Methods for evaluating the effectiveness of teaching
K6 The implications of quality assurance and quality enhancement for academic and professional practice with a particular focus on teaching

Appendix 2: The UKPSF Descriptors (D1–D4)

Descriptor 1 – Associate Fellow	Typical individual role/career stage
Demonstrates an understanding of specific aspects of effective teaching, learning support methods and student learning. Individuals should be able to provide evidence of: I. Successful engagement with at least two of the five Areas of Activity II. Successful engagement in appropriate teaching and practices related to these Areas of Activity III. Appropriate Core Knowledge and understanding of at least K1 and K2 IV. A commitment to appropriate Professional Values in facilitating others' learning V. Relevant professional practices, subject and pedagogic research and/or scholarship within the above activities VI. Successful engagement, where appropriate, in professional development activity related to teaching, learning and assessment responsibilities	Individuals able to provide evidence of effectiveness in relation to their professional role(s) which, typically, will include at least some teaching and/or learning support responsibilities. This teaching and learning role may sometimes be undertaken with the assistance of more experienced teachers or mentors. Typically, those likely to be at Descriptor 1 (D1) include: a. Early career researchers with some teaching responsibilities (e.g. PhD students, graduate teaching assistants (GTAs), contract researchers/post-doctoral students etc.) b. Staff new to teaching (including those with part-time academic responsibilities) c. Staff who support academic provision (e.g. learning technologists, learning developers and learning resource/library staff) d. Staff who undertake demonstrator/technician roles that incorporate some teaching-related responsibilities e. Experienced staff in relevant professional areas who may be new to teaching and/or supporting learning, or who have a limited teaching portfolio
Descriptor 2 – Fellow	**Typical individual role/career stage**
Demonstrates a broad under-standing of effective approaches to teaching and learning support as key contributions to high quality student learning. Individuals should be able to provide evidence of: I. Successful engagement across all five Areas of Activity II. Appropriate knowledge and under-standing across all aspects of Core Knowledge	Individuals able to provide evidence of broadly based effectiveness in more substantive teaching and supporting learning role(s). Such individuals are likely to be established members of one or more academic and/or academic-related teams. Typically, those likely to be at Descriptor 2 (D2) include:

III. A commitment to all the Professional Values IV. Successful engagement in appropriate teaching practices related to the Areas of Activity V. Successful incorporation of subject and pedagogic research and/or scholarship within the above activities, as part of an integrated approach to academic practice VI. Successful engagement in continuing professional development in relation to teaching, learning, assessment and, where appropriate, related professional practices	a. Early career academics b. Academic-related and/or support staff holding substantive teaching and learning responsibilities c. Experienced academics relatively new to UK higher education d. Staff with (sometimes significant) teaching-only responsibilities including, for example, within work-based settings
Descriptor 3 – Senior Fellow	**Typical individual role/career stage**
Demonstrates a thorough under-standing of effective approaches to teaching and learning support as a key contribution to high quality student learning. Individuals should be able to provide evidence of: I. Successful engagement across all five Areas of Activity II. Appropriate knowledge and under-standing across all aspects of Core Knowledge III. A commitment to all the Professional Values IV. Successful engagement in appropriate teaching practices related to the Areas of Activity V. Successful incorporation of subject and pedagogic research and/or scholarship within the above activities, as part of an integrated approach to academic practice VI. Successful engagement in continuing professional development in relation to teaching, learning, assessment, scholarship and, as appropriate, related academic or professional practices VII. Successful co-ordination, support, supervision, management and/or mentoring of others (whether individuals and/or teams) in relation to teaching and learning	Individuals able to provide evidence of a sustained record of effectiveness in relation to teaching and learning, incorporating for example, the organisation, leadership and/or management of specific aspects of teaching and learning provision. Such individuals are likely to lead or be members of established academic teams. Typically, those likely to be at Descriptor 3 (D3) include: a. Experienced staff able to demonstrate, impact and influence through, for example, responsibility for leading, managing or organising programmes, subjects and/or disciplinary areas b. Experienced subject mentors and staff who support those new to teaching c. Experienced staff with departmental and/or wider teaching and learning support advisory responsibilities within an institution

(Continued)

Appendix 2: (continued)

Descriptor 4 – Principal Fellow	Typical individual role/career stage
Demonstrates a sustained record of effective strategic leadership in academic practice and academic development as a key contribution to high quality student learning. Individuals should be able to provide evidence of:	Individuals, as highly experienced academics, able to provide evidence of a sustained and effective record of impact at a strategic level in relation to teaching and learning, as part of a wider commitment to academic practice. This may be within their institution or wider (inter)national settings. Typically, those likely to be at Descriptor 4 (D4) include:
I. Active commitment to and championing of all Dimensions of the Framework, through work with students and staff, and in institutional developments	a. Highly experienced and/or senior staff with wide-ranging academic or academic-related strategic leadership responsibilities in connection with key aspects of teaching and supporting learning
II. Successful, strategic leadership to enhance student learning, with a particular, but not necessarily exclusive, focus on enhancing teaching quality in institutional, and/or (inter)national settings	b. Staff responsible for institutional strategic leadership and policy-making in the area of teaching and learning
III. Establishing effective organisational policies and/or strategies for supporting and promoting others (e.g. through mentoring, coaching) in delivering high quality teaching and support for learning	c. Staff who have strategic impact and influence in relation to teaching and learning that extends beyond their own institution
IV. Championing, within institutional and/or wider settings, an integrated approach to academic practice (incorporating, for example, teaching, learning, research, scholarship, administration etc.)	
V. A sustained and successful commitment to, and engagement in, continuing professional development related to academic, institutional and/or other professional practices	

Appendix 3: Scholarship of Teaching and Learning Transport Map

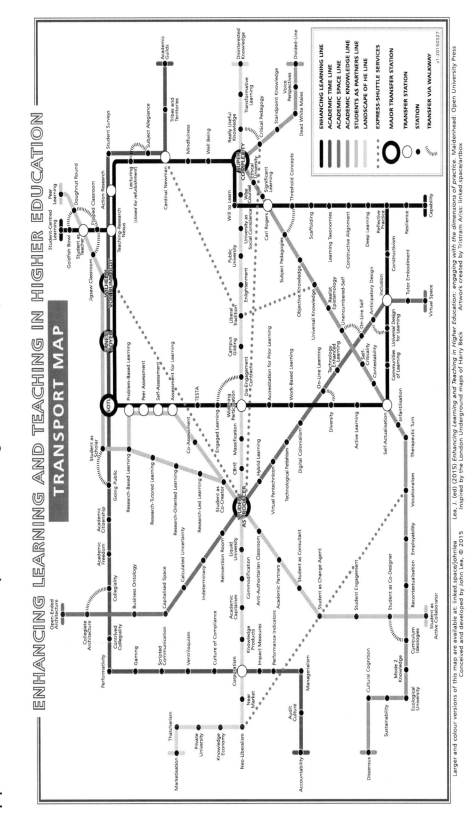

ENHANCING LEARNING AND TEACHING IN HIGHER EDUCATION

TRANSPORT MAP

Larger and colour versions of this map are available at: linked.space/johnlea
Conceived and developed by John Lea, © 2015

Lea, J. (ed) (2015) *Enhancing Learning and Teaching in Higher Education: engaging with the dimensions of practice.* Maidenhead: Open University Press.
Inspired by the London Underground maps of Harry Beck   Artwork created by Tristram Ariss: linked.space/artbox

v1·20150527

Bibliography

Addison, A. (1979) *John Henry Brookes: Craftsman, Educator, Administrator*. Oxford: Oxford Polytechnic Press.

Amiel, T. (2013) Identifying barriers to the remix of translated open educational resources, *The International Review of Research in Open and Distance Learning*, 14(1). Available at: www.irrodl.org/index.php/irrodl/article/view/1351/242 (accessed 6 Jan. 2015).

Amulya, J. (2004) *What Is Reflective Practice?* [Online] retrieved 16 June 2014, from Center for Reflective Community Practice: Massachusetts Institute of Technology.

Andreotti, V. (2006) Soft versus critical global citizenship education, *Policy and Practice: Development Education Review*, 3 (Autumn), 83–98.

Argyris, C. (1976) *Double Loop Learning*. Available at: http://www.instructionaldesign.org/theories/double-loop.html (accessed 14 July 2014).

Aronson, E. (1978) *The Jigsaw Classroom*. Beverly Hills, CA: Sage. Available at: http://www.jigsaw.org/ (accessed 14 March 2014).

Arum, R. and Roksa, J. (2011) *Academically Adrift*. Chicago: University of Chicago Press.

Atherton, J.S. (2013a) *Learning and Teaching: Piaget's Developmental Theory*. Available at: http://www.learningandteaching.info/learning/piaget.htm (accessed 28 June 2014).

Atherton, J.S. (2013b) *Learning and Teaching: SOLO taxonomy*. Available at: http://www.learningandteaching.info/learning/solo.htm (accessed 28 June 2014).

Bailey, C. (1984) *Beyond the Present and the Particular*. London: Routledge.

Bainbridge, A. (2014) Digital technology, human world making and the avoidance of learning, *Journal of Learning and Development in Higher Education: Special Edition on Digital Technologies in Learning Development*. Available at: http://www.aldinhe.ac.uk/ojs/index.php (accessed 6 Jan. 2015).

Ball, L. (2010) *Future Directions for Employability Research in the Creative Industries*. London: HEA.

Ballard, J.G. (2014) *Crash*. London: Fourth Estate.

Barnett, R. (1997) *Higher Education: A Critical Business*. Buckingham: SRHE and Open University Press.

Barnett, R. (2000) *Realizing the University in an Age of Supercomplexity*. Buckingham: Open University Press.

Barnett, R. (2003) *Beyond All Reason: Living with Ideology in the University*. Maidenhead: Open University Press.

Barnett, R. (2007) *A Will to Learn: Being a Student in an Age of Uncertainty*. Maidenhead: McGraw-Hill/ Open University Press.

Barnett, R. (2011a) *Being a University*. London: Routledge.

Barnett, R. (2011b) Developing the university in turbulent times, *Educational Developments*, 12(4): 1–5.

Barnett, R. (ed.) (2012) *The Future University: Ideas and Possibilities*. London: Routledge.

Barnett, R. (2014) *Conditions of Flexibility*. Available at: www.heacademy.ac.uk/conditions-flexibility-securing-more-responsive-higher-education-system

Barnett, R. and Coate, K. (2005) *Engaging the Curriculum in Higher Education*. Maidenhead: Open University Press.

Baron, P. and Corbin, L. (2012) Student engagement: rhetoric and reality, *Higher Education Research and Development*, 31(6): 759–72.

Bauman, Z. (2000) *Liquid Modernity*. Cambridge: Polity.

Baxter Magolda, M.B. (1992) *Knowing and Reasoning in College: Gender-related Patterns in Students' Intellectual Development*. New York: International Publishing Group.

Bayne, S. (2008) Higher education as a visual practice: seeing through the virtual learning environment, *Teaching in Higher Education*, 13(4): 395–410.

Bayne, S. and Ross, J. (2014) *The Pedagogy of the Massive Open Online Course: The UK View*. York: The Higher Education Academy (HEA). Available at: https://www.heacademy.ac.uk/resources/detail/elt/the_pedagogy_of_the_MOOC_UK_view (accessed 10 Oct. 2014).

Becher, T. (1989) *Academic Tribes and Territories: Intellectual Enquiry and the Cultures of Disciplines*. Buckingham: SRHE and Open University Press.

Becher, T. and Trowler, P. (2001) *Academic Tribes and Territories: Intellectual Enquiry and the Culture of Disciplines*, 2nd edn. Buckingham: SRHE and Open University Press.

Beck, J. and Young, M. (2005) The assault on the professions and the restructuring of academic and professional identities: a Bernsteinian analysis, *British Journal of Sociology of Education*, 26(2): 183–97.

Beetham, H. (2014) Post-digital provocations #1–4. Available at: http://design-4-learning.blogspot.co.uk/2014/11/post-digital-provocations-4-in-recovery.html (accessed 6 Jan. 2015).

Bell, H., Stevenson, H. and Neary, M. (eds) (2009) *The Future of Higher Education*. London: Continuum.

Benjamin, W. (1921) Critique of violence, in P. Demetz (ed.) *Reflections, Essays, Aphorisms, Autobiographical Writings*, trans. E. Jephcott. New York: Schocken Books, pp. 277–300.

Berger, J. ([1965] 1998) *The Success and Failure of Picasso*. New York: Vintage Books.

Bergslien, B. (1998) Teaching to avoid the 'CSI effect', keeping the science in forensic science, *Journal of Chemical Education*, 83(5): 690–1.

Bernstein, B. (2003) Social class and pedagogic practice, in B. Bernstein *The Structuring of Pedagogic Discourse*, vol. IV: *Class, Codes and Control*. London: Routledge.

Bernstein, R. (1994) *Dictatorship of Virtue*. New York: Knopf.

Berrett, D. (2012) *How 'Flipping' the Classroom Can Improve the Traditional Lecture*. Available at: http://moodle.technion.ac.il/file.php/1298/Announce/How_Flipping_the_Classroom_Can_Improve_the_Traditional_Lecture.pdf (accessed 14 July 2014).

Biggs, J. and Tang, C. (2007) *Teaching for Quality Learning at University*, 3rd edn. Buckingham: SRHE and Open University Press.

Biggs, J. and Tang, C. (2011) *Teaching for Quality Learning at University*, 4th edn. Maidenhead: SRHE and Open University Press.

Birenbaum, M. (2003) New insights into learning and teaching and their implications for assessment, in M. Segers, F. Dochy, and E. Cascallar (eds) *Optimising New Modes of Assessment: In Search of Quality and Standards*. Dordrecht: Kluwer Academic Publishers, pp. 13–36.

Birnbaum, R. (2001) *Management Fads in Higher Education: Where They Come from, What They Do, and Why They Fail*. San Francisco, CA: Jossey-Bass.

BIS (Department for Business, Innovation and Skills) (2009) *Higher Ambitions: The Future of Universities in a Knowledge Economy*. Available at: http://dera.ioe.ac.uk/9465/ (accessed 6 Jan. 2015).

BIS White Paper (2011) *Students at the Heart of the System*. London: BIS. Available at: https://www.gov.uk/government/news/putting-students-at-the-heart-of-higher-education (accessed 19 Nov. 2014).

Bishop, J.L. and Verleger, M.A. (2013) *The Flipped Classroom: A Survey of the Research*. Available at: http://www.studiesuccesho.nl/wp-content/uploads/2014/04/flipped-classroom-artikel.pdf (accessed 14 July 2014).

Black. P. and Rust, C. (2006) Improving student learning through assessment. *Proceedings of the 2005 13th International Symposium*. Oxford: Oxford Centre for Staff and Learning Development.

Black, P. and Wiliam, D. (1998) Assessment and classroom learning, *Assessment in Education: Principles, Policy and Practice*, 5(1): 7–74.

Blake, N. (2002) Hubert Dreyfus on distance education: relays of educational embodiment, *Educational Philosophy and Theory*, 34(4): 379–85. Available at: http://dx.doi.org/10.1111/j.1469-5812.2002.tb00511.x (accessed 10 Oct. 2014).

Blanden, J. and Machin, S. (2004) Educational inequality and the expansion of UK higher education, *Scottish Journal of Political Economy*, 51: 230–49.

Bloom, A. (1987) *The Closing of the American Mind*. New York: Simon & Schuster.

Bloom, B.S. (ed.) (1956) *Taxonomy of Educational Objectives: the Classification of Educational Goals .Handbook I: Cognitive Domain*. New York: McKay.

Bloom, W. (2001) *The Endorphin Effect: A Breakthrough Strategy for Holistic Health and Spiritual Wellbeing*. New York: Piatkus Books.

Bloom, W. (2005) *Soulution: The Holistic Manifesto*. London: Hay House.

Bok, D. (2005) *Universities in the Market Place*. Princeton, NJ: Princeton University Press.

Boud, D. and Falchicov, N. (1989) Quantitative studies of student self-assessment in higher education: a critical analysis of findings, *Higher Education*, 18: 529–49.

Boud, D., Keogh, R. and Walker, D. (eds) (1985) *Reflection: Turning Experience into Learning*. London: Kogan Page.

Bourdieu, P. and Passeron, J-C. (1979) *The Inheritors: French Students and their Relation to Culture*, trans R. Nice. Chicago: University of Chicago Press.

Bourner, T., Katz, T. and Watson, D. (eds) (2000) *New Directions in Professional Higher Education*. Buckingham: SRHE and Open University Press.

Bovill, C. (2013) Students and staff co-creating curricula: a new trend or an old idea we never got around to implementing?, in C. Rust (ed.) *Improving Student Learning through Research and Scholarship: 20 Years of ISL*. Oxford: The Oxford Centre for Staff and Educational Development, pp. 96–108.

Bovill, C. (2014) An investigation of co-created curricula within higher education in the UK, Ireland and the USA, *Innovations in Education and Teaching International*, 51(1): 15–25.

Bovill, C., Aitken, G., Hutchison, J., Morrison, F., Roseweir, K., Scott, A. and Sotannde, S. (2010) Experiences of learning through collaborative evaluation from a Postgraduate Certificate in Professional Education, *International Journal for Academic Development*, 15(2): 143–54.

Bovill, C., Cook-Sather, A. and Felten, P. (2011) Changing participants in pedagogical planning: students as co-creators of teaching approaches, course design and curricula, *International Journal for Academic Development*, 16(2): 133–45.

Bowen, H.R. (1977) *Investment in Learning: The Individual and Social Value of Higher Education*. San Francisco, CA: Jossey-Bass.

Boyer, E.L. (1990) *Scholarship Reconsidered: Priorities for the Professoriate*. Princeton University, NJ: Carnegie Foundation for the Advancement of Teaching.

Bragg, S. (2007) 'Student voice' and governmentality: the production of enterprising subjects? *Discourse: Studies in the Cultural Politics of Education*, 28(3): 343–58.

Breen, M.P. and Littlejohn, A. (2000) The practicalities of negotiation, in M.P. Breen and A. Littlejohn (eds) *Classroom Decision-Making: Negotiation and Process Syllabuses in Practice.* Cambridge: Cambridge University Press.

Brew, A. (2006) *Research and Teaching: Beyond the Divide.* London: Palgrave Macmillan.

Brigden, D. and Purcell, N. (2013) *Focus: Becoming a Reflective Practitioner Via the HEA.* Available at http://www.medev.ac.uk/newsletter/article/32/ (accessed 9 May 2014).

Brockbank, A. and McGill, I. (1998) *Facilitating Reflective Learning in Higher Education.* Buckingham: SRHE and Open University Press.

Bronner, S.E. (2004) *Reclaiming the Enlightenment: Toward a Politics of Radical Engagement.* New York: Columbia University Press.

Brookfield, S. (1995) *Becoming a Critically Reflective Teacher.* San Francisco, CA: Jossey-Bass.

Brookfield, S. and Preskill, S. (1999) *Discussion as a Way of Teaching: Tools and Techniques for University Teachers.* Buckingham: SRHE and Open University Press.

Brown, G. with Bull, J. and Pendlebury, M. (1997) *Assessing Student Learning in Higher Education.* London: Routledge.

Brown, H. and Ciuffetelli, D.C. (2009) *Foundational Methods: Understanding Teaching and Learning.* Toronto: Pearson Education.

Brown, P., Lauder, H. and Ashton, D. (2008) *Education, Globalisation and the Knowledge Economy.* Teaching and Learning Research Programme (TLRP). Available at: www.tlrp.org (accessed 6 Jan. 2015).

Brown, R. and Carasso, H. (2013) *Everything for Sale: The Marketisation of Higher Education.* London: Routledge.

Brown, S. and Smith, B. (eds) (2013) *Research, Teaching and Learning in Higher Education.* London: Routledge.

Browne Review of HE (2010) *Securing A Sustainable Future for Higher Education.* Available at: http://www.delni.gov.uk/browne-report-student-fees (accessed 19 Nov. 2014).

Bryan, C. (2006) Developing group learning through assessment, in C. Bryan and K. Clegg (eds) *Innovative Assessment in Higher Education.* London: Routledge.

Bryan, C. and Assiter, A. (1995) *The Accreditation and Development of Cognitive Skills Acquired in the Workplace: Report on the ALE Project.* London: University of North London Press.

Bryan, C. and Clegg, K. (eds) (2006) *Innovative Assessment in Higher Education.* London: Routledge.

Bryan, C. and Green, D. (2003) How guided reflection can enhance group work, in C. Rust (ed.) *Improving Student Learning: Theory and Practice – 10 Years on.* Oxford: Oxford Centre for Staff and Learning Development, pp. 316–25.

Bryman, A. (2007) Effective leadership in higher education: a literature review, *Studies in Higher Education*, 32(6): 693–710.

Bryson, C. (ed.) (2014) *Understanding and Developing Student Engagement.* London: Routledge/SEDA.

Bryson, C. and Hand, L. (2007) The role of engagement in inspiring teaching and learning, *Innovations in Teaching and Education International*, 44(4): 349–62.

Buckley, A. (2013) Engagement for enhancement: report of a UK survey pilot. Available at: https://www.heacademy.ac.uk/sites/default/files/Engagement_for_enhancement_FINAL_0.pdf

Buckley, A. (2014) UK Engagement Survey 2014; The Second Pilot Year. Available at:https://www.heacademy.ac.uk/sites/default/files/resources/UKES_report_2014_v2.pdf

Bures, E., Abrami, P., Barclay, A. and Bures, E. (2010) Assessing online dialogue in higher education, in J. Sanchez and K. Zhang (eds) *Proceedings of World Conference on E-Learning in Corporate, Government, Healthcare, and Higher Education 2010.* Chesapeake, VA: AACE.

Burgess, A. ([1962] 2001) *A Clockwork Orange*. London: Penguin Books.

Burroughs, W. (2010) *The Naked Lunch: Restored Text*. London: The Fourth Estate.

Burroughs, W. (n.d.) *Creative Writing, Creating Reading Course*. Available at: http://dangerousminds.net/comments/take_a_creative_writing_course_with_william_burroughs (accessed 6 Jan. 2015).

Campbell, F., Eland, J., Rumpus, A. and Shacklock, R. (2009) *Hearing the Student Voice, Involving Students in Curriculum Design and Delivery*. ESCalate. Available at: http://www.sparqs.ac.uk/ch/E3%20Hearing%20the%20student%20voice%20involving%20students%20in%20curriculum%20design%20and%20development.pdf (accessed 15 March 2014).

Carter, S.L. (1991) *Reflections of an Affirmative Action Baby*. New York: Basic Books.

Cheney, L.V. (1992) *Telling the Truth: A Report on the State of the Humanities in Higher Education*. Washington, DC: National Endowment for the Humanities.

Choi, J.M. and Murphy, J.W. (1992) *The Politics and Philosophy of Political Correctness*. Westport, CT: Praeger.

Clegg, K. and Bryan, C. (2006) Reflections, rationales and realities, in C. Bryan and K. Clegg (eds) *Innovative Assessment in Higher Education*. London: Routledge, pp. 216–27.

Clegg, S., Tan, J. and Saeidi, S. (2002) Reflecting or acting? Reflective practice and continuing professional development in higher education, in *Reflective Practice: International and Multidisciplinary Perspectives*, 3(1), published online (2010) http://www.tandfonline.com/doi/abs/10.1080/14623940220129924#.U20Pj1cRR4w (accessed 9 May 2014).

Collini, S. (2012) *What Are Universities For?* London: Penguin Books.

Colombino, L. (2012) The house as skin: JG Ballard, Existentialism and Archigrams mini environments, *European Journal of English Studies*, 16(1): 21–31.

Cook-Sather, A., Bovill, C. and Felten, P. (2014) *Engaging Students as Partners in Learning and Teaching: A Guide for Faculty*. San Francisco: Jossey-Bass.

Cosgrove, D. (1981) Teaching geographical thought through student interviews, *Journal of Geography in Higher Education*, 5(1): 19–22.

Cotton, D.R.E. and Winter, J. (2010) It's not just bits of paper and light bulbs: a review of Sustainability Pedagogies and their Potential for use in Higher Education, in P. Jones, D. Selby and S. Sterling (eds) *Sustainability Education: Perspectives and Practice across Higher Education*. London: Earthscan, pp. 39–54.

Cowen, J. (2013) Facilitating reflective journaling, *Journal of Learning Development in Higher Education*, 5: 1–17.

CRAC (2013) *The Wider Benefits of International Higher Education in the UK*, BIS Research Paper 128. London: HMSO.

Craig, C. and Gunn, A. (2010) Higher skills and the knowledge economy: the challenge of offshoring, *Higher Education Management and Policy*, 22(3). Available at: http://dx.doi.org/10.1787/hemp-22-5km39qs88zjb (accessed 6 Jan. 2015).

Cuthbert, R. (2010) Students as customers? *Higher Education Review*, 42(3): 3–25.

Dalla Costa, M. and James, S. (1975) *The Power of Women and the Subversion of the Community*. Bristol: Falling Wall Press.

Dall 'Alba, G. and Robyn, B. (2007) An ontological turn for higher education, *Studies in Higher Education*, 32(6): 679–91.

Dean, J. (2012) *The Communist Horizon*. London: Verso.

Dearing, R. (National Committee of Inquiry into Higher Education) (1997) *Higher Education in the Learning Society: Report of the National Committee* (The Dearing Report) London, HMSO. Available at: http://www.educationengland.org.uk/documents/dearing1997/index.html (accessed 19 Nov. 2014).

Deeley, S. (2014) Summative co-assessment: a deep learning approach to enhancing employability skills and attributes, *Active Learning in Higher Education*, 15(1): 39–51.

Deem, R. and Brehony, K. (2005) Management as ideology: the case of 'new managerialism' in higher education, *Oxford Review of Education*, 31(2): 217–35.

Deem, R., Hillyard, S. and Reed, M. (2008) *Knowledge, Higher Education, and the New Managerialism: The Changing Management of UK Universities*. Oxford: Open University Press.

Delanty, G. (2001) *Challenging Knowledge: The University in the Knowledge Society*. Buckingham: Open University Press.

Department for Education (DFE) (1992) *Further and Higher Education Act*. London: HMSO. Available at: http://www.legislation.gov.uk/ukpga/1992/13/contents (accessed 19 Nov. 2014).

Department for Education and Skills (DfES) (2004) *Equipping Our Teachers for the Future*. London: HMSO.

DfES (2003) *The Future of Higher Education*, Cm5753. Norwich: The Stationery Office.

Dinerstein, A. and Neary, M. (2002) *The Labour Debate: The Theory and Reality of Capitalist Work*. Farnham: Ashgate.

Dochy, F. et al. (1999) The use of self-, peer and co-assessment in higher education: a review, *Studies in Higher Education*, 24(3): 331–50.

Double, D. and Wilson, M. (2006) Berthold Brecht on theatre, in P. Thomson et al. *The Cambridge Companion to Brecht*, 2nd edn. Cambridge: Cambridge University Press.

Downes, S. (2005) An introduction to connective knowledge, *Stephen's Web*, 22 Dec. Available at: http://www.downes.ca/cgi-bin/page.cgi?post=33034 (accessed 10 Oct. 2014).

Downes, S. (2012) *Connectivism and Connective Knowledge: Essays on Meaning and Learning Networks*. Ottawa, Ontario: National Research Council Canada. Available at: http://www.downes.ca/files/books/Connective_Knowledge-19May2012.pdf (accessed 10 Oct. 2014).

Drucker, P. (1969) *The Age of Discontinuity: Guidelines to Our Changing Society*. London: Heinemann.

Drucker, P. (1989) *The Practice of Management*. Oxford: Butterworth-Heinemann.

Drucker, P. (1990) *The New Realities*. London: Mandarin.

Drucker, P. [1974] (2011) *Management: Tasks, Responsibilities, Practices*. London: Routledge.

D'Souza, D. (1992) *Illiberal Education*. New York: Vintage Books.

Duah, F. and Croft, T. (2011) Students as partners in mathematics design. Paper presented at CETL-MSOR Conference. Available at: https://dspace.lboro.ac.uk/dspace-jspui/bitstream/2134/9904/3/Duah_Croft_2011final.pdf (accessed 15 March 2014).

Duke, C. (1992) *The Learning University: Towards a New Paradigm?* Buckingham: SRHE and Open University Press.

Dumelow, I., MacLennan, H. and Stanley, N. (2000) *Career and Employment Patterns among British Graduates in Art, Craft and Design: Planning the Future*. Corsham: NSEAD.

Dunne, E. and Owen, D. (eds) (2013) *The Student Engagement Handbook: Practice in Higher Education*. Bingley: Emerald.

Dunne, E. and Zandstra, R. (2011) *Students as Change Agents: New Ways of Engaging with Learning and Teaching in Higher Education*. Bristol: A Joint University of Exeter/ESCalate/Higher Education Academy Publication. Available at: escalate.ac.uk/8064 (accessed 14 Feb. 2014).

Dwyer, C. (2001) Linking research and teaching: a staff-student interview project, *Journal of Geography in Higher Education*, 25(3): 357–66.

Dyer-Witheford, N. (2006) The circulation of the common, paper presented at Immaterial Labour, Multitudes and New Social Subjects: Class Composition in Cognitive Capitalism conference, King's College, University of Cambridge 29 and 30 April. Available at: http://www.fims.uwo.ca/people/faculty/dyerwitheford/Commons2006.pdf (accessed 10 Oct. 2014).

Eagleton, T. (1996) *The Illusions of Postmodernism*. Oxford: Blackwell.

Easton, F. (1997) Educating the whole child, 'head, heart and hands': learning from the Waldorf experience, *Theory into Practice*, 36(2): 87–95.

Ecclestone, K. and Hayes, D. (2008) *The Dangerous Rise of Therapeutic Education*. London: Routledge.

Ecclestone, K., Hayes, D. and Furedi, F. (2005) Knowing me, knowing you: the rise of therapeutic professionalism in the education of adults, *Studies in the Education of Adults*, 37(2): 182–200.

Education and Training Foundation (2014) *Professional Standards for Teachers and Trainers in Education and Training – England 2014*. Available at: http://www.et-foundation.co.uk/wp-content/uploads/2014/05/4991-Prof-standards-A4_4-2.pdf (accessed 5 Jan. 2014).

Eggins, H. and Macdonald, R. (2003) *The Scholarship of Academic Development*. Buckingham: SRHE and Open University Press.

Elton, L. (1992) Research, teaching and scholarship in an expanding higher education system, *Higher Education Quarterly*, 46(3): 252–68.

Elton, L. (2001) Research and teaching: conditions for positive link, *Teaching in Higher Education*, 6(1): 43–5.

Elton, L. (2006) Academic professionalism: the need for change, in C. Bryan and K. Clegg (eds) *Innovative Assessment in Higher Education*. London: Routledge, pp. 209–15.

Elton, L. (2008) Collegiality and complexity: Humboldt's relevance to British universities today, *Higher Education Quarterly*, 62(3): 224–36.

Eraut, M. (1994) *Developing Professional Knowledge and Competence*. New York: Falmer Press.

Eraut, M. (2000) Non-formal learning and tacit knowledge in professional work, *British Journal of Educational Psychology*, 70; 113–36.

European Centre for the Development of Vocational Training (ECDVT) (2013) The shift to learning outcomes and its impacts: taking stock of European policies and practices, Thessaloniki, 21–22 November 2013.

Falchicov, N. and Boud, D. (1989) Student self-assessment in higher education: a meta-analysis, *Review of Educational Research*, 59(4): 431–70.

Fanghanel, J. (2012) *Being an Academic*. London: Routledge.

FELTAG (Further Education Learning Technology Action Group) (2013) *Paths Forward to a Digital Future for Further Education and Skills*. Available at: http://feltag.org.uk/wp-content/uploads/2012/01/FELTAG-REPORT-FINAL.pdf. (accessed 6 Jan. 2015).

Ferman, T. (2002) Academic professional development practice: what lecturers find valuable, *International Journal for Academic Development*, 7(2): 146–58.

Fielden, J. (2011) *Leadership and Management of International Partnerships*. Leadership Foundation for Higher Education. Series 2 publication 7. London: LFHE.

Fielding, M. (2004) 'New Wave' student voice and the renewal of civic society, *London Review of Education*, 2(3): 197–217.

Fish, S. (1994) *There's No Such Thing as Free Speech and It's a Good Thing*. New York: Oxford University Press.

Fisher, M. (2009) *Capitalist Realism: Is There No Alternative?* Ropley: Zero Books.

Fleiszer, D., Fleiszer, T. and Russell, R. (1997) Doughnut rounds: a self-directed learning approach to teaching critical care in surgery, *Medical Teacher*, 19(3): 190–3.

Fontana, D. (1988) *Psychology for Teachers*. 3rd Edition. Leicester: BPS.

Forman, A.E., Baker, P.M.A., Pater, J. and Smith, K. (2011) Beautiful to me: identity, disability, and gender in virtual environments, *E-politics*, 2(2): 1–17.

Fourier, C. (1971) *Design for Utopia: Selected Writings. Studies in the Libertarian and Utopian Tradition*. New York: Schocken.

Fraser, S. and Bosanquet, A. (2006) The curriculum? That's just a unit outline, isn't it?, *Studies in Higher Education*, 31: 269–84.

Freire, P. (1970) *Pedagogy of the Oppressed*. New York: Continuum.

Freire, P. (2003) From pedagogy of the oppressed, in A. Darder, M. Baltodano and R.D. Torres (eds) *The Critical Pedagogy Reader*. New York: Routledge Falmer, pp. 57–68.

Friedman, M. and Friedman, R.D. (1980) *Free to Choose: A Personal Statement*. New York: Harcourt Brace Jovanovich.

Fromm, E. (1977) *To Have Or To Be?* New York: Harper and Row.

Frosh, S. (1991) *Identity Crisis: Modernity, Psychoanalysis and the Self*. London: Macmillan.

Fry, H., Ketteridge, S. and Marshall, S. (eds) (2014) *A Handbook for Teaching and Learning in Higher Education: Enhancing Academic Practice*, 4th edn. London: Routledge.

Fuchs, C. (2008) *Internet and Society: Social Theory in the Information Age*. New York: Routledge.

Fuchs, C. (2011) Cognitive capitalism or informational capitalism? The role of class in the information economy, in M. Peters and E. Bulut (eds) *Cognitive Capitalism, Education and Digital Labor*. London: Peter Lang, pp. 75–119.

Fullan, M. (2008) *The New Meaning of Educational Change*, 4th edn. London: Teachers College Press.

Fuller, S. (2013) Deviant interdisciplinarity as philosophical practice: prolegomena to deep intellectual history, *Synthese*, 190: 1899–916.

Fulton-Suri, J. (2011) *Design Research Through Practice*. Burlington, VA: Morgan Kaufmann.

Furedi, F. (2004) *Where Have All the Intellectuals Gone?* London: Continuum.

Gardner, H. (1993) *Multiple Intelligences: The Theory in Practice*. New York: Basic Books.

Gastil, J. (1997) A definition and illustration of democratic leadership, in K. Grint (ed) *Leadership*. Oxford: Oxford University Press.

Gibbons, M., Limoges, C., Nowotny, H., Schwartzman, S., Scott, P. and Trow, M. (1994) *The New Production of Knowledge*. London: Sage.

Gibbs, G. (2006) How assessment frames student learning, in C. Bryan and K. Clegg (eds) *Innovative Assessment in Higher Education*, London: Routledge, pp. 28–30.

Gibbs, G. (2010) *Dimensions of Quality*. York: HEA. Available at: https://www.heacademy.ac.uk/sites/default/files/Dimensions_of_Quality.pdf (accessed 19 Nov. 2014).

Gibbs, G. (2012) *Implications of 'Dimensions of Quality' in a Market Environment*. York: HEA. Available at: https://www.heacademy.ac.uk/implications-dimensions-quality-market-environment (accessed 19 Nov. 2014).

Gibbs, G. and Dunbar-Goddet, H. (2007) *The Effects of Programme Assessment Environments on Student Learning*. York: Higher Education Academy.

Gibbs, G. and Simpson, C. (2003) Measuring the response of students to assessment: the Assessment Experience Questionnaire. Available at: https://www.uzh.ch/phil/elearning/ssl-dir/wiki/uploads/Main/Gibbs_and_Simpson_2003.pdf (accessed 6 Jan. 2015).

Gibbs, G., and Simpson, C. (2004) Conditions under which assessment supports students' learning, *Learning and Teaching in Higher Education*, 1: 3–31.

Giddens, A. (1984) *The Constitution of Society: Outline of the Theory of Structuration*. Cambridge: Polity Press.

Giddens, A. (1991) *The Consequences of Modernity*. London: Polity Press.

Gilbert, J. K. (2006) On the nature of 'context' in chemical education, *International Journal of Science Education*, 28(9): 957–76.

Gilligan, G. (1982) *In a Different Voice*. Cambridge, MA: Harvard University Press.

Giroux, H. A. (1981) *Ideology, Culture, and the Process of Schooling*. London: Falmer.

Gitlin, T. (1995) *The Twilight of Common Dreams*. New York: Metropolitan Books.

Glancey, J. (2010) University architecture shapes up for a revolution, *The Guardian*, 31 August. Available at: http://www.theguardian.com/education/2010/aug/31/university-architecture-revolution-students (accessed 6 Jan. 2015).

Gordon, N. (2014) *Flexible Pedagogies: Technology Enhanced Learning*. https://www.heacademy.ac.uk/sites/default/files/resources/TEL_report_0.pdf

Gorz, A. (1994) *Farewell to the Working Class: An Essay on Post-Industrial Socialism*. London: Pluto Classics.

Gosling, D. (2001) Educational development units in the UK: what are they doing five years on? *International Journal for Academic Development*, 6(1): 74–90.

Grenfell, M. and James, D. (1998) *Bourdieu and Education: Acts of Practical Theory*. London: Routledge Falmer.

Grossman, R. (2009) Structures for facilitating student reflection, *College Teaching*, 57(1): 15–22.

Grove, J. (2014) Universities to get near 6 per cent cut to most teaching budgets, *Times Higher Education*, 14 March 2014.

Grugulis, I. (2000) The management NVQ: a critique of the myth of relevance, *Journal of Vocational Education and Training*, 52(1): 79–99.

Gulikers, J. T.M., Kester, L., Kirschner, P.A. and Bastiaens, T.J. (2008) The effect of practical experience on perceptions of assessment authenticity, study approach, and learning outcome, *Learning and Instruction*, 18: 172–186.

Gunn, V. and Fisk, A. (2013) *Considering Teaching Excellence in Higher Education: 2007–2013: A Literature Review Since the CHERI Report 2007*. Available at: www.heacademy.ac.uk/sites/default/files/resources/TELR_final_acknowledgements.pdf

Haggis, T. (2003) Constructing images of ourselves? A critical investigation into 'approaches to learning' research in higher education, *British Educational Research Journal*, 29: 8–104.

Haggis, T. (2009) What have we been thinking of? A critical overview of 40 years of student learning research in higher education, *Studies in Higher Education*, 34(4): 377–90.

Hall, R. and Stahl, B. (2012) Against commodification: the university, cognitive capitalism and emergent technologies, *tripleC* 10(2): 184–202.

Halsey, A.H. and Trow, M. (1971) *British Academics*. Oxford: Oxford University Press.

Halsey, A.H. (1992) *Decline of Donnish Dominion*. Oxford: Oxford University Press.

Hardingham, K. and Rattenbury, S. (2007) *Cedric Price: Potteries Thinkbelt: Supercrit#1*. London: Routledge.

Hardt, M. and Negri, A. (2001) *Empire*. Cambridge, MA: Harvard University Press.

Hargittai, E. (2008) The digital reproduction of inequality, in D. Grusky (ed.) *Social Stratification*. Boulder, CO: Westview Press, pp. 936–44.

Hargittai, E. (2010) Digital na(t)ives? Variation in internet skills and uses among members of the 'Net Generation', *Sociological Inquiry*, 80(1): 92–113.

Hargreaves, A. (1994) *Changing Teachers, Changing Times: Teachers' Work and Culture in the Postmodern Age*. London: Cassell.

Harland, T. and Pickering, N. (2011) *Values in Higher Education Teaching*. London: Routledge.

Harper, S. et al. (2008) *Student Engagement in Higher Education: Theoretical Perspectives and Practical Approaches for Diverse Populations*. London: Routledge.

Harvey, D. (1990) *The Condition of Postmodernity: An Enquiry into the Origins of Cultural Change*. Oxford: Blackwell.

Harvey, D. (2000) *Spaces of Hope*. Berkeley, CA: University of California Press.

Hatherley, O. (2011) *A Guide to the New Ruins of Great Britain*. London: Verso.

Hattie, J. and Marsh, H. W. (1996) The relationship between research and teaching: a meta-analysis, *Review of Educational Research*, 66(4:) 507–42.

Hayek, F.A. (1944) *The Road to Serfdom*. London: Routledge.

Haywood, J. (2012) No such thing as a free MOOC, *JISC Blog*, 20 July 2012. Available at: http://www.jisc.ac.uk/blog/no-such-thing-as-a-free-mooc-20-jul-2012 (accessed 10 Oct. 2014).

HEA (Higher Education Academy) (n.d.) Available at: https://www.heacademy.ac.uk

HEA (Higher Education Academy) (2005) *National Professional Standards Framework for Standards in Teaching and Supporting Learning in Higher Education: Consultation Document*. York: Higher Education Academy.

HEA (Higher Education Academy) (2011) UK Professional Standards Framework (UKPSF). Available at: https://www.heacademy.ac.uk/professional-recognition/uk-professional-standards-framework-ukpsf (accessed 8 Dec. 2014).

HEA and HEPI (2014) The HEPI-HEA Student Academic Experience Survey, 2014. Available at: http://www.hepi.ac.uk/wp-content/uploads/2014/05

HEA/QAA (2014) *Education for Sustainable Development: Guidance for UK Higher Education Providers*. Available at: http://www.qaa.ac.uk/en/Publications/Documents/Education-sustainable-development-Guidance-June-14.pdf (accessed 28 Nov. 2014).

Healey, M. (2000) Developing the scholarship of teaching in higher education: a discipline-based approach, *Higher Education Research and Development*, 19(2).

Healey, M. (2003) The scholarship of teaching: issues around an evolving concept, *Journal on Excellence in College Teaching*, 14(2/3): 5–26.

Healey, M. (2014) *Students as Change Agents in Teaching and Learning in Higher Education*. Available at: http://www.mickhealey.co.uk/resources (accessed 15 March 2014).

Healey, M. and Addis, M. (2004) Use of peer and self-assessment to distribute group marks among individual team members: ten years' experience, in M. Healey and J. Roberts (eds) *Engaging Students in Active Learning: Case Studies in Geography, Environment and Related Disciplines*. Cheltenham: University of Gloucestershire, Geography Discipline Network and School of Environment, pp. 116121. Available at: http://www2.glos.ac.uk/gdn/active/student. htm (accessed 15 March 2014).

Healey, M., Flint, A. and Harrington, K. (2014a) *Engagement Through Partnership: Students as Partners in Learning and Teaching in Higher Education*. Available at: https://www. heacademy.ac.uk/sites/default/files/resources/Engagement_through_partnership.pdf (accessed 9 Jan. 2015)

Healey, M. and Jenkins, A. (2009) *Developing Undergraduate Research and Inquiry*. York: Higher Education Academy. Available at: www.heacademy.ac.uk/assets/York/documents/resources/publications/DevelopingUndergraduate_Final.pdf (accessed 14 Feb. 2014).

Healey, M., Jenkins, A. and Lea, J. (2014b) *Developing Research-Based Curricula In College-Based Higher Education*. York: HEA. Available at: http://www.heacademy.ac.uk/resources/detail/heinfe/Developing_research-based_curricula_in_CBHE (accessed 19 Nov. 2014).

Healey, M., Lannin, L., Stibbe, A. and Derounian, J. (2013) *Developing and Enhancing Undergraduate Final-Year Projects and Dissertations*. York: Higher Education Academy.

HEFCE (Higher Education Funding Council for England) (2006) *Higher Education in Further Education Colleges: Consultation on HEFCE Policy*, available at: http://www.hefce.ac.uk/pubs/hefce/2006/06_48/ (accessed 1 Sept. 2014).

HEFCE (Higher Education Funding Council for England) (2013) Student engagement. Available at: www.hefce.ac.uk/about/howweoperate/si/studentengagement/ (accessed 15 March 2014).

HEFCE (n.d.) What we do. Available at: http://www.hefce.ac.uk/whatwedo/wp

HEPI (Higher Education Policy Institute) (2014) Available at: http://www.hepi.ac.uk

Hertz, N. (2001) *The Silent Takeover: Global Capitalism and the Death of Democracy*. London: Heinemann.

HESA (2014) *KIS Collection 2014/15*. Cheltenham: HESA. Available at: https://www.hesa.ac.uk/index.php?option=com_studrec&Itemid=232&mnl=14061 (accessed 19 Nov. 2014).

Hodge, D.C., Nadler, M.K., Shore, C. and Taylor, B.A.P. (2011) Institutionalizing large-scale curricular change: the Top 25 project at Miami University, *Change Magazine*, 43(5): 28–35.

Hollway, W. and Jefferson, T. (2000) *Doing Qualitative Research Differently: Free Association, Narrative and the Interview Method*. London: Sage.

Holmwood, J. (ed.) (2011) *A Manifesto for the Public University*. London: Bloomsbury.

Honeychurch, S. (2012) Taking forward the jigsaw classroom: the development and implementation of a method of collaborative learning for first year philosophy tutorials, *Discourse*, 11(2): 40–52. Available at: https://www.heacademy.ac.uk/resources (accessed 15 March 2014).

hooks, b. (1994) *Teaching to Transgress: Education as the Practice of Freedom*. New York: Routledge.

hooks, b. (1996) Postmodern blackness, in W. T. Anderson (ed.) *The Fontana Post-Modernism Reader*. London: Fontana Press.

Hordern, J. (2014) How is vocational knowledge recontextualised?, *Journal of Vocational Education and Training*, 66(1): 22–38.

Hoult, E. (2012) *Adult Learning and La Recherche Féminine: Reading Resilience and Hélène Cixous*. London: Palgrave Macmillan.

Humboldt, W. von [1810] (1970) On the spirit and organisational framework of intellectual institutions in Berlin, *Minerva*, 8, 242–67.

Hussey, T. and Smith, P. (2002) The trouble with learning outcomes: active, *Learning in Higher Education*, 3(3): 220–33.

Hyland, T. (1994) *Competence, Education and NVQs: Dissenting Perspectives*. London: Continuum.

Jarvis, P. (1992) Reflective practice and nursing, *Nurse Education Today*, 12: 174–81.

Jenkins, A. (2004) *A Guide to the Research Evidence on Teaching-Research Relationships*. York: Higher Education Academy. Available at: https://www.heacademy.ac.uk/node/3617 (accessed 6 Jan. 2014).

Jenkins, A. et al. (1998) Teaching and research: student perspectives and policy implications, *Studies in Higher Education*, 23(2).

Jenkins, A. and Healey, M. (2005) *Institutional Strategies to Link Teaching and Research*. York: The Higher Education Academy. Available at: www.heacademy.ac.uk/assets/York/documents/ourwork/research/Institutional_strategies.pdf (accessed 15 March 2014).

Jenkins, A., Healey, M. and Zetter, R. (2007) *Linking Teaching and Research in Departments and Disciplines*. York: The Higher Education Academy. Available at: https://www.heacademy.ac.uk/node/3890 (accessed 9 Jan. 15).

Jessop, T. (2012) *TESTA: Transforming the Experience of Students through Assessment – Final Project Report*. York: Higher Education Academy.

Jessop, T., El Hakim, Y. and Gibbs, G. (2014a) TESTA in 2014: A way of thinking about assessment and feedback, *Educational Developments*, 15(2): 21–3.

Jessop, T., El Hakim, Y. and Gibbs, G. (2014b) TESTA: the whole is greater than the sum of the parts, *Assessment and Evaluation*, 39(1): 77–88.

Jessup, G. (1991) *Outcomes: NVQs and the Emerging Model of Education and Training*. London: Falmer Press.

Johnson, R. (1979) 'Really Useful Knowledge': radical education and working class culture, 1790–1848, in J. Clarke, C. Critcher and R. Johnson (eds) *Working Class Culture: Studies in History and Theory*. London: Hutchinson.

Jones, P., Selby, D., and Sterling, S. (2010) More than the Sum of their Parts? Interdisciplinarity and Sustainability, in Jones, P., Selby, D., and Sterling, S. (eds.) *Sustainability Education: Perspectives and Practice across Higher Education*. London: Earthscan, pp. 17–38.

Kant, I. ([1784] 2009) *An Answer to the Question: 'What is Enlightenment?'* [trans. H.B. Nisbet] London: Penguin.

Kavanagh, D. (2012) The university as fool, in R. Barnett (ed.) *The Future University: Ideas and Possibilities*. London: Routledge.

Kay, G. and Mott, J. (1982) *Political Order and the Law of Labour*. London: Macmillan.

KCL (2014) *Peer Teaching*. Available at: http://www.kcl.ac.uk/medicine/research/divisions/meded/innovation/peer.aspx (accessed 15 March 2014).

Keddie, N. (ed.) (1974) *Tinker, Tailor…The Myth of Cultural Deprivation*. London: Penguin.

Kelly, G.A. (2003) A brief introduction to personal construct theory, in F. Fransella (ed.) *International Handbook of Personal Construct Psychology*. New York: John Wiley and Sons, pp. 3–20.

Kennedy, D. (1997) *Academic Duty*. Cambridge, MA: Harvard University Press.

Kezar, A. (2014) *How Colleges Change: Understanding, Leading and Enacting Change*. London: Routledge.

Kinsman, B. (1965) *Wind Waves: Their Generation and Propagation Across the Ocean Surface*. New York: Prentice Hall.

Klein, N. (2001) *No Logo*. London: Flamingo.

Knight, P. (2001) *A Briefing on Key Concepts Formative and Summative, Criterion and Norm-Referenced Assessment*, Assessment Series No.7 LTSN Generic Centre. Available at: https://www.heacademy.ac.uk/resources (accessed 6 Jan. 2014).

Knight, P., Tait, J. and Yorke, M. (2006) The professional learning of teachers in higher education, *Studies in Higher Education*, 31(4): 319–39.

Knight, P. and Yorke, M. (2003) *Assessment of Learning and Employability*. Buckingham: SRHE and Open University Press.

Knox, J. (2014) Digital culture clash: 'massive' education in the e-Learning and Digital Cultures MOOC, *Distance Education*, 35(2): 164–77. Available at: http://dx.doi.org/10.1080/01587919. 2014.917704 (accessed 10 Oct. 2014).

Knox, J., Bayne, S., MacLeod, H., Ross, J. and Sinclair, C. (2012) MOOC pedagogy: the challenges of developing for Coursera, *ALT Online Newsletter*, 28, 8 Aug. 2012. Available at: http://newsletter.alt.ac.uk/2012/08/mooc-pedagogy-the-challenges-of-developing-for-coursera/ (accessed 10 Oct. 2014).

Kolb, D. (1984) *Experiential Learning: Experience as the Source of Learning and Development*. London: Prentice Hall.

Kop, R. (2011) The challenges to connectivist learning on open online networks: learning experiences during a massive open online course, *International Review of Research in Open and Distance Learning*, 12(3): 19–38. Available at: http://www.irrodl.org/index.php/irrodl/article/view/882/1689 (accessed 10 Oct. 2014).

Krathwohl, D.R., Bloom, B.S. and Masia, B.B. (1964) *Taxonomy of Educational Objectives: The Classification Of Educational Goals– Handbook II: Affective Domain*. New York: McKay Publishers.

Kreber, C. (ed.) (2008) *The University and its Disciplines: Teaching and Learning Within and Beyond Disciplinary Boundaries*. London: Routledge.

Kreber, C. (2013) *Authenticity in and Through Teaching in Higher Education: The Transformative Potential of the Scholarship of Teaching*. London: Routledge.

Krych, A.J., March, C.N., Bryan, R.E., Peake, B., Pawlina, W. and Carmichael, S.W. (2005) Reciprocal peer teaching: students teaching students in the gross anatomy laboratory, *Clinical Anatomy*, 18(4): 296–301.

Kuhn, T.S. ([1962] 2012) *The Structure of Scientific Revolutions; 50th Anniversary Edition*. Chicago: University of Chicago Press.

Lambert, C. (2011) Psycho classroom, *Social and Cultural Geography*, 12(1): 27–45.

Laurillard, D. (2002) *Rethinking University Teaching: A Conversational Framework for the Effective Use of Learning Technologies*, 2nd edn. London: Routledge Falmer.

Lave, J. and Wenger, E. (1991) *Situated Learning: Legitimate Peripheral Participation*. Cambridge: Cambridge University Press.

Lawton, D. (1983) *Curriculum Studies and Educational Planning*. London: Hodder and Stoughton.

Lawton, R. (2011) Don't underestimate my potential, *Educational Developments*, 12(2): 16–17.

Lea, J. (2009) *Political Correctness and Higher Education: British and American Perspectives*. London: Routledge.

Lea, J. (2011) *Guidance for Awarding Organisations and Practitioners with Regard to the Alignment of Qualifications Available for Teaching in the HE and the FE Sector in England: Report for Lifelong Learning UK*. London: Lifelong Learning UK. Available at: www.heacademy.ac.uk/resources (accessed 8 Dec. 2014).

Lea, J. (2012a) *77 Things to Think About...Teaching and Learning in higher education*. Canterbury: Canterbury Christ Church University. Available at: www.canterbury.ac.uk/Support/learning-teaching-enhancement-unit/77things.aspx (accessed 13 Aug. 2013).

Lea, J. (2012b) The student as customer, British style, *The Chronicle of Higher Education*, 11 July 2012.

Leadbeater, C. (2008) *The Difference Divided: Why Immigration Is Vital to Innovation*. Nesta provocation 06.

Lefebvre, H. (1991) *The Production of Space*. Oxford: Blackwell.

Lefebvre, H. (1996) *Writings on Cities*. Oxford: Blackwell.

Lefebvre, H. (2003) *The Urban Revolution*. Minneapolis: University of Minneapolis Press.

Lewis, D. and Allan, B. (2005) *Virtual Learning Communities: A Guide for Practitioners*. Maidenhead: SRHE Open University Press.

Light, G. (2003) Realizing academic development: a model for embedding research practice in the practice of teaching, in H. Eggins and R. Macdonald (eds) *The Scholarship of Academic Development*, Buckingham: SRHE and Open University Press, pp. 152–62.

Linebaugh, P. (2014) *Stop Thief: The Commons, Enclosures and Resistance*. Oakland, CA: PM Press.

Lingfield, R. [Chair] (2012a) *Professionalism in Further Education: Interim Report of the Independent Review Panel*. London: BIS. Available at: http://www.educationengland.org.uk/documents/pdfs/2012-lingfield1-professionalism-fe-interim.pdf (accessed 14 July 2014).

Lingfield, R. [Chair] (2012b) *Professionalism in Further Education: Final Report of the Independent Review Panel*. London: BIS. Available from: https://www.gov.uk/government/uploads/system/uploads/attachment_data/file/34641/12-1198-professionalism-in-further-education-final.pdf (accessed 14 July 2014).

Little, S. (ed.) (2011) *Staff-student Partnerships in Higher Education*. London: Continuum.

Locke, W. (2008) *The Changing Academic Profession in the UK and Beyond*. London: Universities UK.

Locke, W. (2014) Shifting academic careers: implications for enhancing professionalism in teaching and supported learning. Available at: www.heacademy.ac.uk/node/10079.

Lombardi, J.V. (2013) *How Universities Work*. Baltimore, MD: Johns Hopkins University Press.

Lyotard, J. (1984) *The Postmodern Condition*. Minneapolis, MN: University of Minnesota Press.

Macfarlane, B. (2007) *The Academic Citizen: The Virtue of Service in University Life*. London: Routledge.

Macfarlane, B. (2012) *Intellectual Leadership in Higher Education: Renewing the Role of the University Professor*. London: Routledge/SRHE.

Mainka, C. (2007) Putting staff first in staff development for the effective use of technology in teaching, *British Journal of Educational Technology*, 38(1): 158–60.

Manathunga, C. and Brew, A. (2014) Beyond tribes and territories: new metaphors for new times, in P. Trowler, M. Saunders and V. Bamber (eds) *Tribes and Territories in the 21st Century: Rethinking the Significance of Disciplines in Higher Education*. London: Routledge.

Mann, S. (2001) Alternative perspectives on the student experience: alienation and engagement, *Studies in Higher Education*, 26(1): 7–19.

Mansfield, N. (2003) The subjectivity of money: critical psychology and the economies of post-structuralism, *Critical Psychology*, 8: 129–46.

Marsh, A. (2009) *People Who Love Objects Parts 1–3*. Available at: http://en.wikipedia.org/wiki/Object_sexuality (accessed 6 Jan. 2015).

Marsh, A. (2010) Love among the Objectum Sexuals, *Electronic Journal of Human Sexuality, 13.* Available at: http://www.ejhs.org/volume13/ObjSexuals.htm (accessed 10 Oct. 2014).

Marshall, L. and Morris, C. (eds) (2011) *Taking Wellbeing Forward in Higher Educatio*n: *Reflections on Theory and Practice.* Brighton: University of Brighton Press.

Martin, E., Prosser, M., Conrad, L., Trigwell, K. and Benjamin, J. (1998) *Developing Scholarship in Teaching.* [Online, no longer available].

Marton, F. and Saljo, R. (1976) On qualitative differences in learning: II: Outcome as a function of the learner's conception of the task, *British Journal of Educational Psychology,* 46: 115–27.

Marx, K. ([1867] 1974) *Capital.* Vol. 1. London: Lawrence and Wishart.

Marx, K. (1993) *Grundrisse: Foundations of the Critique of Political Economy.* London: Penguin Classics.

Marx, K. ([1875] 2009) *Critique of the Gotha Programme.* London: Dodo Press.

Marx, K. and Engels, F. ([1848] 2004) *The Communist Manifesto.* London: Penguin.

Maslow A.H. (1943) A theory of human motivation, *Psychological Review,* 50: 370–96.

Mason, M. (ed.) (2008) *Critical Thinking and Learning.* Oxford: Blackwell Publishing.

Mathews, S. (2005) 'The Fun Palace: Cedric Price's Experiment In Architecture and Technology', *Technoetic Arts: A Journal of Speculative Research,* 3(2): 73–91.

Mathews, S. (2007) *From Agit Prop to Free Space: The Architecture of Cedric Price.* London: Black Dog Publishing.

Maxwell, N. (2008) From knowledge to wisdom: the need for an academic revolution, in R. Barnett and N. Maxwell (eds) *Wisdom in the University.* London: Routledge.

Maxwell, N. (2012) Creating a better world: towards the university of wisdom, in R. Barnett (ed.) *The Future University: Ideas and Possibilities.* London: Routledge.

McCulloch, A. (2009) The student as co-producer: learning from public administration about the student-university relationship, *Studies in Higher Education,* 34(2): 171–183.

McGettigan, A. (2013) *The Great University Gamble: Money, Markets and the Future of Higher Education.* London: Pluto Press.

McGoshan, A. and Martin, S. (2014) *From Strategy to Implementation: The Second Evaluation of the Green Academy Programme.* HEA. Available at: https://www.heacademy.ac.uk/sites/default/files/resources/2nd_Green_Academy_Evaluation_2014_FINAL.pdf (accessed 28 Nov. 2014).

McInnerney, J.M. and Roberts, T.S. (2004) Online learning: social interaction and the creation of a sense of community, *Educational Technology and Society,* 7(3): 73–81. Available at: http://www.ifets.info/journals/7_3/8.pdf (accessed 10 Oct. 2014).

McKernan, J. (1996) *Curriculum Action Research.* London: Routledge.

McKernan, J. (2007) *Curriculum and Imagination: Process Theory, Pedagogy and Action Research.* London: Routledge.

McLean, M. (2008) *Pedagogy and the University: Critical Theory and Practice.* London: Continuum.

McNay, I. (1995) From the collegial academy to corporate enterprise: the changing cultures of universities, in T. Schuller. (ed.) *The Changing University?* Buckingham: SRHE and Open University Press.

McNiff, J. (2001) *Action Research: Principles and Practice,* 2nd edition. London: Routledge.

McNiff, J. (2009) *You and Your Action Research Project.* London: Routledge.

McPherson, M.A. and Nunest, J.B. (2008) Critical issues for e-learning delivery: what may seem obvious is not always put into practice, *Journal of Computer Assisted Learning,* 24(5): 433–45. Available at: http://dx.doi.org/10.1111/j.1365-2729.2008.00281.x (accessed 10 Oct. 2014).

Merton, R.K. (1942) *The Sociology of Science: Theoretical and Empirical Investigations.* Chicago: University of Chicago Press.

Merton, R.K. (1947) Patterns of influence: local and cosmopolitan influentials, in R.K. Merton (ed.) *Social Theory and Social Structure*. Glencoe, IL: The Free Press, pp. 387–420.

Meyer, J. and Land, R. (eds) (2006) *Overcoming Barriers to Student Understanding: Threshold Concepts and Troublesome Knowledge*. London: Routledge.

Mezirow, J. (ed.) (2000) *Learning as Transformation: Critical Perspectives on a Theory of Progress*. San Francisco, CA: Jossey-Bass.

Mezirow, J. (2009) An overview on transformative learning, in K. Illeris (ed.) *Contemporary Learning Theories: Learning Theorists... In Their Own Words*. London: Routledge, pp. 90–105.

Mihans, R., Long, D. and Felten, P. (2008) Student-faculty collaboration in course design and the Scholarship of Teaching and Learning, *International Journal for the Scholarship of Teaching and Learning*, 2(2). Available at: http://www.georgiasouthern.edu/ijsot (accessed 15 March 2014).

Mill, J.S. (1867) Inaugural Lecture at the University of St. Andrews, in J.M. Robson (ed.) (1984) *The Collected Works of John Stuart Mill, Volume XXI – Essays on Equality, Law, and Education*. London: Routledge and Kegan Paul.

Miller, A. (2001) *Einstein and Picasso; Space, Time and the Beauty that Causes Havoc*. New York: Basic Books.

Mirowski, P. (2013) *Never Let a Serious Crisis Go to Waste: How Neo-Liberalism Survived the Financial Meltdown*. London: Routledge.

Mittelstrass, J. (2010) The future of the university, *European Review* 18, Supplement No. 1 (Diversification of Higher Education and the Academic Profession. Papers from the Hercules Symposium Turin, Italy 2009, pp. 183–9.

MMU (2013) *Design Your Own Course? A New Role for Students in Programme Development and Curriculum Design*. Higher Education Academy Students as Partners Change Programme. Manchester Metropolitan University Case Study.

Monbiot, G. (2000) *Captive State: The Corporate Takeover of Britain*. Oxford: Macmillan.

Mueller-Vollmer, K. (2011) Wilhelm von Humboldt, in *The Stanford Encyclopedia of Philosophy* (Fall 2011 Edition), ed. E.N. Zalta. Available at: http://plato.stanford.edu/archives/fall2011/entries/wilhelm-humboldt/. (accessed 9 April 2014).

Murphy, D. (2012) *The Architecture of Failure*. Alresford: Zero Books.

Muthesius, S. (2000) *The Postwar University: Utopianist Campus and College*. New Haven, CT: Yale University Press.

Nash, G.B., Crabtree, C. and Ross, E.D. (1997) *History on Trial: Culture Wars and the Teaching of the Past*. New York: Alfred A. Knopf.

Naylor, M. (2005) *Form Follows Idea: An Introduction to Design Poetics*. London: Black Dog Publishing.

Neary, M. (2003) All power to the power workers, emerging from the darkness, electricity and progressive politics in South Korea: a social science fiction, in *Korean Transformations: Power Workers Probation and the Politics of Human Rights*, Resource Centre for Asian NGOs, Sungkonghoe University.

Neary, M. (2010) Student as Producer: a pedagogy for the avant-garde?, *Learning Exchange*, 1(1).

Neary, M. (2012) Teaching politically: policy, pedagogy and the New European University, *Journal for Critical Education Policy Studies*, 10(22): 233–57.

Neary, M. (2014a) Academic not-identity, or the politics of the invisible: a social science fiction, Keynote address to Academic Identity Conference, University of Durham, 9 July.

Neary, M. (2014b) The university and the city: Social Science Centre, Lincoln – forming the urban revolution, in P. Temple (ed.) *The Physical University: Contours of Space and Place in Higher Education*. London: Routledge.

Neary, M. (2014c) Student as Producer: curriculum development, institutional change and reinventing 'the idea of university' as a radical political project, *Educational Development*, 15(1): 10–13.

Neary, M. and Amsler, S. (2012) Occupy: a new pedagogy of space and time, *Journal for Critical Education Policy Studies*, 10(2).

Neary, M., Harrison, A., Crelin, G., Parekh, N., Saunders, G., Duggan, F., Wiliams, S. and Austin, S. (2010) *Learning Landscapes in Higher Education*. Lincoln: University of Lincoln.

Neary, M. and Rikowski, G. (2002) Time and speed in the social universe of capital, in G. Crow and S. Heath (eds) *Social Conceptions of Time: Structure and Process in Work and Everyday Life*. Basingstoke: Palgrave Macmillan.

Neary, M. and Saunders, G. (2011) Leadership and learning landscapes in higher education: the struggle for the idea of the university, *Higher Education Quarterly*, 65(4): 333–52.

Neary, M. and Thody, A. (2009) Learning landscapes: designing as classroom of the future, in higher education, in L. Bell, H. Stevenson and M. Neary (eds) *The Future of Higher Education: Policy, Pedagogy and the Student Experience*. London: Continuum, pp. 30–41.

Neary, M. and Winn, J. (2009) Student as Producer: reinventing the student experience in higher education, in L. Bell, H. Stevenson and M. Neary (eds) *The Future of Higher Education: Policy, Pedagogy and the Student Experience*. London: Continuum.

Neocleous, M. (2000) *The Fabrication of Social Order: A Critical Theory of Police Power*. London and New York: Verso.

Neto, E. (2008) *Stone-Lips-Pepper-Tits-Clove-Love-Fog-Frog*. Available at: http://www.artnet.com/artists/ernesto-neto/stone-lips-pepper-tits-clove-love-fog-frog-a-pxd4D_YM9MBV_G-ecFAS0g2 (accessed 6 Jan. 2015).

Neumann, R. (1992) Perceptions of the teaching-research nexus: a framework for analysis, *Higher Education*, 23(2): 159–71.

Newman, J.H. ([1852] 1996) *The Idea of a University*, ed. F.M. Turner. New Haven, CT: Yale University Press.

Nicholls, G. (2005) New lecturers' constructions of learning, teaching and research in higher education, *Studies in Higher Education*, 30(5).

Nicol, D.J. and McFarlane-Dick, D. (2006) Formative assessment and self-regulated learning: a model and seven principles of good feedback practice, *Studies in Higher Education*, 31(2): 199–218.

Nilsen, S. and Baerheim, A. (2005) Feedback on video recorded consultations in medical teaching: why students loathe and love it – a focus group based qualitative study, *BMC Medical Education*, 5(28).

Nin, A. ([1977] 2008) *Delta of Venus*. London: Penguin.

Nixon, J. (2008) *Towards the Virtuous University: The Moral Bases of Academic Practice*. London: Routledge.

Nixon, J. et al. (1998) What does it mean to be an academic?: a colloquium, *Teaching in Higher Education*, 3(3): 277–98.

NUS (National Union of Students) (2012) *A Manifesto for Partnership*. London: NUS. Available at: www.nusconnect.org.uk/resourcehandler/0a02e2e5-197e-4bd3-b7ed-e8ceff3dc0e4/ (accessed 14 Feb. 2014).

Nussbaum, M. (1997) *Cultivating Humanity: A Classical Defense of Reform in Liberal Education*. Cambridge, MA: Harvard University Press.

Nuttall, G. (1970) *Bomb Culture*. London: HarperCollins.

Nygaard, C., Brand, S., Bartholomew, P. and Millard, L. (eds) (2013) *Student Engagement: Identity, Motivation and Community*. Faringdon: Libri.

O'Mahony, J. (2014) *Enhancing Student Learning and Teacher Development In Transnational Arrangements* (Research report). York: Higher Education Academy.

O'Neill, G. (ed.) (2011) *A Practitioner's Guide to Choice of Assessment Methods Within a Module.* Dublin: UCD Teaching and Learning. Available at: http://www.ucd.ie/teaching/resources/assessment/howdoyouassessstudentlearning/ (accessed 15 Mar. 2014).

Orsmond, P. (2004) *Self- and Peer-assessment: Guidance on Practice in the Biosciences.* Higher Education Academy Biosciences Subject Centre. Available at: ftp://www.bioscience.heacademy.ac.uk/TeachingGuides/fulltext.pdf (accessed 9 Jan. 2015).

Ossa-Richardson, A. (2014) The idea of a university and its concrete form, in P. Temple (ed.) *The Physical University: Contours of Space and Place in Higher Education.* London: Routledge, pp. 131–58.

Panichi, L., Deutschmann, M. and Molka-Danielsen, J. (2010) Virtual worlds for language learning and intercultural exchange: is it for real?, in S. Guth and F. Helm (eds) *Telecollaboration 2.0, Language, Literacies and Intercultural Learning in the 21st Century.* London: Peter Lang, pp. 165–98.

Parry, G., Callender, C., Scott, P. and Temple, P. (2012) Understanding higher education in further education colleges (BIS Research Paper 69). Available at: www.gov.uk/government/publications/understanding-higher-education-in-further-education-colleges (accessed 15 Sept. 2014).

Parsons, D., Hill, I., Holland, J. and Willis, D. (2012) The impact of teaching development programmes in higher education. Available at: www.heacademy.ac.uk/sites/default/files/resources/HEA_Impact_Teaching_Development_Prog.pdf.

Patai, D. and Corral, W.H. (eds) (2005) *Theory's Empire.* New York: Columbia University Press.

Pearman, H. (2014) Cleverer by design, *The Sunday Times,* 17 August. Available at: http://www.thesundaytimes.co.uk/sto/culture/arts/article1445902.ece (accessed 10 Oct. 2014).

Penfold-Mounce, R., Beer, D. and Burrows, R. (2011) The wire as Social Science Fiction, *Sociology,* 45(1): 152–67.

Perkins, D., Jay, E. and Tishman, S. (1993) New conceptions of thinking – from ontology to education, *Educational Psychologist,* 28(1): 67–85.

Pew Research Center (2014) *Online Harassment.* Available online: http://www.pewinternet.org/2014/10/22/online-harassment (accessed 6 Jan. 2015).

Plato (circa. 360 BC) *The Republic.* Harmondsworth: Penguin.

Polanyi, M. (1967) *The Tacit Dimension.* New York: Anchor Books.

Powers, A. (1992) *In the Line of Development: FRS Yorke, E Rosenberg, and CS Mardall to YRM, 1930–1992.* London: RIBA.

Price, P. (2011) *Professional Standards Applying to Teaching and Learning in the HE in FE Sector (England): A Discussion Paper for the Higher Education Academy HE in FE Enhancement Programme.* York: Higher Education Academy. Available at: https://www.heacademy.ac.uk/resources (accessed 8 Dec. 2014).

Prosser, P. and Trigwell, K. (1999) *Understanding Learning and Teaching.* London: SRHE and OU.

QAA (Quality Assurance Agency) (2006) Code of Practice for the Assurance of Academic Quality and Standards in Higher Education, Section 6: Assessment of Students, September 2006. Available at: http://www.qaa.ac.uk/Publications/InformationAndGuidance/Documents/COP_AOS.pdf (accessed 6 Jan. 2015).

QAA (2007) *Outcomes from Institutional Audit: The Adoption and Use of Learning Outcomes.* Gloucester: The Quality Assurance Agency for Higher Education.

QAA (2011) *The UK Quality Code For Higher Education Chapter B6: Assessment of Students and Accreditation of Prior Learning.* Gloucester: QAA. Available at: http://www.qaa.ac.uk/Publications/InformationAndGuidance/Documents/Quality%20Code%20-%20Chapter%20B6.pdf (accessed 6 Jan. 2015).

QAA (2012) *The UK Quality Code for Higher Education* Chapter B3: Learning and Teaching. Gloucester: QAA. Available at: http://www.qaa.ac.uk/publications/information-and-guidance/uk-quality-code-for-higher-education-chapter-b3-learning-and-teaching (accessed 6 Jan. 2015).

QAA (2013a) *Quality Code for Higher Education*. Gloucester: QAA.

QAA (2013b) *Review of Transnational Education in China: 2012, Overview*. Gloucester: QAA.

QAA (2013c) *Guidance on Scholarship and the Pedagogical Effectiveness of Staff: Expectations for Foundation Degree-Awarding Powers and Taught Degree-Awarding Power*. Gloucester: QAA.

QAA (2014) *Review of Transnational Education in UAE: 2013. Overview*. Gloucester: QAA.

Ramsden, P. (2003) *Learning to Teach in Higher Education*. London: Routledge.

Ramsden, P (2008) The future of higher education teaching and the student experience. Available at: http://www.bis.gov.uk/wp-content/uploads/2009/10/HE-Teaching-Student-Experience.pdf (accessed 27 April 2015).

Ramsden, P. and Moses, I. (1992) Association between research and teaching in higher education in Australia, *Higher Education*, 23(3): 273–95.

Ranciere, J. (2004) *The Politics of Aesthetics: Distribution of the Sensible*. London: Bloomsbury.

Readings, B. (1996) *The University in Ruins*. Cambridge, MA: Harvard University Press.

REF (Research Excellence Framework) (2012) *REF 2014: Assessment Framework and Guidance on Submissions*. REF 02.2011. Bristol: REF. Available at: www.ref.ac.uk/pubs/2011-02/ (accessed 3 Aug. 2013).

Revans, R. (2011) *ABC of Action Learning*. Farnham: Gower.

Richardson, V. (1997) *Constructivist Teacher Education: Building a World of New Understandings*. London: Falmer Press.

Riesman, D., Glazer, N. and Denny, R. ([1950] 2001) *The Lonely Crowd*. New Haven, CT: Yale University Press.

Ritzer, G. (2001) Let's make it magical, *Times Higher Education Supplement*, 7 Jan., p. 6.

Robbins Report (1963) *Higher Education Report*. London: HMSO. Available at: http://www.educationengland.org.uk/documents/robbins/robbins1963.html (accessed 19 Nov. 2014).

Rogers, C. (1957) Personal thoughts on teaching and learning, in H. Kischenbaum and V.L. Henderson (eds) (1989) *The Carl Rogers Reader*. New York: Houghton Mifflin.

Rogers, C. (1989) *The Carl Rogers Reader*. Ed. H. Kischenbaum and V.L. Henderson. New York: Houghton Mifflin.

Rogers, C. and Freiberg, H. J. (1994) *Freedom to Learn*, 3rd edn. New York: Merrill.

Rogers, C.R. and Lyon, H. (2013) *On Becoming an Effective Teacher: Person-centered Teaching, Psychology, Philosophy, and Dialogues with Carl R. Rogers and Harold Lyon*. Available at: http://shelf3d.com/i/Carl%20Rogers (accessed 7 July 2014).

Roggero, G. (2011) *The Production of Living Knowledge: The Crisis of the University and the Transformation of Labour in Europe and North America*. Philadelphia, PA: Temple University Press.

Rorty, R. (1989) *Contingency, Irony and Solidarity*. Cambridge: Cambridge University Press.

Rose, G. (1993) *Feminism and Geography The Limits of Geographical Knowledge*. Cambridge: Polity.

Ross, M.T. and Cameron, H.S. (2007) Peer assisted learning: a planning and implementation framework: AMEE Guide no. 30, *Medical Teacher*, 29(6): 527–45.

Rovai, A.P. (2004) A constructivist approach to online college learning, *Internet and Higher Education*, 7(2): 79–93. Available at: http://dx.doi.org/10.1016/j.iheduc.2003.10.002 (accessed 10 Oct. 2014).

Rowland, S. (2006) *The Enquiring University: Compliance and Contestation in Higher Education*. Maidenhead: SRHE and Open University Press.

Rust, C., O'Donovan, B. and Price, M. (2005) A social constructivist assessment assessment process model: how the research literature shows us this could be best practice, *Assessment and Evaluation in Higher Education*, 30(3): 233–41.

Ryan, R.M. and Deci, E.L. (2000) Self-determination theory and the facilitation of intrinsic motivation, social development, and well-being, *American Psychologist*, 55(1): 68.

Sadler, S. (2005) *Archigram Architecture Without Architecture*. Cambridge, MA: MIT Press.

Sagan, O., Candela, E. and Frimodig, B. (2010) Insight on outreach: towards a critical practice, *International Journal of Education through Art*, 6(2): 145–61.

Said, E. (1994) *Representations of the Intellectual*, The 1993 Reith Lectures. London: Vintage Books.

Salmon, G. (2002) *e-Tivities: The Key to Active Online Learning*. London: RoutledgeFalmer.

Sambell, K., McDowell, L. and Montgomery, C. (2012) *Assessment for Learning in Higher Education*. London: Routledge.

Sandover, S., Partridge, L., Dunne, E. and Burkill, S. (2012) Undergraduate researchers change learning and teaching: a case study of two universities in Australia and the UK, *CUR Quarterly*, 33(1): 33–9. Available at: www.cur.org/documents/?CategoryId=7 (accessed 15 March 2014).

Savin-Baden, M. (2003) *Facilitating Problem-Based Learning Illuminating Perspectives*. Maidenhead: SRHE and Open University Press.

Scharmer, C.O. (2009) *Theory U: Leading from the Future as it Emerges*. San Francisco, CA: Berrett-Koehler Publishers.

Schön, D. (1983) *The Reflective Practitioner*. San Francisco, CA: Jossey-Bass.

Schön, D.A. (1991) *Educating the Reflective Practitioner: Towards a New Design for Teaching and Learning in the Professions*. San Francisco, CA: Jossey-Bass.

Schwartz, P. and Webb, G. (2002) *Assessment Case Studies: Experience and Practice from Higher Education*. London: Kogan Page.

Scoffham, S. and Kemp, N. (2014) It's contagious! Developing sustainability perspectives in academic life at a UK university. Paper prepared for The Second World Symposium on Sustainable Development at Universities, Manchester Metropolitan University, September 2014.

Scott, P. (2003) 1992–2002: Where next?, *Perspectives*, 7(3): 71–5.

SEDA (Staff and Educational Development Association) online discussions entitled University teacher conceptions of reflective learning, July 2014, notes available from www.seda.ac.uk

Selwyn, N. (2013) *Distrusting Educational Technology*. New York: Routledge.

Sennett, R. (2008) *The Craftsman*. London: Penguin.

Sharpe, R. (2004) How do professionals learn and develop? Implications for staff and educational developers, in D. Baume and P. Kahn (eds) *Enhancing Staff and Educational Development*. London: RoutledgeFalmer, pp. 132–53.

Sherman, D.L. (2003) Critical theory, in R.C. Salomon and D.L. Sherman (eds) *The Blackwell Guide to Continental Philosophy*. Oxford: Blackwell.

Siemens, G. (2005) Connectivism: a learning theory for the digital age, *International Journal of Instructional Technology and Distance Learning*, 2(1), January 2005. Available at: http://www.itdl.org/journal/jan_05/article01.htm (accessed 10 Oct. 2014).

Simmons, J. (2014) The nature of knowledge in the higher vocational curriculum, in J. Lea (ed.) *Supporting Higher Education in College Settings*. London: SEDA.

Simmons, J. and Lea, J. (2013) *Capturing an HE ethos in College Higher Education*. Gloucester: QAA. Available at: http://www.qaa.ac.uk/publications/information-and-guidance/publication/?PubID=2773#.VBq_j4kshtNI (accessed 19 Nov. 2014).

Skills Commission (2011) *Teacher Training in Vocational Education*. London: Policy Connect.

Slaughter, S. and Rhoades, G. (1994) *Academic Capitalism and the New Economy: Markets, States and Higher Education*. Philadelphia, PA: Johns Hopkins University Press.

Smith, A. and Webster, F. (eds) (1997) *The Post Modern University?* Buckingham: Open University Press.

Smith, D. and James, E. (2008) The utopianist campus: biography, policy and the building of a new university during the 1960s, *History of Education*, 37(1): 23–42.

Smith, H. (2011) *Values in Higher Education: Annotated Bibliography*. CPD4HE: Open Resources on HE Teaching and Learning. Available at: http://vle.bruford.ac.uk/login/index.php (accessed 6 Jan 2015).

Smith, H, Cooper, A. and Lancaster, L. (2002) Improving the quality of undergraduate peer assessment: a case for student and staff development, *Innovations in Education and Teaching International*, 39(1); 71–81.

Smith, M. et al. (2013) Graduate employability: student perceptions of PBL and its effectiveness in facilitating their employability skills, *Practice and Evidence of the Scholarship of Teaching and Learning in Higher Education*, 8(3): 217–40.

Stanek, L. (2011) *Henri Lefebvre on Space: Architecture, Urban Research and the Production of Theory*. Minneapolis, MN: Minnesota University Press.

Steiner, R. (2005) *Theosophy*. Forest Row: Rudolf Steiner Press.

Stephanie, J. et al. (2001) Assessing self- and peer-assessment: the students' views, *Higher Education Research and Development*, 20(1): 53–70.

Sterling, S. (2004) Higher education, sustainability, and the role of systemic learning, in P.B. Corcoran and A.E.J. Wals (eds) *Higher Education and the Challenge of Sustainability: Problematics, Promise, and Practice*. Dordrecht: Kluwer Academic Press, pp. 47–70.

Stevenson, J. et al. (2014) *Pedagogic Stratification and the Shifting Landscape of Higher Education*. Available at: https://www.heacademy.ac.uk/sites/default/files/resources/PedStrat_Finalreport.pdf (accessed 6 Jan. 2015).

Stewart, B. (2014) Networks of care and vulnerability. Online presentation to Scholar14. Available at: http://theory.cribchronicles.com/2014/11/04/networks-of-care-and-vulnerability/ (accessed 6 Jan. 2015).

Stibbe, A. (2013) Work-based learning in the humanities: a welcome stranger? *Practice and Evidence of Scholarship of Teaching and Learning in Higher Education*, 8(3): 241–55.

Sykes, C.J. (1992) *A Nation of Victims*. New York: St Martin's Press.

Tait, J. and Knight, P. (eds) (1996) *The Management of Independent Learning*. London: Kogan Page.

Taylor, C.A. and Dunne, M. (2011) Virtualization and new geographies of knowledge in higher education: possibilities for the transformation of knowledge, pedagogic relations and learner identities, *British Journal of Sociology of Education*, 32(4): 623–41.

Thomas, L. (2001) *Widening Participation in Post-compulsory Education*. London: Continuum Studies in Lifelong Learning.

Thomas, L. (forthcoming) Effective practice in the design of directed independent learning opportunities. Available at: https://www.heacademy.ac.uk/project/350

Thomas, L. and Quinn, J. (2006) *First Generation Entry into Higher Education*. Maidenhead: Open University Press.

Thomas, L. (2012) *Building Student Engagement and Belonging at a Time of Change in Higher Education*. London: Paul Hamlyn Foundation.

Thompson, D. (ed.) (2000) *Stretching the Academy: The Politics and Practice of Widening Participation*. London: NIACE Publications.

Tolsgaard, M.G., Gustafsson, A., Rasmussen, M.B., Hoiby, P., Muller, C.G. and Ringsted, C. (2007) Student teachers can be as good as associate professors in teaching clinical skills, *Medical Teacher*, 29(6): 553–57.

Tomlinson, M. (2014) Exploring the impacts of policy changes on student approaches and attitudes to learning in contemporary higher education: implications for student learning
engagement. Available at: https://www.heacademy.ac.uk/sites/default/files/resources/
Exploring_the_impact_of_policy_changes_student_experience.pdf

Trigwell, K. and Shale, S. (2004) Student learning and the scholarship of university teaching,
Studies in Higher Education, 29(4): 523–36.

Tripp, D. (1993) *Critical Incidents in Teaching: Developing Professional Judgement*. London:
Routledge.

Trow, M. (2010) *Twentieth-Century Higher Education: Elite to Mass to Universal* ed.
M. Burrage. Baltimore, MD: Johns Hopkins University Press.

Trowler, P., Saunders, M. and Bamber, V. (2014) *Tribes and Territories in the 21st Century:
Rethinking the Significance of Disciplines in Higher Education*. London: Routledge.

UNESCO (2002) *Education for Sustainability, from Rio to Johannesburg: Lessons learnt from
a Decade of Commitment*, Paris: UNESCO. Available at http://unesdoc.unesco.org/images/
0012/001271/127100e.pdf (accessed 28 Nov. 2014).

UNESCO (2004) *United Nations Decade of Education for Sustainable Development (2005-14):
Draft International Implementation Scheme*. Paris: UNESCO. Available at http://unesdoc.
unesco.org/images/0013/001399/139937e.pdf (accessed 28 Nov. 2014).

UNESCO (2009) *Bonn Declaration*. Available online at http://www.esd-world-conference-2009.
org/fileadmin/download/ESD2009_BonnDeclaration.pdf (accessed 28 Nov. 2014).

University of Glasgow (undated) *beSoTLed*. Available at: http://www.gla.ac.uk/departments/sotl/
whatissotl/aworkingdefinition/ (accessed 15 March 2014).

Vygotsky, L.S. (1978) *Mind and Society: The Development of Higher Mental Processes*. Cambridge,
MA: Harvard University Press.

Walker, M. (2006) *Higher Education Pedagogies*. Maidenhead: SRHE and Open University
Press.

Warner-Weil, S. and McGill, I. (eds) (1989) *Making Sense Of Experiential Learning: Diversity in
Theory and Practice*. Buckingham: SRHE and Open University Press.

Watson, D. (2000) Lifelong Learning and Professional Higher Education, in T. Bourner, T. Katz
and D. Watson (eds) *New Directions in Professional Higher Education*. Buckingham: SRHE
and Open University Press.

Watson, D. (2007) Does higher education need a Hypocratic oath?, *Higher Education Quarterly*,
61(3): 362–74.

Webster, M. and Buglass, G. (eds) (2005) *The Community Arts Workers: Finding Voices, Making
Choices*. Nottingham: Educational Heretics Press.

Wegerif, R. (1998) The social dimensions of asynchronous learning environments, *Journal of Asynchronous Learning Networks*, 2(1): 34–49. Available at: http://onlinelearningconsortium.
org/read/journal-issues/ (accessed 10 Oct. 2014).

Weinberger, A., Stegmann, K. and Fischer, F. (2007) Knowledge convergence in collaborative
learning: concepts and assessment, *Learning and Instruction*, 17(4): 416–26.

Weller, M. (2011) A pedagogy of abundance, *Spanish Journal of Pedagogy*, 249: 223–36. Available
at: http://oro.open.ac.uk/28774/ (accessed 10 Oct. 2014).

Wenger, E. (1998) *Communities of Practice, Learning, Meaning, and Identity*. Cambridge:
Cambridge University Press.

Wenger, E. (2000) Communities of practice and social learning systems, *Organization*, 7(2): 225–46.
Available at: http://dx.doi.org/10.1177/135050840072002 (accessed 10 Oct. 2014).

Werder, C. and Otis, M.M. (eds) (2010) *Engaging Student Voices in the Study of Teaching and
Learning*. Virginia: Stylus.

Western Washington University (no date) *Teaching-Learning Academy*. Available at: http://
library.wwu.edu/tla (accessed 15 March 2014).

Wilkinson, T. (2014) *Bricks and Mortar: Ten Great Buildings and the People They Made*. London: Fourth Estate.

Williams, J. (2006) The pedagogy of debt, *College Literature*, 33(4): 155–69.

Woods, P., Ashley, M. and Woods, G. (eds) (2005) *Steiner Schools in England*. Research Report RR645. London: Department for Education and Skills, pp. 15–18.

Woolf, V. (2008) *Three Guineas*. Oxford: Oxford University Press.

Young, M.F.D. (1971) *Knowledge and Control*. London: Collier-Macmillan.

Young, M.F.D. (2008) *Bringing Knowledge Back In*. London: Routledge.

Zimmerman, J. (2002) *Whose America: Culture Wars in the Public Schools*. Cambridge, MA: Harvard University Press.

Žižek, S. (2009) *On Violence: Six Sideways Reflections*. London: Profile Books.

Index

TEACHING FOR QUALITY LEARNING AT UNIVERSITY
Fourth Edition

John Biggs and Catherine Tang

ISBN: 9780335242757
eBook: 9780335242764
2011

Teaching for Quality Learning at University, now in its fourth edition, is a bestselling book for higher education teachers and administrators interested in assuring effective teaching. The authors outline the constructive alignment of outcomes based teaching, including how to implement it and why it is a good idea to do so. Clearly organized and written, with practical examples, the new edition is thoroughly updated.

Key features:

- Each chapter includes tasks that offer a 'how-to' manual to implement constructive alignment in your own teaching practices
- Aids staff developers in providing support for teachers
- Provides a framework for administrators interested in quality assurance and enhancement of teaching across the whole university

www.openup.co.uk

RESEARCH PROPOSALS
A PRACTICAL GUIDE

Martyn Denscombe

2012
9780335244065 – Paperback

eBook also available

Whether you are an undergraduate student doing
your final year project, a Masters student writing your dissertation, or a
PhD student applying for acceptance onto a doctoral programme, this practical book will
help you to produce a successful and persuasive research proposal.

Written by an experienced and best-selling author, this handbook uniquely draws a parallel between a research proposal and a sales pitch. The book provides guidance on what to include and what to omit from your proposal and demonstrates how to 'sell' your research idea. Denscombe ably guides you through each stage of the process:

- Choosing a research topic
- Reviewing the literature
- Formulating the research question
- Explaining the research methods
- Estimating the costs and planning the time involved
- Obtaining research ethics approval

With top tips throughout, this book provides an insight to the logic behind research proposals and the way that good proposals address 7 basic questions that readers will ask when they evaluate any proposal.

www.openup.co.uk

WRITING FOR ACADEMIC JOURNALS
Third Edition

Rowena Murray

ISBN: 9780335263028 (Paperback)
eBook: 9780335263035
2013

Writing for publication is a daunting and time-consuming task for many academics. And yet the pressure for academics to publish has never been greater. This book demystifies the process of writing academic papers, showing readers what good papers look like and how they can be written.

Offering a research-informed understanding of the contemporary challenges of writing for publication, this book gives practical advice for overcoming common obstacles such as finding a topic, targeting journals, and finding the time to write. The author offers a range of helpful writing strategies, making this an invaluable handbook for academics at all stages of their career, from doctoral students to early career researchers and even experienced academics.

The third edition has been comprehensively updated to reflect the changing landscape of academic writing, including the most recent research and theory on writing across the disciplines. Drawing on her extensive experience of running writing workshops and working closely with academics on developing writing, Rowena Murray offers practical and tested strategies for good academic writing.

New to the third edition:

- Advice on how to use social media to promote your publications
- More examples from different disciplines and journals
- More advice on how to tackle writer's block
- Extended end-of-chapter checklists
- New evidence that these strategies really work!

www.openup.co.uk

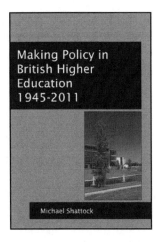

Making Policy in British Higher Education 1945 - 2011

Michael Shattock

ISBN: 9780335241866 (Paperback)
eBook: 9780335241873
2012

This book aims to provide an authoritative account of the evolution of policy in British higher education drawing extensively on previously untapped archival sources. It offers a comprehensive analysis of the policy drivers since 1945 and up to 2011 and of the extent to which, even in the so called golden age of university autonomy in the immediate post-War period, the development of British higher education policy was closely integrated with government policies. In particular, it highlights how the role of the Treasury in determining the resource base for the expansion of student numbers is key to understanding many of the shifts in policy that occurred.

www.openup.co.uk

OPEN UNIVERSITY PRESS
McGraw - Hill Education

Researching Higher Education
Second Edition

Malcolm Tight

ISBN: 9780335241835 (Paperback)
eBook: 9780335241842
2012

This authoritative book couples an overview of the principal current areas of research into higher education with a guide to the processes involved in undertaking such research.

Comprehensively updated throughout, this new edition examines the current state of higher education research with brand new case studies and has been expanded to include North American work.

The book includes:

- Analysis of published research by topic, method, theory and level
- Detailed discussion of selected examples of published research
- Suggestions on under-researched topics
- Guidance on publication outlets

www.openup.co.uk

OPEN UNIVERSITY PRESS
McGraw - Hill Education